WITHDRAWN

HIDDEN®

Tennessee

"Even if you feel you know this state well, the currency of travel information included here is worth the price."
—*Nashville Tennessean*

"*Hidden Tennessee* provides complete travel information for wilderness experiences, restaurants, shops, attractions and musical entertainment."
—*Knoxville News-Sentinel*

"If you like details, trivia and honest-to-goodness helpful information, grab this book and stash it in your travel bag."
—*Savannah Morning News*

"*Hidden Tennessee* excels in outdoor lore and music, with good sections on the blues of Beale Street, Chattanooga's Civil War landmarks (and its Choo Choo), and the natural beauty and amusement of Ruby Falls."
—*Atlanta Journal-Constitution*

HIDDEN ®

Tennessee

Including Nashville, Memphis and the Great Smoky Mountains

Marty Olmstead

FIFTH EDITION

Ulysses Press ®

BERKELEY, CALIFORNIA

Published by: ULYSSES PRESS
          P.O. Box 3440
          Berkeley, CA 94703
          www.ulyssespress.com

ISSN 1524-1289
ISBN 1-56975-485-3

Printed in Canada by Transcontinental Printing

10 9 8 7

MANAGING EDITOR: Claire Chun
PROJECT DIRECTOR: Lily Chou
COPY EDITOR: Lee Micheaux
EDITORIAL ASSOCIATES: Leona Benten, Laura Brancella, Amy Hough
TYPESETTERS: Lisa Kester, Steven Schwartz
CARTOGRAPHY: XNR Productions; Great Smoky
    Mountains map by Stellar Cartography
COVER DESIGN: Leslie Henriques
INDEXER: Sayre Van Young
COVER PHOTOGRAPHY: ©gettyimages.com (pioneer
    homestead)
ILLUSTRATOR: Doug McCarthy

Distributed in the United States by Publishers
Group West and in Canada by Raincoast Books

To Julie

Acknowledgments

When I began researching the first edition of *Hidden Tennessee* in 1996, I had no idea how much I would enjoy it. The first pleasant surprise was the abundant natural beauty. It was a delight to follow winding country roads just to see if there was anything of interest on the way.

The second surprise was how friendly and helpful Tennesseans are. I ought to know: I can't count the times I got lost and had to ask for directions. More than that, locals offered their recommendations for what to see and do and where to eat and sleep. And particularly, where to hear the best music. If Tennessee didn't already have a nickname ("The Volunteer State"), I'd suggest it be called "The Music State," because from the bluegrass in the eastern hills to the country and rock around Nashville to the blues and soul in Memphis, music—both amateur and professional—is everywhere.

Over the years, as I have returned time and again to update this book, I have made real friends and new discoveries. I wish the same for you.

Marty Olmstead
Sonoma, California

What's Hidden?

At different points throughout this book, you'll find special listings marked with a symbol:

◄ HIDDEN

This means that you have come upon a place off the beaten tourist track, a spot that will carry you a step closer to the local people and natural environment of Tennessee.

The goal of this guide is to lead you beyond the realm of everyday tourist facilities. While we include traditional sightseeing listings and popular attractions, we also offer alternative sights and adventure activities. Instead of filling this guide with reviews of standard hotels and chain restaurants, we concentrate on one-of-a-kind places and locally owned establishments.

Our authors seek out locales that are popular with residents but usually overlooked by visitors. Some are more hidden than others (and are marked accordingly), but all the listings in this book are intended to help you discover the true nature of Tennessee and put you on the path of adventure.

Write to us!

If in your travels you discover a spot that captures the spirit of Tennessee, or if you live in the region and have a favorite place to share, or if you just feel like expressing your views, write to us and we'll pass your note along to the author.

We can't guarantee that the author will add your personal find to the next edition, but if the writer does use the suggestion, we'll acknowledge you in the credits and send you a free copy of the new edition.

ULYSSES PRESS
P.O. Box 3440
Berkeley, CA 94703
E-mail: readermail@ulyssespress.com

Contents

Maps

OUTDOOR ADVENTURE SYMBOLS

The following symbols accompany national, state and regional park listings, as well as beach descriptions throughout the text.

▲	Camping		Waterskiing
	Hiking		Windsurfing
	Biking		Canoeing or Kayaking
	Horseback Riding		Boating
	Cross-country Skiing		Boat Ramps
	Swimming		Fishing

ONE

Tennessee Wandering

First came the mountains and the rivers. Then, the pioneers and the presidents. And then the musicians. Whereas geology created one of the most diverse and beautiful landscapes in the country, it was geography that shaped Tennessee's place in history. And it was an in-the-bone love of music that finally defined the three major regions of this wide and narrow state as clearly as any cartographer's pen.

The soaring mountains of East Tennessee are forever associated with the hillbilly music descended from the Scottish, Irish and English ballads of the region's early settlers. Middle Tennessee, a mixture of plateaus and plantations surrounded by bluegrass, has become known the world over as the birthplace of country music, now headquartered in Nashville. Finally, African rhythms led to the creation of an entirely new musical genre, the blues, which are as steady and vital a presence in West Tennessee's Delta Country as the mighty Mississippi that rolls past Memphis, defining the state's western border.

Tennessee is, of course, much more than a place for musical pleasures. Its parks are among the most splendid and diverse in the United States, and outdoor adventurers fill thousands of campsites every spring, summer and fall. Rivers, streams and lakes grace the countryside, and nearly 54 percent of Tennessee's 42,244 square miles are forested or farmed.

Besides the natural splendors, there are the great cities of Memphis, Knoxville, Chattanooga and Nashville, the capital. Knoxville, home of the 1982 World's Fair is headquarters for the University of Tennessee as well as for the Tennessee Valley Authority (TVA), the biggest producer of power in the country. Of all the cities in Tennessee, Chattanooga endured the worst strife in the Civil War, witnessing five major battles in and around Lookout Mountain. Nashville, on the banks of the Cumberland River, has become not only the center of the country music universe, but, increasingly, a power to be reckoned with in all kinds of music recording and publishing. Far away, literally and figuratively, is Memphis, sometimes referred to by Tennesseans who live elsewhere as the capital of northern Mississippi.

Tennessee also has dozens of smaller cities, but its greatest charms lie in the small towns, some no more than villages, that dot the rural landscape—nestled in valleys beside the mountains, hugging the banks of various rivers, or, sometimes, sitting in the middle of seeming nowhere, as if abandoned as the rest of the state progressed into the 20th century. Nowhere else on earth will you find towns like Rugby, a restored utopian community in the Upper Cumberland region, or Jonesborough, a painstakingly preserved part of the state's unique history. Geographic curiosities are almost as appealing: the submerged cypresses of eerie Reelfoot Lake, the dramatic crevice called the Sequatchie Valley, the hot mineral waters that fueled a turn-of-the-20th-century health resort called Red Boiling Springs.

▾ ▾ ▾ ▾ ▾ ▾ ▾ ▾ ▾ ▾ ▾ ▾ ▾ ▾ ▾ ▾ ▾ ▾

The Story of Tennessee

GEOLOGY

The three regions of Tennessee are so geographically distinct, even separate, that they are symbolized by three stars on the state flag. With 42,244 square miles within its borders, the state is so large—432 to north—that it borders on eight other states: Georgia, Alabama, Mississippi, Arkansas, Missouri, miles across and 100 miles from south Kentucky, Virginia and North Carolina. In East Tennessee are the Appalachian Mountains and the Great Valley. Middle Tennessee consists of the Cumberland Plateau, the Central Basin and both the Eastern and West Highland rims. West Tennessee is defined by the Gulf Coastal Plain that culminates in the Mississippi Delta region.

The Appalachian Mountains form the eastern border and are half a billion years old. The Great Smoky Mountains were created more than two million years ago by a massive upheaval of the earth's surface. These mountains, particularly the Unaka Range in the northeast, served as a natural barrier to westward expansion from the original 13 colonies, although gradually they were penetrated by pioneers seeking a home in the open territories that lay beyond. Today, the lakes, rivers and valleys in this portion of the state make it a favorite of sportspeople who fish, hunt, camp and go boating in a scenic wonderland. To the south, the mountains were discovered to contain not only gold, but also copper, which was mined until the Ocoee region resembled a nuclear landscape, although reforestation has been recently successful.

The southern portion of the Great Valley has the Tennessee River as a western border, with the Appalachian peaks to its east. The region has been inhabited for centuries, and was both the physical and the spiritual center of the Cherokee Nation until the early 19th century when the Cherokee were forced into the westward migration known as the Trail of Tears.

A gap in the formidable Cumberland Plateau at the Kentucky border allowed migration through what naturally came to be called the Cumberland Gap. From here south, the region is a diverse topographical mixture of rivers, valleys and forests, along with waterfalls both modest and spectacular, including the 256-foot

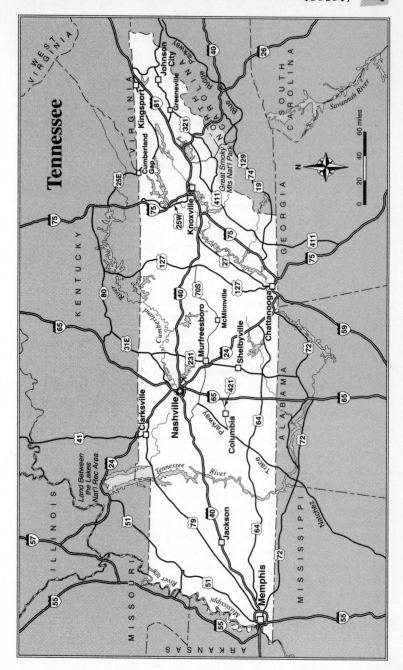

Tennessee

Fall Creek Falls. The forbidding landscape of the Upper Cumberland has always made farming particularly challenging. In fact, horrific winters and other climatic conditions doomed the optimistic English colony of Rugby around the turn of the 20th century.

The fertile bottomlands of the Central Basin, where the Cumberland River flows past Nashville, supported thriving plantations in the late 18th and 19th centuries. The northern portion of Middle Tennessee is replete with lakes and rivers, making it yet another recreational destination, particularly around Land Between the Lakes, which straddles the border with Kentucky.

South of Nashville, rolling pastureland is dotted with farms, plantations and the ranches where the prized Tennessee Walking Horses were developed and are raised today. The agrarian landscape of Tennessee was more defined by small farms growing a mixture of crops than by vast plantations associated with the antebellum South.

The flat expanses of the Gulf Coastal Plain were more suitable for cotton farming. Memphis, on the bluffs of the Mississippi River, became the natural port for shipping cotton as well as hardwoods. Except for some of the cozier hamlets in the southern portion of the Delta, the geology and the scenery are less interesting in West Tennessee than elsewhere in the state.

FLORA

After the frigid winter snows melt high on Roan Mountain, a riot of color explodes in a vast garden of Catawba rhododendrons. Purple, white and pink blossoms thrive in their 600-acre mountaintop home, in one of the largest natural collections of such plants in the world. Soon thereafter, the dainty white blossoms of the wondrously named Dutchman's breeches begin nodding in the breeze deep in the deciduous forests, while in the lower elevations, the intensely fragrant honeysuckle seduces anyone within sniffing distance.

SMOKY MOUNTAINS SHOWCASE

Wildflowers like trillium and iris harbinger the spring, turning late March into a showplace of color. Nowhere is this spectacle more alluring than in late April in the Smokies. The rangers publish a weekly "Bloomin' Report" to let people know which flowering plants of some 1300 species are blossoming at any given time. The rangers recommend the Chestnut Top Trail near the Townsend entrance and a walk up Porter's Creek in the Greenbrier area for looking at rue and wood anemones, bishop's cap, chickweed and four types of violet. Later, almost any trail will do, but for showy orchids, head to the Cosby Nature Trail.

With the warming weather in April, the dogwoods for which Knoxville is famous come alive with their delicate pink and white petals, bearing the sign of the cross in their centers. Dwarf iris is common along the Little River at Metcalf Bottoms; en route, keep an eye out for red columbine and pink bleeding-heart. Flowers bloom a little later at higher elevations, especially along the Balsam Mountain Road, which doesn't even open until the middle of May.

As spring turns into summer, the fields of Middle and West Tennessee burst into a palette of gold and yellow as goldenrod, black-eyed Susan and yarrow blossom into the sunlight. Late in summer, as the weather cools and the days shorten, the leaves on the trees turn to yellow and red before dropping to the forest floor, to replenish the roots and renew the eternal cycle.

Tennessee has more flora to see than blooming flowers. In urban sanctuaries, state parks and national wildlife areas are countless types of shrubs, trees and grasses. From the bald cypress around Reelfoot Lake in the northwest corner of the state to the cherry trees near Frozen Head State Park to the spruce fir forests of the Appalachians, Tennessee is rich with forests, including softwoods like pine and hardwoods such as oak, hickory, dogwood, maple and river birch.

FAUNA

Of the hundreds of species of birds, mammals, amphibians, reptiles and fish in Tennessee, none is more inspiring than the American bald eagle. Flying alone or in pairs, the bald eagle heads south from the Great Lakes and Canada, its great wings spreading six to eight feet and supporting a body that weighs as much as 16 pounds. The adult bird is distinguished by its white head and tail, making it fairly easy to spot.

You can see this living national symbol at Reelfoot Lake, one of the most popular overwintering destinations outside Alaska. Rangers at Reelfoot Lake State Resort Park in northwest Tennessee offer extensive guide and information programs, as well as tours from December to mid-March. In winter and at other times of the year, more than 254 kinds of birds visit Reelfoot, making it a paradise for birdwatchers and even the most casual observer. Bald eagles also are sighted at Land Between the Lakes.

The other most dramatic animal associated with Tennessee is the black bear, *Ursus americanus*, which is considered by many the very symbol of the Great Smoky Mountains. Though there may be as many as 500 of them wandering the backwoods in this national park, they are surprisingly hard to spot. When someone does see one, you can bet there will be a "bear jam" as everyone in the area stops to watch.

Unfortunately, the bears must share their habitat with herds of boars that were accidentally introduced to the area in the early 1900s. Fortunately, there are many more wondrous animals about in these mountains, including a real specialty, dozens of species of salamanders. Untrammeled mountain peaks and a cool, moist climate constitute an Eden for this slippery customer, and dedicated natural historians have even found rare species such as the red-cheeked salamander. Though all salamanders favor darkness and damp, it's possible to find them, particularly after a rainstorm toward the end of a warm day.

Male black bears can weigh well over 200 pounds and may stand up to six feet.

If amphibians aren't your thing, perhaps you'll warm up to white-tailed deer. Unlike many other mountain creatures, the deer population actually thrived after human intrusion. They like clearings and live largely on the forest's edge, habitats that farms and homesites created in abundance.

Occasionally someone reports seeing a mountain lion (or cougar), but officially one hasn't been seen in half a century. Bobcats aren't uncommon though, nor are chipmunks, squirrels, marmots and, along the streams, beavers and river otters. Larger mammals such as elk and bison once flourished in the Smokies, but, like the grey wolf, have long since disappeared.

Songbirds are another delight of a sojourn in the Smokies, as well as elsewhere in the Tennessee mountains. More than 200 species of birds populate the region, including grouse, herons, ducks, vultures, hawks, eagles, quail, turkey, rails, coots, cranes, kingfishers, hummingbirds, woodpeckers, nuthatches, crows and cardinals.

Turtles and lizards comprise many of the 80 species of reptiles and amphibians in this park, and 55 species of native fish can be found here. Most people don't go looking for any of the most common animals—21 kinds of snakes—and, for the most part, snakes don't go looking for them. The only ones hikers need to keep an eye out for are the poisonous varieties, the copperhead and the timber rattlesnake. (Anyone not familiar with how to avoid snakes should check with the park rangers before heading out into the wilderness.)

Trout are the most precious commodity of the mountain streams, but they are outnumbered by minnows and share the aquatic life with crayfish as well as zillions of insects that make flyfishing such a challenge. (See the "Fishing" section below for more information about catching trout.)

State and municipal parks also harbor a diversity of fauna. Canadian geese, wild turkeys, ducks, squirrels, coyotes, skunks and opossums are among the most commonly sighted. Right in Nashville, amazingly enough, you can see great blue herons, belted kingfishers, red and gray foxes, beavers, bobcats, coyotes and rabbits in the woods and meadows of the Radnor Lake State Natural Area.

Tennessee joined the United States in 1796. The 16th state may have come late to the party in the eyes of the original colonists, but its 207-year history is about as colorful as the olden days get, with characters from pioneers such as David Crockett to presidents James K. Polk and Andrew Jackson right up to former Vice President Albert Gore, Jr., who hails from Carthage, Tennessee.

Long before the Spanish explorer Hernando de Soto traipsed the eastern mountains and the western Delta Country in the 1500s, American Indians had created the trails later used by the Europeans. Those pathways have been deepened over the centuries, from the mountains down to present-day Chattanooga, atop the bluffs of the Mississippi River and along the southwest–northeast route, now known as the Natchez Trace. To the north, white men had discovered the Cumberland Gap at least as early as 1673. Tennessee was being invaded from virtually every border.

These immigrants found that the Cherokee and Creek had established thriving towns in the Great Valley and elsewhere in East and Middle Tennessee, while the Chickasaw flourished in the western lands bordering the Mississippi River.

The Chickasaw were not nomads but farmers who raised corn and beans to supplement their hunting and fishing. The arrival of de Soto was only the beginning of their long eviction. The French governor of Louisiana, Sieur de Bienville, ordered a fort built on a bluff in 1739, with the intention of ridding the region of the Anglophile Chickasaw. In 1795 the Spanish built their Fort San Fernando nearby, intensifying their own colonial ambitions. By the time the Americans raised their flag above Fort Adams in 1797, the fate of the Chickasaw was sealed. They had signed such disastrous treaty agreements that the 1819 Jackson Purchase would effectively end all Chickasaw landholding in West Tennessee.

The dispossession of the Cherokee follows a different story line, if anything more tragic than that of the Chickasaw. President Andrew Jackson's support of the Indian Removal Act led to the dreadful Trail of Tears, the forced "relocation" in 1838 of the Cherokee to reservations in the West.

European mistreatment of the Cherokee, however, had begun earlier. In the late 1700s, English fur traders and men called long hunters ("long" because they were gone from home for long periods) were making forays into East Tennessee from Virginia and the Carolinas, gaining the upper hand over the native Cherokee, at least temporarily. A pioneer named William Bean was the first permanent settler in the territory that would become Tennessee. He built his cabin along the Watauga River in the northeast region.

Bean was soon joined by other settlers, who arrived by foot, boat and horseback to squat on land that had been set aside, by treaty, for the Cherokee.

When word of the settlements reached British Colonial officials, the settlers were ordered to evacuate. Instead, some of them joined forces in 1772 to create the Watauga Association, the first self-governing entity of settlers throwing off the yoke of British rule. For the next few years, the Wataugans negotiated their own treaties with the Cherokee, until 1776, when Tennessee was named a county of North Carolina. In 1779 North Carolina ceded her western lands to the federal government, but Congress delayed any action, so settlers from three other counties joined the Wataugans to establish the state of Franklin. In 1784 they established their capital in Jonesborough and appointed John Sevier governor. When North Carolina decided to reclaim the territory, the Franklinites fought for their land but lost badly, leaving the "Lost State of Franklin" as a poignant footnote to history.

In 1789 North Carolina ceded the "Territory South of the Ohio River" to Congress. Appointed governor, William Blount relocated the territory's government to the settlement around James White's fort, established in 1786 on the banks of the Tennessee. This is where Knoxville was founded, in 1791. Five years later, Tennessee joined the Union (the first state to be carved out of national territory), and Knoxville was its capital for the first 16 years of statehood. Tennessee's constitution, which espoused universal suffrage (meaning that free Negroes, as African Americans were called then, could vote), was deemed by Thomas Jefferson the "least imperfect and most republican" of any state's.

Frontiersmen were followed by veterans of the Revolutionary War who, awarded land grants, poured into the new state by land and river, boosting the population to 100,000 by the turn of the century.

One of the first representatives the new state sent to Washington, D.C., was a backwoodsman by the name of Andrew Jackson. By 1829, when Jackson became president, the state had blossomed into prosperity. Steamboats were plying the Cumberland River to Nashville, formerly an 18th-century fur trading post, and Memphis had become a thriving cotton port.

Chattanooga was established in 1839, but did not greatly expand until the railroad arrived in 1850. On the eve of the Civil War, Tennessee voted against secession but when Fort Sumter was attacked, a majority of Tennesseans voted to secede. Pro-Union sentiment remained strong in East Tennessee for a variety of reasons, one of them doubtless that slavery was less a factor there than in the rest of the South.

Amid these internal conflicts, Tennessee was second only to Virginia in terms of violent and bloody battlegrounds. The stories of battles fought at and around Chattanooga, Shiloh, Franklin and elsewhere are discussed in the chapters to follow. Tennessee was the first state accepted back into the Union, in 1866, after former Tennessee governor Andrew Johnson became president. Although Tennessee was spared much of the carpetbagging that plagued the rest of the South, it suffered epidemics, including one of yellow fever that devastated Memphis in 1878.

Despite these and other challenges, Tennessee faced a promising future in the new century. In 1933 Congress established the Tennessee Valley Authority (TVA), the state's most ambitious undertaking. The TVA remains the only federal agency headquartered outside Washington, in Knoxville. In addition to vastly improving the state's water transportation system, it brought hydroelectric power to rural farmers and thousands of others who, at last, really joined the 20th century. Commerce thrived as a result, flood control attracted new residents and the newly created lakes fueled a tourism boom that has yet to peak.

The name "Tennessee" is believed to derive from *Tanasee*, the Yuchi Indian word for "meeting place."

By the 1940s, Tennessee was evolving from an agricultural economy to one supported by manufacturing, though farmland still constitutes nearly 12 million acres and generates more than $2 billion each year. Cattle and dairying, hardwood production, Walking Horse breeding, metal and equipment manufacturing, and transportation all play a major role in the state's economy, as do food production, chemicals, and printing and publishing. Chattanooga and Nashville are prominent insurance centers; Memphis is the second-largest inland port in the United States; Nashville is the world capital of country-music recording; and Lynchburg, home of Jack Daniel's, is one of the country's preeminent distillery towns. The scientific community along the Oak Ridge–University of Tennessee in Knoxville corridor continues to produce breakthroughs in electronics and space-age technologies. Finally, the Great Smoky Mountains National Park and neighboring Pigeon Forge and Gatlinburg attract millions of visitors annually.

Where to Go

The three cities that give the Tri-City Area its nickname—Johnson City, Kingsport and Bristol—are the urban exceptions to the largely rural landscape of **Northeast Tennessee**. The scenic wedge of northeast Tennessee borders both North Carolina, with which it shares Roan Mountain, and Virginia, with which it shares Bristol. Small farms hug the narrow roadsides, which curve gently through the countryside, barely pausing to acknowledge some of the tiny villages that give the region much of its charm. This is the land that gave rise to the Lost State of Franklin and provided the future president, Andrew Johnson, his political start. Jonesborough, founded in 1779, is the oldest city in Tennessee, and its historic district is unparalleled in the state for restoration effort.

South and west is Knoxville, the state's first capital, and its neighbor, Oak Ridge. The Great Smoky Mountains can be easily visited on a day trip from Knoxville, but for a longer sojourn, many visitors opt for lodging in Pigeon Forge and Gatlinburg, the heart of the **Gateway to the Smokies**. Dollywood and smaller entertainment facilities, along with hundreds of discount stores, draw millions of visitors each year.

The **Great Smoky Mountains National Park**, one of the most popular parks in the United States, was fashioned with painstaking care from private lands that once were logged to the brink of disaster. Most of the small communities have vanished into the history pages, but Cades Cove has been preserved to show modern visitors what mountain life looked like in the mid-1800s.

The southern stretches of the Appalachian Mountains harbor towns like Ducktown and Copperhill, where copper ore was once mined. Today, a new industry is revitalizing the **Overhill Region**— a tourist-based industry called whitewater rafting. A five-mile stretch of the Ocoee River here is considered the best whitewater-rafting destination in the country; it was selected for the first Olympic rafting event ever held in natural surroundings, part of the 1996 games headquartered in nearby Atlanta, Georgia.

Inch for inch, **Chattanooga** has more going for it than many cities twice its size. Between the Tennessee Aquarium, part of an ongoing upgrade of the downtown riverfront, and famous Lookout Mountain at the other end of town, a bevy of restaurants, historical buildings and museums—including one just for kids— makes this the most family-friendly city in Tennessee. Visitors can see the town and its attractions in myriad ways: aboard restored trains (no, not the Chattanooga Choo-Choo), free shuttle buses, riverboats and the steep Lookout Mountain Incline.

The dramatic and diverse **Cumberland Plateau** runs from Kentucky down to Chattanooga, marking the eastern and western

TENNESSEE TIME

Tennessee is so wide, in fact, that it is split between two time zones. Northeast Tennessee, Knoxville, the Great Smoky Mountains, Chattanooga and most of the Cumberland Plateau lie in the eastern time zone. Nashville and points west are in the central time zone. Thus if you drive from Chattanooga to Nashville, you gain an hour, shaving an hour off the trip—at least, according to the clock. And if you drive from Nashville to Chattanooga, bear in mind you will arrive an extra hour late.

borders of Middle Tennessee. This is wild and rugged land, home to some of the state's most spectacular parks and most unusual towns, including the wonderfully preserved Rugby, founded in the last century as a utopian community. Backcountry hiking, fishing and antique shopping are among the diversions that draw adventuresome visitors.

Nashville hardly needs an introduction. Ever since the first guitar was twanged in Ryman Auditorium, the town has been in the forefront of country music. Country has won fans far outside what used to be a niche. The capital is home to dozens of music publishing firms, some of the biggest in the business, and restaurants and hotels have increased in sophistication to accommodate the influx of newcomers from California and elsewhere. The Grand Ole Opry has moved to Opryland, a sprawling entertainment complex not far from The Hermitage, Andrew Jackson's estate, one of the premier tourist attractions in Middle Tennessee.

On the outskirts of Nashville and farther south, old towns like Franklin and Columbia still have their antebellum homes, most of them in private hands but several open to the public, part of what's known as the **Heritage Trails**. Some of the most horrific fighting in the Civil War occurred right at Franklin, where places like the Carnton Plantation and the Carter House have been restored as poignant reminders of the conflict. The rolling countryside down around Shelbyville is world headquarters for raising Tennessee Walking Horses. Winding country roads lead to villages like Bell Buckle and Wartrace, offering some of the best antique shopping in Tennessee.

Lakes and rivers in **Northwest Tennessee and the Delta Country** provide exceptional recreational opportunities for lovers of the outdoors. Land Between the Lakes, straddling the border with Kentucky, offers more than boating and fishing; there is also The Homeplace-1850, one of the state's finest living-history museums. In the farthest corner of this portion of the state, Reelfoot Lake attracts American bald eagles and other birds who flock to the region each winter. In the Delta Country closer to Memphis are towns like Nutbush and Henning, hometowns, respectively, to rock star Tina Turner and Pulitzer Prize–winning author Alex Haley.

Memphis is the most populous city in Tennessee and, although it's on the state's western border on the banks of the Mississippi River, it feels in many ways the most Southern of all. This is the home of the blues, that uniquely American musical genre, as well as of Graceland, the mansion where Elvis chose to live the last years of his life. Between the nightclubs of Beale Street and the barbecue joints scattered around town, Memphis has a lively nightlife scene, as well as numerous museums and institutes of higher learning.

Southwest Tennessee, stretching from the outskirts of Memphis to the Natchez Trace, is the least touristy region of the state.

It's a favorite destination for Civil War buffs, who find endless pleasure in exploring the battlefields of Shiloh, as well as for folks who like to hunt and fish, particularly around Pickwick Reservoir. The Natchez Trace, a historic route between Natchez, Mississippi, and Nashville, was on the verge of disappearing into history until the National Park Service began constructing a highway approximating the old trail. The northernmost stretch of the road was paved in 1996, and now travelers can enjoy a peaceful, scenic 200-mile drive entirely within Tennessee.

When to Go

Picking the best time to visit Tennessee depends on what you want to do and see. To a lesser extent, it depends on how important bargains are to you. Spring and fall are the peak seasons just about everywhere, except for the town of Gatlinburg, where the ski slopes are a big wintertime draw. At the other extreme, summer is ideal for lake swimming, canoeing and waterskiing. In fact, many mountain attractions are closed during the dead of winter, particularly the month of January.

SEASONS

It should be noted that weather conditions can change swiftly and dramatically at higher elevations. Anyone traveling to the mountains of Tennessee—or to any wilderness area—should take plenty of water, rain gear and emergency supplies in case of sudden storms.

Tennessee is large enough, with sufficient variation in elevations, to have several climatic zones. In the eastern mountain towns, for instance, January's average high temperature is 50°; low is about 29°. At the other end of the state, Memphis's winters average 41°.

In July, the average high temperature in Gatlinburg is 87°; the low, about 60°. In Memphis, it's about 81°, which means there are some insufferably hot Delta days in July and August. Both ends of the state receive roughly the same amount of rain, right around 50 inches a year.

Nashville, close to the geographical center of the state, averages 80° in July, when 100° days are not uncommon, and the humidity is almost as high. In January, Nashville's temperature averages 37°, and the likelihood of rain is higher than at the height of summer.

The sparkling days of spring and fall are especially popular with folks who enjoy the great outdoors. Wildflowers and flowering trees and shrubs change the face of the state in spring, when the grayness disappears in a brilliant blur of pink, white and green. Autumn finds the leaves changing colors in the mountains, making it the second-most popular time of year to visit the Great Smoky Mountains.

CALENDAR OF EVENTS

Gateway to the Smokies WinterFest events take place throughout the month in Pigeon Forge, which makes the most of the season with musical entertainment, sports and automobile shows, art exhibits, nature walks and talks, Trolley Tours, factory discount outlet sales and more.

Northwest Tennessee and the Delta Country Reelfoot Eagle Watch Tours begin this month and extend into March. Rangers lead groups on guided walks to look at wildlife, particularly the American bald eagles that nest here each winter on the outskirts of Tiptonville.

Memphis Elvis Presley's Birthday Celebration is held early in the month at The King's regal residence, Graceland, featuring a reception, a banquet and a special proclamation ceremony, during which visitors can tour the Memphis mansion.

Gateway to the Smokies As living proof that Tennessee's oral tradition includes the spoken word as well as song, the Smoky Mountain Storytelling Festival is held early in the month in Pigeon Forge.

Nashville In early February, the Music Valley Antiques Market of Nashville gathers more than 70 dealers—of paintings, porcelains and furnishings—under one roof, with speakers on horticulture and antiques and a flower sale. For one-stop antique and craft shopping, the place to be the second weekend of this month is the All American Heart of Country Antiques Show at the Gaylord Opryland Resort. More than 140 vendors not only sell their art, textiles and furniture, but also offer lectures and other information.

Southwest Tennessee This part of Tennessee is bird dog country, as evidenced by the presence of the National Bird Dog Hall of Fame and the nearby Ames Plantation in Grand Junction, which hosts the National Field Trial Championships for 11 days in the middle of the month.

Northeast Tennessee At the Bristol International Raceway in the Tri-City Area, the Busch and Nextel NASCAR Races are held toward the end of the month.

Gateway to the Smokies Amateur magicians make rabbits jump out of hats and perform other inexplicable feats at the Winter of Carnival of Magic, held at the Gatlinburg Convention Center the first weekend of the month.

Nashville At the end of the month, Tin Pan South brings the largest week-long songwriters' festival to Nashville.

Northwest Tennessee and the Delta Country If you like old-time country music, prick up your ears and head up to Clarksville for the **Tennessee Old-Time Fiddlers Championship**, a two-day festival featuring the best fiddlers from around the country.

APRIL   **Gateway to the Smokies**   Knoxville's dogwood trees have a habit of blooming just in time for the annual three-week-long **Dogwood Arts Festival**, an extravaganza headquartered in Market Square, a hub of arts-and-crafts booths, food vendors and entertainment. From there, buses depart to tour up to 60 miles of dogwood trails around the city and county, and festival-goers are also encouraged to tour some 100 private and public gardens. The last weekend is capped with a huge country music concert. Dolly Parton returns to her hometown of Pigeon Forge each spring to kick off **Dollywood's Festival of Nations**, a five-week celebration of food, culture and entertainment. Toward the end of the month, the **Annual Spring Wildflower Pilgrimage** includes a hike through the Great Smoky Mountains as well as spectacular indoor displays at the Gatlinburg Convention Center.

Heritage Trails   They call it **Mule Day**, but it's actually a long weekend early in the month honoring this otherwise unsung hero of the countryside. Mule shows, arts-and-crafts booths, food and entertainment, a talent contest, square dances, a flea market and, best of all, the big parade make this one of Columbia's most popular events.

Northwest Tennessee and the Delta Country   The **World's Biggest Fish Fry** is held each April in Paris, during which more than 10,000 pounds of fish (accompanied by hush puppies and coleslaw) are consumed.

MAY   **Cumberland Plateau**   The food, dance, music, poetry, crafts and other cultural aspects of the mixed heritage of the town of Rugby add up to a long weekend called the **Festival of British and Appalachian Culture**.

Memphis   The **Memphis in May International Festival** runs the whole month, a smorgasbord of blues and other musical and cultural performances. It's one big party, with nearly 100 events including a festival on Beale Street, a barbecue contest and wall-to-wall food and entertainment.

Southwest Tennessee   Pickers from all over entertain thousands of fans each Memorial Day weekend at the **Summertown Bluegrass Reunion**, with much clogging, square dancing and buck dancing going on. There's a repeat over Labor Day.

JUNE   **Northeast Tennessee**   Way up on Roan Mountain near Elizabethton, the **Rhododendron Festival** is held mid-month at the peak of bloom in one of the world's largest natural rhododendron gardens.

Chattanooga   During the wildly popular **Riverbend Festival**, internationally known entertainers perform county, classical, blues and rock in a week of activities that include the "Bessie Smith Strut," a day in honor of native jazz and blues queen Smith, capped with a fireworks display, at venues throughout the city. The **Sewanee Summer Music Festival** is a classic affair that begins this month and continues through August, with some 30 orchestra, chamber music and solo concerts by students (at the University of the South) as well as guest artists.

Northwest Tennessee and the Delta Country   Beauty pageants, horse shows, pet shows and peach "everything" are part of the celebrations at the annual **Tennessee Peach Festival** the last weekend in June in Brownsville.

JULY

Cumberland Plateau   Conjuring up the early days of Red Boiling Springs, the town hosts a **Folk Medicine Festival** each summer, a weekend that reminds folks of the reason this town was founded as a spa at the turn of the 20th century. The festival includes workshops and seminars as well as medicine shows and music and magic performances.

Heritage Trails   A parade replete with mules, goats and bicycles highlights **Uncle Dave Macon Days**, a weekend featuring old-time music and competitions in fiddling and banjo playing and buck dancing, held on the grounds of Cannonsburgh Pioneer Village in Murfreesboro. There are also crafts booths, historical displays and plenty of good food.

AUGUST

Heritage Trails   Shelbyville is the site of the annual **Tennessee Walking Horse Celebration**, an extravaganza held the last ten days of the month at Celebration Grounds. This is the best chance anytime, anywhere, to see 2000 of these extraordinarily graceful thoroughbreds strut their stuff.

Memphis   Summertime gets really hot during **Elvis Week**, a citywide, week-long celebration of the life and music of the King. Nearly 100 artists and musicians spend the first weekend of the month in Jackson, performing and meeting fans at **The Rockabilly Festival**.

SEPTEMBER

Gateway to the Smokies   In a state where fireworks are available at practically every interstate offramp, it's really saying something to note that the largest fireworks display in the Southeast takes place on the downtown Knoxville Riverfront each Labor Day, an event called **Boomsday**.

Cumberland Plateau   Marbles are the topic at Standing Stone Park's **Marble Festival and National Championship Rolley Hole Tournament**, where festivities include marble making, marble playing and marble trading, along with some marble-unrelated activities to round out the event.

Nashville The **Tennessee State Fair** is a classic summertime event, usually over the second weekend, including a midway with games and rides, 4-H Club events, crafts, needlework and antiques as well as a huge livestock and agricultural component. A family-oriented, alcohol-free weekend, the annual **African Street Festival** in Nashville involves 100 merchants from 25 states, ethnic-food concessions, children's storytelling, art and fashion shows and lots of music: rap, reggae, blues, jazz and gospel.

Heritage Trails In Franklin, Dixieland jazz is the music of choice at the **Franklin Jazz Festival**, held over Labor Day weekend on the town square and surrounded by food booths and plenty of kegs of beer. No place else but Bell Buckle would host a quaint old-fashioned **Quilt Tour**, an exhibition and home tour held on the third Saturday of the month, with demonstrations, seminars, music and food. Of course the antique shops will be open for those who can't resist taking home a handmade example. Ten historic homes and churches on the National Register of Historic Places open their doors each September for the **Majestic Middle Tennessee Fall Tour** in the Columbia area.

Memphis Mud Island is the site of a three-day celebration of the diversity of the South called the **Memphis Music and Heritage Festival**, sponsored by the river town's own Center for Southern Folklore.

OCTOBER **Northeast Tennessee** Rescued from near-extinction, the venerable art of storytelling is revived and thriving in Jonesborough early in the month. The **National Storytelling Festival** is a famous event that just gets bigger and better all the time; each year, a book and a book-on-tape are released of the competition's winning 'tellers. The founder of the United Nations is honored with old-time crafts, Gospel music, storytelling and museum tours at the **Cordell Hull Folk Festival** in Byrdstown.

Chattanooga A combination boating and foliage event, the **Fall Color Cruise and Folk Festival** is one of the largest gatherings of watercraft in the Southeast. Folks flock to Chattanooga during the last two weekends of the month to admire the changing fall foliage, to check out the arts-and-crafts exhibits and to attend the folk festival.

NOVEMBER **Gateway to the Smokies** Oak Ridge's **Foothills Craft Guild**, the oldest chartered Craft Guild in Tennessee, presents its **Annual Show and Sale**, including a juried show and demonstrations, with special guest artists and musicians, at the Knoxville Convention Center during a long weekend mid-month. **WinterFest**-ivities begin this month in Gatlinburg and Pigeon Forge, with music and crafts and special sales at the factory discount stores. Seven antique malls and shops get decked out for the holidays in time to host the late-November **Goodlettsville Antique Festival**.

Heritage Trails The annual **Native American Indian Association's Pow Wow** in Tullahoma brings together American Indians from throughout North America for a weekend of storytelling, traditional dancing, foods, crafts and fine arts displays from many different tribes.

Nashville In mid-month, the Nashville Arena comes alive with the sound of hoofbeats during the **Longhorn Championship Rodeo**, an event in which only the top 72 North American cowboys and cowgirls compete in six different contests, with a theme that changes each year. This is the final championship rodeo of the year for Nashville's own national touring big-league rodeo company.

Northwest Tennessee and the Delta Country November is a good time to visit Land Between the Lakes for **The Homeplace-1850 Harvest Festival**. It's so all-American there are even demonstrations of apple butter–making skills, wagon rides, storytelling and other types of entertainment appropriate to mid-19th-century America.

Gateway to the Smokies **Christmas in Old Appalachia** is a special holiday presentation at Norris' Museum of Appalachia, a living-history museum with authentic log cabins and farm implements from the early days of East Tennessee settlement.

DECEMBER

Cumberland Plateau Christ Church Episcopal, the beautiful chapel with the lovely stained glass, offers a special service during **Christmas at Historic Rugby**. During two Saturdays in December, visitors tour historic buildings by candlelight, listen to classical music and watch actors in period costume portray the holiday festivities of the town's founding families.

Heritage Trails The **Carter House Candlelight Tour of Homes** in Franklin visits several historic homes that have been dressed up to offer treats and music during the first weekend.

Memphis If you find yourself in River City on New Year's Eve, join the revelers at the **Bury Your Blues Blowout on Beale New Year's Eve Celebration**, an event that happens on the street and in the clubs that line this historic street where the blues were born.

The Tennessee Department of Tourist Development is a wonderful resource of information about the state and its attractions. For further details on a specific area, visitors are directed to local agencies, either convention and visitors bureaus or, in the smaller towns, the chambers of commerce. ~ 320 6th Avenue North, Nashville, TN 37243; 615-741-2159, 800-462-8366, 888-243-9769, fax 615-741-7225; www.tnvacation.com.

Before You Go

VISITORS CENTERS

The **Knoxville Convention and Visitors Bureau** is located near Old Town. ~ 601 West Summit Drive; 865-523-7263, 800-727-8045; www.knoxville.org, e-mail tourism@knoxville.org.

Visitors can pick up hundreds of brochures and have just about any travel-related questions answered by a friendly, well-trained staff at the **Chattanooga Area Convention and Visitors Bureau**. ~ 2 Broad Street; 423-756-8687, 800-322-3344; www.chattanoogafun.com, e-mail inquiries@chattanoogacvb.com.

In Nashville, where the state department of tourism is located, check out the local **Convention and Visitors Bureau**. ~ 211 Commerce Street; 615-259-4700, 800-657-6910; www.nashvillecvb.com. There is also a **Tourist Information Center** at the Gaylord Entertainment Center at 5th Avenue and Broadway, where you can get brochures and information on area attractions. ~ Exit 85 off Route 65; 615-259-4747, 800-657-6910. If you're flying into town, especially if you're arriving before or after normal working hours, check out the **Nashville International Airport Welcome Center** on the baggage-claim level; it's open from 6:30 a.m. to 11 p.m. daily.

In Memphis stop by the **Visitors Information Center**, which is open daily and on Sunday afternoons. ~ 119 North Riverside Drive; 901-543-5333. The **Memphis Convention and Visitors Bureau** is located downtown. ~ 47 Union Avenue; 901-543-5300, 800-863-6744, fax 901-543-5350.

You'll find **State Welcome Centers** on Route 81, near Bristol, at the Virginia–Tennessee border; on Routes 75 and 24, near Chattanooga, by the Georgia border; on Route 75, near Jellico, by the Kentucky border; and on Route 155, near the Missouri border north of Memphis.

PACKING

The good news is you can travel just about anywhere in Tennessee, save churches and deluxe restaurants, in a pair of blue jeans and a shirt or a turtleneck. There is no bad news. The key to successful packing for a trip to this diverse state is summed up in one word: layering. Pack a windbreaker, sweater, rain hat, raincoat and, in winter, a down parka for the upper elevations. A good compromise is a down vest and a warm hat, which should not take up too much room in your carry-on. If you're doing business, you'll need a suit (or at least a coat and tie) in the big cities, unless you're in the music business, which is more casual (although some recent arrivals can still be spotted in Armanis and Bruno Maglias). If you plan to dine in fine hotel restaurants or other top spots, you'll need a dress or coat and tie. Tennesseans take a fairly casual attitude toward dress, especially in the mountains. In fact, you'll feel overdressed if you go to Pigeon Forge in anything much more formal than a T-shirt. But please, no cutoffs, anywhere, except in a canoe.

LODGING

Old homes, some of them mansions, are being converted into bed-and-breakfast inns practically every month throughout Tennessee. The great news for travelers is that the cost of living in the state lags far behind that in New England and California, which have led the B&B boom in the United States. In many cases, you can spend the night in an antebellum B&B and be served a generous hot Southern-style breakfast for less than what you'd pay for a room in a medium-priced hotel. In virtually every case, the inn-keeper knows the local lore, the lay of the land and exactly how to get to an out-of-the-way restaurant that the townsfolk love but are almost never advertised. Imagine enjoying an early-morning cup of coffee while rocking in a chair on a porch overlooking the mountains, or a historic town, or simply a quiet woodland, and you've got the picture.

> Tennessee State Parks is a wonderful resource for accommodations throughout the state. ~ 401 Church Street, Nashville, TN 37243; 800-867-2757; www.tnstateparks.com.

Lodging in the big cities is dominated by chain hotels that are much the same the world over, though in Tennessee they are graced with touches of Southern hospitality and, usually, grits and fresh biscuits on the breakfast menu. Some grand old hotels have retained their original charm; others have reclaimed their ties to tradition through remodeling and upgrading. A handful, we are happy to report, remain legends in their own right.

Along the interstates, of course, it's hard to find any place to stay other than a chain motel. Even the mom-and-pop motels that only a few years ago retained some remnants of individuality have been swallowed by bigger companies and turned into cookie-cutter accommodations. It is still possible to find little gems where personality and affordability are not mutually exclusive. This book lists every one we could discover.

While there is only one place to spend the night with a roof over your head in the Great Smoky Mountains National Park, motels and condominiums are plentiful elsewhere in Tennessee's mountains. Pigeon Forge and Gatlinburg are particularly blessed with an abundance of lodging choices, including a preponderance of country inns unmatched elsewhere in the state.

An additional source of lodging is supplied by none other than the great state of Tennessee. We're not just talking about primitive campsites. Several of the parks offer fine accommodations, in some cases the best possible choice for miles around. Many of the parks are located on lakes, in the mountains or beside rivers and waterfalls, and boast the best views available. The prices are not bargain-basement level, but you are unlikely to feel over-charged, either. These are not the kinds of places where you are going to get room service, but you probably didn't decide to visit a state park if you were expecting caviar and champagne delivered at midnight.

If you're traveling during a less-than-peak season (which varies throughout the state), remember that prices fluctuate. Wherever you lay your head in Tennessee, don't do it without checking to see if you qualify for a discount by virtue of the season or even a club membership such as AAA or AARP. Anyone on a strict budget can find great deals in the shoulder seasons around March and October, when iffy weather can break in your favor, and you might get a first-rate room that would rent for much more a week earlier or later.

In *Hidden Tennessee*, accommodations are described in the same order as sights and restaurants, to make it convenient for the traveler to tour the local attractions neighborhood by neighborhood. The range of rates printed at the end of each description refers to high-season rates, those charged for two people on a weekend at the optimum time to visit a particular place. In other words, an inn that qualifies as deluxe in spring might offer some budget rates in the dead of winter.

Budget lodgings are priced at less than $60 for two people. *Moderate*-priced lodgings run anywhere from $60 to $100 (occasionally, at the same establishment). For these rates, you can expect a little more in the way of space, service or amenities. Lodgings qualified as *deluxe* cost $100 to $140 a night, usually because of the quality of the accommodations or for the uniqueness of the situation. It is rare in Tennessee to have to pay for more than you get, as long as you stay out of chain hotels in downtown locations, which vary widely in value. In Tennessee, *ultra-deluxe* accommodations, those costing more than $140 a night, are few and far between. Believe it or not, some can be found in the state parks; others are in extraordinarily gracious homes or in the finer rooms in truly grand hotels, or in places that provide an extraordinary level of comfort, privacy and service.

DINING

There's a lot more to food in Tennessee than barbecue and biscuits, though some are bound to ask, "Why?" Until you've had the best of both, served in generous proportions in a home-style restaurant (not casual, but *home-style*), you might not understand why these two foodstuffs are so beloved.

Tennessee may be landlocked, but its many rivers and streams supply an almost endless bounty of delectables. Mountain trout are the most delicate, and after you taste them you just may decide to take up fishing yourself, to get even closer to the source. Catfish are the most popular and ubiquitous fish; you'll find them prepared every which way, but fried, with tartar sauce, is best. You can also get fresh shrimp, crab and oysters, and, in the home

That's
Good Eatin'

The classic Tennessee meal is called "meat-and-threes," which is not unique to Tennessee except for the nomenclature. Whenever you have lunch or dinner at the most popular local spot in any given town, you'll always find meat-and-threes meals on the menu.

Actually, menu is too formal a word in many instances; sometimes there is no written menu, just a sign on the wall or a friendly waiter who will point to a series of tables where steam rises from deep dishes. The phrase "meat-and-threes" derives from the fact that, for one set price, customers get a choice of one meat dish and three vegetables. It is rare to be charged more than $7 for a meat-and-threes meal, especially when it is served buffet style.

Meat choices inevitably include roast or fried chicken, pork chops and/or chicken-fried steak. Numbering among the moist vegetables selections are usually some kind of greens (collard, turnip, mustard), corn, carrots, beets, baked beans, sweet potatoes and/or mashed potatoes.

There is a menu variation of this that is likely to include portions of, say, fried onion rings or a choice of baked potato, coleslaw and the like. All these goodies usually come with biscuits, often made in the back and quite simply irresistible: hot, fluffy and oozing with butter. And just when you think you'll never eat another bite, that nice waiter will start telling you about the fresh pies—sweet potato, pecan, buttermilk.... What a way to end a meal!

state of Federal Express, naturally just about anything can be flown in fresh that day from just about any place on the planet.

Visitors looking for more elegant or exotic fare, be it Continental, Cantonese or California cuisine, will find it almost exclusively in the big cities of Memphis, Nashville, Knoxville and Chattanooga.

In particular, Memphis and Nashville offer the widest range of cuisine, from expensive dinners served in absolutely elegant surroundings to holes-in-the-wall where locals go when they want a fast, cheap lunch. There are, of course, fabulous exceptions. Just outside of Jonesborough, for example, Cajun is the specialty at a restaurant located in a former general store that may take several attempts to locate off a series of increasingly narrow country roads. Sensational home-cooked meals are one of the main draws to a bed and breakfast way up in remote Rugby, which has only one restaurant to its name. At an interstate intersection outside Murfreesboro is an outpost of a Memphis-based barbecue joint that might well convert a vegetarian to the virtues of 'cue. On the outskirts of Pigeon Forge is a tiny restaurant famed for the imagination and exuberance of its chef, who performs his magic in a galley kitchen that would fit inside most New York City apartments. And it would be a shame to leave Gatlinburg without sampling the sample made-from-scratch muffins and other treats in a log cabin with an Austrian-style tearoom. These are the hidden gems of Tennessee, and this book goes out of its way to lead you to their doors.

Outside urban centers, though, trendy ethnic food such as Thai cuisine is a rarity. But if it's exotic you want, Tennessee cooking might just fill the bill. That is, if you're from out of state.

The restaurants recommended in *Hidden Tennessee* are, like the lodging and attractions segments, grouped geographically. Each chapter includes suggested restaurants in various price ranges, as indicated at the end of each description. In each case, the price category reflects the average price of a single dinner entrée; in virtually every instance, lunch costs less. Restaurants classified as *budget* price their entrées at an average of $10. Many ethnic and most home-style establishments fall into this category, or in the budget-to-moderate range. *Moderate*-priced restaurants list most of their entrées between $10 and $16. *Deluxe* establishments, where you can expect more and better service and fancier food, charge between $16 and $24 for most entrées. Restaurants classified as *ultra-deluxe* price their entrées at $24 and above. These are relatively rare birds in Tennessee, and tend to be linen-tablecloth establishments with superior service and good wine lists.

If you grew up around coastal waters, don't confuse freshwater catfish with those that swim in salty rivers. The two are as different as night and day.

The more expensive restaurants tend to have longer life spans than their cheaper counterparts. Still, food service is a volatile business so if you call or arrive at a recommended spot only to find it has closed, don't hesitate to ask for recommendations from your hotel or inn or even from people you meet casually. Everyone likes to talk about his or her favorite spots to eat, and if you discover some jewels omitted from this book, please write and let us know about them.

All restaurants listed in this guide serve lunch and dinner unless otherwise noted.

LIQUOR LAWS

Like several other Southern states, Tennessee has no statewide laws about which types of alcoholic beverages may be sold and consumed. The rules vary from county to county. One regulation is consistent, however; no liquor may be carried into or consumed within state park boundaries. Laws are most lenient in the big cities; liquor stores and wine lists can be found in just about every neighborhood. But even in the big cities, liquor sales are often restricted on Sunday, when you might be allowed to buy liquor only after noontime or at a place that also serves food. Even in counties designated as "dry," beer is almost always sold, but wine is grouped with hard liquor and available only in "wet" counties. Regardless of local liquor laws, Tennessee's many wineries can serve and sell their products in their own tasting rooms.

TRAVELING WITH CHILDREN

If you've traveled with your children before, you won't have to make many adjustments to tour Tennessee. The major cities of Memphis, Nashville, Knoxville and Chattanooga all have attractions geared to children, from zoos to discovery museums to outdoor parks and activities such as those offered at nature centers. Many state parks have nature programs and plenty of pint-size activities. The only places not really geared to kids are the remote backroads, unless you're en route to a lake or unless your kids like stopping at out-of-the-way diners and the occasional antique shop.

If you are traveling by air, try to reserve bulkhead seats where there is plenty of room. Take along extras you may need, such as diapers, changes of clothing, snacks and toys, or small games. When traveling by car, be sure to take along the extras, too. Make sure you have plenty of water and juices to drink; dehydration can be a subtle problem.

A first-aid kit is a must for any trip. Along with adhesive bandages, antiseptic cream and something to stop itching, include any medicines your child's pediatrician might recommend to treat allergies (particularly if you visit in spring), colds, diarrhea or any chronic problems your child may have.

If you plan on getting out on any of Tennessee's lakes, take extra care with children's skin the first few days. Tender young skin can suffer severe sunburn before you know it. Hats for the kids are a good idea, along with liberal applications of a good sunscreen. Never take your eyes off children when you're near lakes or streams.

All-night stores are scarce in rural areas, and stores in small towns often close early. You may go a long distance between stores that can supply you with essentials, so be sure to be well-stocked with diapers, baby food and other necessities when on the go.

WOMEN TRAVELING ALONE

Tennessee's big cities require the same precautions travelers would observe anywhere. Women should not walk the streets alone after dark, and although it's tempting to attend nighttime street festivals in places like Beale Street, it's not a good idea to do it alone. It is better not to let strangers know you are traveling alone or where you are staying or planning to travel. The more rural areas are somewhat safer, but at the same time, women traveling alone are considered something of an anomaly outside the big cities. It's best to avoid accommodations at motels in industrial areas or other places where there is no real neighborhood after dark. When requesting reservations at hotels and motels, ask for rooms near the elevator or facing a central courtyard rather than find yourself in a remote location. For more hints, get a copy of *Safety and Security for Women Who Travel* (Travelers' Tales).

GAY & LESBIAN TRAVELERS

Very few places in Tennessee could be described as gay-friendly. Outside the big cities, few lodgings, restaurants, nightclubs or cafés specifically cater to gays and lesbians. Only Nashville and Memphis could be said to have any sizable gay communities; elsewhere, these communities are virtually invisible to the non-gay traveler.

The **Rainbow Community Center** in Nashville provides meeting space. Bulletin boards, notebooks and pamphlets are filled with information ranging from gay-friendly organizations to local happenings. They sponsor a variety of activities as well. Their number is staffed Wednesday and Friday between 6 p.m. to 9 p.m. ~ 703 Berry Road, Nashville; 615-297-0008; www.rainbowcommunitycenter.org.

The **Memphis Gay & Lesbian Community Center** runs an extensive recording that lists restaurants, cafés and nightclubs that welcome gays. The switchboard is staffed from 7:30 to 11 p.m. ~ 892 South Cooper Street, Memphis; 901-278-6422; www.mglcc.org.

The **Rock MCC** has a ministry to the lesbian, gay, bisexual and transgender community, sponsoring socials several times a year and two services on Sunday. ~ 1601 Faust Street, Chattanooga, TN 37404; 423-629-2737.

Local and regional gay and lesbian publications can usually be found in the larger bookstores in any city. While you're in Mem-

> The staggering number of Tennessee residents that donated time and effort to the War of 1812 and the Mexican War garnered Tennessee its nickname, "The Volunteer State."

phis, pick up the free monthly tabloid *Triangle Journal News*. It covers news and features pertaining to gays and lesbians, and also includes a handy list of resources for metropolitan Memphis. ~ 901-454-1411; www.memphistrianglejournal.com. The Nashville-based *Query*, a free statewide tabloid, comes out weekly with news, arts and entertainment, sports and leisure features of interest to the lesbian and gay community. ~ 615-298-4532.

SENIOR TRAVELERS

The AARP offers membership to anyone over 50. Benefits of AARP membership include travel discounts with a number of firms. ~ 601 E Street NW, Washington, DC 20049; 800-424-3410; www. aarp.org, e-mail member@aarp.org.

Elderhostel offers reasonably priced, all-inclusive educational programs in a variety of locations throughout the year. ~ 11 Avenue de Lafayette, Boston, MA 02111; 877-426-8056, fax 877-426-2166; www.elderhostel.org.

Be extra careful about health matters. In addition to the medications you ordinarily use, bring along the prescriptions for obtaining more. Consider carrying a medical record with you—including your medical history and current medical status as well as your doctor's name, telephone number and address. Make sure that your insurance covers you while away from home.

DISABLED TRAVELERS

Providing helpful information for disabled travelers are the Society for Accessible Travel & Hospitality at 347 5th Avenue, Suite 610, New York, NY 10016 (212-447-7284; www.sath.org, e-mail sathtravel@aol.com); the MossRehab ResourceNet at Moss-Rehab Hospital, 1200 Tabor Road, Philadelphia, PA 19141 (215-329-5715; www.mossresourcenet.org); and Flying Wheels Travel at 143 West Bridge Street, Owatonna, MN 55060 (507-451-5005, fax 507-451-1685; www.flyingwheelstravel.com).

Travelin' Talk, a network of people and organizations, also provides assistance. ~ P.O. Box 1796, Wheat Ridge, CO 80034; 303-232-2979; www.travelintalk.net, e-mail travelin@travelintalk. net.

Access-Able Travel Service has worldwide information online. ~ www.access-able.com.

FOREIGN TRAVELERS

Passports and Visas   Most foreign visitors need a passport and tourist visa to enter the United States. Contact your nearest United States embassy or consulate well in advance to obtain a visa and to check on any other entry requirements.

Customs Requirements   Foreign travelers are allowed to carry in the following: 200 cigarettes (1 carton), 50 cigars or 2 kilograms (4.4 pounds) of smoking tobacco; one liter of alcohol for personal use only (you must be 21 years of age to bring in alcohol); and US$100 worth of duty-free gifts that can include an additional quantity of 100 cigars. You may bring in any amount of currency, but must fill out a form if you bring in over US$10,000. Carry any prescription drugs in clearly marked containers. (You may have to produce a written prescription or doctor's statement for the customs' officer.) Meat or meat products, seeds, plants, fruits and narcotics are not allowed to be brought into the United States. Contact the **United States Customs Service** for further information. ~ 1300 Pennsylvania Avenue NW, Washington, DC 20229; 877-287-8667; www.customs.treas.gov.

Driving If you plan to rent a car, an international driver's license should be obtained before arriving in the United States. Some car rental agencies require both a foreign license and an international driver's license. Many also require a lessee to be at least 25 years of age; all require a major credit card. Seat belts are mandatory for the driver and all passengers. Children under the age of six or 60 pounds should be in the back seat in approved child safety restraints.

Currency United States money is based on the dollar. Bills come in denominations of $1, $2, $5, $10, $20, $50 and $100. Every dollar is divided into 100 cents. Coins are the penny (1 cent), nickel (5 cents), dime (10 cents) and quarter (25 cents). Half-dollar and dollar coins are rarely used. You may not use foreign currency to purchase goods and services in the United States. Consider buying traveler's checks in dollar amounts. You may also use credit cards affiliated with an American company such as Interbank, Barclay Card and American Express.

Electricity and Electronics Electric outlets use currents of 110 volts, 60 cycles. To operate appliances made for other electrical systems, you need a transformer or other adapter. Travelers who use laptop computers for telecommunication should be aware that modem configurations for U.S. telephone systems may be different from their European counterparts. Similarly, the U.S. format for videotapes is different from that in Europe; National Park Service visitors centers and other stores that sell souvenir videos often have them available in European format on request.

Weights and Measures The United States uses the English system of weights and measures. American units and their metric equivalents are: 1 inch = 2.5 centimeters; 1 foot (12 inches) = 0.3 meter; 1 yard (3 feet) = 0.9 meter; 1 mile (5280 feet) = 1.6 kilometers; 1 ounce = 28 grams; 1 pound (16 ounces) = 0.45 kilogram; 1 quart (liquid) = 0.9 liter.

▼▼▼▼▼▼▼▼▼▼▼▼▼

Outdoor Adventures

CAMPING

Backcountry sites, tent-only sites, RV hookups and rustic cabins account for many of the lodging choices in Tennessee. The state park system has done an outstanding job of creating and maintaining campsites throughout the state. In addition, there are numerous private campgrounds, particularly near lakes and streams outside the state park system. In the eastern mountains, most of the latter are closed from October through March due to inclement weather, however. Rates vary from park to park, but public sites typically cost about $13 per night for two people. The **Tennessee State Department of Tourism** publishes an annual vacation guide that lists private campgrounds in each locale. For a copy, contact the department. ~ 320 6th Avenue North, Nashville, TN 37243; 615-741-2159, 800-462-8366, fax 615-741-7225.

Tennessee Valley Authority reservoirs and other lakes are extremely popular with boating enthusiasts. At the bigger ponds, such as Dale Hollow Lake, boat rentals are readily available.

BOATING & CANOEING

One of the most thrilling sports Tennessee has to offer is guided canoe and kayak trips, either along fairly smooth rivers in the southern part of the state or through the whitewater rapids of the Cherokee National Forest and the Ocoee region. Rentals are available, and many reputable outfitters can arrange trips for kayakers of all levels, from young children to experienced enthusiasts.

Swimming, waterskiing, jetboating and floating on inflatable rafts are popular activities in the summer. People have drowned in Tennessee waters, but accidents are easily avoided when you respect the power of the water, heed appropriate warnings and use good sense.

WATER SAFETY

Wherever you swim, never do it alone. Always swim in designated areas, preferably where there are lifeguards. Exercise caution in the use of floats, inner tubes or rafts; unexpected currents can be hazardous.

If you're going canoeing or whitewater rafting, always scout the river from land before the first trip, and check available literature. Rivers may have danger areas such as falls, boulders, rapids and dams.

There's fish in them thar lakes as well, not to mention rivers, streams and creeks. There are more than 30 kinds of fish swimming around, most of them edible, including bass (striped, largemouth, smallmouth and white), crappie, catfish, walleye, stripers, rockfish and trout. The type of fishing permit you will need varies, according to what you will be fishing for. There is a wide range of experiences whether you prefer a light fly rod or heavy bait-casting tackle. Almost everywhere there's good fishing, there's a good bait shop to supply and guide you. With few exceptions, anyone over the age of 13 will need a permit, which is available from sporting-goods stores, hardware stores, county court clerks, boat docks and all regional offices of the **Tennessee Wildlife Resources Agency**. Three-day permits cost $10 (no trout) or $20 (all species). For a booklet detailing the regulations,

FISHING

contact the agency. ~ P.O. Box 40747, Nashville, TN 37204; 615-781-6500; www.state.tn.us/twra.

HIKING

Most Tennessee state parks distribute free trail guides at the appropriate ranger stations. If you like to plan in advance, you should contact the individual park, which is described in each chapter in the "Parks" sections. The most popular hiking parks are Roan Mountain, Frozen Head, Radnor Lake, South Cumberland and Natchez Trace.

You might want to sign up for one of the dozens of annual outings sponsored by the **Smoky Mountain Hiking Club**. ~ P.O. Box 1454, Knoxville, TN 37901; 865-694-0160; www.smhclub.org.

BIKING

The Tennessee Department of Transportation has established a network of cycling routes along paved highways in different regions. For a copy of these maps, contact the **Bicycle Coordinator**. ~ James K. Polk Building, 505 Deaderick Street, Suite 700, Nashville, TN 37243-0349; 615-741-5310; www.tdot.state.tn. us/bikeroutes/procedures.htm. In addition, mountain bikes are welcome on many hiking and horse trails in various state parks. Bicycle shops offering rentals are few and far between, so if you want to cycle, take your own wheels or make advance reservations. See individual listings in each chapter in the "Parks" sections for details.

TWO

Northeast Tennessee

This, locals are eager to tell you, is where it all began. Not only the state of Tennessee, but the whole westward migration, not to mention a couple of attempts at independence that had little to do with the Revolutionary War.

The region is often called the Tri-City Area, but that chamber-of-commerce term doesn't do justice to its charms: historic Jonesborough, Roan Mountain and scenic two-lane roads stretching like ribbons through the sparsely populated countryside. The most appealing parts of the First Frontier lie not in the Big Three—Bristol, Johnson City and Kingsport—but in the little towns and along the byways.

Hugging the Appalachian Mountains, this region is quite removed from the commercialism and imported entertainment of the gateway cities in the Great Smoky Mountains. The neighborhoods here are inhabited chiefly by people who either have never left or have left and returned, unable to resist its special appeal. Instead of theme parks and traffic snarls, there are quiet country roads where you might not see another car for miles, and if you do, odds are the driver won't tailgate you, anyway. In Erwin, Rogersville and Blountville, it is the locals who fish the streams, who run the great state parks, who keep alive out-of-the-way restaurants that few tourists ever find. Don't look for much nightlife. In fact, some of the most popular places to eat board up before 8 p.m., and you could risk going hungry anywhere on a Monday night without advance planning.

The past is present in these parts, a worthwhile destination for families seeking to impart a sense of history to their children. Pick and choose carefully, however, lest you risk hearing your seven-year-old whining, "Do we have to see another place where some old dead guy used to live?" Some of the best bets for kids are the living-history museums where they can see what daily life was like a century or more ago.

Besides the historical sites, there is wondrous beauty here, not only in the mountains but in the hills and valleys. Bordered by Virginia and North Carolina, which are so close you can easily wind up in either state without realizing it, the Tri-City Area extends beyond the borders of Tennessee. In fact, Bristol straddles the state line, split between Tennessee and Virginia. Yet the people who live here have a lot to be proud of when it comes to state history. Their story is one that is echoed, over and over, in many other parts of Tennessee.

Two hundred years ago, pioneers entered this part of Tennessee from Virginia's Shenandoah Valley and, to a lesser extent, over the rugged Appalachians. Lured by fertile fields and bountiful game, they came overland as well as by boat, raft and canoe along the many tributaries of the Tennessee River. They settled along the Holston, Nolichucky and Watauga rivers, and, knowingly or not, began squatting on land preserved by treaty for the Cherokee. In 1771 British officials became aware of the fact and instructed the settlers to evacuate. In defiance, some of the pioneers took steps to protect the land they had worked so hard to tame. In 1772 the settlers of Sycamore Shoals, now part of Johnson City, created the Watauga Association, the first self-governing entity of settlers striving to be free from the yoke of England. As such, the Wataugans for several years negotiated their own treaties with the Cherokee, encouraging infusions of even more immigrants. The leaders of the Cherokee met with Richard Henderson, the land speculator, at Sycamore Shoals in 1775—a negotiation that led to the largest private real estate transaction in the United States. The so-called Transylvania Purchase involved 20 million acres of Indian land being made available for white settlement. Dragging Canoe, one of the disgruntled chiefs, led a contingent of some 300 Indians in an attack on Fort Watauga. In 1777 North Carolina created Washington County, which incorporated the region northeast of Tennessee.

During the Revolutionary War, the Sycamore Shoals served as the gathering point for a group known as the Overmountain men. These volunteers crossed the Appalachian Mountains to play a crucial role in the American defeat of the British troops at the pivotal Battle of King's Mountain in South Carolina. Their story is told in an exceptional slide program at the Sycamore Shoals State Historic Area.

Jonesborough, unquestionably the oldest town in Tennessee, was founded in 1779, just three years after the signing of the Declaration of Independence. Five years later, when North Carolina ceded her western lands, Jonesborough found itself in limbo. Congress failed to act within the specified amount of time, so the residents of Greene, Sullivan and Washington counties, along with the Wataugans, established the state of Franklin (in honor of Benjamin Franklin) and made Jonesborough its capital and John Sevier its governor in 1784. Franklin applied to the Continental Congress for admission to the Union but lost its bid by a single vote. Undeterred, Franklinites went their independent way, at least for a while. When North Carolina decided to reclaim the territory, the settlers fought back, and, after many skirmishes and battles, lost decisively. The state of Franklin is history, but the independent attitude of the locals is not. Tennessee became a state in 1796.

When Jonesborough was laid out in 1780, great care was taken to construct buildings that would withstand the ravages of time and temperature. The townspeople were quite successful: Jonesborough's downtown area is chockfull of so many 18th-century structures that after a massive restorative effort in the late 1960s, the town became the first in the state to be named a National Register Historic District.

This corner of Tennessee is rife with more history. This is where David Crockett was born, and where Andrew Johnson, destined to become the 17th president of

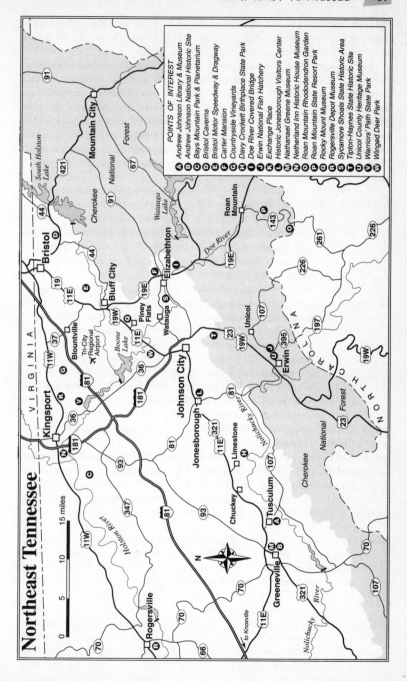

Northeast Tennessee

POINTS OF INTEREST

Ⓐ Andrew Johnson Library & Museum
Ⓑ Andrew Johnson National Historic Site
Ⓒ Bays Mountain Park & Planetarium
Ⓓ Bristol Caverns
Ⓔ Bristol Motor Speedway & Dragway
Ⓕ Carter Mansion
Ⓖ Countryside Vineyards
Ⓗ Davy Crockett Birthplace State Park
Ⓘ Doe River Covered Bridge
Ⓙ Erwin National Fish Hatchery
Ⓚ Exchange Place
Ⓛ Historic Jonesborough Visitors Center
Ⓜ Nathanael Greene Museum
Ⓝ Netherland Inn Historic House Museum
Ⓞ Roan Mountain Rhododendron Garden
Ⓟ Roan Mountain State Resort Park
Ⓠ Rocky Mount Museum
Ⓡ Rogersville Depot Museum
Ⓢ Sycamore Shoals State Historic Area
Ⓣ Tipton-Haynes State Historic Site
Ⓤ Unicoi County Heritage Museum
Ⓥ Warriors' Path State Park
Ⓦ Winged Deer Park

the United States, lived and died. Greeneville has lagged behind Jonesborough in organizing its historic sites, and it is a much bigger, busier town, but the downtown area is compact enough to be explored on foot.

Johnson City, Bristol and Kingsport are the big cities in northeast Tennessee, but their innate charms are so dwarfed by industry and commerce that they are not as appealing as tourist destinations. The outskirts of these cities have much to recommend them, however, as does nearby Rogersville, a small town that grew up on the stagecoach line and still maintains its early-19th-century ambience. The northeast Tennessee mountains do see some snow most winters, averaging about 16 inches a year. Summertime temperatures average roughly 73°; winter about 35°. The area gets about three inches of rain every month, and more during July.

▼▼▼▼▼▼▼▼▼▼▼▼▼▼▼▼▼▼▼▼▼

Greeneville to Johnson City

Greeneville, one of Tennessee's oldest cities, is the southernmost city in northeast Tennessee, located less than a two hours' drive from both Bristol and Knoxville. The historic downtown district is surrounded on three sides—west, south and north—by chain motels and fast-food joints, so you must persevere to find the good stuff.

Neighboring Limestone, to the north, isn't so much a town as a location consisting of narrow two-lane roads and a couple of intersections, an inn and Davy Crockett Birthplace State Park.

The historic town of Jonesborough, named after Willie Jones of Halifax, North Carolina, was one of the earliest planned communities in the United States. Chartered by North Carolina in 1779, it became the first capital—before Greeneville—of the state of Franklin. Today, more than 150 structures in various architectural styles (mostly dating from the mid-1800s) compose the conveniently compact Jonesborough Historic District, which was restored in 1969 and placed on the National Register of Historic Places.

Johnson City is the most centrally located town in the triangle of northeast Tennessee, while nearby Erwin—also easily accessible from Jonesborough—is worth a visit for the drive alone. It's particularly spectacular during the spring, when honeysuckle and fruit trees bloom.

SIGHTS

The 17th president wasn't born in **Greeneville**, but he might as well have been because he's considered a native son and has spawned something of a cottage industry. There are other historical sights in the neighborhood, however, although the downtown neighborhood is just getting its act together for tourists.

Greeneville's namesake, among other notable regional figures, is remembered at the **Nathanael Greene Museum**, housed in what looks like an old school building downtown. Extensive exhibits in nine galleries tell the story of Greene County's history. Displays cover the role of the county during the Civil War and other eras, as well as more specific local lore, such as the fascinating story of how Horse Creek was named for the fact that Indians used to raid the settlers' farms to steal horses and reconvene by the creek. Closed Sunday and Monday. ~ 101 West McKee Street, Greeneville; 423-636-1558.

If you are driving from Greeneville toward Jonesborough, the first town you come to is **Tusculum**. Take a break and stretch your legs with a walk through the **Tusculum College** campus, the 28th college founded in the United States in 1794. It not only is pretty but also contains a number of historic buildings, including a cabin where Andrew Johnson once resided. Also here is the **Andrew Johnson Library and Museum**, which has Johnson family papers, books and manuscripts, as well as family silver, the bed Johnson died in and his wife's rocking chair. The library also houses nearly 200 Civil War–era newspapers from all over the country. Closed weekends. ~ 60 Shiloh Road, Tusculum; 800-729-0256, library 423-636-7348; www.tusculum.edu.

Continuing in a northeasterly direction from Tusculum, look for the turnoff to **Limestone**. We hate to break it to you, but Davy Crockett was not born on a mountaintop after all, but in fact right here in Greene County. And he never went by "Davy," either; he always signed his name "David." There are many Crockett sites around Tennessee—after all, he was a busy man, holding down the jobs of hero, warrior and backwoods statesman while trying to make a buck. Crockett was born August 17, 1786, on the banks of the Nolichucky River near the mouth of Limestone Creek. A plaque marks the approximate spot at the **Davy Crockett Birth-**   ◄ HIDDEN

AUTHOR FAVORITE

sights   Andrew Johnson's humble beginnings as a tailor's apprentice are acknowledged in the tailor's shop that is part of the fascinating **Andrew Johnson National Historic Site**. Other exhibits in the visitors center, museum and the 1830s family home explain his rise in politics and his ascension to the presidency following Abraham Lincoln's assassination. Serious history buffs will be most interested in tracing the events leading to Johnson's impeachment; with one more vote against him, he would have been forced from office. Related sites include the nearby Homestead and the Andrew Johnson National Cemetery, where the 17th U.S. president is buried. A hilltop monument marking his burial spot is inscribed, "His faith in the people never wavered." Fee for tours. ~ College and Depot streets, Greeneville; 423-638-3551; www.nps.gov/anjo.

place State Park, and a cabin much like the one Crockett must have grown up in is also open to the public. ~ 1245 Davy Crockett Park Road, Limestone; 423-257-2167.

The shortest route from the park to the charming town of **Jonesborough** is via Route 321, which is less congested north of Tusculum than right around Greeneville. The town is just a couple of blocks off the highway; signage is quite clear. To get an overview of the town's symmetrical pattern, climb to the top of North Main Street and look down.

Before embarking on a walking tour of the Jonesborough Historic District, arm yourself with a map from the **Historic Jonesborough Visitors Center** and your own imagination. The visitors center also offers guided tours daily except Sunday. ~ 117 Boone Street, Jonesborough; 423-753-1010, 866-401-4223.

After an extensive restoration program in 1969, this downtown became the first in the state to be named a national historic district, and much of its charm stems from the fact that most of the 40 18th- and 19th-century buildings on this walking tour are still lived in or used. The old-time ambience is enhanced by the brick sidewalks, lampposts and wrought-iron fencing along Main Street.

Located inside the town's visitors center, the **Jonesborough- Washington County History Museum** has a well-done time line that starts with the pioneer days, includes Jonesborough's Union sympathizing during the Civil War and ends at 1913. There are lifestyle artifacts—Victorian interiors, farm tools, apparel—and displays about the nation's first abolitionist newspaper, published here in the early 1800s. Pick up a walking-tour map of the historic district here. Closed January and February. Admission. ~ 117 Boone Street, Jonesborough; 423-753-1015.

Only a couple of blocks away from the visitors center are some of the town's most significant buildings. Of particular interest is the **Chester Inn,** the oldest frame structure in Jonesborough, now housing the National Storytelling Center on the street level. President Andrew Jackson once practiced law in Jonesborough and stayed here. ~ 116 West Main Street, Jonesborough.

A few doors down is the **May-Ledbetter House.** The first periodicals printed in support of abolition, the *Emancipator* and the *Manumission Intelligencer*, were printed in Jacob Howard's print shop, which stood here. ~ 130 West Main Street, Jonesborough.

Next door, travelers on the Great Stage Road linking the eastern seaboard to the western wilderness once stayed over at the **Mansion House,** a fine example of Federal-style architecture. ~ 200 West Main Street, Jonesborough.

Farther down the street, the **Griffith-Lyle House** was once home to a pioneer photographer in the early days of that art form. ~ 303 West Main Street, Jonesborough.

Located a couple of blocks away, the **Salt House** was built in the late 1840s and used as a store, post office, grocery, warehouse and, during the Civil War, salt-rationing headquarters. ~ 127 Fox Street, Jonesborough.

Discover Jonesborough's Times & Tales Tour has won awards for guiding visitors around the town, including visits to historic homes, probably because of the way the guides interweave anecdotes and storytelling into their spiels. ~ 117 Boone Street, Jonesborough; 423-753-1010.

The mockingbird, Tennessee's state bird, really gets around—it's also the state bird in Arkansas, Florida, Mississippi and Texas.

Leave the driving to the guy with the reins from **Historic Jonesborough Carriage Tours** and sit back for a horse-drawn carriage ride—completely narrated, of course—through the historic district. ~ 119 East Main Street, Jonesborough; 423-753-2903.

One of the loveliest short drives (less than half an hour) in northeast Tennessee is the trip from Jonesborough up to **Erwin** via Route 81, a winding two-lane road that passes by small farmsteads and alongside streams that gush in springtime.

You probably won't want to order sushi after a tour of the **Erwin National Fish Hatchery**. Constructed in the 1890s, it's one of the oldest hatcheries operated by the U.S. Fish and Wildlife Service. Its mission: produce millions of healthy rainbow-trout eggs every year for various fish management programs around the country. Indoor and outdoor tanks hold four strains of rainbow, from hatchling to the age of three years. The older fish are stocked in local streams. Closed weekends. ~ 520 Federal Hatchery Road, Erwin; 423-743-4712; southeast.fws.gov/erwin.

Sharing the grounds with the hatchery is the **Unicoi County Heritage Museum**. It's housed in a turn-of-the-20th-century white-frame house, containing relics from the early 1900s, including Blue Ridge Pottery (made hereabouts in a factory that closed in the '50s), old wedding dresses and even some American Indian relics. A Civil War display features memorabilia and historical documents. Upstairs is "Main Street," where two bedrooms were combined in order to install a miniature downtown, with replicas of an apothecary shop, Clinchfield railroad, doctor's office and barbershop. Originally built as the residence for the superintendent of the Erwin National Fish Hatchery, the ten-room house was saved from demolition and transformed into a museum in 1982. Closed Monday through Friday from October through April. ~ 1715 Johnson City Highway, Erwin; 423-743-9449; www.unicoi.tn.us/heritage.html.

◄ *HIDDEN*

About a half-hour north of Jonesborough, you will reach the city limits of **Johnson City**. You can choose to head left and follow Route 19W up toward Rocky Mount Historic Site in the

Text continued on page 38.

David Crockett,
"King of the Wild Frontier"

Okay, class, first of all, he wasn't "born on a mountaintop"—but he was born in Tennessee, on the banks of the Nolichucky River. David Crockett, who would go on to make a name for himself (which he always signed David, by the way, not Davy) as warrior, hero, pioneer industrialist and backwoods statesman, was born in modest circumstances to John and Rebecca Hawkins Crockett in Greene County, on August 17, 1786. Ten years later, the same year Tennessee joined the Union, the Crockett family opened a tavern on the road between Knoxville and Abingdon, Virginia. A couple of years later, David was hired out to one Jacob Siler, who was driving a herd of cattle to Rockbridge County, Virginia. Siler attempted to detain the 12-year-old worker by force after the drive was complete, but David escaped, rejoining his family in a matter of months. This was the first of many exploits that helped create a legend around the name Crockett.

Crockett, like many folks on the frontier, didn't stay in one place too long. There seem to be as many markers claiming his presence as there are East Coast plaques declaring George Washington Slept Here. And he has much in common with other politicians, staging comeback after comeback, sometimes after having been reported literally, not just politically, dead.

The monument to his early days in Limestone is a replicated log cabin in the state park that bears his name. After marrying Mary (Polly) Finley in Jefferson County, and having two sons, Crockett left East Tennessee for a place along the Elk River in Lincoln County in 1811. Two years later, the family moved again, this time to Franklin county, near present-day Alabama, to a homestead Crockett named Kentuck. Shortly thereafter, Crockett signed up for the militia to avenge an Indian attack on an Alabama fort and, serving under Andrew Jackson, took part in a retributive massacre of an Indian town. After a busy three months of service, Crockett got home in time for Christmas. But the next fall, he re-enlisted, returning home again just in time to learn Polly had given him their first daughter. Polly died the next summer and Crockett married again in 1816, this time to a widow with children of her own.

In 1817, having survived a bout of malaria so serious his family was informed he had died in Alabama, Crockett moved his family to Lawrence county, where there is another park named in his honor. At this point, the former militia lieutenant became a justice of the peace, his first move towards a career as a statesman. Sure enough, within a year he became the town commissioner of Lawrenceburg. He settled into a place at the head of Shoal Creek, where he established a water-powered industrial complex complete with powder mill, grist mill and distillery. All of this was washed away in a flood in 1821, the same year he resigned his justice of the peace position in order to run successfully for the state legislature.

The Cocketts moved again the following year, this time to the far western region of the state. Crockett was elected from that district and served his third and last state term. When it was suggested, largely as a joke, that he run for Congress, Crockett did just that, though unsuccessfully. In the meantime, he nearly died again in a boat wreck on the Mississippi, after which he was brought to Memphis and urged to give Congress another shot. Crockett was reelected in 1829, the year Andrew Jackson became president. He split with Jackson on several issues and, after a campaign in which he argued against the president's policies, lost his bid for reelection.

It was round this time that the earliest books were written about Crockett, the first a biography by Mathew St. Clair Clarke and the second, an autobiography, one of a number of tomes penned by Crockett (some with the aid of writers). Then, in 1836 Crockett joined Sam Houston in Texas and, on March 6, was captured and executed after Santa Anna's army seized the Alamo.

What made Crockett such a figure was not merely his military or even political exploits, but his way with words—which he exploited in the almanacs he published—and his style of dress. He had a sly wit, salted with a bit of raunchy backwoods humor, and was widely liked during his years in Washington. Such a figure was irresistible fodder for writers and, later, movie and television producers.

In 1872 the play *Davy Crockett; Or, Be Sure You're Right, Then Go Ahead* opened and ran for 24 years here and in England. Then came the movies, first a film called *Davy Crockett—in Hearts United*, and then a variety of other silent films. The first "talkie" came out in 1937, but Crockett was not really immortalized until 1955, the peak of the Crockett craze. The frontier hero will forever be remembered by audiences as looking a lot like the actor Fess Parker who played him in a series of TV shows produced by Walt Disney.

At the David Crockett State Park in Lawrenceburg, David Crockett Days are celebrated each August with an array of frontier-style activities from tomahawk throwing to blacksmithing, along with a Crockett film festival.

Overmountain Area, or take Route 19W in a southerly direction to find one of the best-hidden attractions in all of Tennessee. It would be a good idea to call the site to make sure you have the right directions before you exit Johnson City.

HIDDEN ► If you can ignore the power lines in the distance beyond the **Tipton-Haynes State Historic Site**, you can almost imagine the place as it looked when Colonel John Tipton bought it in 1784. He built the first home here, a log cabin; when Tennessee legislator Landon Carter Haynes took over the property in the mid-1800s, he built the frame farmhouse that now encases the log cabin. The place is most famous as the site of the Battle of the Lost State of Franklin, a fateful skirmish between Tipton, a North Carolina militia leader, and John Sevier, the only governor of Franklin, a short-lived sovereign state established in 1779. In addition to the horse barn, granary and Haynes' old law office, you should stop by the visitors center to see artifacts from the area that date back to prehistoric times. Admission. ~ 2620 South Roan Street, off Route 81, Exit 31, Johnson City; 423-926-3631.

Johnson City Chamber of Commerce/Convention and Visitors Bureau can give you more information about the area. ~ 603 East Market Street, Johnson City; 423-461-8000, 800-852-3392; www. johnsoncitytn.com.

LODGING An exception to the chain and/or under-par motels along the Route 11E Bypass, the two-story **Charray Inn** has clean rooms that are slightly bigger than average, although the color scheme is a slightly depressing brown and blue. Half of the 36 rooms are nonsmoking. Executive suite and a conference room. ~ 121 Serral Drive, Greeneville; 423-638-1331, 800-852-4682; www.charray inntour.com. BUDGET.

AUTHOR FAVORITE

I was awakened by the "hoo-hoo-whooo" of owls on the hill behind the **Hawley House**, the oldest house in the oldest town in Tennessee. Now a three-bedroom inn decorated with quilts, folk art and comfortable four-poster beds and other antiques, the 1790s home was built of dove-tailed chestnut logs constructed on a native limestone rock foundation. Occasional trains trundle past, but after a while you don't notice the sound. Rocking chairs on the long veranda offer views of several other historic structures. Hearthside-cooked dinners are available in winter, and picnic baskets are available in good weather. ~ 114 East Woodrow Avenue, Jonesborough; 423-753-8869, 800-753-8869; www.hawleyhouse.com, e-mail bandb1793@xtn.net. MODERATE TO ULTRA-DELUXE.

The **General Morgan Inn and Conference Center** is a major, full-service hotel in the heart of downtown. The 51 large rooms have high ceilings, marble vanities and plenty of amenities; however, if you can ask for an outside room (instead of one that faces in on the lobby), you'll get a better night's sleep. There's a restaurant on the ground floor plus an ultra-deluxe presidential suite. ~ 111 North Main Street, Greeneville; 423-787-1000, 800-223-2679, fax 423-787-1001; www.generalmorganinn.com, e-mail generalmanager@generalmorganinn.com. MODERATE.

An old homestead on a bluff above the Nolichucky River, the **Thistle Place** has a double-decker porch with bright white railings and three guest rooms. It's close to town and to the mountains that surround it on three sides. The elegant decor includes a combination of authentic and reproduction Olde English antiques. Check out the English-style garden, with its butterfly-friendly plants and century-old maple trees. A full breakfast is included in the rate, as is afternoon tea. ~ 6 Sanford Circle, Greeneville; 423-639-8202; e-mail ashworth@greene.xtn.net. MODERATE.

◄ HIDDEN

The **Blair-Moore House**, an 1832 residence on the National Register, has been decorated with taste and flair. The overall effect is a sophisticated early American inn, with lots of stenciling and comfortable furnishings appropriate to a 19th-century home. There are two rooms on the second floor, a suite with a private entrance on the first, and a back porch with views of an English-style garden. ~ 201 West Main Street, Jonesborough; 423-753-0044, 888-453-0044; www.blairmoorehouse.com, e-mail blairmoorehouse@aol.com. DELUXE TO ULTRA-DELUXE.

The original version was built in 1891 in a nearby location and has long since burned down. But in 1999, the finishing touches were put on its namesake, the all-new **Carnegie Hotel**, complete with stained-glass ceilings and first-class service that could probably compare with its namesake. The 141 rooms and suites on the upper five floors are large and furnished with updates of the old antiques, boasting modern flourishes such as Egyptian cotton sheets, internet service and private fax machines. The stately structure also houses a restaurant, a casual eatery and a spa/salon. Small pets are allowed. ~ 1216 West State of Franklin Road, Johnson City; 423-979-6400, fax 423-979-6424; www.carnegie hotel.com, e-mail info@carnegiehotel.com. DELUXE.

Davy Crockett could never have envisioned a log home on the scale of the **Jam n Jelly Inn**. A huge stone chimney anchors one end of this two-story contemporary log structure, which has a spacious front porch and a large covered deck in the back. All six guest rooms (one on the main floor) are furnished with antique reproductions, queen-size beds and TVs. (The inn's library stocks both books and videos.) Amenities include a ten-person hot tub and full breakfast. ~ 1310 Indian Ridge Road, Johnson

◄ HIDDEN

City; 423-929-0039, fax 423-929-9026; www.jamnjellyinn.com. MODERATE.

DINING   **The Tannery**, set in an old white-brick tannery building, is one of the few places open for lunch in downtown Greeneville. A few tables and an open kitchen are about the only things to look at, but this is a luncheon spot, not a romantic restaurant. The entire menu consists of sandwiches, salads and a few soups. No dinner. Closed weekends. ~ 117 East Depot Street, Greeneville; 423-638-2772. BUDGET.

The most elegant food in town—trout filet, veal chops, Thai stuffed chicken and eggplant with fresh pasta—is served on white linen in suitable surroundings at **Bistro 105**. Your favorite mixed drink will gladly be served from the full-service bar. Dinner reservations recommended. Closed Sunday and Monday. ~ 105 East Main Street, Jonesborough; 423-788-0244, fax 423-753-0012; www.bistro105.com. DELUXE.

Located on Courthouse Square next to the courthouse, the **Dogwood Lane Café** is a favorite local gathering and dining place for casual meals and homemade specials such as grilled salmon, fettuccine, sirloin and vegetarian stir-fry (plus a nightly special). On weekends, a pianist plays on the baby grand. No dinner Sunday through Tuesday. Closed Monday. ~ 109 Courthouse Square, Jonesborough; 423-913-1629. MODERATE.

A souped-up delicatessen, the contemporary **Main Street Cafe** serves sturdy sandwiches (pastrami, vegetarian, club, BLT) and the town's best selection of salads. Half a dozen are listed, plus on Friday, the Fatash, with Greek ingredients and pita chips. Try the Key lime pie, a house specialty. Closed Sunday. ~ 117 West Main Street, Jonesborough; 423-753-2460. BUDGET TO MODERATE.

On the grounds of the Carnegie Hotel, **Wellington's** is filled with original paintings and antique architectural details, all surrounded by mahogany and cherry woods. House specialties include crab cakes, cashew-crusted salmon, pan-seared filet of beef and, of course, beef Wellington (they use Angus beef). Upscale salads and sandwiches are available at lunch and dinner. ~ 1216 West State of Franklin Road, Johnson City; 423-979-6500. DELUXE.

The **Peerless Restaurant** is owned by a Greek family, but there's no sign of that heritage in the decor, and scarcely any in the menu. There are Grecian salads (tomatoes, olives, cucumbers), and some vegetables, such as zucchini and green beans, get sort of a Mediterranean treatment. The emphasis is on seafood and steaks, including a generous prime rib. Closed Sunday. ~ 2531 North Roan Street, Johnson City; 423-282-2351, fax 423-282-4224. MODERATE TO DELUXE.

Who can resist a shop called **Ye Olde Tourist Trappe**? Located   **SHOPPING**
right across the street from the Andrew Johnson home, it's the
place for small antiques and mementos, plus collectibles like quilts,
toys and wreaths, most of them handcrafted. ~ 204 East Depot
Street, Greeneville; 423-639-1567.

Up the street, some 50 dealers have come together at the
Greeneville Antique Market, creating one-stop shopping convenience for fans of antiques and collectibles. There's 14,000 square
feet of goodies spread over two-and-a-half stories; surely you'll
find something you want. ~ 117 West Depot Street, Greeneville;
423-638-2773.

Dedicated hounds will seek out **Ledford's Antiques**—if you   ◄ *HIDDEN*
follow the signs carefully from Route 11E en route to Johnson City
(hint: look on the right after the signs for Davy Crockett Birthplace State Park) you may actually find it. The store is in a brick
Greek Revival building, built in the 1840s and formerly home to
a general mercantile, and the furnishings look as if they've been
there all along. "We don't have much after 1850," allows proprietor Erlene Ledford. Closed Monday and Tuesday. ~ 234
Gravel Hill Road, Limestone; 423-257-3293.

If you're interested in a truly American craft, you'll love **Tennessee Quilts**, where locally handcrafted quilts, wall hangings
and other fabric-based goods are as much decoration as they are
merchandise. Custom work is available. Closed Sunday. ~ 114
Boone Street, Jonesborough; 423-753-6644.

Even non-equestrians can find some attractive boots and belts
at **Deer Ridge Farm & Saddlery**, though most of the merchandise
in this tiny store is meant to be worn by horses. The shop will also

AUTHOR FAVORITE

Even locals have trouble pinpointing the **Harmony Grocery**, an
outpost of Cajun cuisine tucked away among the hills and dales between
Route 181 and Old Route 81. Dinners are served on the ground floor of a
green wooden building dating from the 1850s, when it was a general store.
Since the mid-1980s, its stained-glass windows and pristine canned goods
have helped cozy up the ambience of one of the region's favorite places
to eat. Especially if you're partial to red beans and rice with andouille
sausage, boneless breast of duck, pan-fried veal with Creole sauce, pork
chops, crawfish étouffée or various blackened seafoods. Reservations
recommended. ~ 1121 Painter Road, Harmony; 423-348-6183. MOD-
ERATE TO DELUXE.

make custom boots. Closed Sunday. ~ 131 East Main Street, Jonesborough; 423-753-6046.

The **Pig & Slipper** stocks a goodly supply of antiques and collectibles such as stenciled lampshades, Victorian reproductions and china. ~ 117 East Main Street, Jonesborough; 423-753-2141.

Located in an 1840s building where salt was rationed during the Civil War, the **Salt House** is the place to shop for dollhouses, antiques and handcrafts. ~ 127 Fox Street, Jonesborough; 423-753-5113.

Photography, painting, prints and sculpture by regional artists in various styles and media are exhibited for sale at **Acorns & Ivy**. ~ 100 North Cherokee Street, Jonesborough; 423-753-8823.

The **Jonesborough Art Glass Gallery** offers blown glass, custom stained glass, pottery and jewelry created by more than 100 local and regional craftspeople. ~ 101 East Main Street, Jonesborough; 423-753-5401.

The specialties at **Mulberry Corner Used and Rare Books** include local and regional subjects, history, military and Southern writers and literature. ~ 121 West Main Street, Jonesborough; 423-753-913-0575.

Mahoney's Sportsman Paradise is an impressively well-stocked source of serious outdoor wear and gear, but you can also find gadgets and accessories such as the top-rated Casa del Mar sunglasses, a favorite among people who spend a lot of time in nature. ~ 830 Sunset Drive, Johnson City; 423-282-5413.

HIDDEN ► The **Farmhouse Gallery & Gardens** features wildlife paintings by Johnny Lynch. There's a display garden here as well, where you can check out perennials, wildflowers and herbs. ~ Old Erwin-Johnson City Highway off Route 181, 21 Covered Bridge Lane, Unicoi; 423-743-8799.

NIGHTLIFE   **Down Home** features a variety of musical groups Wednesday through Saturday, from acoustic folk guitarists to R&B. Cover. ~ 300 West Main Street, Johnson City; 423-929-9822.

PARKS   **DAVY CROCKETT BIRTHPLACE STATE PARK** 🏃 🚲 ⚓ 🚣 ⚒

HIDDEN ► Located upstream from the Nolichucky River falls, this 105-acre historic park is not going to impress you with its majesty, but it does claim one distinction: a simple cabin built on the site of Davy's birthplace. The park has three large picnic shelters, a playground and a swimming pool (closed Monday, and Labor Day through Memorial Day) and allows fishing in Limestone Creek. A visitors center has exhibits devoted to the life and exploits of the legendary pioneer. Other facilities include restrooms, showers and picnic tables. Day-use fee, $3. ~ 1245 Davy Crockett Park Road, Limestone; 423-257-2167.

▲ There are 65 campsites with water and electricity; $17.25 RV, $13.75 tent site.

WINGED DEER PARK 🏃 🚣 🚤 🚣 ⚓ A conveniently located sports complex, Winged Deer offers softball and soccer fields, plus two miles of lighted, paved woodland trails. Guided hikes and nature programs are also offered. You'll find restrooms, playgrounds and picnic areas here. ~ Route 11E, Johnson City; 423-283-5815.

Overmountain Area

A small town (population around 13,000) in the foothills of the Appalachian Mountains, Elizabethton (pronounced with the accent on "beth") is the site of an early pioneer fort and where independence from Britain was first declared by American settlers who belonged to the Watauga Association. Elizabethton's outskirts have some charm, and the area has a couple of nifty historical attractions. From downtown, you can take either Route 19E to Roan Mountain, or Route 321 to Scenic Route 67 for a beautiful drive up to quiet little Mountain City.

SIGHTS

If you could visit only one site in this region, you should make it the **Sycamore Shoals State Historic Area**, about a 45-minute drive from Limestone between Johnson City and Elizabethton. Its main drawing card is an excellent audio-visual show, "The Overmountain People," that explains what happened in the region during the time of the Revolutionary War. The pioneers' attitude toward the lush, fertile lands west of the Appalachians—"tame it and claim it"—pitted them against the American Indians, naturally. Sycamore Shoals played a significant role in the events of the late 18th century; it was here that the Cherokee sold some 20 million acres of land to an American company, setting the stage for subsequent conflicts. Aside from the video, there's a reconstruction of Fort Watauga, which had been built nearby and served as a refuge for settlers fleeing the Cherokee in 1776. ~ 1651 West Elk Avenue, Elizabethton; 423-543-5808.

> Elizabethton is where one of the largest land purchases in the history of the United States (the 1775 Transylvania Purchase) took place.

For additional information about the town and Carter County, visit the **Elizabethton/Carter County Chamber of Commerce.** They will arm you with brochures, maps and even souvenirs. ~ 500 19E Bypass, Elizabethton; 423-547-3852, 888-547-3852; www.tourelizabethton.com, e-mail info@tourelizabethton.com.

The oldest mansion in Tennessee is the **John and Landon Carter Mansion,** built by this prominent northeast Tennessee family on the banks of the Watauga River between 1775 and 1785. Just think: construction on this simple clapboard two-story home began before there even was an entity called the United States of America. Today, more than 90 percent of the materials in the interior are original, including hand-carved panels, crown molding and landscape paintings on the fireplace moldings that may be the earliest paintings in Tennessee. Be sure to walk around the grounds, especially the cemetery where you'll find the Carter family gravesites. Closed Monday and Tuesday and from September through May. ~ 1013 Broad Street, Elizabethton; 423-543-6140.

Crossing the river only a short drive from the Carter home, the **Doe River Covered Bridge** is the oldest bridge of its type still in use in Tennessee. Built in 1882 and closed only briefly for repairs, it spans the river for 134 feet. It was considered an engineering feat when it was built, sufficiently elevated to have withstood the great flood of 1901 (which destroyed the county's other Doe River bridges). The interior has been renovated over the years, but it is still charming and exceptionally photogenic. ~ Off Route 19E, Elizabethton; 423-547-3852.

From the covered bridge, a 16-mile drive down a four-lane highway leaves the commercial strip behind as it climbs the mountain at a low incline with sweeping curves, taking you to **Roan Mountain State Resort Park** (see "Parks" section below).

After touring Roan Mountain, retrace your route on Route 19E through Elizabethton to the intersection with Route 19W. One of the oldest homes in the region can be found just south of that intersection. You can almost literally step back in time at the **Rocky Mount Museum**, one of Tennessee's handful of living-history sites maintained to show what life was like in olden times. In this case, it's from the day of your visit back to the same day and month of 1791. No tours from mid-December through February and Sunday through Monday the rest of the year. The **Massengill Museum of Overmountain History** is in a modern

AUTHOR FAVORITE

sights The ten-mile drive up from the ranger station to the **Roan Mountain Rhododendron Garden** took me longer than expected. Flanked by forests, the curving road tempted me to stop at a number of scenic vista points. The 600-acre garden, at a breathtaking elevation of some 6200 feet, claims one of the world's largest collections of these plants in the world. The biggest show of purple and pink Catawba rhododendrons blossoms each June. Keep an eye out for the site of the long-gone Cloudland Hotel, which has unsurpassed views of the surrounding terrain. ~ Located 12 miles past Roan Mountain State Resort Park.

building, with exhibits on the early days of the Southwest Territory ("Territory of the United States south of the river Ohio"), including things like a rickety old wagon, Southern earthenware and old bustles. Behind the museum are restored buildings (a residence, a kitchen, a springhouse, a smokehouse, a weaving cabin) and gardens; out front you can see the orchard, sheep pasture, pigpen and barn. The two-story log house was the original capitol of the Southwest Territory, headed by William Blount. Members of an 18th-century family, in period dress, go about their daily business, which—depending on the time of year—may include planting, harvesting, blacksmithing, open-hearth cooking or weaving. Closed Sunday in winter. Admission. ~ 200 Hyder Hill Road, Piney Flats, just north of Winged Deer Park; 423-538-7396, 888-538-1791.

LODGING

To the north, a beautiful detour off the well-traveled roads of Route 421 and Route 91 leads to tiny Mountain City, about 30 scenic miles from Elizabethton. The town has little to recommend except for its location on the edge of the Cherokee National Forest and an exceptional inn. **Butler House Bed and Breakfast** is a two-story brick home that was begun before the Civil War and, like many others in the region, incomplete until years later, in 1870. Built for the family of a prominent Tennessee congressman, it sits amid 15 acres of hilly, wooded land with trails for walking. Closer to the stately house (now on the National Register of Historic Places) is a well-kept lawn and garden. Fourteen-foot ceilings give the four sizable guest rooms an airy, light feeling, a nice counterpoint to the period furniture used throughout. The best amenity, though, is the two-story veranda overlooking the garden. ~ 309 North Church Street, Mountain City; phone/fax 423-727-4119, 800-219-7737. MODERATE TO DELUXE.

DINING

It's a little out of the way, but most locals know it's worth a drive to **Ridgewood Restaurant**. The menu consists mainly of sandwiches, hamburgers and barbecued pork; if you're in the neighborhood between Elizabethton and Bluff City, you ought to check out this classic. Forget asking for the barbecue recipe—it's been a secret since the place opened in 1948. Closed Sunday. ~ 900 Elizabethton Road (Old Route 19E), Bluff City; 423-538-7543. MODERATE.

SHOPPING

You can find an assortment of gifts and antiques on East Elk Avenue in downtown Elizabethton. One such example is **Duck Crossing Antique Mall**, which carries a hodgepodge of antiques on four floors. Closed Sunday. ~ 515 East Elk Avenue, Elizabethton; 423-542-3055.

At **Sycamore Shoals Antiques**, the resident proprietor can give a history lesson on goodies such as her chandeliers from the White House. ~ 1788 West Elk Avenue, Elizabethton; 423-542-5423.

PARKS

ROAN MOUNTAIN STATE RESORT PARK 🏃 🏕 🚣 🎣 Ten miles below the peak (which is in North Carolina), this stunning 2156-acre park makes a wonderful half-day excursion, even if you never get out of your car other than to appreciate the sensational views. Spring is an excellent time to visit, though you should check the weather forecast before heading up, since the region is subject to rapidly changing conditions. With luck, any lingering fog will lift by midmorning, the clouds dispersed by rising temperatures. Rainbow, brown and brook trout populate the Doe River, one of the state's best trout streams (which is stocked with rainbow twice a month from March until mid-June). Keep an eye out for wildlife (deer, fox, skunk, chipmunks, bobcats and the occasional bear) as well as some 180 species of wildflowers from spring until fall. Geology buffs will appreciate that the rocks here, known as Roan Mountain gneiss, are found nowhere else in the world. At the top of the mountain, just west of the North Carolina state line, take the road toward the Rhododendron Garden. Park facilities include a visitors center, a gift shop, playgrounds, volleyball courts, covered shelters, picnic tables, basketball courts, a pool, restrooms and bathhouses; a restaurant is located on the premises; except in winter, there are fruit and vegetable stands along the highway. ~ Located 20 miles south of Elizabethton, 3 miles from the town of Roan Mountain on Route 143; 423-772-3303, 800-250-8620.

▲ There are 107 campsites (87 with water and electricity); $17-25 for RVs and trailers, $10.50 for tent-only. Thirty cabins are available for $99 a night.

▼▼▼▼▼▼▼▼▼▼▼▼▼▼

Bristol to Rogersville

Close to the very northeast corner of Tennessee, Bristol straddles the Virginia state line. In fact, State Street's center line is the exact dividing point between the two states. In all the hubbub over Nashville, most folks forget that Bristol is the birthplace of country music: the first country-and-western music was recorded in Bristol by the Carter Family and Jimmie Rodgers, back in 1927. Downtown Bristol has a historic district consisting of 18th- and 19th-century structures, but beyond that there isn't much to look at. The surrounding countryside, however, is entrancing. Four miles down the road, the tiny downtown area of Blountville and its centerpiece, the Chester Inn, are in the process of restoration.

Southwest of Bristol, Kingsport was known for the William King boatyard, located along the Holston River back around 1800. The Netherland Inn Historic House Museum, located across the old stagecoach road, became the stopover of choice. More historic, and infinitely more compact, is nearby Rogersville, where the entire downtown is on the National Register of Historic Places.

A **lighted sign** on State Street (the boundary between Virginia and Tennessee) proclaims that Bristol, Virginia, and Bristol, Tennessee, are "a good place to live." Erected in 1910, the sign, believe it or not, is on the National Register of Historic Places. ~ State Street between Edgemont and Pennsylvania avenues, Bristol.

SIGHTS

Nearby, a **monument** memorializes Bristol as the birthplace of country music when the Carter Family and Jimmie Rodgers recorded here in 1927. ~ At the intersection of Edgemont Avenue and State Street, Bristol.

Stop by the **Bristol Chamber of Commerce** for information about the town. ~ 20 Volunteer Parkway, Bristol; 423-989-4850, fax 423-989-4867; www.bristolchamber.org, e-mail info@bristol chamber.org.

To the west of town off Route 421, you'll find the **Bristol Caverns**, one of northeast Tennessee's oldest attractions. After all, they have been around some 200 million years. These days, the folks who manage the caves are pretty casual. In fact, your guide may well be wearing overalls and perhaps even say "Shucks." But that's because he may no longer be enthralled by these caverns, which have exceptionally large rooms and so many changes in elevation that only physically fit visitors should plan on making the full tour, even though the temperature is always about 60°. (That's okay; anyone not up for a strenuous hike need only wait in the picnic area for the rest of the group to return.) Tours depart about every 20 minutes and cover some of the paths used by Indian warriors as an attack-and-escape route in their skirmishes with settlers. With some stalactites and some stalagmites the size of tree trunks, the Bristol Caverns are some of the best in the state. And there's enough indirect lighting to warrant toting a camera. Admission. ~ 1157 Bristol Caverns Highway, Bristol; 423-878-2011; www.bristolcaverns.com.

◆◆

START YOUR ENGINES

South of Bristol Caverns is an out-of-the-way attraction. If you like cars—especially NASCAR—you may already know about the **Bristol Motor Speedway & Dragway**. It's the world's fastest half-mile track—maybe it's those ultra-high-banked curves—and hosts seven major NASCAR events every year. Admission. ~ 151 Speedway Boulevard, Bristol; 423-764-1161; www.bristolmotorspeedway.com.

WALKING TOUR
Rogersville

Compact, intact and oh-so-historic, Rogersville makes an ideal town for strolling. Most of the notable buildings are within a few blocks of each other, and the streets are blessedly flat. Begin your walk at ground zero, Town Square, at the intersection of Main and Depot streets, where four squares have remained almost intact since 1787.

OVERTON LODGE   The Overton Lodge No. 5 F. & A.M. sits on the northeast corner of the square. Chartered in 1805, it was built in 1839 and named after Andrew Jackson's law partner, John Overton.

RHEA ARMSTRONG HOUSE   Head west on Main Street (left from Town Square) to the Rhea Armstrong House, built in 1881 and notable for its stately pillars. ~ 119 West Main Street.

CHAMBERS BUILDING   Cross the street to see the Chambers Building, a brick building dating to about 1818. ~ 120 West Main Street.

ROGERSVILLE PRESBYTERIAN CHURCH   Continue west on Main Street, take a right onto Rogers Street, then left onto Kyle Street. The Rogersville Presbyterian Church was constructed in 1840 and still harbors the original pew in the balcony where family servants worshipped. ~ 309 West Kyle Street.

300 BLOCK OF WEST MAIN STREET   Retrace your steps to Main Street and turn right. On your right, you will see several 19th-century homes on this block, including the **Margraves House** (301 West Main Street). and the **Armstrong House** (311 West Main Street). Cross the street

Heading south from Bristol on Route 81, keep an eye out for exits to **Blountville**. Hand-lettered signs keep hope alive as you *HIDDEN ▶* make turn after turn in search of **Countryside Vineyards**, which has a nice tasting room and even nicer tasting room hosts. They make chardonnay and 15 other varieties of wine, many created from European grape varieties rarely available in the U.S., as well as the sweet wines that are so popular in these parts of the country. ~ 658 Henry Harr Road, Blountville; 423-323-1660.

To get to Kingsport, return to Route 81 and continue south to exits for Route 36N and Route 181N.

HIDDEN ▶   The **Netherland Inn Historic House Museum** looks exactly like the stagecoach stop it was in the 18th and 19th centuries. The white three-story wooden structure is located on the old Great

to the **Kirckbaum House**, which was made of homemade brick and sports a hedge of English boxwood believed to have been planted early in the 18th century. ~ 324 West Main Street.

SMITH HOUSE   Continue west and cross the street to reach to the end of this part of the historic district, marked by the Smith House, which once was a stagecoach inn on the Atlanta-to-Washington Stage Line. ~ 413 West Main Street.

ROGERS CEMETERY   Cross West Main Street again and turn right down Rogers Road. Located on your left will be the Rogers Cemetery, where you can find the graves of town founder Joseph Rogers and his wife as well as those of Davy Crockett's grandparents, who lost their lives in a massacre.

SOUTH ROGERS STREET   At the bottom of this block turn left onto Crockett Street and take the first left to head up Rogers Street, where on the left you can see the 1786 **Rogers Tavern**. ~ 205 South Rogers Street. Next door is the **Pettibone Double House**, which consists of two houses made of logs beneath the clapboard siding. ~ 207 South Rogers Street.

OLD PRESBYTERIAN CEMETERY   Continue up Rogers Street to the next corner and turn right onto Washington Street. On your right near Depot Street will be the Old Presbyterian Cemetery, established in 1826. Continue east on Washington Street and turn left onto Depot Street to return to the Town Square.

FURTHER INFORMATION   For more information or for a copy of this tour and one of the east side of town, visit the **Rogersville Heritage Association**. ~ 415 South Depot Street; 423-272-2186; www.rogers villeheritage.org.

Stage Road; today, it's restored and furnished with period pieces and costumes from the inn's heyday. In the back of the main building are three log cabins including the tiny Log Cabin Children's Museum, where kids may enjoy seeing how their peers lived more than a century ago. Closed Tuesday through Friday and from November through April. Admission. ~ 2144 Netherland Inn Road, Kingsport; 423-246-7982; www.netherlandinn.com.

The friendly folks at the **Kingsport Area Chamber of Commerce** are always ready to dispense travel advice. ~ 151 East Main Street, Kingsport; 423-392-8800, 800-743-5282, fax 423-246-7234; www.kingsportchamber.org.

Exchange Place is a little rundown these days, but that adds   ◀ HIDDEN
to the authenticity of this mid-19th-century farmstead. It got its

name as both a stage stop and a place to exchange state currencies between Tennessee and Virginia. From time to time, special events like crafts and early household demonstrations are held among the eight old log buildings that once constituted the Preston farm. Closed Monday through Wednesday and from November through May. ~ 4812 Orebank Road, Kingsport; 423-288-6071; www. exchangeplace.info.

Day and night, the **Bays Mountain Park and Planetarium** has plenty to offer visitors, even those who aren't necessarily hikers or bikers. The place really bustles on weekends throughout the year, thanks to a full array of activities, including wildlife programs (wolves, venomous snakes and bats, to name a few of our favorite creatures). Guided wildflower walks are offered in April and May; during the summer, visitors can take barge rides or moonlight hikes. For more sedentary fun, check out the regularly scheduled shows in the planetarium. The observatory has several reflector telescopes, plus one with an eight-inch refractor. Be sure to get something to eat before you head out to the park, as there are no cold-drink machines or concessions of any kind on the premises. Additional fees are charged for certain nature programs and planetarium shows. Admission. ~ 853 Bays Mountain Park Road, Kingsport; 423-229-9447, fax 423-224-2589; www.bays mountain.com, e-mail baysmtn@baysmountain.com.

Historic **Rogersville** is off the beaten path, 25 miles southwest of Kingsport via Route 11W. The highway bypasses town, so keep an eye peeled for the Route 70 exit sign and head east.

The first paper in the state was printed in Rogersville in 1791; the first railroad paper in the world was published in the early 1800s.

When you arrive in Rogersville, stop by the **Rogersville/Hawkins County Chamber of Commerce** and pick up detailed walking-tour brochures. ~ 107 East Main Street, Suite 100; phone/fax 423-272-2186; e-mail hawkinschamber@intermediatn.net.

You can also get them from various merchants around town. These guide visitors to a number of sites within the six-block **Rogersville Historic District**, which encompasses numerous historic houses, buildings and sites.

The **Hawkins County Courthouse**, built in 1836 with Palladian windows and brick columns, is the oldest original courthouse still in use in Tennessee. ~ Corner of Main and Depot streets, Rogersville; 423-272-7359.

Originally built around 1837 as courthouse offices, the **Shelburne Law Offices** also functioned at one point as a hotel and hospital. ~ 100 West Main Street, Rogersville.

Constructed in the late 1700s, the **Pettibone Double House** stands as one of Rogersville's earliest structures. Underneath the clapboard siding, the houses are actually made of logs. ~ 207 South Rogers Street, Rogersville.

Rogers Cemetery is where you'll find the founder of Rogersville, Joseph Rogers, and his wife resting in peace. Also buried here are the grandparents of David Crockett, who were killed in their cabin by a Cherokee attack in 1777. ~ Rogans Road, Rogersville.

You can learn a thing or two about Rogersville history at the **Rogersville Depot Museum.** On permanent display are exhibits about Rogersville's printing history as well as artifacts of daily Rogersville life in the early years. You can also catch revolving exhibits such as quilt shows, art exhibits and photography. Open Tuesday through Thursday or by appointment. Admission. ~ 415 South Depot Street, Rogersville; 423-272-1961.

The accommodations at the **MeadowView Conference Resort and Convention Center** are dull as dishwater—unless you have a room with a view. Rates are higher during the week, when business travelers check in. It's not close to anything in particular but it is appreciated by conventioneers as well as by golfers, who can play on the par-71 layout or just fool around on the practice range and green. There's a passable restaurant on the ground floor of the seven-story, 195-room hotel. ~ 1901 Meadowview Parkway, Kingsport; 423-578-6600, 800-820-5055, fax 423-578-6630; www.meadowviewresort.com. MODERATE TO DELUXE.

LODGING

The **Kyle House Bed and Breakfast**, an 1832 Federal-style home constructed of handmade brick, served as headquarters for Confederate officers during the Civil War. Now on the National Register of Historic Places, it has eight fireplaces, antique chandeliers and other antebellum features. The former smokehouse is now a pottery studio. There's cable TV in all three rooms. ~ 111 West Main Street, Rogersville; 423-272-0835; www.kylehousetn.com, e-mail sltaliaferro@yahoo.com. MODERATE.

The **Home Place Bed & Breakfast** is on the outskirts of Rogersville, about ten miles southwest of downtown. Built as a log cabin in the early 19th century, this expanded still-cozy inn has four guest rooms decorated with family heirlooms. And what a family it's been: ancestors of the present owner raised their children in this house, and another ancestor, Joseph Rogers, founded the town that bears his name. The inn's first floor has been converted into a restaurant. ~ 132 Church Lane, Mooresburg; 423-921-8424, 800-521-8424; www.homeplacebb.com, e-mail pris-rogers@bellsouth.net. BUDGET TO MODERATE.

◄ HIDDEN

A pretty old house has been transformed into the **Troutdale Dining Room**, where they like to say, "We make everything but the butter." You could make a meal out of a couple of appetizers like eggplant roulade or semi-boneless marinated quail. Or go all out by ordering one of the entrées; they all come with salad or fresh veg-

DINING

etables. Among more than a dozen choices are trout, scallops, lamb, veal and a selection of filet mignons. Closed Sunday and Monday. ~ 412 6th Street, Bristol; 423-968-9099, fax 423-968-5385; www.thetroutdale.com. DELUXE.

HIDDEN ►

Located out of sight on a lower level of the Colonial Heights Shopping Center, **Motz's** is thronged with locals who get off work around 5 p.m. and head straight for dinner. The specialty is pasta, but there are also steaks, seafood, pizza, calzones, veal and lots of chicken dishes. Don't expect ambience: the color scheme ranges from light pink to dark pink with green plastic ivy. ~ 4231 Fort Henry Drive, Kingsport; 423-239-9560, fax 423-349-2772. BUDGET TO MODERATE.

Who would ever expect to find a fast-service restaurant in sleepy downtown Rogersville, especially one that's open 24 hours most days? **Oh, Henry** is not a chain, either. Indeed it would be hard to duplicate the overwhelming nondescriptness of this corner spot. Still, the plastic tablecloths and placemats are clean and the service, downright cheerful. Basically, it's a "meat-and-threes" place, meaning you order a meat and three vegetables and pay very little money. The selection's pretty good, including pork chops, country ham and catfish, and the salads are fresh and crisp. Closed Sunday. ~ 201 Main Street, Rogersville; 423-272-0980. BUDGET.

HIDDEN ►

On the ground floor of the Home Place Bed & Breakfast, the **Lattice Room** serves up entrées such as pork loin, roast beef with gravy, grilled chicken, country ham and honey baked ham. Both lunch and dinner include country-style vegetables, homemade rolls and desserts. Regulars are especially fond of the salad luncheon, which includes three or four salads of the diner's choice. ~ 132 Church Lane, Mooresburg; 423-921-8424; 800-521-8424. BUDGET.

SHOPPING   A number of interesting stores line downtown Rogersville.

Beale Pottery specializes in locally handcrafted pottery. Closed Sunday and Monday. ~ 116 East Main Street, Rogersville; 423-272-3879.

You'll find a mountain of antiques to sort through at the 10,000-square-foot **Mountain Star Antique & Craft Mall**, where more than ten rooms are chock-full of timeworn treasures. They also carry Boyds bears and rabbits, and figurines such as bear stones and doll stones. Closed Sunday. ~ 122 East Main Street, Rogersville; 423-274-2920.

NIGHTLIFE   In Bristol, the **Paramount Center for the Arts** sets the stage for a variety of performances throughout the year. Call to find out what's scheduled at this restored 1931 art-deco movie house. ~ 518 State Street, Bristol; 423-274-2920.

Entertaining the masses for over 30 years, **Theatre Bristol** puts on musicals, comedies, dramas, children's theater and occasional cabaret. Performances are at the Paramount and at the Theatre Bristol Artspace. ~ 512 State Street, Bristol; 423-968-4977.

Kingsport is home to a burgeoning arts scene. The **Kingsport Renaissance Center** hosts a number of shows throughout the year and boasts an art gallery exhibiting regional and local works. ~ 1200 East Center Street, Kingsport; 423-392-8415. The **Kingsport Theater Guild** puts on plays and musicals at the center. ~ 423-392-8427. The **Kingsport Renaissance Players**, composed of senior citizens, also entertain with their performances at the center. ~ 423-392-8400. The **Kingsport Symphony Orchestra** performs a variety of concerts throughout the year. ~ 400 South Wilcox Street, Kingsport; 423-392-8423.

WARRIORS' PATH STATE PARK 🚶 🐎 ⛴ 🏕 🚤 🎣 ⛳   **PARKS**
Close to a commercial hub but seemingly in another time zone, this 970-acre gem is named for its proximity to ancient war and trading paths favored by the Cherokee and offers all kinds of activities at the Patrick Henry Reservoir. It has more activities for kids than most other state parks: the Olympic-size swimming pool has a waterslide, and there's an 18-hole course and putting green (and pro shop). If you really want to get away from it all, there are nine miles of hiking trails. Or you can take a horse or pony ride along two miles of woodland trails or book a campsite on an island in the reservoir. The park has a snack bar, and full-service restaurants are nearby. ~ Take Exit 59 off Route 81, east to Route 36, on Hemlock Road near Kingsport; 423-239-8531.

> Naturalists call the mountainous tip of the state "East of Eden" because of the extensive recreational opportunities.

▲ There are 135 sites; $17.25 with water and electrical hookup; $11.25 for tent sites.

BAYS MOUNTAIN PARK 🚶 🚵 🚣 ⛳ A 44-acre lake, a planetarium and observatory (with an eight-inch refractor telescope and several reflector telescopes), a farmstead museum and an interpretive nature center make this 3000-acre nature preserve a perennial favorite with families—and nature lovers of all ages, for that matter. Gray wolves, ducks, herons, beavers, rabbits, bobcats and squirrels can sometimes be observed on the nature trails that crisscross the park; deer sightings are almost inevitable. There are 25 miles of trails to hike. They range in length from 300 feet to 4.8 miles and can be connected to make a full day of hiking. Facilities are limited to restrooms. Day-use fee, $3. ~ 853 Bays Mountain Park Road, Kingsport; 423-229-9447; www.baysmountain.com, e-mail baysmtn@baysmountain.com.

▾ ▾ ▾ ▾ ▾ ▾ ▾ ▾ ▾ ▾ ▾ ▾ ▾

Outdoor Adventures

Northeast Tennessee offers some of the best recreational possibilities in the state. It contains more than 232,000 acres of national forest, 156 miles of the Appalachian National Scenic Trail, waterfalls, golf courses and riding and hiking trails, as well as lakes, rivers and creeks for rafting, boating and fishing.

FISHING

Fishing is fantastic on the six TVA lakes: Boone, Cherokee, Douglas, Fort Patrick Henry, South Holston and Watauga. Trout, bass and crappie provide the most popular fishing in northeast Tennessee. Cherokee and Douglas are the major lakes, although South Holston and Watauga are also worthwhile.

At **Cherokee Lake**, expect to find largemouth bass in April and May and smallmouth bass, March through May. Crappie can be fished from the middle of April through May and again in the fall, in October and November. You can troll for catfish in the summer off the lake's rocky banks.

At **South Holston**, fish for bass in May and June, September and October; trout fishing is good from March through May. On summer nights, try trolling near the dams. In general, **Watauga** is good for night fishing. Three species of trout—brook, rainbow and brown—are found in the waters of the **Doe River**. Because they are wild, flyfishing allows you to imitate, with flies, the trout's natural food source. Several brook trout streams meet above **Roan Mountain State Resort Park**, where the Doe River is born. These are good fishing waters. For details on where to go, call 423-772-3303, 800-250-8620.

RIVER RUNNING

Canoers, kayakers and rafters flock to this part of Tennessee, particularly to the upper reaches of the Nolichucky and French Broad rivers. If you want to shoot the rapids (Class I–III) of the Watauga River, call Charles or Martha Shell at **B-Cliff Whitewater Rafting**. ~ 423-542-2262, 800-592-2262. **Russell Fork Expeditions, Inc.** specializes in advanced whitewater adventures as well as instruction in kayaking, rafting and rescue clinics. Based near Mountain City, they take trips into Russell Fork Gorge, Wilson's Creek,

AUTHOR FAVORITE

Canoeing down the Watauga River is so relaxing on a warm summer day that after a while I don't care if I catch any trout or not. The best guides to the river are the friendly folks from **Mahoney's Sportsman Paradise**, who are experts at finding (and catching) trout on the Watauga and other rivers in the Tri-Cities area. ~ 830 Sunset Drive, Johnson City; 423-282-5413.

Watauga Gorge, Watauga Lake, Spring Creek and the south fork of the Holston River. ~ P.O. Box 37, Shady Valley, TN 37688; 423-739-9326, 800-843-3675. Other outfitters include **Cherokee Adventures Whitewater Rafting** ~ 423-743-7733, 800-445-7238; **Nantahala Outdoor Center** ~ 704-488-2175, 800-232-7238; **Russell Fork Expeditions, Inc.** ~ 423-739-9326, 800-843-3675; and USA **Raft** ~ 423-743-7111, 800-872-7238. Cherokee Adventures and USA Raft also offer rafting on the Nolichucky River.

Roan Mountain offers what may be the only cross-country skiing in any state park in the South. Three trails, totaling about eight and a half miles, are available for skiers who bring their own equipment. The season opens after the first major snowfalls, usually mid-December, and lasts into early March. ~ Route 143; 423-772-3303, 800-250-8620.

SKIING

GREENEVILLE TO JOHNSON CITY Everything else in town seems to be named for our 17th president, so why not a golf course? The semiprivate **Andrew Johnson Golf Club** has a few large hills to make the par 70 something of a challenge. You may want to rent a cart for this one. The 18-hole course is a couple of miles southeast of Route 70, just off Route 321. ~ 615 Lick Hollow Road, Greeneville; 423-636-1476, 800-421-2149. A popular public golf course located near downtown Greeneville, the **Kinser Park Golf Course** has nine holes with a par 36. ~ 780 Kinser Park Lane, Greeneville; 423-639-6406. You may have trouble keeping your mind on business at **Twin Creeks Golf Course,** an 18-hole, 72-par course with panoramic views of the East Tennessee mountains. A full-service pro shop and a large putting green are among the amenities. ~ 90 Chuckey Highway, Chuckey, five miles north of Greeneville; 423-257-5192.

GOLF

BRISTOL TO ROGERSVILLE The original 18 holes at **Tri-Cities Golf Course** date back to the 1960s; another nine holes on slightly hillier terrain were added in 1994. The par on any 27-hole combination is 70. Carts available. ~ 2354 Feathers Chapel Road, Blountville; 423-323-4178. If you've been wanting to play some golf but don't know anyone who belongs to a club—or even anyone who plays golf—your best bet is the **Camelot Golf Course.** The original nine holes were laid out in 1970, including a par-4 hole that has been upgraded to a par 5, thanks to a creek in front of the green that makes it impossible to just roll the ball right up there. The par for all 18 holes is 73. ~ Guntown Road, Rogersville; 423-272-7499.

Kinser Park, located along the Nolichucky River in Greeneville, has two public tennis courts. Call ahead to make sure nets are up. ~ 710 Kinser Park Lane, Greeneville; 423-639-5912.

TENNIS

It snows about 16 inches in an average winter in Johnson City, but from spring through fall, you can play on any of the five tennis courts at the **Metro-Kiwanis Park**. ~ Guaranda Drive, Johnson City; 423-283-5824.

RIDING STABLES

Flintlock Farm leads all-day rides on horses or mules through mountains and valleys, through running streams and across farmlands. Lunch is included, or riders may opt to stay at the Flintlock Lodge. The trail rides are designed for small groups of experienced adult riders. No children under 12 are allowed. ~ 790 G'Fellers Road, Chuckey, about seven miles northeast of Greeneville; 423-257-2489, 866-472-4434.

Warrior's Path Riding Stables offers guided trail rides through scenic woodlands. ~ Warrior's Path State Park, 1882 Fall Creek Road, Kingsport; 423-323-8543.

BIKING

Northeast Tennessee is blessed with a network of country roads, but few of them have designated bike paths and drivers are not accustomed to sharing the open road with bikers. There's plenty of mountain biking in the area, however.

Although bicycles are not allowed on the Appalachian Trail, mountain bikers have access to the **Cherokee National Forest** except for hiking trails and designated wilderness areas. For information on more than 70 miles of roads around the Nolichucky Ranger District, call 423-735-1500. Another 125 miles of unpaved roads await bikers in the Unaka Ranger District; call 423-735-1500 for details. Try the **Rock Creek Park Loop**, and pay attention because the views are incredibly distracting. Finally, near Elizabethton are more jeep roads in the Watauga Ranger District. ~ 423-735-1500.

Cherokee Adventures Whitewater Rafting leads guided mountain bike trips in northeast Tennessee, from March through October. ~ 200 Jonesborough Road, Erwin; 423-743-7733, 800-445-7238.

Johnson City, designated as a Bicycle Friendly Community by the League of American Bicyclists, has three routes throughout the city with wide shoulders and bikeways. You can get a map from the **City of Johnson City**. ~ 423-434-6000.

Bays Mountain Park has about 35 unpaved miles of trails. You must register your bike for the day for a $2 fee before getting a sticker and a trail map.

HIKING

All distances listed for hiking trails are one way unless otherwise noted.

OVERMOUNTAIN AREA The Cherokee National Forest covers some 625,000 acres in eastern Tennessee, split between the northeast and the southeast by the Great Smoky Mountains National Park. The northern division of the forest has 275 miles of trails, and

there are another 100 miles along the Appalachian Trail. Not all
the trails are in good condition, but two are highly recommended.

The **Iron Mountain Trail** (17 miles) starts at about 3700 feet,
near the peak of Iron Mountain near Elizabethton. A difficult
trail, it runs along the crest of Iron
Mountain, which peaks at 4000 feet, af-
fording views of Shady Valley and Holston
Mountain to the west, and Laurel Creek
Valley and the mountains along the North
Carolina border on the east side. Parking space
is scarce at the Cross Mountain trailhead but
more plentiful at Sandy Gap or Camp A-Hi-S-Ta-
Di at the north end of the trail.

The Overmountain Victory Trail in
Roan Mountain State Resort
Park was used by Revolutionary
War soldiers on a march from
Sycamore Shoals to Kings
Mountain in South
Carolina, site of a pivotal
battle.

Another difficult but popular route is the **Holston Mountain Trail**. It extends a little over eight miles
(plus a one-mile road hike) along the crest of Holston Mountain
to Flint Mill Trail. Along the way are vistas of South Holston
Lake on the west and the Iron Mountain on the east. The trail
climbs to 3700 feet and eventually intersects with the Appalachian Trail. For specifics, contact the Watauga Ranger District,
246 Route 91, Elizabethton; 423-735-1500.

BRISTOL TO ROGERSVILLE   Roan Mountain State Resort Park
has seven trails in varying degrees of difficulty. The longest is **Chestnut Ridge** (4.3 miles). Experienced hikers prefer the stretch of the
Appalachian Trail that crosses the Roan High Knob. ~ Route 143;
423-772-3303.

Kingsport's **Greenbelt** offers several hiking options along fairly
level ground. One stretch (1.75 miles) is at Netherlands Road at
the Boatyard-Riverfront Park. Another longer portion (4.25 miles)
is accessed via the parking lot at the Kingsport Mall off Eastman
Road. ~ 423-229-9457.

Transportation

Most of northeast Tennessee is accessible only by state
highways or local roads. **Route 81** is the exception,
running from Knoxville to Bristol, with exits for Greeneville, Jonesborough, Johnson City (via **Route 181N**) and Kingsport (via **Route 181S**). The main thoroughfare linking Greeneville,
Jonesborough, Johnson City and Bristol is **Route 11E**. Traffic becomes very congested around Greeneville and Johnson City; use
the bypass whenever possible. Bristol is linked to Kingsport by
Route 81 as well as **Route 11W**, which continues west to Rogersville. Elizabethton is on **Route 19E**, a scenic segment of which runs
from 11E all the way up Roan Mountain near the North Carolina border.

CAR

AIR

Tri-City Regional Airport is in the middle of the triangle made by
Johnson City, Kingsport and Bristol, almost exactly equidistant

from all three. It is served by America Connection, Delta Connection, Northwest Airlink and US Airways. ~ 2525 Route 75, Blountville; 423-325-6000; www.triflight.com. The nearest major airport is the **McGhee Tyson Airport** in Knoxville, which offers more extensive service. ~ 423-325-6000; www.tys.org. (See "Transportation" in Chapter Three for more information.)

BUS   **Greyhound Bus Lines** (800-231-2222; www.greyhound.com) offers passenger service to three cities in northeast Tennessee. There are stations in Johnson City at 137 West Market Street; in Kingsport at 325 1/2 Cherokee Street; and in Greeneville at 1060 West Andrew Johnson Highway.

CAR RENTALS   The best place to arrange for automobile rental is the Tri-City Regional Airport. Within the airport are outlets for **Avis Rent A Car** (800-230-4898), **Budget Rent A Car** (800-527-0700), **Enterprise Rent A Car** (800-325-8007), **Hertz Rent A Car** (800-654-3131) and **National Interrent** (800-227-7368). Just across the road is **Thrifty Car Rental** (800-847-3489). More car-rental companies can be found in Knoxville, the closest major airport. The city of Knoxville is about 70 miles southwest of Greeneville, and about two hours' driving time from Bristol.

PUBLIC TRANSIT   **Johnson City Transit** offers bus service throughout the city. ~ 423-929-7119. For transportation to and from the Tri-City Regional Airport, visitors can use their hotel's shuttle service. **Kingsport Transit** does the same for its city. ~ 423-224-2613.

For getting around Bristol, the cheapest route is the **Bristol Tennessee Transit** bus line. ~ 423-989-5586.

TAXIS   Greeneville has no municipal bus system, but you can always call a cab from either the **Greeneville Cab Company** (423-636-0123) or **Yellow Cab** (423-638-5252).

For getting around Johnson City, to the airport or neighboring towns call **WW Cab** (423-928-8316).

Tri-City Cab (423-246-9037) serves the Kingsport area.

The city of Elizabethton has no muni transit, but does have a couple of taxi companies: **Graham Cab** (423-542-2171) and **Black and White Cab** (423-542-4161).

THREE

Gateway to the Smokies

To the millions of people who flock to the attractions in Pigeon Forge, schuss the slopes of Gatlinburg or flock to the Great Smoky Mountains National Park to see the stunning display of autumn leaves, Knoxville is little more than a refueling station. But this city, the third largest in the state, is of historic interest. Home to the University of Tennessee and site of the 1982 World's Fair, Knoxville now has a newer attraction in its restored Old City. This renovated warehouse district has several blocks of restaurants, boutiques and antique stores with merchandise almost as old as the city itself.

It all started when James White came to town—or actually, to the banks of the Tennessee River—and set up his farmstead in 1786. He settled in with his wife and six kids, chickens, horses and cows, later adding outbuildings to accommodate the many, many pioneers who followed in his footsteps. A well-to-do militiaman from North Carolina, White purchased some 1000 acres, never dreaming that this stop on the river would become a town, then a city, then the first state capital.

After William Blount was appointed governor of the "Territory South of the Ohio River," he decided to move the capital from northeast Tennessee to a more central location, specifically the settlement around White's fort. The city was founded in 1791. Five years later, Tennessee became the 16th state to join the Union, and Knoxville was its capital for the first 16 years of statehood.

Blount's decision was a sound one. Knoxville lies in a green valley 936 feet above sea level, surrounded by seven lakes created by the Tennessee Valley Authority, which is headquartered here. Some 174,000 people live in the city today, with more than half a million in the greater metropolitan area. If you asked every one of them why they choose to live in Knoxville, probably 100,000 would mention the distinct seasons. The city's climate is temperate, with an annual average temperature of about 59°, dropping to 30° in the dead of winter and up to 87° in summer. It gets a good deal of rain, about 50 inches in an average year, but only about a foot of snow. That's okay: there's plenty of that in the Great Smoky Mountains, which are visible from the Sunsphere and other tall structures.

59

It's an outdoorsy kind of town, and the presence of the University of Tennessee probably enhances the casual lifestyle. You'll see plenty of business suits downtown, but not in the rest of Knoxville. It's not a very touristy town, although thousands of people visit Knoxville en route to the Great Smoky Mountains National Park, which is about a two-hour drive to the east.

Between Knoxville and the park lie several towns, including Sevierville (pronounced "seVERE-ville"), Pigeon Forge and Gatlinburg. Sevierville is pretty and small, but offers less to visitors than its neighbors, two adjacent towns that could hardly be more different from each other.

Sevierville's first settler was probably an Indian trader named Isaac Thomas, who moved to the area in 1783 following the Revolutionary War. In 1795, the Territorial Legislature established a town and county seat named Sevierville in honor of John Sevier, the prominent frontier hero who became a leading Tennessee politician. The town grew slowly; there were fewer than 600 people in 1900. While the downtown neighborhood has been slow to ignite, the outskirts have seen a great deal of development spurred, no doubt, by the success of tourism in neighboring Gatlinburg and Pigeon Forge.

Who would ever have thought little ol' Pigeon Forge would become one of the top tourist attractions in the Southeast? Who would ever have thought little ol' Dolly Parton, who left home with nothing in her knapsack but a lot of talent and gumption, would become one of the most famous and beloved performers of her generation? Parton may have put Pigeon Forge on the map big-time when she helped launch Dollywood in 1986, but since then the place has mushroomed with a gazillion amusements for both young and old. Pigeon Forge's sprawling outlet malls are so popular they even outdraw Dollywood, especially during the winter months. The various musical venues around town have a combined total of more than 10,000 seats; though the emphasis is on contemporary country music, you can also hear gospel and some toned-down rock-and-roll. The town prides itself on being a family place, and a majority of the citizens figure that by remaining "dry," they can preserve that reputation forever.

For better or worse, they haven't preserved much else. Thirty years ago, there were two traffic lights in what was then a farming community. By 1982 the World's Fair in Knoxville, only 40 miles to the west, began drawing attention to the region. Riding on the coattails of that city as well as Gatlinburg, Pigeon Forge was raking in about $72 million in tourist trade. These days, the town averages $500 million per year in tourism revenue. The town knows its business, and to keep the momentum, it's gobbling up the surrounding countryside in a feeding frenzy. There is precious little open space left, but everybody knows that just up the road, there is more open space in the Smokies than they'll ever get around to enjoying.

Although Gatlinburg has been a mountain resort destination for decades, it has grown more slowly than Pigeon Forge. Gatlinburg's first hotels were operating well before Dolly Parton was even born, capitalizing on their proximity to scenic wilderness areas just outside the city limits.

Situated at 1292 feet, the town developed along the banks of the Little Pigeon River, which flows down from Mount LeConte and is still a part of the town's identity. If you spend any time at all in Gatlinburg, you won't be surprised that the Ogles were the first-known settlers because dozens of businesses (and people!) go by that name today. The Ogles were followed by families from North Carolina and Virginia; now many of the town's 5000 residents trace their ancestry to English, Scottish and Irish people. Established as White Oak Flats in 1935, the village was too remote to grow much. It wasn't until the early part of this century that Pi Beta Phi, a national sorority, opened a school in what had become Gatlinburg (named after an early shopkeeper, Radford Gatlin). Most of the mountain children got their first education at the school, which later evolved into an arts-and-crafts institution, giving rise to the many artisans who populate the region today. After the Great Smoky Mountains National Park was established in 1934, Gatlinburg developed as a tourist resort. More than 70 million people live within a 400-mile radius, which may account for the more than 9 million people who visit the park each year, many of whom choose lodging in the many motels, inns and chalets of Gatlinburg. Snowfall averages 50 inches a year. January's average high temperature is 50°; low is about 29°. In July, the average high temperature is 87°; the low, about 60°.

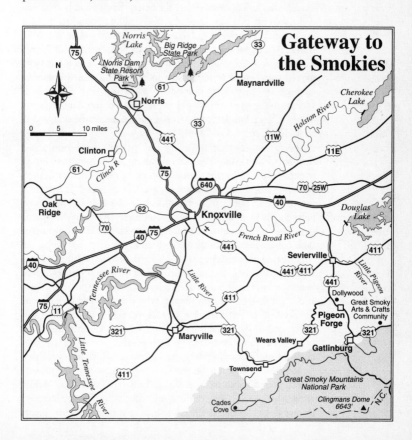

Gateway to the Smokies

▼▼▼▼▼▼▼▼▼▼
Knoxville

Founded on the banks of the Tennessee River, Knoxville has sprawled in every direction. The downtown area is home to the city's historic mansions, the business district, the University of Tennessee and World's Fair Park, site of the 1982 exposition. The major shopping malls and many of the city's restaurants are found along Kingston Pike, which also is the main thoroughfare to many of the nicer neighborhoods.

SIGHTS

One Vision Plaza, opened in 2004 in a renovated early-20th-century building, offers tourism and sports information. Also in the plaza are a coffee shop and the headquarters of WDVX radio. ~ 301 South Gay Street, Knoxville; 865-523-7263, 800-727-8045; www.knoxville.org, e-mail tourism@knoxville.org.

Most forts are named simply to honor some long-gone hero, but not the **James White's Fort**. Touring this living-history museum, with its stockaded walls and brick walkways, you can easily imagine the Indians just beyond the fence, the pigs and horses bedded down on one side, and the lanky White trying to build a house with doorways tall enough to accommodate his 6'4" frame. White brought his wife and six kids here from North Carolina in 1786, built a two-story log cabin (which has been moved some yards to its present location) and added buildings as more and more settlers used the place as a way station convenient to the river. The on-site manager is a descendant of James White. Closed Sunday, and Saturday in winter. Admission. ~ 205 East Hill Avenue; 865-525-6514.

For a leisurely tour of the city and environs, book passage on the **Star of Knoxville**. You can hop aboard a 90-minute sightseeing cruise along the Tennessee River or opt for lunch or dinner-and-entertainment excursions aboard this two-tier, 325-passenger riverboat, with an open-air deck for basking in the sun or taking a little moonlit stroll. ~ Tennessee Riverboat Company, 300 Neyland Drive; 865-525-7827, 800-509-2628; www.tnriverboat.com, e-mail capt@tnriverboat.com.

Situated only a stone's throw from the river, the **Blount Mansion** is of such significance that it's one of only seven registered historical landmark buildings in Tennessee. It was the home, from 1792 to 1800, of William Blount, who was the only governor of the Southwest Territory (the area of the U.S. south of the Ohio River) and whose name is on the United States Constitution. One of the first frame houses to be built on this side of the Appalachian Mountains, it looked quite modern at the time, with sharp lines distinguishing it from the log structures nearby. The numerous shuttered windows inspired the Indians to call it the "house with many eyes." Guided tours, including living-history interpretations, lead through the house, which has many original pieces

Text continued on page 66.

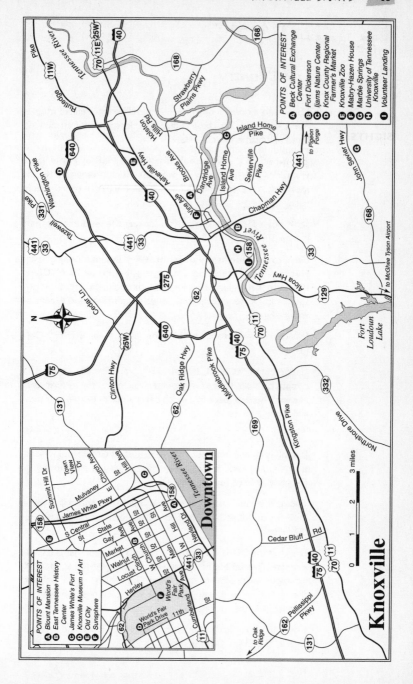

POINTS OF INTEREST
A Beck Cultural Exchange Center
B Fort Dickerson
C Ijams Nature Center
D Knox County Regional Farmer's Market
E Knoxville Zoo
F Mabry-Hazen House
G Marble Springs
H University of Tennessee Knoxville
I Volunteer Landing

POINTS OF INTEREST
A Blount Mansion
B East Tennessee History Center
C James White's Fort
D Knoxville Museum of Art
E Old City
F Sunsphere

Downtown

Knoxville

Three-day Weekend

Gateway Country

Day 1
- Check into a hotel in downtown Knoxville or the refined **Maplehurst Inn** (page 72). These choices are close to major attractions, some of which are listed below.

- Bounce off to the **Women's Basketball Hall of Fame** (page 67), which tells the story of women's rising prominence in the sport. Take time to dribble a few balls on the partial courts before taking off.

- Settle down for lunch at one of the inexpensive restaurants around Market Square.

- Drive to the **University of Tennessee Knoxville** campus (page 66). Among the interesting sights here is the **Frank H. McClung Museum**, famed for its geological, anthropological, archaeological and natural history collections, as well as a really good exhibit on ancient Egypt.

- Experiment with exotic Thai food for dinner at the **Stir Fry Cafe** (page 75).

- Catch a show at the **Carousel Theatre** (page 80) on the U-T campus or head downtown for entertainment at the historic **Tennessee Theatre** (page 80), which offers a mix of live performances and classic movies.

Day 2
- Take off early and head out in the direction of Great Smoky Mountain National Park. Search for good deals at the **Pigeon Forge Factory Outlet Mall** (page 103).

- Shoot the rapids and enjoy other rides and entertainment at **Dollywood** (page 87). Pick up lunch at one of several places in the theme park.

- Drive up the hill to **Gatlinburg** (page 89), a town that started as a summer retreat but now welcomes visitors year-round, especially if there's enough snow to ski at **Ober Gatlinburg**. At any rate, take the tram ride up the slope and get your picture taken with the mountains in the background.

- Check into the **Gatlinburg Inn** (page 94) or a bed and breakfast such as the **Eight Gables Inn** (page 95).

- Get cozy at the **Park Grill** (page 100) for a dinner of lamb chops or Moonshine chicken, then mosey over to nearby Pigeon Forge and catch a show at the **Classic Country Theater** (page 107).

Day 3

- Kick off the morning with a hearty breakfast at the **Burning Bush** (page 100).

- Get out in the fresh mountain air for some exercise. Try your hand at fishing by signing up with **Old Smoky Outfitters** (page 109). Or climb aboard a horse and see the countryside from atop a saddle. Golf your heart out at one of the area's hilly courses.

- Complete the day with a tasty lunch in Sevierville at the **Rocky River Brewery & Grille** (page 101) or the **Applewood Farmhouse Restaurant** (page 101).

as well as some period furnishings. Look around the grounds at the separate kitchen building—there are occasional demonstrations—and the office where Blount drafted the Tennessee Constitution. Closed January and February. Admission. ~ 200 West Hill Avenue; 865-525-2375, 888-654-0016, fax 865-546-5315; www.blount mansion.org, e-mail info@blountmansion.org.

Before visiting the nearby World's Fair Park, take a detour to the **University of Tennessee Knoxville**. For a map of the campus, take Cumberland Avenue south from Henley Street to the entrance at Volunteer Boulevard. After a block, look for the visitors kiosk on the right, where you can pick up information and a parking permit. Founded as Blount College in 1794, the university began as a nonsectarian institution in a period when most institutions of higher learning were linked to one religious denomination or another. Known for a time as East Tennessee University, the school changed locales over the decades, finally coalescing as the University of Tennessee on a hill west of the city center. Some of the oldest buildings can be found on the crest of "The Hill," including the Austin Peay Building, originally built in 1911 as the Carnegie Library. The school has a faculty of 1200 and a student body of about 26,000, ranging from freshmen to postdoctoral students. Fifteen colleges and schools at UT offer nearly 300 degree programs. ~ 865-974-1000; www.utk.edu, e-mail admissions@utk.edu.

HIDDEN ►

Housed in a red-brick building deep in the University of Tennessee campus, the **Frank H. McClung Museum** is regarded as a general museum, with outstanding exhibits in anthropology, archaeology, decorative arts and medicine. Its unique appeal, however, lies in its extremely informative displays on the state's natural history, especially its extraordinarily diverse geology. Models, paintings, photographs and maps tell the story so well that ideally, everyone who plans to drive around Tennessee's backroads would visit this museum first. The McClung has one of the Southeast's best collections of American Indian artifacts, some of

sights

AUTHOR FAVORITE

My favorite house in Knoxville is the 1834 **Crescent Bend** mansion, which overlooks a particularly pretty stretch of the river. Also known as the Armstrong-Lockett House, it is furnished in 18th-century antiques, decorative arts and English silver from 1640 to 1820. Allow time to stroll among the five fountains in the impeccably manicured formal Italian gardens that descend from the house to the waterfront. Closed Monday and from January through February. Admission. ~ 2728 Kingston Pike; 865-637-3163, fax 865-637-1709; www.korrnet.org/cresbend.

which date from ancient times, as well as a permanent exhibit on ancient Egypt. ~ 1327 Circle Park Drive; 865-974-2144, fax 865-974-3827; mcclungmuseum.utk.edu

Volunteer Landing opened in 1999 between the university and the Tennessee River. A complex that when completed will amount to $40 million worth of improvements along a mile of riverfront, it already features several restaurants and will eventually include shops, office buildings and condominiums. The centerpiece of the Landing is the **Gateway Regional Visitors Center**, whose exhibits focus on the abundant natural resources of the Southern Highlands, the entire region's cultural resources, and the technological resources of the Department of Energy's nearby Oak Ridge Complex. Visitors can get information on local attractions through electronic media or by asking a staff member. The center is at the foot of the James White Parkway. ~ 900 Volunteer Landing; 800-727-8045; www.volunteer-landing.com.

When the **Women's Basketball Hall of Fame** (WBHOF) opened in 1999, it shined a long-overdue spotlight on the achievements of more than a century of female athletes from around the world. The best feature is an inspiring video, "Hoopful of Hope," that tells the story of the sport and many individuals. Exhibits include a timeline, a simulated locker room where you can hear various coaches discussing strategy, and the world's biggest basketball: a 20,000-pound, 30-foot-wide sphere. Visitors who take time to play on one of the mini-courts here may feel that regulation balls weigh that much, especially if they haven't done any lay-ups recently. The gift shop carries sports memorabilia with the logos of contemporary pro teams. Admission. ~ 700 Hall of Fame Drive; 865-633-9000, fax 865-633-9294; www.wbhof.com.

Retrace your route on Cumberland Avenue to the intersection with 11th Street and you will practically be at **World's Fair Park & Festival Center**, where the Sunsphere tower remains the most visible symbol of the 1982 event. The fair came and went in the course of the summer, leaving in its wake an open space that is used for public events, but none of the new commercial and residential buildings that were expected to revitalize the neighborhood. Bounded by Henley Street, Cumberland Avenue, World's Fair Park Drive and a pedestrian viaduct that closed off Clinch Avenue, the park is mostly open space.

You can see the **Sunsphere** from blocks and blocks—and sometimes miles—away. And vice versa. That was the goal when the 300-foot-tall tower, topped with a golden ball, was constructed for use as a restaurant at the 1982 World's Fair. Today, visitors are allowed to ride the elevator to the top for a bird's-eye view of the city and surrounding landscape, but the restaurant has long since gone. ~ World's Fair Park, 810 Clinch Avenue; 865-525-1791, 800-727-8045; www.knoxville.org.

Historic Knoxville

You'll need a car or bicycle to make the rounds of Knoxville's historic sites, which include antebellum mansions, a Confederate cemetery and an 18th-century farmstead.

JAMES WHITE'S FORT   Start your exploration of regional history where Knoxville got its start: at James White's Fort (page 62) on East Hill Avenue, where you can get a glimpse of pioneer life. Continue east on East Hill, then turn left onto Mulvaney Street to the intersection of Summit Hill Drive. Turn right and head east until the street turns into Dandridge Avenue, home to two notable historic sites.

MABRY-HAZEN HOUSE   Stop at the Mabry-Hazen House (page 70), a two-story frame residence with some fascinating background, including a stint as headquarters for both factions during the Civil War. Two blocks beyond the house is the four-acre **Confederate Cemetery** (page 71).

BECK CULTURAL EXCHANGE CENTER   Return to Dandridge Avenue and continue east to the fork with Brooks Avenue. On your left will be the Beck Cultural Exchange Center (page 71), which has exhibits on African-American citizens of Knoxville.

OLD CITY   Return on Dandridge back to Summit Hill Drive. Just past the James White Parkway, turn right onto South Central Street and proceed to the intersection with Jackson Avenue. Park your car and wander around Old City (page 70). This area thrived during the 19th century and many of the buildings have been rescued and turned into restaurants and shops.

Arm yourself with brochures and maps at the **Knoxville Convention and Visitors Bureau Tourist Information Center Office** in the old City Hall building. Closed weekends. ~ 800 Volunteer Landing Lane; 865-523-7263, 800-727-8045, fax 865-673-4400; www.knoxville.org.

The stunning, multilevel **Knoxville Museum of Art** is so entrancing that it's a pity the five beautiful galleries offer such a limited number of artworks. The museum, made of Tennessee pink marble, was designed by well-known museum architect Edward Larabee Barnes, and is itself a work of art. It does have small exhibits donated by private local collectors, mostly paintings and quilts, but its main appeal lies in the visiting exhibits devoted to a single artist or medium. Check the schedule before going out of

EAST TENNESSEE HISTORY CENTER   After investigating Old City, retrace your path on South Central and continue about six blocks to Clinch Avenue. Turn right for three blocks and you will be at the intersection with Market Street. On your left will be the East Tennessee History Center (page 70), a repository of myriad objects relating to this part of the state, dating back to pre-pioneer days.

MARBLE SPRINGS STATE HISTORIC FARMSTEAD   When you leave the museum, continue west on Clinch Avenue for three blocks to Henley Street (Route 441) and turn south (left). It will take about 25 minutes to reach your next destination. Route 441, also known as the Chapman Highway, continues south; exit at Route 168 (John Sevier Highway) and go right (west) a couple of miles until you see the signs for Marble Springs State Historic Farmstead (page 72). This 37-acre 18th-century farm has been restored and visitors can take tours explaining the life and times of one of Tennessee's heroes, John Sevier.

BLOUNT MANSION   Return to Knoxville proper via Route 441. After you cross the Tennessee River, turn right on East Hill Avenue, as if you were returning to the James White's Fort. On your right after you pass Gay Street, you will see the parking lot and welcome center for the Blount Mansion (page 62). A tour of the home and grounds will tell you a lot about the early days of Tennessee's statehood.

CRESCENT BEND   From the mansion, head west on Hill Avenue and turn left at Walnut Street for one block. This is the route to Neyland Drive (Route 158), which will take you past Volunteer Landing and on out to Crescent Bend (page 66). Also known as the Armstrong-Lockett House, this is a restored 1834 home with spectacular gardens right on the banks of the river.

your way to tour this attraction. Closed Monday. Admission. ~ 1050 World's Fair Park Drive; 865-525-6101, fax 865-546-3635; www.knoxart.org.

Confederate Memorial Hall (Bleak House) was one of the Confederate headquarters in 1863. The unusual Tuscany-style architecture is actually typical of the period, but most of its contemporaries have since been torn down. The hall is furnished in period pieces, although very few are original. Look closely: bullet holes in the walls are chilling evidence of the hall's role in the Confederate/Union battle. A library (located in the hall's former ballroom) houses an impressive collection of first editions, and a museum provides further information about the building's historical significance. The grounds are particularly lovely. Closed

Thursday, and Saturday through Monday, except by appointment. Fee for tours. ~ 3148 Kingston Pike; 865-522-2371; www.knoxvillecmh.org.

Compact and informative, the **East Tennessee History Center** covers the gamut of local history, with special emphasis on the last two centuries. This is not a stodgy museum; it comes alive with exhibits like the one on David ("Be sure you are right, then go ahead") Crockett, a large relief map of the region that shows where the rivers flow and another map of the vast Cherokee nation. The exhibits are well done, grouped chronologically to show the development of the region from pioneer days through the Revolutionary War, the struggle for statehood, the Trail of Tears, the Civil War, the Depression, the establishment of Great Smoky Mountains National Park, TVA, Oak Ridge and the development of Knoxville. The gift shop is also excellent, with games for kids and rack after rack of book on local topics. ~ 600 Market Street; 865-215-8830; www.east-tennessee-history.org.

Knoxville was founded in 1791 and named after General Henry Knox, President Washington's secretary of war.

Alex Haley, the late author known all over the world for *Roots* and other books, grew up in west Tennessee and later made Knoxville his home. He is honored with the 13-foot bronze **Alex Haley Statue**, which was commemorated in Haley Heritage Square at Morningside Park. ~ 1600 Dandridge Avenue; 800-727-8045.

The most charming commercial neighborhood in Knoxville, a section known as **Old City**, lies a short drive (or a long walk) from downtown. The easiest way to reach it is via the James White Parkway (Route 158), which offers an Old City exit as it veers north from the Tennessee River. The heart of this section of town, which thrived in the 19th century before being all but abandoned, is intersected by Jackson Avenue and Central Street. Old warehouses now contain restaurants, shops, nightclubs and the offices of architects and other nonindustrial concerns. Lively by day, the district is also a popular destination after dark, with a variety of musical venues in the restored buildings. ~ 800-727-8045.

HIDDEN ►

You must insist that your tour guide recount the dramatic personal stories pertaining to the three generations who lived in the **Mabry-Hazen House**. They would make a miniseries fit for television, with the last Hazen daughter living out her spinster days here after a soured love affair. Thanks to her bequest, this 1858 hilltop home, now on the National Register, is restored and its regal rooms filled with hundreds of period pieces, from horsehair sofas to family portraits to dolls and toys. The home's proximity to Fort Hill led to its occupation by Confederate troops. Closed Sunday and Monday. Admission. ~ 1711 Dandridge Avenue; 865-522-8661, fax 865-522-8471; www.korrnet.org/mabry, e-mail mabryhazen@yahoo.com.

Situated two blocks behind the Mabry-Hazen House is the **Confederate Cemetery**. Four acres in size and part of the Mabry-Hazen House Museum, this is where the bodies of 1600 soldiers are interred. Closed Sunday and Monday. ~ Bethel Avenue; 865-522-8661.

It's too bad the **Beck Cultural Exchange Center** is so far off the   ◀ HIDDEN
beaten track because in a regrettable way the location symbolizes the underpublicized achievements of so many black citizens, as they are called in these exhibits. This remodeled residence houses photographs, oral histories, biographical sketches, fine art, newspapers and books. A glance at the photographs lining the Pioneer Stairway tells part of the story: Charles Canseler, Knoxville's first male black schoolteacher in 1864; William F. Yardly, the first black lawyer (1872); and Cal Johnson, a former slave who owned Knoxville's only horse-racing track. One room is dedicated to the state's first black governor, William H. Hastie, and features many of his personal artifacts. The center also maintains 350 videos and classic black films from the 1930s and 1940s as well as a library and resource center. Closed Sunday and Monday. ~ 1927 Dandridge Avenue; 865-524-8461, fax 865-524-8462; www.korrnet.org/beckcec, e-mail beckcec@korrnet.org.

The hilly layout of the **Knoxville Zoo** makes it seem intimate because you can see so much in such a short space, although it stretches over some 33 acres. Shaded walkways zigzag up and down gentle slopes past well-done exhibits. Have a kitty back home? Check out the big cats here, including African lions and snow leopards. There's a petting zoo and an amphitheater for bird shows. Children can feed the llamas, get up close to the silverback gorilla and watch the river otters play in their habitat. The latest exhibits include the Stokely African Elephant Preserve and Grasslands Africa. Admission. ~ 3500 Knoxville Zoo Drive, Exit 392 off Route 40; 865-637-5331, fax 865-637-1943; www.knoxville-zoo.org, e-mail knoxzoo@knoxville-zoo.org.

If the zoo hasn't tired out the little ones, detour to the nearby **East Tennessee Discovery Center**. One of those "learning is fun" hands-on museums, this place may amuse the kids for a few hours while leaving your conscience at peace. Aquariums, an insect collection, live reptiles (you might want to skip the giant hissing cockroaches and black widow spider), comparatively harmless kaleidoscopes, and a simulated space shuttle are among the permanent exhibits. Closed Sunday and occasional days in June and July. Admission. ~ 516 North Beaman Street (Chilhowee Park); 865-594-1494; www.etdiscovery.org, e-mail etdc@bellsouth.net.

For a pleasant midday break from touring, find your way to the **Ijams Nature Center**, an oasis beside the Tennessee River southeast of downtown. Pronounced "eye-ams," the 150-acre site was the home of Alice and Harry Ijams. On the premises are a nature center building and an educational facility that houses a small museum with nature-related exhibits. The grounds are planted with wildflowers and a variety of trees that offer spring and summer shade. The center offers an array of naturalist programs, as well as special events such as performances by the Knoxville Symphony. Closed Sunday from November through March. ~ 2915 Island Home Avenue; 865-577-4717, fax 865-577-1683; www.ijams.org.

A short drive from the urban density of Knoxville proper is a carefully preserved, 37-acre 18th-century farm that gives you an idea of how grueling daily life could be in those times. **Marble Springs State Historic Farmstead** was established as a way station by John Sevier, the Revolutionary War hero who was given a land grant in recognition of his service, served as governor of the Lost State of Franklin and was elected twice to the U.S. Congress. Sevier himself spent relatively little time here. Although only a few original Sevier possessions have been recovered, some pieces, such as a cherry desk, are in the restored home, which, along with several newer outbuildings, you can tour on your own or with a guide. Closed Monday. Admission. ~ 1220 West Governor John Sevier Highway; 865-573-5508.

LODGING   As befits the Maplehurst Park neighborhood on the edge of the business district and not far from the University of Tennessee campus, the **Maplehurst Inn** is refined and residential, marked by a small yellow canopy, a pair of antique lanterns and a modest sign. Most of the 11 rooms on the first and second floors have king-size beds with desks and sitting areas. The view from the Penthouse extends over the Tennessee River to encompass the outline of the Smokies. The basement has been converted to a sizable common room where a full breakfast and afternoon tea are served. ~ 800 West Hill Avenue; 865-523-7773, 800-451-1562; www.maplehurstinn.com, e-mail sonny@maplehurstinn.com. MODERATE TO ULTRA-DELUXE.

Accommodations at the **Hotel St. Oliver** are likely to remind you of a nice home in a big city. The structure, which dates from the 1870s, has 24 rooms on two upper floors. Sophistication permeates the place; all of the rooms are different, linked by style and accouterments such as lithographs and fine art reproductions. Some have jet tubs, and the corner suite is large enough to inspire a long stay. ~ 407 Union Avenue; 865-521-0050, 888-809-7241, fax 865-521-9227; www.hotelstolivertn.com. BUDGET TO DELUXE.

HIDDEN ▶   The grandest inn in Knoxville is tucked away on 16 wooded acres quite a way from downtown. **Maple Grove Inn**, indeed, seems worlds away. Like many a Tennessee bed and breakfast, it came into existence as a home and antiques assortment grown out of control. Not to worry: there's plenty of room in this

14,000-square-foot mansion for an eclectic collection of furniture, from four-poster beds to settees, arranged with an interior decorator's talents. The original Georgian-style structure, which has been expanded extensively, was built in 1799. Today it's closer to a resort than a B&B, with tennis courts, a pool, terraces and decks, six spacious rooms and two enormous suites. ~ 8800 Westland Drive; 865-690-9565, 800-645-0713, fax 865-690-9385; www.maplegroveinn.com, e-mail info@maplegroveinn.com. DELUXE TO ULTRA-DELUXE.

Unfortunately, quaint B&Bs and historic inns aren't as plentiful in Knoxville as one might hope. There are, however, the usual litany of chain hotels, some of which are more comfortable than others. You might try the **Hilton Knoxville Downtown**, a looming 18-story complex with a pool, a fitness center and a restaurant and lounge. Although the 317 guest rooms promise blandness, the sheer size of the place means a great view of the Tennessee River, and it's located just a block from the university. ~ 501 West Church Avenue; 865-523-2300, fax 865-525-6532. DELUXE.

DINING

One of the better places to eat on Market Square is **The Tomato Head**. Although it's not fancy—an old brick building, with seating outside beneath blue awnings—it's dependable for gourmet pizzas (with ingredients such as gorgonzola, lamb, tofu and smoked salmon), sandwiches, calzones, salads and fresh breads. ~ 12 Market Square; 865-637-4067. BUDGET TO MODERATE.

A one-way street down from Market Square leads past a block of rowhouses to reveal a delightful surprise. **Chesapeake's** is in a restored historic brick building that beckons with a blue awning. A little blackboard lists specials that enhance the kind of menu you might find up east. From Maine lobster to Maryland crab cakes to grilled shrimp, the house specialty is seafood. Don't look too long at the saltwater aquarium—you might end

AUTHOR FAVORITE

The most charming place in town for breakfast or lunch is the **Crescent Moon Café**. Housed in the ground floor of a historic three-story brick building, this friendly restaurant features a cozy room as well as an interior courtyard. The name of the game is healthy food, freshly made soups, salads, sandwiches and pastas, often made with organic ingredients. Breakfast and lunch are served and the café serves dinner on the first and third Fridays of each month by reservation only. Closed Saturday and Sunday. ~ 718 Gay Street; 865-637-9700; www.crescent mooncafe.com, e-mail terriatthemoon@juno.com. BUDGET.

up ordering the chicken. ~ 500 Henley Street; 865-673-3433; www.chesapeakes.com. DELUXE TO ULTRA-DELUXE.

Imagine a Woody Allen movie shot in New York's Russian Tea Room and you have an image of **Lucille's**. Elegant and vaguely European, this is the kind of place where you'll feel comfortable in black tie before a formal event, or in street clothes or even more casual attire. The common denominator may well be a love of the perfect martini—or it may be a class ring from the University of Tennessee, although fans of UT's football opponents also seem at home here. Seasonal sea bass and salmon dishes star on a menu that also covers the pasta, steak and chicken bases. ~ 106 North Central Avenue; 865-637-4255, fax 865-637-0502. MODERATE.

The most famous place to dine in Knoxville is **Regas The Restaurant**, which has been in business since it started as a coffee shop in 1919. The place is huge, and on busy nights it's astonishing how room after room is jam-packed. At these times, service can be excruciatingly slow and you may spend more time than you care to in the gargantuan bar. Best bets are Angus beef and fresh seafood dishes, although the Southern classics are also good. ~ 318 North Gay Street; 865-637-3427, fax 865-637-7799. MODERATE TO ULTRA-DELUXE.

HIDDEN ▶ Located on the third floor of the University of Tennessee Boathouse, the **Tennessee Grill** reveals grand views of the river and Neyland Stadium. You'll know you're in "Big Orange" country the second you walk in the door and see all the U-T sports memorabilia lining the walls and, most likely, U-T sports clips playing on four large-screen TVs. In addition to chicken, seafood, steak and pasta dishes, this casual restaurant offers daily specials: chicken, shrimp, rib or catfish platters and prime rib, Monday through Friday respectively, plus Sunday brunch. ~ 900 Neyland Drive; 865-862-8657, fax 865-862-8658; www.tennesseegrill.com. BUDGET TO MODERATE.

RIPE FOR THE PICKING

Sample Amish butter, select fruits and cheeses and soft drinks for a picnic, buy an ice cream cone for less than a dollar or pick up some local honey, jam or pickled vegetables for souvenirs at the **Knox County Regional Farmer's Market**. It's a huge enclosed space, where a lot of Knoxvillians do their major marketing, but there's plenty of ready-to-eat fare, as well as crafts and plants. Closed Sunday morning. ~ 4700 New Harvest Lane close to East Towne Mall, Exit 8 off Route 640; 865-524-3276, fax 865-522-4833.

At **Litton's Market and Restaurant**, a brick-and-glass-fronted neighborhood hangout, steak, burgers and seafood are the order of the day. A giant room, rimmed with plants, contains simple tables and a couple of booths, with a pair of glass cases displaying the day's selection of tempting pies and cakes. If it's crowded, just put your name and the number in your party on the greaseboard and wait to be called. If you know it's going to be more than a few minutes, check out the duck pond across the street. Closed Sunday. ~ 2803 Essary Drive; 865-688-0429. BUDGET TO MODERATE.

The bulk of inexpensive, ethnic and chain restaurants are clustered on the west side of Knoxville.

Dining on the road wearing thin? **Naples Italian Restaurant** is a lovely combination of informal neighborhood dining and food you'd rarely manage to prepare for yourself. Red tablecloths and intimate booths are the perfect setting for the comforting, flavorful soups, pasta and fish dishes. The ravioli comes stuffed with your choice of shrimp, lobster or beef, and you'll have your pick of sauces as well, such as tomato, butter or alfredo. If you can save room, there's an excellent crème brûlée for dessert. No lunch Saturday and Sunday. ~ 5500 Kingston Pike; 865-584-5033. BUDGET TO DELUXE.

The Plum Tree provides an oasis of serenity on busy Kingston Pike. Inside a red wooden building topped with a golden dragon, a warren of booths and small rooms is decorated in the red-and-gold color combination signifying good fortune to the Chinese. You'll feel lucky, too, when you see the extensive menu of cooked-to-order dishes including the standard shrimp, beef, chicken, pork and vegetable entrées. The Plum Tree has some not-so-traditional offerings as well, including moo-shu seafood and fish in ginger sauce. If you want to pass on the serenity, call ahead to arrange pickup at their drive-through window. ~ 7052 Kingston Pike; 865-588-2002. BUDGET.

Chili pepper icons in the menu's margin denote particularly spicy dishes at the **Stir Fry Cafe**. The indoor-outdoor restaurant looks like a chain, probably because it's in a shopping center, but is one of a kind. You'll find Thai–Chinese food—curries, Szechuan bean curd, twice-cooked pork and a host of vegetable and other choices, some hot, some stir-fried and none with MSG (except the soups). There are some great deals here, especially a spinach salad with the café's special Thai dressing. It's very popular with the 20- to 30-year-olds looking for a quick, tasty bite on their way home from work. ~ 7240 Kingston Pike; 865-588-2064, fax 865-584-1841. BUDGET TO MODERATE.

Sometimes you may not be in the mood for ambience. You may just want to eat and get on with it. For cheap, fast food, you can take your pick of some 200 items (including Mongolian grill

Text continued on page 78.

The Tennessee
Valley Authority

Unless you live in Tennessee, you probably haven't thought much about the Tennessee Valley Authority (TVA) since high school civics class. Today, with energy and power considerations fueling worldwide debate and even declarations of war, it's a lot more interesting to know that the TVA, headquartered in Knoxville, is the nation's largest producer of electric power.

The TVA is many things: it's a federal corporation, a regional economic development agency and a national Environmental Research Center. It operates nuclear plants and coal-fired plants as well as the dams and recreational areas with which most people associate the entity. As owner of some 41,000 square miles, it harnesses the power of the Tennessee River, the fifth largest river system in the U.S., for power production, flood control, water quality, recreation and navigation.

More than eight million people—not only in Tennessee but also in parts of Georgia, Alabama, Mississippi, Kentucky, Virginia and North Carolina—depend on the TVA for energy.

How did such a vast enterprise come to be?

In these enlightened times, it's easy to forget that concerns about balancing the needs of man and the country's natural resources are a relatively new phenomenon. Around the turn of the century, however, people were just beginning to realize how the abundant resources of the New World had been alarmingly depleted over three centuries of settlement. Gifford Pinchot, who was chief U.S. forester under President Theodore Roosevelt, spent a lot of his waking hours pondering the various aspects of natural resources—forests and soil, wildlife and streams, minerals and human nature. Finally it dawned on him that there was "unity in this complication."

Quoted in *A History of the Tennessee Valley Authority*, Pinchot observed, in 1907, "Here were no longer a lot of different, independent, and often antagonistic questions, each on its own separate little island, as we had been in the habit of thinking. In place of them, here was one single question with many parts. Seen in this new light, all these separate questions fitted into and made up the one great central problem of the use of the earth for the good of man."

This idea—one of unifying resource development—lay the groundwork for the establishment of the TVA in 1933. By then, of course, the country was still reeling from the economic devastation of the Depression. Franklin Delano Roosevelt had just been inaugurated, and people everywhere were looking to him for salvation, but nowhere more desperately than in the economically devastated Tennessee Valley. Because of the unique route of the Tennessee River (520 miles from Knoxville to the Mississippi River, conduit to the Gulf of Mexico) and because of extreme navigational problems around Muscle Shoals, Alabama, the idea of a regional federal agency in the Tennessee Valley had been championed for years by Nebraska Senator George Norris. When Roosevelt realized how the idea of the TVA fit his New Deal plan for revitalizing the economy, he backed Norris' efforts, and Congress passed the Tennessee Valley Authority Act in 1933.

Within three months, construction began on the TVA's first hydro-electric dam, which had been planned as a Corps of Engineers project on the Clinch River in northeast Tennessee.

Despite continual bouts of opposition to its expansion, even to its very existence, the TVA expanded until it is now a nearly $7 billion corporation, employing nearly 13,000 people in offices throughout the region as well as at 11 coal-fired plants, 3 nuclear plants, 29 hydroelectric dams and 1 pumped storage unit. At the turn of the millennium, TVA added energy from the renewable sources of sun, wind and methane gas. While the system was designed for flood control, navigation and the generation of electricity, recreation is one of the best-loved byproducts of TVA's success. TVA lakes in Tennessee include Kentucky, Pickwick, Tim's Ford, Nickajack, Chickamauga, Watts Bar, Fontana, Tellico, Fort Loudoun, Melton Hill, Douglas, Davy Crockett, Fort Patrick Henry, Boone, Cherokee, South Holston, Watauga and Norris. On the border with Kentucky, the Land Between the Lakes is a National Recreational Area with 300 miles of undeveloped shoreline managed by the TVA (see page 281 for more information). Fishing, best in the spring and late fall, is allowed at all of them, and many TVA reservoirs offer hiking or biking trails, camping facilities and access to wilderness areas. ~ 865-632-2101; www.tva.gov, e-mail tvainfo@tva.gov.

and, for dinner, seafood) at the huge spread at **Number One China Buffet**. ~ 6300 Papermill Drive; 423-212-3788. BUDGET.

Knoxville has its own outpost of **Corky's Ribs & BBQ**, the regional chain that got its start in Memphis. Arguably serving the best hickory-smoked ribs and barbecue in eastern Tennessee, this is the place to get your fix—with all the fixin's including irresistible fresh bread for mopping up the sauce. ~ 260 North Peters Road; 423-690-3137. BUDGET TO MODERATE.

Bare wood floors, a huge bar and big-screen television tuned to sports are the major draw at **Kingston Alley**. Their specialties include chicken lasagna and a "gourmet" meat loaf, and they also serve pizza, pasta, steak and seafood. ~ 7355 Kingston Pike; 423-766-0464. BUDGET TO MODERATE.

SHOPPING Chocoholics alert! You can watch chocolate and other candies being made Monday through Friday at the **South's Finest Chocolate Factory**. Although a plate-glass window prevents overzealous fans from participating in the process, all manner of sweets are displayed for sale in the retail store. It's appropriate that all this goes on in a seven-story building constructed in 1919 expressly for a candy manufacturer (the now-defunct Red Seal company). ~ 1060 World's Fair Park; 865-522-2049, 800-522-0874; www.chocolatelovers.com.

Across the street and up a steep slope is an unlikely variation on a shopping center in the form of three Victorian houses. **Art & Antiques Gallery** is in the green one, with two floors of original works by some 40 local artists in various media. Careful shopping will reveal some good buys in watercolors, tapestries, stained glass and prints. Closed Monday. ~ 1012 Laurel Avenue; 865-525-7619.

The most fun place to window-shop in Knoxville is in Old City. Antique shops, bookstores and boutiques are arrayed along some four city blocks around South and North Central streets and West and East Jackson avenues.

One of the largest and best-stocked antique stores in East Tennessee, **Jackson Antique Marketplace** is a sprawling, 24,000-square-foot mecca where you can find clocks, linens, toys, lamps,

VISIONS OF SOUTHERN APPALACHIA

While some traveling shows perform here, concerts, dance and festivals dedicated to preserving theatrical aspects of southern Appalachian culture are the mainstays at the **Laurel Theatre**, housed in a former church on the National Register of Historical Places. ~ 1538 Laurel Avenue; 865-522-5851.

fireplace accessories and all manner of less likely objects. ~ 111 East Jackson Avenue; 865-521-6704.

Jewelry, lighting, fragrances and such home decor as beaded curtains are among the pretty things at **Earth to Old City**. ~ 22 Market Square; 865-522-8270.

Vagabondia stocks natural-fiber women's fashions and accessories from FLAX, April Cornell, Planet and Peter Carroll, among other designers. ~ 27 Market Square; 865-525-5842.

At **Back 40**, you can find original art-like products—from letterpress posters promoting special events, music acts and theater shows to handmade, woodcut fine art prints. ~ 413 South Gay Street; 865-522-1812.

The **Knoxville Center** shopping mall has more than 120 stores plus a food court and full-service restaurants. ~ Exit 8 off Route 640; 865-544-1500.

Topographical maps, lake maps, globes, 3-D maps, compasses, celestial maps, state atlases—if you're going absolutely anywhere at all, find the way with help from **The Map Store**. Closed Saturday and Sunday. ~ 900 Dutch Valley Drive; 865-688-3608, 800-678-6277.

A store devoted to gifts for corporate chieftains is such a good idea you'd think someone would franchise it. That's exactly what's going on at **The CEO Agenda**, a cool store with business items, travel gear, leather goods, writing instruments, gadgets, golf accessories, desktop gizmos and more. Closed Sunday. ~ The Shops at Bearden Place, 5809 Kingston Pike; 865-584-1660.

On the west side of the city, you can find more than 130 shops at **West Town** shopping mall, which also has a food court and full-service restaurants, as well as a nine-theater movie complex. ~ 7600 Kingston Pike (near the West Hills exit off Routes 40/75); 865-693-0292.

Lucille's is the hip spot for sipping a martini and catching some cool jazz. In nice weather, the band sets up on the patio Friday through Sunday nights (they advertise 9:30 p.m., but nothing seems to get going until at least 10). Cover. ~ 106 North Central Avenue; 865-637-4255.

NIGHTLIFE

Locals were thrilled with the opening of **Blue Cats**, a rock club finally big enough to host popular acts that used to skirt Knoxville for greener pastures. The excellent acoustics may also contribute to the club's lure, attracting artists like the Cowboy Junkies and Michelle Shocked. There's a full-service bar, and a restaurant in the courtyard. Cover. ~ 125 East Jackson Avenue; 865-544-4300; www.bluecatslive.com.

Across the street is the edgier **Pilot Light**. There will be bands here you've probably never heard of, but that's part of the fun.

There's usually a free film night on Sunday. Cover. ~ 106 East Jackson Avenue; 865-524-8188; www.thepilotlight.com.

One of a handful of 1920s-era movie palaces still in use today, the rococo-style **Tennessee Theatre** is the site of various stage productions, but it mostly shows movie classics accompanied by a Wurlitzer (and a bag of popcorn). ~ 604 South Gay Street; 865-522-1174; www.tennesseetheatre.com.

OPERA, SYMPHONY, BALLET AND THEATER   With its various ensembles, the **Knoxville Symphony Orchestra** performs more than 300 concerts annually, accompanied by visiting professionals in both its classical and pops series. ~ 406 Union Avenue; 865-291-3310; www.knoxvillesymphony.com.

The biggest production of the year for the **City Ballet** is its annual *Nutcracker* ballet, but it also presents other dances throughout the year at the Knoxville Civic Auditorium. ~ 1060 World's Fair Park Drive, 7th floor; 865-544-0495; www.knoxballet.org.

The **Knoxville Opera Company** produces four performances a year, including operas, concerts and musicals, accompanied by the Knoxville Symphony, in both the Tennessee Theatre and the Knoxville Civic Auditorium. ~ 612 East Depot Avenue; 865-524-0795; www.knoxvilleopera.com.

The **Carousel Theatre**'s "theatre-in-the-round," one of the country's first arena theaters, attracts musicals, comedies, drama and dance performances. ~ 1714 Andy Holt Boulevard on the UT campus; 865-974-5161; www.clarencebrowntheatre.org.

The **Tennessee Theatre**, which reopened in early 2005 after a two-year restoration of the historic 1920s movie palace, now features film as well as music, dance and drama performances. ~ 604 South Gay Street; 865-522-1174; www.tennesseetheatre.com.

PARKS

HIDDEN ▶

FORT DICKERSON   You have to look closely to find the remains of the Civil War fortifications, but this pocket park south of the Henley Street Bridge has other charms. Union general Ambrose Burnside had his troops build a fort of earthworks on top of this hill, a wonderful location from a militaristic point of view, because from this position, it would be possible to shell most of the city just north of the river. In fact, Union troops did turn back Confederate cavalry, although the latter were advancing from the south. The park is used for peaceable purposes now; there are a few picnic tables in the shade and public restrooms, but other than that it's just the kind of place you'd go to take a nap on a Sunday afternoon. ~ From downtown, take Henley Street south across the river, go an eighth of a mile and turn right to go up the hill.

IJAMS NATURE CENTER   In an unusual set up, Ijams Nature Center is contained within a city park on the banks of the Tennessee River (the exact locale is considered Lake Loudoun). The 150-acre property was the residence of Alice and Harry Ijams, avid birdwatchers who left a legacy for all to enjoy. The nature center building home houses a small museum with small exhibits like birds nests and reptiles. But the main attraction is Mother Nature. Trails connect gardens, woods and meadows, a kind of urban wonderland where birds and humans can both enjoy wild-flowers and a diverse assortment of trees—white ash, tulip poplar, hickory and beech. ~ 2915 Island Home Avenue; 865-577-4717; www.ijams.org.

Oak Ridge Area

America's "Secret City" was built during World War II as part of a massive effort to complete the Manhattan Project. Officials selected the semirural area in the hills northwest of Knoxville as an ideal site, partly because it was so unlikely. It was constructed according to military requirements for isolation yet it was accessible to highways and railways. Some 3000 people were living in the area in 1942; they were pledged to secrecy and given only months to move out so the plant, plus an entire town, could be constructed. In a matter of months, a new city, with facilities for development of the material for atomic weapons, was built on a 60,000-acre tract less than an hour from downtown Knoxville. Few people outside of high-ranking government officials knew the whole story, and security was tightly monitored. The city is ten miles long and two miles wide, stretching through a valley and up a hillside called Black Oak Ridge, which inspired the innocuous-sounding name of Oak Ridge. In less than three years, Oak Ridge's population soared to 75,000, making it the fifth-largest, if unknown, city in Tennessee.

> The world's first gram quantities of plutonium were created at the Oak Ridge National Laboratory.

After the bombs were dropped in Japan and the war ended, many of the plants and facilities were converted to peacetime use. The homes, schools and other buildings used during the war were opened to the public in 1949, and in 1955 the Atomic Energy Commission sold the federally owned land and homes to the people of Oak Ridge. The city, incorporated in 1959, now has a population of nearly 28,000 people, many of whom are highly educated and technically trained as a result of the wartime relocation. The world's largest and oldest nuclear reactor, housed in the Oak Ridge National Laboratory (ORNL), was decommissioned in 1963. Today, ORNL is the site of projects ranging from coal technology to genetics and energy conservation, although you'll have to marvel from afar because the lab is not open to the public.

Oddly enough, neighboring Norris could also be called a company town. The first dam the Tennessee Valley Authority built was on the Clinch River north of Knoxville. As construction began in 1933, a town was needed to house the engineers and construction workers. There's not much to see, tourism-wise, except on the outskirts of town.

SIGHTS   Visiting **Oak Ridge** today, you wouldn't necessarily be aware of its history until you began touring some of the extremely unusual sites in this town, which at first glance resembles the average American small town.

Your first stop in Oak Ridge should be the **American Museum of Science & Energy**, where you can see *Ten Seconds that Shook the World*, a documentary on the decision to drop the first atomic bomb. You can also fiddle with interactive exhibits, attend scheduled live demonstrations and take a self-guided tour. Closed Monday. ~ 300 South Tulane Avenue, Oak Ridge; 865-576-3200; www.amse.org, e-mail information @amse.org.

In 1943, the height of construction in Oak Ridge, houses were completed at the rate of one every 30 minutes.

Walking- and driving-tour maps of the Oak Ridge area are available at the desk in the museum, as well as at the **Oak Ridge Convention and Visitors Bureau** right next door. Closed Sunday and Saturday from November through May. ~ 302 South Tulane Avenue, Oak Ridge; 865-482-7821, 800-887-3429; www.oakridgevisitor.com, e-mail orcvb@oakridgevisitor.com.

The **Children's Museum of Oak Ridge** makes World War II, and the role Oak Ridge played in it, make sense. Though the focus is mostly local, there are other exhibits here, including a 19th-century pioneer homestead, a walk-in dollhouse, a nature area and displays on foreign countries including Japan and Norway. Closed Sunday during the summer. Admission. ~ 461 West Outer Drive, Oak Ridge; 865-482-1074; www.childrensmuseumofoakridge. org, e-mail chmor@bellsouth.net.

The **Oak Ridge Art Center** shows off a permanent collection of abstract expressionism, American modern, primitive and other contemporary styles in different media—painting, sculpture, pottery, photography. It also has revolving exhibits. ~ 201 Badger Avenue, Oak Ridge; 865-482-1441; www.kornet.org/art, e-mail orarts37830@cs.com.

HIDDEN ▶   If you're not already intrigued by the story of Tennessee's mountain people, you surely will be after you visit the **Museum of Appalachia**. A bona-fide must-see attraction, the museum is a 65-acre spread, with 30 authentic log structures, a display building, a gift and snack shop and the Appalachian Hall of Fame. John Rice Irwin has devoted his life to collecting memories and memorabilia of the "old people" of his grandparents' community in southern Appalachia, and has curated them with a mother's care and a son's respect. Goats, sheep and chickens wander about the well-kept grounds, which visitors traverse on a self-guided tour with the help of a detailed printed guide. You start at the Hall of Fame, where photographs and prose bring the people seemingly to life; also here is an extensive exhibit of artifacts like Cherokee baskets and American Indian trade bottles, ceremonial items and pottery. From Roy Acuff's fiddle to farming tools, the collection encompasses some 250,000 pieces. The log buildings include an old jail cell, a couple of residences and other structures likely to be found in rural Appalachia; if you're lucky, somebody will be fiddlin' on the porch when you visit. Admission. ~ 2819 Andersonville Highway, Clinton; 865-494-7680; www.museumofappalachia.com, e-mail musofapp@icx.net.

If you're heading out to Norris Dam, take a detour into the city of **Norris**, just east of the Museum of Appalachia. Don't expect a lot of pizzazz; the interesting thing about this place is how it came to be built in the first place. It's a planned community, constructed by the Tennessee Valley Authority (TVA) to house the engineers and other employees who worked on the Norris Dam project in the early 1930s. After the dam was finished in 1937, the town became residential. Today it's incorporated and listed on the National Register of Historic Places. Spacious and preternaturally suburban in ambience, Norris is composed of homes that vary only slightly, mostly with different facades of brick, stone, board, cinder block and shingles, flanked with manicured lawns that may remind some movie buffs of the town in *Stepford Wives*.

More kinds of mousetraps were in use in the late 1800s than are on the market today. The phrase "sleep tight" came from the practice of tightening the jacks on rope beds for a better night's rest. "Reading between the lines" stems from the turn-of-the-20th-century habit of saving paper by writing a response between the lines on the original correspondence. These are but a few revelations awaiting visitors to the **Lenoir Museum**. East Tennessee history is illuminated by exhibits on the daily lives of turn-of-the-20th-century residents, with some 5000 items arranged in displays on dairying, food preparation, wood and metal working and American Indians. A nearby threshing barn and 18th-century grist mill are adjuncts to the museum. Closed Monday and Tuesday from Labor Day to November 15, Monday through Friday from November 15 to April 15, and Monday and Tuesday from April 15 to Memorial Day. ~ Norris Dam State Resort Park, 2121 Route 441, two miles downstream from the dam, Norris; 865-494-9688, fax 865-426-9494.

The first dam built by the Tennessee Valley Authority, **Norris Dam and Lake** is a popular getaway spot for Knoxvillians, and if you've never seen a big dam, it's worth detouring off Route 75 for a peek. You can visit the overlooks at the 265-foot dam, which impounds a lake nearly 130 miles long. ~ Five miles northwest of Norris on Route 441.

LODGING   The only places to stay in town are chain motels. A good choice may be the **Hampton Inn**, since it has 20 suites (two with jet tubs) and 18 studios with refrigerators and microwaves among its 62 rooms. Amenities include an indoor pool, sauna, fitness center and whirlpool. ~ 208 South Illinois Avenue, Oak Ridge; 865-482-7889, fax 865-482-7493. BUDGET.

DINING   The town's got Chinese and Mexican, why not Greek? For this, locals may steer you toward the **Magnolia Tree Restaurant**, where you can sample moussaka and dolmas or stick to American standards like steaks, catfish, burgers and milkshakes. Closed Sunday. ~ 1938 Oak Ridge Turnpike, Oak Ridge; 865-482-5853. BUDGET TO MODERATE.

A well-kept secret in this "secret city," the **Jefferson Fountain/ Restaurant** serves home-cooked breakfast and lunch, including their specialty Myrtle Burger, in an old pharmacy building. No dinner. Closed Sunday. ~ 22 Jefferson Circle, Oak Ridge, 865-482-1141. BUDGET.

Something different in Oak Ridge is **The Bleu Hound Grille**, a chef-owned place where the menu—emphasizing fresh, local organic products—changes with the seasons. The restaurant is one of the few in these parts with a full bar and wine list. Closed Sunday and Monday. ~ 80 East Tennessee Avenue, Oak Ridge; 865-481-6101. MODERATE TO DELUXE.

Located in an unassuming building off the main drag, **Ayala Mexican Restaurant** has surprisingly numerous offerings. Peruse the menu while nibbling on the piping-hot corn chips and spicy salsa that appear at your table, which will probably be instantly. There are the usual burritos, enchiladas and fajitas, plus house specialties like *tacos de carbon* (charbroiled sirloins strips on steaming, soft tortillas), steak *rancheros* and *pasilla* chicken. Green walls are sparsely decorated with the requisite sombrero and brightly colored blankets. Oh, and brace yourself for a lot of south-of-the-border music in the foreground. ~ 299 Oak Ridge Turnpike, Oak Ridge; 865-483-6397. BUDGET TO MODERATE.

SHOPPING   Right across the street from the Museum of Appalachia, the **Appalachian Arts Craft Shop** is a regional destination for fans of quilts, woodcarvings, dolls, pottery, weaving, jewelry, baskets and other crafts. The shop is one of the oldest crafts cooperatives in the country. Housed in a former country store, the co-op offers classes and workshops as well as reasonably priced merchandise, contemporary pieces utilizing traditional skills. ~ Route 61, one mile east of Exit 122 of Route 75, Clinton; 865-494-9854.

You're in antique country. For leisurely browsing try **Granny's Attic** (9221 Oak Ridge Highway; 865-927-5553) or **Out House Antiques** (374 Warehouse Road; 865-482-7466).

Shades of Mickey Gilley! Urban cowboys or the real thing, fans of two-step and line dancing come to a screeching halt at **Cotton Eyed Joe**, a 25,000-square-foot monument to boot-scooters everywhere and a little piece of Texas in eastern Tennessee. Pay your cover to the lady in the horse trailer with a livestock trough full of cold beer and check out the deejay's digs in the cab of an 18-wheeler that has burst through the back wall. More than a dance club, Cotton Eyed Joe offers roping in one corner, nine pool tables in another, a mechanical bull against one wall and huge bars at either end. They sell a record-breaking amount of beer here except for every Monday during summer and the first Monday of every month the rest of the year, which are alcohol-free nights with the cover going to local charities. Admission. ~ 11220 Outlet Road (off Lovell Road at Exit 374 off Route 75), Oak Ridge; 865-675-4563; www.cottoneyedjoes.com.

NIGHTLIFE

The **Oak Ridge Community Playhouse**, founded in 1943, produces several Broadway and off-Broadway classics throughout the year, including dramas, musicals and comedies. ~ Jackson Square, Oak Ridge; 865-482-9999; www.orplayhouse.com.

The **Oak Ridge Symphony Orchestra** has been performing since 1944, and is composed of about 60 percent professional musicians. The group presents five concerts a year, a schedule augmented with other shows including soloist events, local showcases and chorus performances. ~ Oak Ridge Civic Music Association, P.O. Box 4271, Oak Ridge, TN 37831; 865-483-5569.

The historic grist mill at Norris Dam State Resort Park grinds meal most days during the summer.

You can listen to local bands, shoot pool or check out sports on the big-screen TV at the **Buffalo Grille and Bar**. If you're hungry, order buffalo wings or ostrich burgers. Closed Sunday. ~ 205 Oak Ridge Turnpike, Oak Ridge; 865-481-0515.

NORRIS DAM STATE RESORT PARK 🏃 🛶 ⛺ 🚤 ⛴ ⛵ Arranged on the shores of Norris Lake, this picturesque park's 4000 acres include caves, streams, virgin forestland, hiking trails and more amenities than do most other state parks, plus access to 800 miles of shoreline. During the summer, a park naturalist and a ranger offer activities for adults and kids, including guided walks, float and cave tours, movies and arts-and-crafts programs. Badminton, volleyball, football and other equipment can be signed

PARKS

out at the park office or ranger station. Picnic areas are equipped with tables and grills; playgrounds are nearby at both the east and west sites. Also here is the Lenoir Museum, with a pioneer museum, an 18th-century grist mill and a threshing barn. Staff is on hand to describe East Tennessee pioneer life. ~ Located in Lake City, 20 miles northwest of Knoxville; 865-426-7461, 800-543-9335.

▲ There are 90 campsites, 75 with electrical and water hook-ups; $14 to $17 per night. Ten three-bedroom deluxe-priced cabins and 19 rustic cabins (one-week minimum stay; available in summer only) are arranged in a quiet wooded setting; they are furnished with electrical appliances, utensils for cooking and serving and bed and bath linens.

BIG RIDGE STATE PARK 🏃 🚣 🛝 🚤 🛶 Sporting its own beach along the shoreline of Norris Reservoir, this rugged 3687-acre area was developed in the 1930s by the TVA and the Civilian Conservation Corps as a demonstration park. In warm weather, the placid lake is good for swimming and fishing. Nature exhibits, play areas and 19 cabins (rented by the week during the summer) make it popular with families. You'll also find a visitors center with nature exhibits and a play area, tennis courts, hiking trails and a seasonal snack bar. ~ Located 12 miles east of Route 75 on Route 61 west of Maynardville; 865-992-5523, 800-471-5305, fax 865-992-0619.

▲ There are 3 backcountry campsites, a group campsite for 120 people and 50 campsites; $14 per night for campsites and $17 for RVs.

▼▼▼▼▼▼▼▼▼▼▼▼
Gatlinburg Area

Pigeon Forge is a narrow swath of a town, where new motels, restaurants, shopping malls and family-style entertainment have obliterated any real personality. It's a kind of theme park, except for some charming inns and restaurants off the beaten track. The town got its name from the pigeons that used to flock to the iron forge by the river.

Gatlinburg is separated from Pigeon Forge by only a few miles, but they are worlds apart. While the main access to the Smokies from the west is here, there is also an entrance point in nearby Townsend, a town that's mostly hidden from view by hills and mountains. Despite a tourism boom that has almost blotted out its old-fashioned features, Gatlinburg has retained some of its charm. Its ace in the hole is the Great Smoky Arts and Crafts Community, an area east of downtown that got its start in the 1930s as a crafts show and now claims over 70 craft shops.

SIGHTS   Most people go to **Pigeon Forge** for one of two reasons: to shop at the more than 300 discount outlets and specialty stores, or to spend a day at Dollywood. Or both. The attractions lined up along Parkway are mostly family oriented, such as miniature golf. There's not much history to be seen here; almost everything you're likely to see has been built in the last ten years, with the exception of the Old Mill area.

The 1830 **Old Mill** is, thankfully, not restored, replaced or replicated. Right out of central casting, this rambling, multilevel wooden structure is the oldest operating mill in the United States. For decades, farmers would drop off wagons full of kernel corn and water power would turn the mill wheel to grind it, processing two pounds in only 30 seconds at 22 mph. Later, the farmers would return to collect their bags of flour and grits. Today, you can buy similar products here, as well as cornmeal or corn flour. The tour through this creaky, dusty old place is actually fun, and you get to touch, or even sample, the various grades of grind. The next-door souvenir shop sells the goodies, as well as a ton of other stuff, from books to quilting patterns. Admission for tour. ~ 160 Old Mill Avenue, Pigeon Forge; 865-453-4628; www.old-mill.com, e-mail postmaster@old-mill.com.

The **Pigeon Forge Department of Tourism** is the place to go for guidance before you start taking in all the glitter and lights. ~ 2450 Parkway, Pigeon Forge; 865-453-8574, 800-251-9100; www.mypigeonforge.com, e-mail inquire@mypigeonforge.com.

DOLLYWOOD   To Dolly Parton's legions of fans, Pigeon Forge is synonymous with Dollywood, the 120-acre entertainment complex just a mile away from the heart of town. Rides, restaurants, shops and more than 40 musical performances a day keep visitors busy for hours. Don't expect to see singer-actress Parton, who makes scarce after the seasonal opening in April of each year, but do expect to see a lot of her likeness. These are the major features within the park, along with their amenities.

> Dollywood's repeat business is ensured by the park's policy of introducing a new attraction every year since its opening in 1986.

Daredevil Falls affords thrill-seekers a water-soaked, 60 m.p.h. freefall down a 60-foot ersatz mountain cascade.

Jukebox Junction harks back to the '50s, with Red's Diner serving hand-patted burgers and other classics, doo-wop sounds in the background and shops featuring poodle skirts and other memorabilia of the time. Live entertainment: "Let the Good Times Roll," rock-and-roll of the era. Ride: Rockin' Roadway, a '50s car ride through this seven-acre sight.

The Village is where you'll find the wonderful, one-of-a-kind antique Dentzel Carousel, where the marvelously painted animals will take you back to your childhood in a heartbeat. Also nostalgic is the Dollywood Express, a coal-burning steam train that was part of the original complex and still makes five-mile roundtrips all daylong. Then there's *Heartsong*. First of all, you have to admit it's well done, no matter how you feel about Dolly Parton. That said, it's a lot to swallow. Inside the "naturound" Heartsong Theatre, a film narrated by Dolly, and accompanied by Dolly's songs, deals with Dolly's memories of and feelings about this part of the world. The cool thing about it is the animation and the sensory experiences—from fireflies to actual rainfall—afforded the audience.

At *Rivertown Junction*, in the heart of the park, the Smoky Mountain River Rampage is a lite whitewater rafting adventure that usually creates long lines. The junction is also home to old-fashioned country food outlets, from french fries and other greasy foods to country-style meats and vegetables (not that there's always a difference). You can watch glass blowing, tour a replica of Dolly's two-room childhood home, shop for bait, tackle and other fishing accoutrements and listen to Back Porch Theatre, a revue of Dolly's music by kinfolks and friends.

Country Fair is a good stopping place for kids (there's a second swing ride for grownups), bumper cars, games, face painting and a log flume ride. If swings are too tame, there's the Tennessee Twister (a Tilt-a-Whirl) and a 60-foot Ferris wheel. The food is the kind of fare that would garner blue ribbons at a county fair.

Showstreet is where you'll find the Friendship Gardens, planted with 35,000 growing things. There's a restaurant called the Backstage (the most upscale dining spot in the park) and other show biz–related distractions. This area is an odd mix of glitz and gardens; the shops, for instance, vary between Hollywood star-related items and nature-based gift and collectibles.

Dreamland Forest hosts the Dollywood Celebrity Theatre, where top-name entertainers perform. Except for the water toboggan, things are fairly tame, with craft demonstrations, homemade candies and glass-blowing demonstrations.

DOLLYWOOD STORY

Dollywood's origins date to the 1960s, when an entertainment complex called "Rebel Railroad" ran a steam train, a general store, a blacksmith shop and a saloon. Gradually, it grew, incorporating the old Robert F. Thomas Church in 1973 and becoming "Goldrush Junction" and, in the late '70s, "Silver Dollar City." Meanwhile, the story goes, Dolly Parton had long dreamed of having her own attraction in the neighborhood of her childhood. In 1986 she joined the existing management and lent her name to the complex. Since then, Dollywood has doubled in size, attracting more than two million people in 2002, while keeping some of the park's natural landscape intact so that there are plenty of trees and lots of shade on hot summer days.

Craftsmen's Valley is the soul of Dollywood in many ways, and not only because it's where you'll find the old church. There are Appalachian crafts—brooms and dulcimers, as well as carriage works, blacksmiths, woodworkers, a grist mill and so on—throughout this cozy corner of Dollywood. This is also the place to try Sugar Mountain Funnel Cakes, barbecue, Granny Ogle's Ham 'N' Beans (Ogle is a local name you'll see all over the place) and, to top off your day, pork rinds.

A poor rural family with 12 children is bound to develop its imagination more than today's average 2.5-television household. Dolly, then, would be the imagination expert. Her *Adventures in Imagination*, a $10-million showpiece includes, among other themed attractions, a fully operational donut factory. Once you've achieved a suitable sugar high, proceed to *Chasing Rainbows*, a museum of memorabilia from Dolly's life and impressive career. Wonder how you'd look as a peroxide blonde? You'll find out at the animated wig stations. There are photographs, costumes, a Dolly-narrated video and tons of other artifacts. Most of the collection is interactive and suitably "behind the scenes," so despite its high profile you'll have a sense of intimacy with the likable star. There's also a simulated tour through the Smoky Mountains via air and water, with Dolly as a guide. If you're prone to motion sickness, you may want to hit this one before the donut factory. Closed December 30 to April, most weekdays in November and December, and on select days during every other month except June and July. Admission. ~ 1020 Dollywood Lane, Pigeon Forge; 865-428-9488, 800-365-5996; www.dollywood.com, e-mail guestservices@dollywood.com.

Make a stop at the **Gatlinburg Chamber of Commerce** before painting the town. ~ 811 East Parkway, Gatlinburg; 865-436-4178, 800-267-7088; www.gatlinburg.com, e-mail info@gatlinburg.com. The **Smoky Mountain Visitors Bureau** is also invaluable. ~ 201 South Washington Street, Maryville; 800-525-6834; www.smokymountains.org.

The **Great Smoky Arts and Crafts Community**, located east of downtown, proffers wooden and leather goods, weavings, pottery and Appalachian brooms, as well as New Age–type crafts like wearable art and clever glass sculptures. See the feature in this chapter for more information. ~ 800-565-7330; www.artsandcraftscommunity.com

The **Smoky Mountain Winery** makes 24 varieties, most of them sweet but some, like its sauvignon blanc, more on the dry side. This being Gatlinburg, you are allowed to sample, for free, some of their wares in the cozy stone tasting room, and though there is no formal tour, you can rummage about the casks, barrels and tanks to get an idea of how wines are made. This winery has no vineyards of its own, but buys grapes from growers located only about 30 miles away. ~ 450 Cherry Street, Suite 2, Gatlinburg; 888-765-9463; www.smokymountainwinery.com.

Well, we suppose there are enough to go around. Why else would there be a **Guinness World Records Museum** in this mountain town? If nature pales, you can always take a peek at the unnatural, such as the most tattooed lady (okay, her likeness). For more bigger, badder, smallest, worst, slowest and fastest, hie thee to this temple to overachievement. Admission. ~ 631 Parkway, Gatlinburg; 865-436-9100; www.guinness-gatlinburg.com.

You don't have to ski to enjoy a chairlift ride at **Ober Gatlinburg Ski Resort & Amusement Park**. In fact, it doesn't even have to be winter. Whatever the weather, you'll first take the aerial tramway (the biggest in the country) two and a half miles up from downtown. A 120-passenger tram departs every 20 minutes. The views are even better from the chairlift, which takes you to the top of the mountain, where you'll find a snack bar and several telescopes for closer views of the Great Smoky Mountains. If you don't want to go all the way up, you can opt to disembark at a way station and return via a simulated bobsled ride.

The amusement park has various attractions and activities, including three waterslides, miniature golf, go-carts, a trampoline, an ice-skating rink and something called the Spider Web, for which you snap on a giant space suit and fling yourself at a Velcro wall, hoping to stick. (Tip: It's harder than it looks. Get a running start.) Finally, there is the black-bear habitat, a zoo-quality setting of three huge concrete "cages" where bears, and sometimes their small offspring, can be viewed playing or, more likely, sleeping. Closed the second and third weeks of March. Admission. ~ 1001 Parkway, Gatlinburg; 865-436-5423; www.obergatlinburg. com, e-mail sun@obergatlinburg.com.

Just off the Parkway between Pigeon Forge and Sevierville is a complex with a store and two restaurants. If you get a chance to taste the apple butter they make at the **Apple Barn Cider Mill & General Store**, you'll probably end up toting several jars of it home with you. Established in 1976 by a former pharmacist, the complex raises Rome Beauty, Red Delicious, Winesap and other varieties and sells the sweet crunchy fruit in this former barn, where the corn crib has been turned into a cider room. Over the years, the business has taken over not only the barn but the family home, now the site of a restaurant. ~ 230 Apple Valley Road, Sevierville; 865-453-9319, fax 865-453-4060; www.applebarn cidermill.com.

As you approach Sevierville along the Winfield Dunn Parkway (Route 66), you'll find a number of attractions on the far side of Route 411. Ignore, for a moment, the stuffed bear and the humongous elephant head nailed to the wall. In this environment, a display of weaponry seems benign, even expected. Of course, it's the **Smoky Mountain Knife Works**, a store-cum-museum spread over three floors. Among the displays are pocket knives, special blades, knives with inlaid handles, "character" knives based on Dick Tracy and the like, and lots more, including an enlightening exhibit depicting various blades like razor, punch and sheepfoot, in case you were wondering. Unfortunately, the exhibits are poorly labeled. ~ 2320 Winfield Dunn Parkway, Sevierville; 865-453-5871, 800-251-9306, fax 865-428-5991; www.eknife works.com.

About five miles down the road toward Route 40 is another gotta-be-unique "museum." There are two kinds of people in the world: those who would go out of their way to see **Floyd Garrett's Muscle Car Museum** and those who whimper with boredom at the idea. According to the establishment, in 1997 two guys drove down here from Pennsylvania and couldn't tear themselves away for five and a half hours. The stock changes a little bit when the owner is offered a deal he can't refuse, but he regularly displays dozens of hot cars from his 90-car collection. Admission. ~ 320 Winfield Dunn Parkway, Sevierville; 865-908-0882; www.musclecarmuseum.com.

> Built by the Seth Thomas Clock Company of Thomaston, Connecticut, and installed in 1896, Sevierville County Courthouse's clock tower was manually wound, struck on the hour and half-hour, had four faces and cost $1396.

A little closer to Route 40, the **McIntosh Grist Mill** at Maplewood Farms is a modest affair, but at least it allows visitors to see where grits come from. You can watch the various types of corn meal being processed the way things were done a century or more ago. And you can buy some to take home. ~ 2510 Winfield Dunn Parkway, Kodak; 865-932-7637, 800-545-1360.

Double back on Highway 66 (Winfield Dunn Parkway) towards Dolly Parton Parkway and turn left onto Main Street. You're heading for a glimpse of a town that probably looks much the same as it did in 1950. The **Sevierville County Courthouse** is worth at least a drive-by to see the Tower Clock. There's a small exhibit inside that explains the history. By the mid-19th century, large clock parts—like those used here—could be industrially cast. The courthouse, designed by A. S. Hotchkiss and built in 1895–96, is an unusually fine example (especially locally) of Beaux Arts Classicism. Now on the National Register of Historic Places, it was restored for the Sevierville County American Revolution Bicentennial in 1976. The clock, removed from the tower in 1974 and repainted, was placed in an exhibit in the courthouse. ~ Corner of Bruce Street and Courthouse Avenue, Sevierville.

On the Courthouse Lawn is the **Dolly Parton Statue**, unveiled in 1987 to honor the popular country singer/actress who is still probably the most famous graduate of Sevier County High School (class of '64).

HIDDEN ► From Sevierville, you'll need a local map to find **Harrisburg Covered Bridge**, which you can reach by continuing along Route 411 towards Newport. The bridge was built in 1875 by Elbert Stephenson Early, who owned Newport Mills. One of a handful of covered bridges remaining in Tennessee, it was threatened with collapse until a 1972 restoration by the local chapter of the Daughters of the American Revolution. ~ Located about three-tenths of a mile from the junction of Routes 339 and 411.

LODGING The 102-room **Mountain Trace Inn** is family owned and family oriented. The only reason it's not called a motel is because it's four stories tall and has some above-average amenities. Namely, both an outdoor and an indoor pool, the latter with a tiny hot tub next to it. The layout is simplicity itself, only it has better lighting than most motels. Some feature fireplaces and/or kitchenettes. ~ 130 Wears Valley Road, Pigeon Forge; 865-453-6785, 800-453-6785, fax 865-453-1334; www.mountaintraceinn.com. DELUXE TO ULTRA-DELUXE.

Looking more like something out of Las Vegas than the Tennessee mountains, the 420-room **Grand Resort Hotel and Convention Center** carries on the grandeur with a five-story waterfall. And that's in the lobby. Accommodations include standard rooms as well as jacuzzi and honeymoon suites, some with kitchenettes and fireplaces. While the hotel obviously courts business travelers, its size means it has many amenities families would like as well. Both the indoor and outdoor pools are heated. The onsite restaurant serves three daily buffets. ~ 3171 Parkway, Pigeon Forge; 865-453-1000, 800-251-4444, fax 865-428-3944; www.grandresorthotel.com. BUDGET TO DELUXE.

Perhaps the most unusual accommodations in town (and the closest to Dollywood) can be found at the (deep breath here) **HIDDEN ►** **Evergreen Cottage Inn and Forge Mountain Honeymoon Village**. Certainly you'll find the most variety. The cottage has two up-

FLIGHT OF FANTASY

Ever thought of skydiving but never had the nerve? **Flyaway Indoor Skydiving** lets you act out your fantasy. The indoor skydiving simulator, one of several in the country, depends on a vertical wind tunnel to keep you buoyed up, mimicking the conditions of diving without any of the downside risks. Admission. ~ 3106 Parkway, Pigeon Forge; 865-453-7777, 877-293-0639; www.flyawayindoorskydiving.com, e-mail gsflyaway@aol.com.

stairs rooms, one with a black walnut bed covered in an antique wedding ring quilt, the other with a high-back oak bed and views of the town; both have spa tubs and river rock wood-burning fireplaces. Next door, the Honeymoon Village has 11 suites on two floors; guests can reserve private times at the eight-person hot tub in a gazebo across the road. Finally, there is the cute Shamrock, a two-bedroom cottage with jacuzzi, fireplace and screen porch. ~ 34161 Householder Street, Pigeon Forge; 865-453-4000, 800-264-3331, fax 865-429-0240; www.gocabins.com. MODERATE TO DELUXE.

Hilton's Bluff Bed & Breakfast Inn is a contemporary coun-   ◄ HIDDEN
try inn about half a mile from central Pigeon Forge. Its best fea-
ture, aside from its seclusion on two acres atop a little bluff, is the half-screened porch that runs along both floors. Furnished with oak rocking chairs and shaded by oak, redbud and hardwood trees (there are more varieties of hardwood in the Great Smokies than anywhere else except the Himalayas), it affords views of the surrounding foothills. In summertime, you can smell the honey-suckle and listen to the katydids chirping you to sleep at night. The rooms don't have a whole lot of personality: pastels, com-plementary coverlets and wall-to-wall carpeting and, in five of the rooms, whirlpool baths. All of the rooms have private balconies or decks. The inn has a rec room with a pool table, a small library and a stone fireplace in the "den," which has a 22-foot cathedral ceiling. ~ 2654 Valley Heights Drive, Pigeon Forge; 865-428-9765, 800-441-4188; www.hiltonsbluff.com, e-mail info@hiltonsbluff.com. MODERATE TO DELUXE.

The five-story **Music Road Inn** has 140 rooms and suites, each with a refrigerator, microwave and private balcony. The suites also have jacuzzis and/or fireplaces. The accommodations feel residential rather than institutional, despite the fact that this property is popular for meetings and conventions. If you have kids in tow, the indoor and outdoor pools could be your ticket to peace and quiet. ~ 314 Henderson Chapel Road, Pigeon Forge; 865-429-8803, 866-429-8803; www.musicroadinn.com, e-mail info@musicroadinn.com. DELUXE TO ULTRA-DELUXE.

The **Wonderland Lodge** is a voyage back in time . . . in this   ◄ HIDDEN
case, to the original Wonderland Hotel that once existed in Elk-
mont, deep in the Great Smoky Mountains. Though built in 1992, this two-story lodge re-creates many aspects of the original, with a large granite fireplace in the two-story lobby, specially made rocking chairs on the veranda overlooking Cove Mountain and simple decor in all the rooms. Set on a knoll, it has 29 rooms and manages another dozen cabins nearby. Sharing the ground floor with a restaurant are the more modest accommodations, which have rough wood or white-painted walls, handsome patterned drapes, dark green carpeting and ceiling fans. Decor is rustic,

with a single chair, lamp and table and open closets. The second-floor rooms are a little fancier, with unobstructed views of Cove Mountain and prints by local artist Randall Ogle. All the rooms are air conditioned. ~ 3889 Wonderland Lane, Wears Valley; 865-436-5490, 877-428-0779; www.wonderlandlodge.com, e-mail smokylodge@aol.com. BUDGET TO MODERATE.

The **River Terrace Resort & Convention Center is** a meandering complex of low- and high-rise structures blessedly off the main drag. The Mountain Tower rooms are huge, with in-room spa baths, textured walls, teal carpeting and, unfortunately, windows that just flat refuse to open. There are 205 rooms in all, two pools and not a lot of amenities. ~ 240 River Road, Gatlinburg; 865-436-5161, 800-251-2040, fax 865-436-7219; www.riverterrace.com, e-mail rivert@riverterrace.com. MODERATE TO DELUXE.

A river runs, well, practically through it. The **Quality Inn Creekside** is on the same site as the former LeConte Creek Inn, one of the first lodges in the area. Today, the approach is through a parking lot, but once there, guests find peace and quiet and yes, that gurgling stream. The 67 rooms and suites are simple, nicer than motels but not quite up to hotel standards, with refrigerators and microwaves in every room. Accommodations are arranged in four two-story buildings. One building (36 rooms) has balconies facing the creek and 13 rooms have jacuzzis. ~ 125 LeConte Creek Drive, Gatlinburg; 865-436-4865, 800-473-8319, fax 865-436-0139; www.qualityinncreekside.com, e-mail info@qualityinn creekside.com. MODERATE TO DELUXE.

The **Terrace Motel** is a nice, 20-room affair where cabins have little porches facing the usually quiet Roaring Fork Creek. Guests

MAPLE OPERATION

Old maps of Gatlinburg from the '30s show only four hotels. In all that time, the two-story **Gatlinburg Inn** has been operated only by the Maples family, who built it in 1937. Such notables as Tennessee Ernie Ford, Liberace, Dinah Shore and Lady Bird Johnson have stayed here, as well as Boudleaux and Felice Bryant, who wrote the local anthem, "Rocky Top," in the hotel. History and rusticity are the hallmarks of the Gatlinburg Inn, where 67 rooms and suites still have their original maple furnishings and the colorful country print wallpaper looks as if it, too, is original. Amenities are basic, but it's centrally located and has one tennis court and a front veranda with rocking chairs when you're too tired to go on playing shuffleboard. It's the kind of place couples return to for their 25th or 50th wedding anniversary. Closed November through March. ~ 755 Parkway, Gatlinburg; 865-436-5133, fax 865-436-4005. MODERATE TO DELUXE.

can choose these cottages (single or double) or one of the motel-type accommodations in a two-story structure in the back. Little touches like vibrating beds (!), in-room coffee and the little patios make this an endearing spot. Plus, it accepts small pets. ~ 396 Parkway, Gatlinburg; 865-436-4965; e-mail terracemotel@aol.com. MODERATE.

The **Open Hearth Hotel** is one of those hotel/motels that seems somehow homier than most. Which is saying something, since it's six stories high. Maybe it's the balconies, or the setting behind the creek, or maybe it's the rooms. All 86 rooms and suites have refrigerators, some have fireplaces, balconies and/or kitchens; with a heated pool, an outdoor hot tub, a tennis court and landscaped gardens, as well as conference facilities, it calls itself a resort. ~ Hemlock Street (Traffic Light 2), Gatlinburg; 865-436-6166, 800-233-4663, fax 865-436-2117; www.openhearth hotel.com. MODERATE TO DELUXE.

The **Greystone Lodge at the Aquarium** is a great big thing, with 257 rooms, some with jacuzzis or fireplaces. The rooms are big and done in color schemes like peach-and-blue but basically this is a motel with window dressing. There's a nice heated pool. ~ 559 Parkway, Gatlinburg; 865-436-5621, 800-451-9202, fax 865-430-4471; www.greystonelodgetn.com, e-mail staywithus@aol.com. MODERATE TO DELUXE.

Eight Gables Inn is not some old home that's been converted into a B&B. It was built as one in 1990, and the present owners are proud to have a five-diamond AAA status. It's a little *grande* for the setting, but it is spacious—9000 square feet—and exquisitely appointed. As the name suggests, some of the 20 rooms are octagonal, with names like Cloud Nine. One room is done in creamy Battenburg lace, another is wall-to-wall lavender. Four rooms, two with private entrances, share the ground floor with a huge double parlor that boasts a baby grand piano; a staircase worthy of Scarlett O'Hara leads to the eight upstairs accommodations. Wrapped around all this is a gracious porch, where guests can snooze away a summer afternoon in hammocks. Eight Gables is out of the way, but close enough to golf courses, hiking and riding trails and Dollywood. Dinner is served Tuesday, Thursday and Saturday by reservation. ~ 219 North Mountain Trail, Gatlinburg; 865-430-3344, 800-279-5716; www.eightgables.com, e-mail eightgables@eightgables.com. ULTRA-DELUXE.

Hippensteal's Mountain View Inn harks back to the days when ◄ *HIDDEN* Gatlinburg was quaint and quiet. The views of the Smokies—Greenbriar Pinnacle, Mount LeConte and Mount Harrison, left to right—are spectacular from the wraparound porch of this modern structure, built in 1990 at an elevation of 2500 feet. The inn is a replica of Gatlinburg's oldest hotel (once run by Lisa Hippensteal's parents but now closed), right down to the rocking chairs. Before you book one of the eleven rooms here, you should make sure you like the artwork of owner Vern Hippensteal, one of the area's leading watercolorists, and probably the most prolific. His landscapes cover virtually every vertical surface, to the point one wonders why they bothered with wallpaper in the first place. If you like your accommodations decorated to the *n*th degree, this is the place for you. Rooms are spacious, with antique armoires, fireplaces, reading chairs, whirlpool tubs and many other attractive conveniences, and the hosts are warm and gracious. ~ Grassy Branch Road, Gatlinburg; 865-436-5761, 800-527-8110, fax 865-436-8917; www.hippensteal.com, e-mail vern hippensteal@aol.com. ULTRA-DELUXE.

HIDDEN ►

One of the most attractive accommodations near the Smokies, the **Richmont Inn** has a lot going for it. Once you get over the stunning architecture—inspired by the cantilevered barns particular to Appalachia—the hand-hewn long walls, treated pine and slate floors and 13-foot beamed ceilings (and piped-in classical music) aren't too much of a surprise. Fourteen rooms contain a mixture of English antiques, French paintings, Oriental rugs, heart of pine floors and other accoutrements collected by Jim and Susan Hind, who moved here from Knoxville in 1990 and built the place from scratch. Each room is named after, and decorated to honor, a particularly outstanding Tennessean, from a church circuit rider to a dulcimer maker to the Cherokee scholar who invented his tribe's alphabet. The crowning glory, literally, is the top-floor, top-drawer Nanye-hi (Nancy Ward) Room, named for the Cherokee chieftainess who urged peace between her nation and the United States. American Indian basketry and blankets, and paintings depicting the woman considered the most beautiful Cherokee of all, make this high-ceilinged room a particular joy. The inn now features a restaurant serving dinner. Full breakfast and a candlelight dessert are included in the rates. ~ 220 Winterberry Lane, Townsend; 865-448-6751, fax 865-448-6480; www.richmontinn.com, e-mail richmont inn@aol.com. DELUXE TO ULTRA-DELUXE.

The 1830 Old Mill supplied electricity to Pigeon Forge until the 1940s, when the TVA began producing the town's power.

The three-story, 100-room **Oak Tree Lodge** is conveniently located near the Tanger Five Oaks Mall between Pigeon Forge and Sevierville. It's nicely kept, with an antebellum-looking porte cochere adding a grace note. Opened in 1990, it was expanded in 1998 so the rooms are not all the same; the ones in the new wing have interior entrances and a color scheme leaning to magenta and green. Some have balconies, refrigerators and/or coffee makers. ~ 1620 Parkway, Sevierville; 865-428-7500, 800-637-7002, fax 805-429-8603; www.oaktennlodging.com. MODERATE TO ULTRA-DELUXE.

When you just want a place to lay your head and have no interest in paying big bucks for the experience, spots like the **Green Valley Motel North** are perfect. This 58-room pit stop has clean accommodations with decent lighting and plaster walls edged in patterned wallpaper. Some rooms have spa baths or fireplaces. ~ 1544 Parkway (Route 441), Sevierville; 865-453-4066, 800-426-4066, fax 865-429-8133. MODERATE.

Who would guess that the unassuming **River View Inn** has a secret weapon? From the front, it looks like a generic white two-story motel. But when you step across a room and open the back door, you're looking at the gentle Little Pigeon River, with ducks and marsh and the mountains beyond. The 50 rooms are nice enough, and some feature jacuzzis, waterbeds or kitchenettes. ~ 423 Forks of the River Parkway, Sevierville; 865-428-6191, 800-447-2601, fax 865-428-7116. MODERATE TO DELUXE.

◄ HIDDEN

The best food in Pigeon Forge comes out of a kitchen in the back of a glorified mobile home far from the glitter and glow of the Parkway. **Chef Jock's Tastebuds Cafe** may not look like much, but no one seems to care. In a scantily adorned white room with 42 seats, chef Jock (a.k.a. Giacomo Lijoi) turns out ambitious dishes such as sea scallops, roasted range chicken breast and a number of imaginative pastas. The chef and his kitchen staff may be seen greeting patrons from behind a neck-high counter, or heard belting out lyrics to piped-in pop tunes from the '60s. It's an experience not to be missed. Closed Sunday and Monday, and the first three weeks of January. ~ 1198 Wears Valley Road, Pigeon Forge; 865-428-9781; www.tastebudscafe.com, e-mail chefjock@vic.com. MODERATE TO DELUXE.

DINING

◄ HIDDEN

East Tennessee's paean to the be-bop-a-lu-la '50s, the **Bel Air Grill** claims to serve the best cheeseburgers anywhere. Don't believe it? Okay, try any of nine steak dishes, or chicken or shrimp or salmon or snacks like stuffed jalapeños. Albums (those vinyl disks of yore) by the likes of Elvis, Frank Sinatra, Patti Page and Johnny Mathis adorn the walls, along with photos and posters of classic cars of the era. Family oriented, with booths and well-spaced tables split among two rooms, the Bel Air may be ersatz, but it's well-done ersatz. ~ 2785 Parkway, Pigeon Forge; 865-429-0101, fax 865-453-1554. MODERATE TO DELUXE.

Nightly piano music accompanies the excellent Italian menu at **Santo's**, a family-owned restaurant located on the Parkway. Try the veal piccata, shrimp scampi or sautéed chicken breast with spinach and garlic over fettuccine. In addition, there's pizza (try it with the fried mushrooms) and a children's menu. All the entrées come with salad or soup, and steaming hot garlic sticks. Bring a bottle of good red wine to complete the experience.

Closed Sunday. ~ 3270 Parkway, Pigeon Forge; 865-428-5840; www.santositalianrestaurant.com, e-mail info@santositalian restaurant.com. MODERATE.

They should serve breakfast all day at the **Old Mill Restaurant**, because the servings are so generous they could suffice for dinner. Console yourself with traditional fried specialties: calf liver, chicken, pork chops, catfish or trout. Or opt for lighter fare like chicken and dumplings (!), pot roast, sugar-cured ham, grilled ribeye or the signature corn chowder. Bare wood, high beamed ceilings, plank floors and round oak tables are a perfect backdrop for the tree-shaded stream that flows just outside the huge plate-glass windows of this multilevel restaurant, built in 1830. ~ 164 Old Mill Avenue, Pigeon Forge; 865-429-3463, 865-429-2511; www.old-mill.com, e-mail postmaster@old-mill.com. MODERATE TO DELUXE.

HIDDEN ▶   An out-of-the-way spot is the **Wonderland Lodge and Hotel Restaurant**. Whether or not you're staying at this hideaway, you can have breakfast and dinner in the large lobby-level dining room. The most expensive items at night are the country ham and full dinners, with a choice of fried chicken (dark or white), steak and gravy, rib-eye, catfish, or pork chops, with two vegetables and a salad. À la carte choices include shrimp, pinto beans and cornbread, vegetables, chicken, salads and sandwiches and homemade desserts like cobbler and pecan pie. The restaurant is usually closed weekdays in winter; call ahead. ~ 3889 Wonderland Lane, Wears Valley; 865-436-5490; www.wonderlandlodge. com, e-mail smokylodge@aol.com. BUDGET TO MODERATE.

Even if it didn't have its very own waterfall, **The Atrium** would be a pleasant environment for breakfast or lunch. Lots of windows and a cheery decor are well suited to eye-openers like crêpes, waffles, a dozen types of pancakes, and both Southern and standard breakfast items. Lunch is more pedestrian, an unin-

REELING FOR CATFISH

Look for the giant catfish hoisted above a manmade waterfall and you'll be closing in on **Huck Finn's Catfish Restaurant**. They really work the theme here, with a picture of Huck purportedly reeling in a catfish on the mighty Mississippi prominently displayed. At any rate, inside is one huge room on one side, and a series of smaller ones on the other, with old fishing signage, farm implements and fishing paraphernalia strung about. Catfish comes in many guises, and besides chicken and steak there are delicacies like 'gator tail and chicken livers. ~ 3330 Parkway, Pigeon Forge; 865-429-3353, fax 865-429-1894. MODERATE.

spired but serviceable list of entrées, salads and sandwiches. No dinner. ~ 432 Parkway, Gatlinburg; 865-430-3684, fax 865-436-0325. BUDGET.

Plaid tablecloths, lots of bare wood, Tiffany-style lampshades and a veritable school of fake fish set the stage at the **Smoky Mountain Trout House**, where they serve trout caught daily at about 2 p.m. (how the fish know to show up remains a mystery); you can order yours almondine, dilly, parmesan, grilled, pan fried, broiled or "Eisenhower," with corn meal breading and bacon flavorings. It is possible to get prime rib, chicken, catfish or shrimp as well, but then why would you go to the Trout House? ~ 410 Parkway, Gatlinburg; 865-436-5416. MODERATE.

Open every day from late morning until well after dinnertime, the family-style **Brass Lantern** keeps things in the middle of the road. Steak, chicken, trout, pasta and a list of sandwiches should accommodate everyone in the family at this brass-railed, plant-filled downtown spot. ~ 710 Parkway, Gatlinburg; 865-436-4168, fax 865-436-4376. MODERATE.

Once you get over the juxtaposition of seeing a forested mountain poking up behind the pulapas, the idea of a Mexican restaurant in the Smokies seems like a good one. **No Way Jose's** is a rainbow of bright, low-budget decor in vibrant pinks, limes and blues. In winter, the interior rooms are cozy; with the least bit of warmth, the patio is the place to be. Along with the usual tacos, tostadas and enchiladas, this upbeat restaurant offers specials such as grilled chipotle chicken, caliente burritos, chimichangas and deep-fried ice cream. Tortillas and tamales are made fresh on the premises every day and the only oil used in the kitchen is canola. ~ 555 Parkway, Gatlinburg; 865-430-5673. BUDGET TO MODERATE.

One of the few semi-elegant restaurants in the Smokies, **Legends by Max** has glossy green walls, a glossy bar in the middle and sports coverage on the glossy television. Although it's odd to have your Italian food served with a Southern accent, the menu is decent, with entrées like lasagna, and all-you-can-eat spaghetti marinara. You can eat lightly around the main events by choosing hearty sandwiches, side orders or Major League desserts such as chocolate cheesecake and bread pudding. ~ 650 Parkway, Gatlinburg; 865-436-7343, fax 865-436-7342. MODERATE.

The Best Italian Café & Pizzeria looks like every other pizza parlor in the whole world—cozy tables overlit with Tiffany-style lampshades—but it's the place locals often end up when they want a good dinner and an excellent value. There's nothing extraordinary about the list of pastas, but TBICP does have unusual pizzas like the Brazilian Bechamel as well as other main courses including veal florentine. ~ 968 Parkway, Gatlinburg; 865-430-4090, fax 865-436-2378; www.bestitalian.com. MODERATE.

The **Park Grill** is a grand lodge-like affair, constructed of a veritable forest of Idaho spruce that make it the handsomest restaurant in town. In a wide-open setting like this, New York strip, lamb chops and Moonshine chicken seem appropriately hearty fare, but there are many seafood, pasta and vegetarian dishes, as well as a sizable offering of appetizers. This is where people in the know go after a show, to top off the evening with a cappuccino and power dessert. (Management, by the way, makes it clear on the menu that only standing dead trees were harvested for construction.) Dinner only. ~ 1110 Parkway, Gatlinburg; 865-436-2300, fax 865-436-2836; www.peddler-parkgrill.com. MODERATE TO DELUXE.

If you have a choice at the **Burning Bush**, ask to be seated in one of the slate-floored solarium rooms, which are set in a glade that is totally green in spring and summer. The main rooms are not quite as attractive; they are paneled in pine and have small stained-glass windows placed high on the wall. This place buzzes day and night, with an extensive menu ranging from pork chops to duckling, with plenty of grilled meats and light dishes to boot. ~ 1151 Parkway, Gatlinburg; 865-436-4669, fax 865-436-3525; www.burningbushrestaurant.com. MODERATE TO DELUXE.

HIDDEN ► Restaurants don't come much more adorable than the **Wild Plum Tea Room**, a haven of gentility convenient to many crafts shops. You enter the gentrified log cabin through a screened porch (where you will probably wait after signing up) to find about three dining rooms that seat a total of roughly 60 people. The intimate tables and lace tablecloths are joined by pretty nature prints on the walls. Everyone orders the chicken salad, but there are several choices of dainty soups, special sandwiches and seasonal desserts, such as pumpkin pie and Amaretto bread pudding. It's a small menu, so everything that comes out of the kitchen is perfectly executed. Don't leave without trying the Wild Plum tea and muffins. Lunch only. Closed Sunday and from mid-December through February. ~ 555 Buckhorn Road, Gatlinburg; 865-436-3808. BUDGET.

HIDDEN ► The mansion-sized dining room of the **Eight Gables Inn** is converted into the Magnolia Tea Room at lunchtime. To the tune of classical music in the background, guests sip homemade tea and nibble on fresh breads, sandwiches of cheese, chicken or turkey, homemade soups, pasta salads and similar delicacies. Bare wood floors and an abundance of windows make this one of the most spacious places to restore vigor on the road. Closed Saturday through Monday and Wednesday. ~ 219 North Mountain Trail, Gatlinburg; 865-430-3344; www.eightgables.com, e-mail eight gables@eightgables.com. BUDGET.

If you're intrigued by ghost stories, as well as stunning settings, the **Greenbrier Restaurant** is definitely worth a stop. The management loves to tell the "legend" of the jilted bride that killed herself here, but it's probably the view that keeps folks coming back. High on a hillside above Gatlinburg, the circa-1939 log cabin is surrounded by floor-to-ceiling windows and sports a cozy fireplace to boot. The menu is heavy on the butter, but some of the fish dishes can be ordered baked or blackened; in general the offerings are pretty tasty. ~ 370 Newman Road, Gatlinburg; 865-436-6318; www.greenbrierrestaurant.com. MODERATE TO DELUXE.

Set amid 65 acres and supplied by some 4000 apple trees, the **Applewood Farmhouse Restaurant** gives visitors a chance to experience the rural lifestyle without having to do the heavy lifting. Seating is in several rooms—the Country Kitchen, the Keeping Room, Orchard View—at barewood tables or booths with decidedly un-corny wallpaper. After breakfast, which may include house specialties like toad-in-the-hole (eggs fried in bread . . . or vice versa) along with traditional selections, the menu gets progressively shorter as the day wears on. Chicken and dumplings, country fried steak, roast turkey, applewood grilled pork loin and grilled trout share the honors with vegetable platters and other treats. Sunday dinner is served in the afternoon in various price categories. Winter hours vary. ~ 240 Apple Valley Road, Sevierville; 865-428-1222. BUDGET TO MODERATE.

Sevierville's growth has brought a spate of shopping centers such as Governor's Crossing, which is where **Rocky River Brewery & Grille** opened in 1998. Naturally, there's a big fermentation tank near the entrance of this great big room where open beams and a soaring ceiling afford a barn-sized spaciousness. The food is not country-style, however, but rather a more urban melange of grilled shrimp and chicken, smoked pork loin, pastas, beef dishes and appetizers such as quesadillas. Oh, the beer: ale, lager, stout, pale ale, red ale and Heidelberg Hefeweizen, a traditional unfil-

FORBIDDEN CAVERNS

From Sevierville, it's a pretty 15-minute drive out Route 411 to **Forbidden Caverns**. One of Tennessee's many commercial caves, it is known for its numerous grottoes, a crystal-clear stream, towering natural chimneys and manmade lighting effects. Human exploration of the caves dates from 1919; moonshiners used the caves as late as the '40s to create the "white lightnin'" for which these hills became famous. The tour of caves takes about an hour and goes as deep as 650 feet from the surface. Closed December through March. ~ 455 Blowing Cave Road, Sevierville; 865-453-5972; www.smokymtnforbiddencaves.com.

tered German-style wheat beer. ~ 1444 Hurley Drive, Sevierville; 865-908-3686, fax 865-908-6114. MODERATE TO DELUXE.

Look for the orange rooftop that announces the **Chiang House Restaurant**. It's a hybrid, a Chinese place that also serves Japanese cuisine such as teppanyaki—there's even a sushi bar. It's a trip: chefs cook on a hibachi at your table, wearing kimonos and Chinese-style caps. ~ 624 Parkway, Sevierville; 865-428-5977. BUDGET TO MODERATE.

HIDDEN ▶

For something quick and cheap, especially en route to the Forbidden Caverns, look for the CitGo station at the intersection of Routes 441 and 339. **The Grill at Layman's Market** has working lunches of pinto beans, sandwiches, chicken and a steak plate. Nothing fancy but at least it's home-cooked. ~ 1779 Route 339, Sevierville; 865-429-8131. BUDGET.

SHOPPING

There are dozens of almost interchangeable crafts stores located beyond the Old Mill along Middle Creek Road and Old Mill Avenue. You can pick up a dulcimer, should you be so inclined, at **Pigeon River String Instruments**. They also have a great selection of videos and CDs featuring "music of the mountains." Closed Sunday. ~ 7 Millstone Village (off Mill Stone Avenue), Pigeon Forge; 865-453-3789.

The **Old Mill General Store** is the place to buy grits and cornmeal ground at the adjacent mill, as well as souvenirs, hickory walking sticks, quilting patterns and all sorts of kitsch. ~ 160 Old Mill Avenue, Pigeon Forge; 865-453-4628; www.old-mill.com.

More people come to shop in Pigeon Forge than to visit Dollywood or any other attraction. The big pull is the hundreds of stores in various outlet malls where discounts of up to 70 percent are a major incentive. The larger ones include the **Belz Factory Outlet World**, which is home to 80 stores including Burlington Brands (865-428-6401), Fossil (865-428-2334), Hush Puppies (865-428-6555), Izod (865-429-0834), Jockey (865-428-9303),

---

HOW DO YOU LIKE THEM APPLES?

They've got a lot more than apples at **The Apple Barn Cider Mill & General Store**: apple butter, apple pies, apple jams and jellies, country ham and bacon, crafts and gifts. In addition, you'll find a cider-pressing room, a candy and chocolate factory, a winery and an ice creamery at this early 1900s cattle barn. ~ 230 Apple Valley Road, Sevierville; 865-453-9319, 800-421-4606; www.applebarncidermill.com, e-mail visit@applebarn cidermill.com.

Maidenform (865-428-9979), Naturalizer (865-429-8260) and Van Heusen (865-428-9394). ~ 2655 Teaster Lane, Pigeon Forge; 865-453-7316.

Lenox, Royal Doulton, Wedgwood and Spode are all represented at **Factories' Outlet China & Gift Mart.** ~ 2680 Parkway, Pigeon Forge; 865-453-5679.

At **Pigeon Forge Factory Outlet Mall,** known locally as "the red-roof mall," you'll find Black & Decker (865-428-3307) and Mikasa (865-453-5482), among others. ~ 2850 Parkway, Pigeon Forge; 865-428-2828.

The **Tanger Factory Outlet Center** has Coach (865-429-0772), Easy Spirit (865-908-7060), Eddie Bauer (865-453-0468), Faberware (865-453-1323) and Liz Claiborne (865-453-3593), plus dozens of other shops. ~ 161 East Wears Valley Road, Pigeon Forge; 865-428-7002, 800-408-5775.

If you spend any time in the mountains, you'll probably wind up wanting to own a nice pair of boots. The buys are good at **Stages West,** which claims to be the biggest boot outlet in the Smokies. If Tony Lama, Durango or Justin don't ring your chimes, maybe you should start at the other end with a Stetson hat, or accessorize with bolo ties and boot bracelets. And if you're planning to do any square dancing, this is the place to get outfitted. Closed Sunday. ~ 2765 Parkway, Pigeon Forge; 865-453-8086; www.stageswest.com.

Boyd's Bear Country has been dubbed "119,000 square feet of every teddy bear imaginable" since it opened in 2004. ~ 149 Cates Lane, Pigeon Forge; 888-654-6215.

Nature lovers will find two floors of paradise at **Beneath the Smoke,** which is devoted to the great outdoors, especially the Great Smoky outdoors. From books, photographs and videos to tick repellents and high-tech gear, well-known photographer Ken Jenkins has amassed a wide assortment to lure you . . . or help you lure the fish. Closed Sunday. ~ 467 Parkway, Gatlinburg; 865-436-3460; www.kenjenkins.com.

The Cellar, in the same building as the Smoky Mountain Winery, is the place to buy wine accessories, baskets, bar accessories and the like, as well as some actual wines. ~ Winery Square at Route 321N; 865-436-7142.

No signs of actor Woody Harrelson lately at **The Hemp Store,** but odds are he'd think this merchandise was far out. Shoulder bags, clothing, shoes, socks and even lingerie are made from hemp and sold here. ~ 411 Parkway, Gatlinburg; 865-436-8300.

If some of the lace and linens at various bed-and-breakfast inns have caught your fancy, head to **Mr. Tablecloth,** where hand-embroidered linens, napkins, runners, aprons and more, many of them created with Battenburg, Venice, Cluny or other styles of

Text continued on page 106.

Great Smoky Arts & Crafts Community

There is a community of artisans hard at work in the shadow of the blue smoke, far away—literally and figuratively—from the factory outlets of Pigeon Forge. Members of the Great Smoky Arts and Crafts Community continue to live and work to preserve a way of life that was first established in these mountains more than 200 years ago. Independent and hardworking, these artisans revere the dignity of producing one-of-a-kind pieces with their hearts, minds and hands. Stained glass, brooms, quilts, jewelry, dolls, glass, candles, pewter, woodcarvings, scrimshaw, pottery and clothing are only a few of the works of art produced by the people still practicing these crafts, despite the modern-day obsession with fads, mass production and impersonal service. The community claims to be the largest group of independent artisans in North America.

The Great Smoky Arts and Crafts Community is more than a group; it's actually a place, as well. An eight-mile loop runs from downtown Gatlinburg to Route 321, along Glades Road to the intersection with Buckhorn Road, and back to Gatlinburg again via Route 321. Along this route are some 78 shops offering a wide array of goods and vendors including food, accommodation rentals and services such as antique-clock restoration. In many cases, visitors are welcome to talk to the artisans (with their permission, of course) and sometimes even to watch them as they go about their traditional work.

There is plenty of parking along the way, but it's a lot less hassle if you leave the car at your hotel or in a lot downtown and hop a trolley. You can take the Orange Trolley from downtown, transferring at City Hall on Route 321N to the Yellow Trolley. This trolley departs the parking lot at

City Hall every half hour. A $1 ticket gives you day-long on-and-off privileges. Brochures, with maps and details on what is available, are handed out free at most locations in the Great Smoky Arts and Crafts Community. If there's a particular artisan you want to visit, it's best to call ahead, particularly during the winter months, when some shops close for the season. Members usually post a sticker attesting to their good standing in the community, but there are also some worthwhile stores on this route that, for one reason or another, don't belong to the organization.

Some of the best shopping is in the roadside clusters, such as the one across Glades Road from Powdermill Road. Of special interest here is **The Church Mouse Gallery**, in a century-old church building, where regional paintings, prints and crafts are the main focus. ~ 865-436-8988. Next door, the **Cliff Dwellers Gallery** sells contemporary and traditional crafts, including furniture, pottery, glass, baskets, gourds and wearable art. ~ 668 Glades Road, Gatlinburg; 865-436-6921.

Another place for one-stop shopping is near the intersection of Glades Road and Route 321N. **Lucite by Louise** is the spot for napkin holders, keychains, Christmas ornaments and other knick-knacks. ~ 865-430-8849. **Scrimshaw, Knives & Silversmithing** sells American Indian handcrafts as well as knives—and the supplies to make them. This is also a good place to have jewelry repaired. Closed Sunday. ~ 865-430-3496. If you're thinking ahead to holiday gifts, look around. **Future Relics**, one of the very best shops in the Smokies, features ceramics, vintage glass and jewelry such as handcrafted bracelets that seem to fly out of the store. ~ 865-436-4423. All types of handcrafted candles, fragrance oils, oil lamps and potpourri distinguish **Candles By Dick and Marie** in the Morning Mist Village Shop. ~ Gatlinburg; 865-430-9148.

Other shops en route are too numerous to list but one deserves special mention. **Earthwalk**'s merchandise is a blend of New Age and American Indian crafts, jewelry and books. Closed Sunday. ~ 865-436-2271, 877-327-8492.

lace, are top drawer. ~ 205 Airport Drive, Gatlinburg; 865-430-3081, 800-626-7542.

Feel guilty about leaving Fido or Muffin behind? Take them a souvenir from **Just Furr-Pets**. ~ 143 Forks of the River Parkway, Sevierville; 865-774-0170.

Downtown Sevierville isn't exactly a mecca for shoppers, but if you are in the market for antiques, roll around to **Wagon-Wheel Antiques**, which has an eclectic collection, mostly of chests and other large furniture, not all of which is at big-city prices. ~ 131 Bruce Street, Sevierville; 865-429-4007.

Eileen's Collectibles specializes in goodies for the hot-rod fancier in your family—NASCAR products, die-cast models and the like. ~ 1605 Winfield Dunn Parkway, Sevierville; 865-428-4696.

Antiques and collectibles including Indian artifacts, vintage signs, glassware, guns, knives, dolls and more are jammed into the **Riverside Antique Mall**. ~ 1442 Winfield Dunn Parkway, Sevierville; 865-429-0100.

The Country Peddler General Store has an outstanding collection of local crafts such as quilts, along with the kind of collectable stuff you can see anywhere, coast to coast. But there's a lot of cute merchandise, and some great stocking stuffers. ~ Maplewood Farms, 2510 Winfield Dunn Parkway, Kodak; 865-932-7637.

It's always holiday time at **Tennessee Christmas**. No matter what kind of ornaments you like to collect, you can probably find something to match it here, along with lots of other decorations. ~ Maplewood Farms, 2510 Winfield Dunn Parkway, Kodak; 865-932-7637.

NIGHTLIFE Regularly voted "Best Show in the Smokies" and "Best Live Country Show in America" by the Country Music Association, **Country Tonite** offers an evening of variety with the area's largest award-winning cast of singers, dancers and comedians. ~ 129 Showplace Boulevard, Pigeon Forge; 865-453-2003, 800-792-4308; www.countrytonitepf.com.

One of the newest productions in town, the **Black Bear Jamboree Dinner & Show** includes a country feast and an award-winning cast that belts out country, Broadway, bluegrass, gospel and rock from the early days. Admission. ~ 119 Music Road, Pigeon Forge; 865-908-7469.

Perhaps only in Pigeon Forge could Dolly Parton's **Dixie Stampede Dinner and Show** not only open, but even prosper. Inside a 35,000-square-foot enclosed stadium, 1000 tiered seats overlook a horseshoe-shaped arena, providing a rider's-eye view of the proceedings at this happening on horseback. Costumed men and women perform various maneuvers, races and feats of derring-do that mostly have a South vs. North theme, but it's all in good family fun. Although the schmaltz-o-meter goes way off the charts whenever the horses are offstage, you've got to love a show that stars world-class racing ostriches. Waiters dressed as either Confederate or Union soldiers mete out rations of barbecue, bread and corn, which you have to eat without utensils. The experience certainly primes the audience for some down-home belly laughs. The show schedule varies, so call ahead. Admission. ~ 3849 Parkway, Pigeon Forge; 865-453-4400, 800-356-1676; www.dixiestampede.com.

Charlie, brother Jim and son Charlie Bob make it a true family affair at the **Smith Family Theater**, singing country, oldies, bluegrass and gospel, interspersed with some comedy bits, at this theater, which opened in a new venue in 2004. ~ 2330 Parkway, Pigeon Forge; 423-429-8100, 866-399-8100; www.smithfamily theater.com.

Move over, Babe, and make room for the other barnyard animals at **The Comedy Barn Theater**. Magicians, musicians, fire-eaters and the now-legendary Arnold the Mind-Reading Pig are among the entertainers at the big red barn. The show schedule varies in January and February, so call ahead. Admission. ~ 2775 Parkway, Pigeon Forge; 865-428-5222, 800-295-2844; www. comedybarn.com.

The **Louise Mandrell Theater** stars the singer/dancer/musician in a high-energy production featuring nine singers and dancers and an eight-piece orchestra playing big band, gospel, country and rock-and-roll tunes. Closed January through March. Admission. ~ 2046 Parkway, Pigeon Forge; 865-453-6263, 800-768-1170.

The tram lifts nightlifers up to Ober Gatlinburg's **Heidelberg Restaurant**, which has a large dancefloor. Dinner show and dance music, including lots of polkas, provided by a German band. ~ 148 Parkway, Gatlinburg; 865-430-3094.

Two new, original shows are presented each season at **Sweet Fanny Adams Theatre**. The idea here is smiles, laughs, or a chance to sing-along. You won't find any dark dramas, just light entertainment suitable for the family. Admission. ~ 461 Parkway, Gat-

---

THERE AIN'T NOTHING LIKE A SONG

For a trip down memory lane, traipse over to the **Classic Country Theater** for a two-and-a-half-hour songfest of tunes made famous by the likes of Hank Williams, Patsy Cline, Tammy Wynette, Loretta Lynn, Conway Twitty, Elvis Presley and others, along with some gospel and bluegrass. Admission. ~ 125 Music Mountain Drive, Pigeon Forge; 865-774-7469, 866-430-8422; www.classiccountrytheater.com.

linburg; 865-436-4039, 877-388-5784; www.sweetfannyadams theatre.com.

Even some Big City Slickers might be forced to chuckle at the country slapstick on view at **Elwood Smooch's Ole Smoky Hoedown**. Fiddles and banjos, clowns and corny jokes are meant for the whole family to enjoy but if the name Elwood Smooch doesn't ring any bells (think "Hee Haw"), you'll probably be happier off playing laser tag. The show schedule varies, so call ahead. ~ 570 East Parkway, Gatlinburg; 865-428-5600, 888-231-6444; www. olesmokyhoedown.com.

The futuristic and dimly lit "war zone" at **Fort Fun** is a great setting for an invigorating game of laser tag. You get a gun, a vest and a little advice, and are then set loose to fight each other and a mysterious stranger. Admission. ~ 716 Parkway, Gatlinburg; 865-436-2326.

A popular local family worked for years to bring to life their dream, in the form of **Southern Nights Music Theater.** There's definitely a talent gene at work here—they all seem able to sing and dance—but maybe they should find an in-law who can streamline the show. Admission. ~ 1304 Parkway, Sevierville; 865-908-0020, 865-908-0600.

PARKS   **PATRIOT PARK** Named for the Patriot missile exhibited here (one of only four in the United States), this quiet greensward sits beside the Pigeon River. There's lots of trees and greenery in season; it's a nice spot to walk off a big dinner, especially on spring and summer evenings. You'll find picnic tables, a half-mile lighted walking path and soccer fields. ~ Middle Creek Road, Pigeon Forge; 865-428-3113.

PIGEON FORGE CITY PARK This riverside park has a mile-and-a-quarter walking trail that's lit at night, a picnic pavilion with grills, a basketball court, playgrounds, a field for baseball and softball, tennis courts, a volleyball court and a soccer field. ~ On McGill Street off Wears Valley Road, Pigeon Forge; 865-428-3113.

▼▼▼▼▼▼▼▼▼▼▼▼▼▼
Outdoor Adventures
From the bass that populate Norris Lake to the trout brimming in the mountain streams of the Smokies, this area is an angler's paradise.

FISHING   **OAK RIDGE AREA** Norris Lake is the place to go after striped bass. The average specimen is about 15 pounds, but fish twice that size are not a rarity.

Bubba's Striper Fishing offers both day trips throughout the year and night trips in summer on a 22-foot cutty cabin (heated in winter). All you have to do is lug along what you want to eat and drink and an ice chest for your day's catch. ~ Norris Dam Marina; 865-689-3244.

GATLINBURG AREA   The rivers and streams in the Gatlinburg area are rife with trout; guides can show you the ropes.

Whether you know how to fish or not, you can head out with **Old Smoky Outfitters** to some of the most challenging streams in the country; you'll have a choice of full- or half-day trips for flyfishing or bass fishing, or even camping overnight. "On the Stream" trips include trout fishing in stocked waters, float trips on the Little Pigeon River, boat fishing on Great Smoky Finger Lakes and bass fishing on Douglas Lake. Overnight trips lead into the backcountry, with lodging in one of the company's base camps. All guides, equipment, camping gear and meals are included in the price. All you have to do is dress appropriately—natural olives, tans or grays, arranged in layers, with polarized sunglasses, hats and rain gear. ~ 511 Parkway, Gatlinburg; 865-430-1936; www. oldsmoky.com.

For information about recreation on TVA lakes, contact the Department of Tourism for the State of Tennessee, 320 6th Avenue North, Fifth Floor, Nashville, TN 37243; www.tnvacation. com.

How about a stream you can call your own? The **Smoky Mountain Angler** has its own six-mile private stream where you're just about guaranteed to catch rainbow trout. You can opt for a half day or a full day of fishing, and all equipment will be provided. Don't worry about an ice chest; all fishing is strictly catch-and-release. There is also a store on the premises with a full line of fishing gear. ~ 376 East Parkway, Gatlinburg; 865-436-8746; www.smokymountainangler.com.

RiverSports Outfitters, Inc., offers instruction on Hiwassee Lake. They rent and sell all the clothes and equipment you can possibly need, and also book rafting trips through their Whitewater Company. ~ 2918 Sutherland Avenue, Knoxville; 865-523-0066.

RIVER RUNNING

Two-hour trips on the Pigeon River out of Hartford can be arranged through the **Nantahala Outdoor Center**. The excursions run on Class II to Class IV rapids, and part of the trip goes under a bridge along the legendary Appalachian Trail. Some trips are suitable for beginners. ~ 800-232-7238; www.noc.com.

Even families who've never canoed together can find happiness on the Big Pigeon, Lower Pigeon and Nantahala rivers. You have a choice of excitement levels with **Rafting in the Smokies**. This outfit offers three different outings in the area from April through October. The five-mile Big Pigeon River excursion lasts one and a half hours on the water, with 12 Class III spots and three Class IV (rivers are graded from low, Class I, to high, Class VI). Trips depart from Hartford, about a 45-minute drive from Gatlinburg. A milder eight-mile outing on the Nantahala lasts two and a half hours of river time, mostly on Class II rapids with a couple of Class III. The trip runs through the Nantahala Forest gorge in North Carolina, and the departure point is 90 minutes from Gatlinburg in North Carolina. ~ Route 321 North, Gatlinburg; 865-436-5008, 800-776-7238; www.raftinginthesmokies.com.

DOWNHILL SKIING
Two quad chairs and one double have the capacity to lift 6000 skiers per hour up to the slopes at **Ober Gatlinburg Ski Resort.** Seven tree-lined slopes and one open hill are mostly intermediate, with two beginner and two advanced runs. The steepest incline is on the long Grizzly Trail, which drops 556 feet over its 3800-foot length. Closed mid-March to early December. ~ 1001 Parkway, Gatlinburg; 865-436-5423; www.obergatlinburg.com.

GOLF
KNOXVILLE Resident PGA pros are on staff at the **Royal Oaks Golf Course,** which is located out by the Knoxville airport just in case your plane is delayed. There are three nine-hole courses and equipment rentals. ~ 4411 Legends Way, Maryville; 865-984-4260, 888-681-0194.

Four holes along a creek and two by a lake add to the scenery at the semiprivate **Willow Creek Golf Club,** which claims to have best back nine in East Tennessee. ~ 12003 Kingston Pike, Knoxville; 865-675-0100.

GATLINBURG AREA There aren't many places to shoot golf like the **Bent Creek Golf Village,** where a creek meanders through a hilly, even mountainous, 18 holes. Gary Player designed the course back in the early '70s and golfers probably think about him when they get to No. 14, a par-3 hole that runs straight down a mountainside. ~ 3919 East Parkway, Gatlinburg; 865-436-3947, 800-251-9336.

A large indoor rink at Ober Gatlinburg Ski Resort & Amusement Park allows skating throughout the year. ~ 1001 Parkway, Gatlinburg; 865-436-5423; www.obergatlinburg.com.

The **Gatlinburg Municipal Golf Course,** designed by William Langford, is best known for Hole 12, a.k.a. "Sky Hi," a 194-yard-long challenge that drops 200 feet from tee to green. ~ Dollywood Lane, Gatlinburg; 865-453-3912.

You can see Mount LeConte from the fifth hole at **Eagle's Landing Golf Club** and there is water on 16 holes, so don't make any careless wagers on your first day at this course. Oh, and watch out for the wildlife, since the club is part of an Audubon Cooperative Sanctuary. Other than that, enjoy your seven-mile walk around the 18-hole, par-72 course. The steep greens fee includes a cart. ~ 1556 Old Knoxville Highway, Sevierville; 865-429-4223.

TENNIS
One of the few sets of courts in Knoxville that have night lights can be found in **Tyson Park.** ~ 2351 Kingston Pike. Other city courts are at **Harriet Tubman Park,** which has three night lights

and four hard courts. ~ 332 Harriet Tubman Street. You can also practice your lobs at **Fountain City Park**. ~ 3701 Ludo Road. For details, contact the Knoxville Park and Recreation Department at 865-215-2090.

McCarter's Stables, Inc. offers one- to four-hour excursions along scenic trails running deep into the Great Smoky Mountains National Park. They can provide lead horses for children. Closed in winter. ~ Near the Sugarlands Visitors Center, Gatlinburg; 865-436-5354.

RIDING STABLES

Walden Creek Riding Stables offers rides ranging from an hour to overnight. Most will take you past a 1900 cabin and an old moonshine still, and through several streams and valleys. There are buggy rides as well, should you have children and/or senior citizens in your group. ~ 2709 Walden Creek Road, Sevierville; 865-908-6700; www.waldencreekstables.com.

If you're fascinated by the lore surrounding Cades Cove, sign up for a half-hour, one-hour or two-hour guided ride (faster rides are available for experienced riders) with **Davy Crockett Riding Stables, Inc.** Open by appointment only in winter. ~ 505 Old Cades Cove Road, Townsend; 865-448-6411.

Experienced guides also lead trips into the foothills at **Middle Creek Riding Stables**. ~ Off Dollywood Lane, a half-mile past the Dollywood entrance, Pigeon Forge; 865-428-8363.

You can find some flat places to bike in Knoxville, but true cycling enthusiasts will love the scenic hills around Oak Ridge.

BIKING

KNOXVILLE The **Third Creek Bike Trail** is a paved three-and-a-half-mile stretch of "greenway" that connects the University of Tennessee neighborhood with West Knoxville. It extends from Tyson Park (2351 Kingston Pike) out to Sutherland Avenue.

OAK RIDGE AREA Some of the best mountain biking around is on a network of trails at the **Norris Watershed**. Extremely popular with locals, the area offers loops from 5 to 20 miles in length, starting with a leg-warming two-mile hill near the parking lot at the Lenoir Museum in Norris Dam State Resort Park. ~ Located in Clinton, 20 miles northwest of Knoxville; 865-426-7461, 800-524-3602.

Bike Rentals Bikes can be rented or serviced (or bought) at **West Bicycles**. Closed Sunday. ~ 11531 Kingston Pike, Farragut; 865-671-7591.

This area is, after all, the gateway to the Great Smoky Mountains National Park, so there's no shortage of nearby trails. Aside from the granddaddy of all parks, however, look to state parks for some wonderful walking opportunities. All distances listed for hiking trails are one way unless otherwise noted.

HIKING

KNOXVILLE Knoxville's **Ijams Nature Center** is an 150-acre bird/nature sanctuary on the banks of the Tennessee River with several easy foot trail loops totaling one mile winding through woods and meadows and across streams and along the bluffs of Fort Loudoun Lake. One segment, Serendipity Trail, is handicapped accessible, a four-foot paved trail with some slight elevations through forests where many of the native trees are identified with Braille markers. From there, a paved area links up with another quarter-mile handicapped-accessible trail; the Universal Trail leads through woods and meadows. ~ 2915 Island Home Avenue; 865-577-4717.

OAK RIDGE AREA There are eight access points to Oak Ridge's **North Ridge Trail** (7.5 miles), a moderately difficult trail along the north side of Black Oak Ridge. The most popular entry point for this trail is on Illinois Avenue just north of West Outer Drive; the early part of the trail rises uphill to over 900 feet before leveling off.

Norris Lake is another prime hiking destination. The 3.1-mile loop through the Tennessee Valley Authority's 125-acre **River Bluff Small Wild Area** provides a good range of experiences for a trail its length. This National Recreation Trail is particularly popular during spring wildflower displays and is especially known for its trout lilies. It leads hikers through old-growth hardwoods, a 40-year-old pine forest, past towering bluffs and alongside the Clinch River just as it comes from beneath Norris Dam. Rated easy, the trail has lengths of moderate grades. ~ Off Route 441, west and downstream of Norris Dam; 865-632-2101.

Another TVA trail on Norris Lake offers a different experience. Also in the National Recreation Trail inventory, the **Hemlock Bluff Small Wild Area** (7 miles) trail is notable for its excellent views of Norris Lake, bluffs overlooking the lake, hemlock stands, old homestead sites and stone fence remnants. Hikers need to remember the area is heavily hunted in the fall. Rated moderate to fairly difficult. ~ About 20 miles west of New Tazewell; 865-632-2101.

▼ ▼ ▼ ▼ ▼ ▼ ▼ ▼ ▼ ▼

Transportation

CAR

AIR

The main approach to Knoxville from the west is via **Route 40** and **Route 75**. Route 40 intersects the city on a roughly east–west axis. Route 75 runs north–northwest from central Knoxville. From downtown Knoxville, **Route 441** leads southwest toward Pigeon Forge and Gatlinburg. **Route 640** is a perimeter highway that runs in a semicircle around Knoxville's north side.

Several major airlines service **McGhee Tyson Airport**, located 12 miles southwest of downtown Knoxville. Airlines include Delta,

Northwest, United and US Airways. Commuter airlines servicing
Knoxville are AirTran, American Eagle and ComAir. ~
www.tys.org.

Greyhound Bus Lines has a terminal in Knoxville at 100 East
Magnolia Avenue. ~ 865-522-5144, 800-231-2222; www.grey
hound.com.

BUS

A number of car-rental agencies can be found at McGhee Tyson
Airport. They are **Alamo Rent A Car** (800-327-9633), **Avis Rent
A Car** (800-230-4898), **Budget Rent A Car** (800-527-0700),
Hertz Rent A Car (800-654-3131), **National Rent A Car** (800-
227-7368) and **Thrifty Rent A Car** (800-847-3489).

CAR RENTALS

K-Trans operates the municipal bus system throughout Knoxville. **Knoxville Trolley Lines** operate three lines downtown, with
the Blue Line extending north to Hall of Fame Drive and the
Orange Line extending to the University of Tennessee campus.
The Green Line visits the arts district, the World's Fair Park, and
the Cumberland Avenue Strip. They both run every five to twenty
minutes on weekdays and are free. For fares, schedules and pickup
points, call 865-637-3000.

PUBLIC TRANSIT

The **Fun Time Trolley** provides cheap transportation throughout Pigeon Forge, at 100 stops marked by the sign of the bear.
Trolleys run from 8:30 a.m. until midnight April through October, and 10:30 a.m. to 10 p.m. November and December except
for Thanksgiving, Christmas Eve and Christmas Day. Fare is 25
cents each time you board a trolley and you must change trolleys
for Dollywood and Wears Valley Road points. The trip to Gatlinburg costs 75 cents. ~ 865-453-6444, fax 865-429-7349.

The **Gatlinburg Mass Transit Department** runs the Red
Trolley out to Airport Road and the length of Parkway, and the
Pink Trolley runs down to Dollywood in Pigeon Forge, all for 25
cents a ride, from 8 a.m. to midnight (hours are slightly shorter
in winter). The Yellow Trolley runs out into the Glades, home of
the Great Smoky Mountain Arts and Crafts Community, from
10 a.m. to 6 p.m., for $1 a ride. ~ 865-436-3897; www.gatlinburg
trolley.org.

Nearly 20 taxicab companies offer transportation within Knoxville and to and from the airport and surrounding communities.
At least one, **AAA Taxi** (865-531-1930), accepts credit cards.
Other major services include **ABC Airport Taxi Service** (865-970-
4545) and **Paradise Taxi** (865-525-9580).

In the Gatlinburg area, you can hitch a ride with **C & O Cab**
(865-436-5893) and **A&R Taxi** (865-429-3531).

TAXIS

FOUR

Great Smoky Mountains National Park

The most magical national park in the United States, the beloved "Smokies" are loaded with history, beauty and lore. The ridges of this part of Appalachia, which the American Indians called *Shaconage*, or "place of blue smoke," roll toward the horizon in waves of pristine splendor.

Or nearly pristine. Like every place else on the planet, the Great Smoky Mountains National Park is threatened by manmade hazards, from industrial pollution that drifts in from the east to automobile exhaust emitted within the park's boundaries. (Even the wild boars that have yet to be routed from the park are a problem caused by humans; in 1920 more than 100 of them escaped from a private game preserve in Murphy, North Carolina, and they've been tearing up the mountainside ever since.) In October, when hundreds of thousands of people drive bumper-to-bumper to get a peek at the spectacular autumn colors, the park sometimes seems in danger of being loved to death. Nearly ten million visitors descend (or ascend) upon the Smokies every year, making it the most popular national park in the United States.

Springtime is nearly as busy as fall, thanks to the balmy mountain air, the wildflowers and other warmer-weather attractions. The park is open year-round, however, and by avoiding the most popular weekends, visitors can indeed have a peak experience in the Smokies. Late April and early May are the best times for viewing wildflowers, which are followed by the blossoms of rhododendrons, at their most profuse in June and July. July is the wettest month, and sudden thunderstorms are common. (Remember that although the higher you go, the cooler it is, afternoon temperatures regularly hit 90° below altitudes of 3000 or 4000 feet.) By September, deciduous trees begin changing their color; the show of yellow, gold, orange and red leaves is usually most awesome in mid-October.

The Smokies are home to 100 species of native trees—more than are found in any other national park in North America and more species than are found in all of northern Europe. Nearly 95 percent of the park is forested; about one-fourth of that is old-growth forest, one of the largest such blocks remaining in

North America. Here, too, are another 1400 species of flowering plants—about 10 percent of them are considered rare—and approximately 4000 kinds of non-flowering plants.

Within the park's 800 square miles is a tremendous diversity of wildlife; more than 230 species of birds, 66 mammals, 50 fish and 73 different reptiles and amphibians. (There are 27 species of salamanders alone, making this something of a national headquarters for the moisture-loving creatures.)

The climate and the environment vary tremendously between the lowest elevations (800 feet at the mouth of Abrams Creek) to the highest (6643 feet, the summit of Clingmans Dome). The difference is so great that it can be snowing on the peaks while spring wildflowers are bobbing in the breeze in meadows along the lower slopes. Throughout this paradise, more than 600 miles of streams and rivers run through ridges and valleys, fed by more than 80 inches of annual rainfall on the peaks.

The park, authorized by Congress in 1926, was created from lands in both North Carolina and Tennessee. Unlike most other American national parks, which were formed from existing government lands, the Smokies belonged to private individuals or companies. The mountainsides were a gold mine for logging companies; from the early part of this century until the park's establishment, nearly 65 percent of the forest had been logged. The lumber was carried out of the area via railroads, and many of the 1200 farms there existed mostly to feed the loggers.

Logging not only deforested what is today the park, but also devastated natural habitats and induced widespread erosion, which in turn clogged streams with sediment and reduced the opportunity for the forests to replenish themselves. It's very unlikely the park would have ever become a reality had it not been for the efforts of private individuals—from John D. Rockefeller, Jr., who contributed some $5 million toward the purchase of parklands, to a St. Louis librarian named Horace Kephart, who came up with the idea of preserving the Smokies as a national park after having visited the fresh-air mountains for his health.

Finally obtained by the federal government and proclaimed a national park on June 15, 1934, the parcel comprises 520,197 acres, roughly split along 70 miles of the eastern Tennessee–western North Carolina border. It is one of 43 International Biosphere Reserves in the United States.

The Great Smoky Mountains were created between two and three million years ago by a gargantuan upheaval of the earth's surface. Ice Age glaciers did not stretch this far south; as a result, the region is alive with an unusual biological diversity. Species of plants migrated southward ahead of advancing glaciers during the Ice Age, but when the thaw began and the glaciers retreated, they left many of these northern plants in the Smokies. As temperatures normalized, some of these northern species relocated to higher and cooler elevations, allowing the southern plant species to reclaim the lower slopes.

Before the Smokies were formed, sedimentary deposits of soil, sand, silt and gravel were layered on top of each other, hardening over millions of years. Known as the Ocoee series, this large mass contains rocks so ancient that no fossils have ever been discovered.

The Smokies are a popular day trip for folks from Knoxville and smaller cities and towns. On the North Carolina side, Bryson City and nearby Cherokee are two major access points. In Tennessee, Gatlinburg and Townsend abut the park (and Pigeon Forge, which is chockablock with motel rooms, is just down the road from Gatlinburg), and are logical overnight spots for those who don't want to camp out or make the lengthy hike (or horseback ride) to LeConte Lodge, the only accommodation within the park's boundaries. Many come to picnic or take short hikes, to fish or hunt, and some—although this is hard to believe—never get out of their cars.

Those who do abandon their vehicles to take a closer look are following in the footsteps of the first-known inhabitants, the Cherokee. They named this special place for the color of the haze that so often floats like gossamer above the mountains, softening every vista. The "blue smoke" is caused mostly by terpenes, hydrocarbon molecules released by trees that break down in sunlight, reforming into bigger molecules large enough to refract the sun's rays. The phenomenon is most intense in the fall, adding yet another color to nature's vivid autumn palette.

SIGHTS

Other discoveries await the visitors, however, no matter where in the park they visit. The **flora** and **fauna** alone are spectacular. In the cove hardwood forests are buckeye, maple, yellow poplar, basswood, oak and silverbell, along with the elegant trillium and the comical-looking Dutchman's breeches (the flower of which looks like billowing trousers hung out to dry in the breeze). Above these, the northern hardwood forest is predominantly composed of birch, beech and other broad-leafed trees. The Fraser fir and red spruce flourish above 4500 feet, where the blue haze settles in. Also in the spruce fir forests are blackberry and mountain berry shrubs and wildflower communities.

On hikes, it is not uncommon to spot red or gray foxes, even though these animals are known to be nocturnal in nature. White-tailed deer, chipmunk, squirrels and marmots are found in different areas while river otters and beaver—a reintroduced species—are likely to be spotted in and around streams. The great horned owl is one of five owl species in the park, and songbirds comprise some of the more than 230 species that either live in or regularly visit the region. Listen for the thumping sound of the ruffed grouse, the rustle of wild turkey or the rat-a-tat-tat of woodpeckers. The list seems endless.

Keep an eye out for snakes. Only two species, the copperhead and the timber rattlesnake, are poisonous. If you don't know how to avoid them, ask a ranger to explain.

The other animal no one wants to mess with is the black bear, the largest mammal in the Smokies. Good places to look are in hollow trees; bears like to den in them, often 20 to 50 feet above the forest floor. They don't hibernate, so keep your eyes open even during the winter. Whenever a bear is sighted near (or on) a road, traffic comes to a standstill so get out your camera. This phenom-

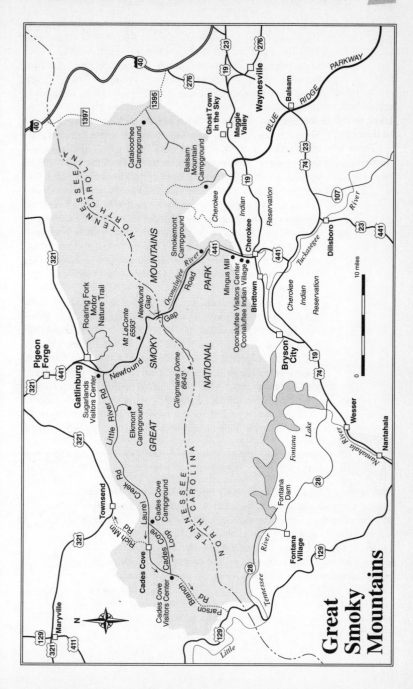

Great Smoky Mountains

enon (known jocularly as a bear jam) is most likely to happen on the Cades Cove Loop, Roaring Forks Motor Trail, Newfound Gap Road and around the Cosby Campground.

For general information about the park, contact the Park Superintendent, Great Smoky Mountains National Park, 107 Park Headquarters Road, Gatlinburg, TN 37738; 865-436-1200; www.nps.gov/grsm.

Park headquarters are in the **Sugarlands Visitors Center**, a contemporary building close to Gatlinburg. Here you can see a slide presentation and exhibits on natural history (including mounted specimens of park animals in re-creations of natural habitats, such as a rather unimposing stuffed black bear) and pick up an armload of information, including maps, campsite directory and backcountry camping permits if you need them. If you have time, check out the reproductions of journals written by early park naturalists. Rangers are usually available to answer questions; formal talks and slide shows are presented regularly from spring through fall, depending on the weather. ~ On Newfound Gap Road near Little River Road; 865-436-1200, 865-436-1230; www.nps.gov/grsm.

For a brief introduction to the park, cross the road from the visitors center and look for signs; it's not far from the entrance to Cherokee Orchard Road, which leads to the five-and-a-half-mile **Roaring Fork Motor Nature Trail**. To reach it from Gatlinburg, take Airport Road one mile out of town, then turn onto the one-way Park Drive. The speed limit on this loop is 10 mph and the tour takes about 45 minutes. You'll go through virgin forest, past pioneer farmsteads long since abandoned, beside streams and, in summer, within view of blooming wildflowers. Near the start of the trail you'll be on **Cherokee Orchard Road**, named for

sights

AUTHOR FAVORITE

I enjoy imagining the early settlers who cleared the trees, planted orchards and fields and built homes in picturesque **Cades Cove**. You can drive the 11-mile, one-way loop based on the grades and turns of wagon roads created more than a century ago. The population of the cove peaked at 685 in 1850; by the time the park was established, about 500 people lived here. Keep an eye out for the deer and wild turkey that roam Cades Cove throughout the year. From mid-April through September, you can check out the Cades Cove Visitors Center, which has exhibits on turn-of-the-20th-century life in the area. You can also pick up brochures and inexpensive maps here. The Visitors Center is open daily.

the 796-acre commercial orchard and nursery that operated in the 1920s and 1930s. Roaring Fork, a village established in the early 1800s, still has some log cabins and a cemetery. Close to the end of the loop, look for a sporadic waterfall called **The Place of a Thousand Drips**, which changes from a leak to a torrent after particularly rainy periods. (Closed in winter.)

You will gain nearly 3000 feet in altitude if you drive the length of Newfound Gap Road (Route 441), which starts at 2000 feet and rises to the **Newfound Gap Overlook** at 5048 feet, right at the Tennessee–North Carolina state line. Making the drive from the lowlands to the mountainous crest has been compared to traveling from Georgia to Canada, in terms of the variety of plant life you could see en route. Trees range from pine oak and southern cove hardwood, which thrive in lower elevations, to northern hardwood and spruce fir, the higher you go. Newfound Gap itself is almost exactly in the center of the park; it's a cut through the crest at 5048 feet, a good place for taking in the view.

A good view of Chimney Tops, the dramatic pinnacles that reveal the powerful force that created the Appalachian Mountains, is, naturally, from the **Chimney Tops Overlooks** along Newfound Gap Road. (Alternatively, you can hike to the cliffs on a steep, four-mile roundtrip trail.)

You can see **Clingmans Dome**, the 6643-foot peak of the park, from all over the Smokies. You can also see much of the Smokies from an observation platform off Clingmans Dome Road (usually closed from December until April). Allow an hour to drive the curvy scenic road that leads up the slope. The views en route are great, but for an unparalleled view, you have to trek a tough half mile from the parking lot to the platform, which rises above the forest of spruce and fir trees. The parking lot is seven miles southwest of Newfound Gap. Try visiting late in the season, between the time the leaves fall and the snow falls. Under a full moon, the scene is hard to beat.

Nearby **Mount LeConte**—at 6593 feet, the third-tallest peak in the park—draws hikers and backpackers by the vanload. Many of them come to get a sunrise or sunset view from a couple of rocky outcroppings on the summit, Cliff Top and Myrtle Point. The park's only lodging is on this mountain, but you can't get very close in a car.

Newfound Gap Road is the starting point for just about every drive in the Smokies. Another possibility is Little River Road, accessible from the Sugarlands Visitors Center. It runs beside the river en route to the best spot in the Smokies (at least, the best spot for nonbackpackers): **Cades Cove**. (Along the way, you'll spot the turnoff for the Elkmont Campground.) See page 118 for more information.

The North Carolina portion of the park has attractions of its own. Drop by the **Oconaluftee Visitors Center** at the southern entrance to the park at the far end of Newfound Gap from the Sugarlands entrance on the Tennessee side. Here you can walk through the **Mountain Farm Museum**, a replica of a small family farmstead typical of the mid-19th century, including a collection of authentic log cabins and a collection of barnyard animals. From spring through October, folks costumed in period dress perform living-history demonstrations at the farm. ~ 828-497-1900.

The Cherokee called the Chimney Tops Overlooks Duniskwalguni, *or Forked Antlers.*

To see a working corn mill, drive about half a mile north of the center. The water-powered **Mingus Mill** was built in 1866 by the son of the first permanent settler in the region, operated for half a century and was reopened in 1968 by the park service as an educational exhibit. Pick up a souvenir pound of fresh stone-ground cornmeal as a memento.

LODGING

HIDDEN ►

Who says you don't have a choice of lodging in Great Smoky Mountains National Park? You can choose among several accommodations at the only game in town, **LeConte Lodge**. Situated so deep in the park that you have to get there by foot (on a four-hour hike via the shortest and steepest of five trails) or by hoof, it offers room for 50 guests, either in rustic cabins or group sleeping lodges. Double bunk beds in the cabins make them a good choice for several people or a small family. Ten to 13 people can fit into one of the lodges, which, like the cabins, are warmed by kerosene heaters and lit by kerosene lamps. There's no electricity, and it was considered a pretty big deal when a privy building with flush toilets was added to the complex. All accommodations have their own basin, but forget about taking a shower during your stay. Meals are served family style in the lodge dining room. Everyone is generally so pleasantly fatigued that they go to sleep after dinner and awake with the sun. Needless to say, there's no disco, no bar and no TV. Instead of staring at the tube, folks rock on the porch and stare off into the distance, which is where all the bright lights and automobile traffic are. Rates may include breakfast and dinner; advance reservations are required. The lodge accepts reservations for the upcoming season beginning October 1. Closed mid-November to mid-March. ~ 250 Apple Valley Road, Sevierville; 865-429-5704; www.lecontelodge.com. BUDGET TO ULTRA-DELUXE.

CAMPING

The park offers 1008 developed campsites at ten campgrounds (closed November through February), and another 100 primitive campsites on backcountry ridges. Sixty backcountry sites are available on a first-come, first-served basis. Permits are required for backcountry camping at the other sites. The permit is free at campgrounds, visitors centers (except Cades Cove) and ranger stations and covers up to eight people. For backcountry reservations, call 865-436-1231.

In addition, there are ten developed campgrounds (though none have trailer hookups), two of which are open year-round. In Tennessee, **Cades Cove** has 161 sites off Cades Cove Loop about 23 miles from Newfound Gap Road. In North Carolina, **Smokemont** has 440 sites off Newfound Gap Road, Signpost 19. These are quite popular, and reservations are required between May 15 and October 31. Fees range from $12 to $20 per night. To book a site for up to seven days during the high season (or 14 days during the rest of the year), call 800-365-2267; reservations.nps.gov.

The seven other campgrounds open in spring when the weather allows and remain in operation through October. They include **Abrams Creek** (16 sites), **Cosby** (175) and **Look Rock** (92) on the Tennessee side, and **Balsam Mountain** (46), **Big Creek** (12), **Cataloochee** (27) and **Deep Creek** (108) on the North Carolina side.

To help siphon off traffic at the campsites during peak season, the park has some 18 shelters backpackers can reserve for one-night stands. Closed on three sides, they are bear-proofed with a chain-link fence on the fourth side. Most are sprinkled at eight- to ten-mile intervals along the Appalachian Trail.

SHOPPING

With all the souvenir shops in gateway towns—not to mention the discount outlets in Pigeon Forge—perhaps shopaholics can survive a visit to the Smokies without buying more than a map. But if you are interested in learning more about the park through books and videotapes, drop into either the **Sugarlands** or the **Oconaluftee visitors center**.

If you've arrived at the park unprepared for hiking, get back down to Gatlinburg to **The Happy Hiker**, which sells the appropriate boots and other gear. ~ 905 River Road, Gatlinburg; 865-436-6000; www.happyhiker.com.

NIGHTLIFE

In the mountains, nightlife consists mostly of listening for the sound of bears trying to get into your food pack. However, there are **ranger programs** such as walks and slide shows, usually at one of the visitors centers and sometimes at the campsites. For a schedule, call 865-436-1200.

The **Great Smoky Mountains Railway** offers gourmet and wine dinner excursions on a regular schedule from mid-March until November. There are also murder-mystery dinner outings on a more limited basis. All trains depart from North Carolina depots. ~ Dillsboro, NC; 800-872-4681; www.gsmr.com.

Outdoor Adventures

FISHING

Before you head out, check road and weather conditions by calling 865-436-1200.

The brook trout, which have lived in the streams of this region for centuries, are the only native trout species in Great Smoky Mountains National Park. Threatened by the introduction of the rainbow trout (by loggers) and the brown trout (by a single stocking in 1900), the brook trout were placed under park protection in 1975. In other words, don't even think about taking one out of the water.

Except for the protected native brook trout, it's pretty much open season in the open waters of the Great Smoky Mountains, as long as you use the approved type of bait and have the proper permits. The bait list is short: artificial flies and lures only. No worms, pork rinds or anything you pick up on the stream bank. Spring and fall are the best times to fish; the trout are hungry and active. In late spring, you have to compete with hatches, which supply plentiful food; in summer, the fish tend to head for deeper, cooler waters; in winter, the fish's metabolism is slowed and it doesn't need to eat as much—except on sunny days, when good fishers can get lucky. For information and guidance, check with park personnel.

Some of the best places to fish in Tennessee are the West Prong of the Little Pigeon River in Gatlinburg and Abrams Creek, which flows out of Cades Cove and takes rainbow trout with it. In North Carolina, try the Raven Fork and Oconaluftee River, which flow together upstream of Cherokee; Deep Creek as it exits the park near Bryson City; and the streams that run into Fontana Lake.

A couple of guide services are available in nearby Gatlinburg. Whether you know how to fish or not, you can head out with **Old Smoky Outfitters** to some of the most challenging streams in the country; you'll have a choice of full- or half-day trips for fly- or spin fishing, or even camping overnight. All guides, equipment, camping gear and meals are included in the price. All you have to do is dress appropriately—natural olives, tans or grays,

AUTHOR FAVORITE

I like the catch-and-release program almost as much as the trout do. For one thing, I don't have to carry an ice chest. For another, I can tell whoppers because there are no fish to count at the end of the day. If you don't know your way around the mountains, I suggest signing up for a day or a half-day with a guide from **Smoky Mountain Angler.** You get to fish in their private six-mile stream. ~ 466 Brookside Village Way, Gatlinburg; 865-436-8746; www.smokymountainangler.com.

arranged in layers, with polarized sunglasses, hats and rain gear.
~ 511 Parkway, Gatlinburg; 865-430-1936.

The **Nantahala Outdoor Center** offers half-day excursions on
both the French Broad and the Nantahala (pronounced "nan-ta-
hay-la") rivers. Depending on where you go, this could be a good
option for people with little experience on the water, since the
rapids are Class II and Class III. ~ 13077 Route 19W, Bryson City,
NC 28713-9114; 800-232-7238; www.noc.com.

**RIVER
RUNNING**

Avoid the hassle of driving and sign up for a tour of the top
Smokies sights with **Rocky Top Tours, Inc.,** which provides pickup service at Pigeon Forge and Gatlinburg locations. Best of all,
you'll get a knowledgeable local guide who can tell you about
Cades Cove and other points of interest. ~ 2638 Parkway, Gatlinburg; 865-429-8687, 877-315-8687; www.rockytoptours.com.

TOURS

The Great Smoky Mountains Railway has three depots on
the North Carolina side of the park. Using vintage trains on the
original logging tracks—all restored—this outfit offers a variety
of excursions, from half-day sightseeing trips to twilight outings
and Saturday dinner outings. Schedule varies. ~ 800-872-4681;
www.gsmr.com.

Scenic Helicopter Tours flies nine different sightseeing excur-
sions ranging from just a few minutes to 40 minutes in length.
Closed part of January and February. ~ 2491 Parkway, Pigeon
Forge; 865-428-6929.

Smoky Mountain Tours offers top-notch van tours through
the park; picnic lunches can be arranged. ~ Pigeon Forge; 865-
453-0864, 800-882-1061.

Horses can be rented by the hour or half-day from concessions
within the park's boundaries, most of them located near campgrounds at **Cades Cove** (865-448-6286), where you can also take
hayrides from April through October. Another option is
Sugarlands, on Newfound Gap Road near the Sugarlands park
headquarters (865-430-5020). Park rules dictate that all rides
within the park must be accompanied by guides provided by the
stables.

**RIDING
STABLES**

One-hour, four-mile and two-hour eight-mile guided rides are
offered by **Smoky Mountain Stables** in Gatlinburg. Closed from
after Thanksgiving through Easter. ~ 865-436-5634.

Steep terrain, narrow roads and heavy traffic make bikes an uncommon sight in the Smokies. Unless you have your own bike or
tote one from as far away as Knoxville, your best bet is to rent
one at the Cades Cove campground. The 11-mile loop is closed

BIKING

Text continued on page 126.

Black
Bears

The only species of bear found in the eastern United States, Ursus americanus is the largest mammal in the Smokies, both figuratively and literally. The black bear symbolizes these mountains in the minds of many, and when it attains full stature, it dwarfs every other warm-blooded creature. The only animal that comes close in weight is the wild boar, which is definitely not a beloved symbol, but a destructive pest.

Approximately 500 black bears live in the park. Since full-grown bears weigh in at between 200 and 400 pounds, you'd think they'd be impossible to miss, but there are no guarantees of what the locals call a "bear jam." That's when someone sights a bear and cars stop in their tracks so people can watch. (Preferably, with the windows rolled up.) It still counts as a sighting if the bears you see aren't exactly black. Some have fur in shades of blond or cinnamon to dark brown.

Born blind, hairless, toothless and tiny (8 to 12 ounces), black bears are usually one of a set of twins. They are born during their mother's winter rest, normally in January or February. In fact, she may even sleep through their first waking hours. The cubs typically weigh about four pounds by the time the female emerges from her den sometime between March and May. And boy, is everybody hungry. The bears don't necessarily hibernate, but they don't eat (which is just as well, since worthwhile food sources are negligible in the wintertime mountains), nor do they drink or eliminate wastes. They survive by consuming their own body fat, and by spring, have lost up to one-third of their weight.

By this time, the males have already emerged from their own dens on the ground. All the bears begin searching for food, mostly early or late in the day and usually close to their dens, sleeping during the middle of the day. When the weather begins to warm up, the bears' diet changes from roots and grasses to berries and other spring-ripening fruit, as well as beetles, yellow jackets, ants and even some small mammals.

Summertime is for foraging the wealth of flora—particularly blackberries, raspberries, huckleberries and blueberries—and fauna in the forest, and for mating. Young bears compete with their older colleagues, often violently, for access to the most desirable females, which are ready to mate by the age of three and a half. Hikers may come across tree trunks scarred with claw marks or even bites, which may be a way bears mark their territory during the breeding season.

There's an interesting quirk to the reproductive process in *Ursus americanus*. The female doesn't ovulate until after mating, and then the fertilized egg does not implant immediately on the uterine wall, as it does in mammals such as humans, but remains unattached for up to five months, until the female is safely ensconced in her winter den, usually 15 to 20 feet above the ground.

In the meantime, the bears are downing acorns and chestnuts that abound in the late summer. When the weather turns cold in late October and November, the bears head for their winter dens to await the thaw that usually begins in February.

Each spring, like clockwork, some visitor or another will come across a cub that has been separated from its mother. Occasionally, the mother will return unexpectedly, which is definitely not something you want to have happen to you. If she doesn't appear, some folks will try to bottle-feed the cub, an even worse idea, since it will probably not survive if it becomes accustomed to handouts.

Bears who are fed, at any age, by humans become real problems, developing aggressive and unpredictable behavior. Many bears have had to be destroyed following confrontations with humans, some of them fatal. For this reason rangers have installed bear-proof garbage cans so that bears won't be tempted, and constantly instruct backpackers to hang their food supplies from a tree at a safe distance from their sleeping bags. Bears are intelligent, but they can't read labels. If you have a bottle of suntan lotion, it might smell like coconut to the animals, whose sense of smell is extremely keen. Along the same lines, bears have been conditioned to recognize the form of an ice chest, usually a good source of food. Keep any items that might remotely be construed as edible in the trunk of your car, out of sight. Bears have been known to pry open car doors to get something to eat. This is not the bears' fault; it's their nature. Bear these facts in mind when you head to the mountains, and you and the fabulous black bear will get along just fine.

to automobile traffic Saturday mornings until 10 a.m. beginning the second Saturday in May and ending the last Saturday in September.

HIKING

More than 900 miles of hiking and riding trails crisscross the park. All hiking trails are one way unless otherwise noted. The **Appalachian Trail** (AT) accounts for 70 miles within the park, which can be accessed at Newfound Gap, Clingmans Dome, Fontana Dam and at the end of Route 32 just north of Big Creek Campground. Every year, some 100 hikers walk the entire 2100-mile trail between Georgia and Maine, a trip that takes four to six months. Clingmans Dome is the highest point of the AT. A popular moderate eight-mile (roundtrip) section runs from Newfound Gap to Charlies Bunion and back, passing through a forest of spruce and fir where you can enjoy vistas, as you gain an elevation of 980 feet along the path.

Wherever you hike, remember to dress in layers and carry rain gear, since weather changes quickly in the mountains. If you should find yourself in the middle of a thunderstorm, remember to stay off the balds (see below) and out of open areas such as meadows, where you're more apt to be struck by lightning. And take plenty of water; you won't find much in the way of shelter or facilities in the park beyond the occasional picnic table.

If you've got time for only one hike in Great Smoky Mountains National Park, consider the **Abrams Falls Trail** (5 miles roundtrip). It's an easy, mostly flat hike that leads to the 20-foot falls for which it's named. In all, there's an elevation gain of just 340 feet. The trailhead is at the parking lot at the west end of the Cades Cove Loop Road.

For a hike that incorporates some flat portions but culminates in a steep climb, head for the **Alum Cave Bluffs Trail** (10 miles roundtrip). The first third of the trail goes through Arch Rock's tunnel, created by erosion. Then it's on to the steep part, Alum Cave Bluffs, nearly a mile atop a 100-foot bluff. The home stretch, about 3 miles, takes you to Mount LeConte. Trailside cables give hikers something to grip as they traverse the cliffs. The trail, which begins at Newfound Gap Road between Newfound Gap and Chimney Tops, has an elevation gain of 2800 feet.

Throughout the Appalachians, you can see what are called "balds," which look like, well, bald spots—open unforested fields along mountain ridges that may have been created by fires or overgrazing. **Andrews Bald** (4.4 miles roundtrip), on the North Carolina side of the park, is easiest to reach. Popular with day hikers, it's at the end of a two-mile trek south of Clingmans Dome. Try it in springtime if you want to see fabulous displays of intensely colored azaleas. Not accessible by car from December through April.

If you're camping at Deep Creek in North Carolina, there are some good trails nearby. For cheap thrills, it's hard to beat the easy **Indian Creek Falls Trail** (1.5 miles), which follows the creek to a 60-foot waterfall. Start just past the Deep Creek ranger station and campground. Walk around the gate and up a small grade to where you can see Tom Branch Falls. In spring, you'll be accompanied by wild geranium, anemone, trillium, phlox and flowering dogwood trees. At .7 mile from the gate, turn right to stay on Indian Creek Trail, which was partly cleared for an intended road project, long since abandoned. In another 200 feet, a side path drops down on the left for a view of the wide cascade known as Indian Creek Falls.

For details on these and other hiking trails, check with the park rangers at 865-436-5615.

Transportation

CAR

The northern entrance to the park is two miles south of Gatlinburg on **Route 441**, a two-lane road known within the park as Newfound Gap Road. The 33-mile highway links the northern entrance with the southern one, which is at Cherokee, North Carolina. The park is also accessible from Townsend via Little River Road, usually a less-crowded route.

AIR

The closest major airport in Tennessee is Knoxville's **McGhee Tyson Airport**. See Chapter Three for information on flights and car rentals.

In North Carolina, the **Asheville Airport** is about 60 miles east of the park.

FIVE

Overhill Region

As the Appalachians stretch south from the Smokies, they encompass the southern region of the Cherokee National Forest and mountain towns. Down from the foothills are a number of small cities sandwiched between the scenic wilderness and the commercial corridor of Route 75.

Today, the so-called Overhill Region of Tennessee, located southwest of Knoxville, is prized for its rivers and its tranquil scenic beauty, as well as for its excellent fishing and hunting opportunities. Its towns are now being "discovered," but in fact these places have a history all their own. And the new tourists shouldn't feel like Johnny-come-latelies; after all, the river itself arrived only recently, in a matter of speaking.

Not since the copper-mining boom of the 1800s has this region received so much attention. The Tennessee Valley Authority (TVA) harnessed the 40-mile Ocoee River for hydroelectric power. Dammed into reservoirs, the river was occasionally diverted from its natural course along wooden flumes built on the mountainsides. From these flumes, the water plunged hundreds of feet, creating the power to turn turbines. In the early 1980s, one of the support trusses failed, returning the Ocoee to its ancient course for a stretch of several miles. Immediately, word of a beautiful wild river spread throughout the rafting community. Although the TVA repaired the flume, the stretch of rapids was already becoming known as the best place to raft in the southeastern United States; it seemed a shame to turn all those people away.

Finally, a compromise was struck. Through a lease and permit system, designated sections of the river are allowed to flow from between 50 and 116 days a year. During that time from Monday through Thursday, rafters can find Class III or better rapids on a five-mile stretch of the Middle Ocoee. After a joint effort by the TVA, the U.S. Forest Service and the Tennessee Ocoee Development Authority, the river was more or less remodeled, at a cost of some $25 million. The flow was manipulated with sandbags, the river's banks enhanced with natural-looking, pebble-flecked concrete and the original graffiti preserved in the nomenclature of certain points, such as Smiley Face and Calihan's Ledge. Some 300,000 people visited in 1995, supporting a $40 million industry.

The presence of such a stunning river provides a vivid counterpoint to another distinctive feature of the southern Appalachian landscape: the barren hills of Copper Basin.

Long before these hills were denuded, the Cherokee had rights to the land. The Cherokee Nation had been headquartered nearby in Georgia, but after that state passed a law in 1830 declaring all Cherokee laws null and void, they were forbidden even to hold council meetings. The Cherokee relocated their capital to Red Clay, Tennessee, and petitioned Congress and President Andrew Jackson for help in reclaiming their lost territory. Jackson, however, intent on moving all the American Indians west of the Mississippi, made the Indian Removal Act one of his top priorities. The Cherokee surrendered their land around Ducktown and Copperhill, and it was put up for sale. The offer attracted few takers, since there were virtually no roads in the area. Finally, a white settler named John Rogers purchased 40 acres in 1839, followed by a few optimistic gold prospectors. Instead of the gold so plentiful in Georgia, they found iron and copper. By 1850 copper had become a sought-after mineral, and the Hiwassee Copper Mine was established in what was called Hiwassee before its name was changed to Ducktown.

In 1899 the Tennessee Copper Company took over the operation of most of the Copper Basin mines, building a new smelter in McCays, which they renamed Copperhill. In those days, enormous copper roasters were used to process the iron ore; trees were yanked from the hillsides to provide timber fuel for the roasters. What finished off the vegetation, though, were the sulphur dioxide fumes released by the roasters. Eventually, the toxic fumes created a 56-square-mile area of freakishly bare red hills.

In the past few decades, reforestation efforts have succeeded, but some hillsides have been left alone as a history lesson, if nothing else. Indeed, some have objected to the reforestation, finding a strange beauty in the sight of the bare hills.

Down the road, gold was discovered in Coker Creek long before the 1849 California gold rush. Interest faded quickly, since the gold was too fine to separate from ore, but not before white settlers replaced the local Cherokee.

Several of the flatland towns, such as Tellico Plains, were originally Cherokee villages established along the Hiwassee, Tellico and Little Tennessee rivers. The British referred to them as Overhill Towns, since they could be found several miles "over the hill" from North Carolina. Except for several place names and the Sequoyah Birthplace Museum (owned and operated by the Cherokee), contemporary visitors will see little evidence of the Cherokee culture.

Sweetwater, Vonore and Loudon

Loudon is close enough to Knoxville almost to qualify as a suburb, while Sweetwater and Vonore (population of about 1160) seem to belong more to the mountains. Throughout the area, fairly direct country roads provide a convenient and scenic alternative to the larger highways.

SIGHTS

HIDDEN ►

The largest underground lake in the United States, the Lost Sea lies 500 feet beneath a hillside on the eastern outskirts of Sweetwater. Even though you can see only about a quarter of the whole thing, the **Lost Sea** is an awesome sight and a fabulous place to be on a hot or rainy day because it's entirely underground. Thirty years ago the cave system—part of a much larger system known as Craighead Caverns—was opened to the public. For a while it was designated a nuclear fallout shelter and loaded with supplies to help an estimated 30,000 people survive a disaster. Now the sea has been drained somewhat so that visitors can walk down a long passageway to the underground cavern that contains the lake, where they can view only about four and a half acres of the nearly 18 acres that make up the entire lake. Few people have ever seen all of it; the American Indians were reluctant to venture much farther than the mouth of the cave, not knowing what predators or other terrors lurked within the lightless interior. Later, bootleggers brewed moonshine in the caves. The combination boatride/walking tour takes about an hour, but seems shorter. Admission. ~ 140 Lost Sea Road, Sweetwater; 423-337-6616; www.thelostsea.com.

To the northeast, via Route 68 and Route 411, on the shores of Tellico Lake, the **Sequoyah Birthplace Museum** honors not only the man who developed the Cherokee syllabary in the early 1800s, but also other cultural and historical aspects of the Cherokee people. In addition to crafts such as handwoven baskets, this modern museum displays artifacts such as tools derived from two decades of archaeological work in the Little Tennessee Valley. Behind the museum building, the Cherokee Memorial contains a common grave with the remains of 18th-century Cherokee excavated from burial sites that would have been lost when the Tellico Reservoir was completed. Admission. ~ 576 Route 360, Vonore; 423-884-6246; www.sequoyahmuseum.org.

On the other side of this same peninsula, you can visit the 1200-acre **Fort Loudoun State Historic Area,** which encompasses the remains of the fort as well as the Tellico Blockhouse. Today, despite the restoration efforts of the TVA, all that remains of the complex are the foundations and outlines of buildings as they existed around 1799. After a particularly bloody conflict (in which the local militia attacked and killed several Cherokee), the local Cherokee petitioned Governor Blount to built a fort, or blockhouse, for their own safety. In fact, the place became a haven of peace and order on the often-lawless frontier and, later, a lively trading post. Today, visitors have to use their imaginations to envision how this fort looked in the late 1700s, when it was a major stopover point for westbound travelers. ~ 338 Fort Loudoun Road, Vonore; 423-884-6217.

A few miles east of Route 75, about halfway between Knoxville and Chattanooga, and about halfway between Sweetwater and Madisonville, **Orr Mountain Winery** is tucked away around a few country road corners. On a clear day, you can see Mount LeConte and Starr Mountain from the little knoll where the winery sits. You can take a tour of the winemaking facilities, taste the products and pick up a sample of something nice and light for a picnic. Perhaps Tellico Rose or a white or red varietal produced from estate grapes would do the trick. Closed Monday and Tuesday most of the year. ~ 355 Pumpkin Hollow Road, Madisonville; 423-442-5340.

◄ HIDDEN

The two-story **Best Value Sweetwater Inn** is exceptionally attractive for its price range. The 140 accommodations (including two suites don't quite live up to the white-columned pretentiousness of the portico, but they are slightly larger than average. Comfortably furnished with padded chairs at the little square table by the window, they are decorated monochromatically in

LODGING

Overhill Region

colors such as teal and cream. Two pools and an indoor hot tub are just the ticket after a long day of touring. Small pets allowed. ~ 180 New Highway 68 at Exit 60 from Route 75, Sweetwater; 423-337-3513, fax 423-337-3514. MODERATE TO DELUXE.

DINING

Ashley's at the Sweetwater Inn is pleasant, as hotel dining rooms go, and the food is a cut above average. The small menu ranges from steak and seafood to liver and onions. ~ 180 New Highway 68 at Exit 60 off Route 75, Sweetwater; 423-337-3317. MODERATE.

Sweetwater is not exactly a destination dining spot, but you can at least find some affordable food at **China East Chinese Restaurant**. Tangerine beef, Hunan shrimp, scallops, chicken, curries and pork dishes star on a menu of more than 50 items at this sparely decorated storefront spot. ~ 793 Route 68, Sweetwater; 423-337-2800. BUDGET TO MODERATE.

SHOPPING

A friendly "Welcome, Y'all" sign hangs over the door at the **Country Store**. The stuff here is hard to categorize but on a given day you might find a cuckoo clock, antique and collectible glass, a ceramics booth with work by a local artist, a carved wooden Indian, old tools and a half-priced section. ~ 121 County 308 Road, Sweetwater; 423-337-6540.

PARKS

FORT LOUDOUN STATE HISTORIC AREA A 1200-acre park sits where the British built their first fortifications on the western frontier in 1756. Located at the tip of the peninsula that's also home to the Sequoyah Birthplace Museum, the park— encompassing the remains of the fort and the 1794 Tellico Blockhouse—overlooks the serene Tellico Reservoir and the Appalachian Mountains in the background. Excavations made prior to the fort's reconstruction turned up artifacts displayed in the interpretive center. There are picnic areas within view of Fort Loudoun Lake, and a couple of four-mile hiking trails within the gently sloping park. Other facilities include restrooms, picnic tables, a boat dock and a fishing pier. ~ 338 Fort Loudoun Road, Vonore; 423-884-6217; www.fortloudoun.com.

▾ ▾ ▾ ▾ ▾ ▾ ▾ ▾ ▾ ▾
Athens

The largest city in the area with more than 12,000 residents, Athens is surrounded by rich farmland that made it a prosperous, well-to-do town in the early 19th century. It is home to Tennessee Wesleyan College, originally established in 1857 as Athens Female College. An excellent museum and a compact downtown imbue the town with much of its character.

SIGHTS

The **Athens Area Chamber of Commerce** has brochures on local attractions, lodging and historical sights, as well as a guide to the

downtown area. ~ 13 North Jackson Street; 423-745-0334; www.
athenschamber.org.

One of the best attractions in the Athens area is found off the
beaten track on the northeast side of town. If you like ice cream,
you'll scream for the treats at the **Mayfield Dairy Farms Visitors**   ◄ *HIDDEN*
Center. It's not only kids who melt at the notion of touring this family-run dairy; grownups will like the feeling of a flashback to the
'50s. It's just so darned wholesome. In addition to
the bottling line and the production of ice cream
and novelty items, the tour provides answers to such
perplexing questions as how do they get the stick into
ice cream treats. What really counts is the little shop and
fountain in the visitors center where you can sample the
wares yourself. Closed Sunday. ~ 4 Mayfield Lane; 423-
745-2151, 800-629-3435; www.mayfielddairy.com.

> The first cottage cheese
> was made in the family
> kitchen of Mayfield
> Dairy Farms by
> Goldie Denton
> Mayfield herself.

From the dairy, it's a short drive to Madison Avenue,
which leads directly to downtown. It's kind of unusual that the
Living Heritage Museum is housed in a contemporary building,
but it matters little. Founded by Muriel Mayfield of Mayfield
Dairy fame, the museum is the community's attic. Here are
Cherokee moccasins and Victorian satins, spinning wheels and
quilts, in all nearly 30 exhibit areas arranged on three floors. Displays explicate the county's history, from before the first white
settlers arrived, through the pioneer years, the Civil War and the
development of the region as manufacturing began to supplant
farming as the community's economic base in the 1930s. Best of
all, it's a lively, friendly place where visitors find it easy to absorb
a sense of history. Admission. ~ 522 West Madison Avenue; 423-
745-0329; www.livingheritagemuseum.com.

If you're traveling with a small pet, you'll be relieved (if not as-   **LODGING**
tounded) to learn you can take it with you to the **Days Inn** in
Athens, located near the junction of Route 75 and Route 30.
Some rooms have microwaves, refrigerators and whirlpool baths,
making this two-story, 55-room motel a good choice in the usually undistinguished chain category. Amenities include a pool
and a coin-operated laundry. ~ 2541 Decatur Pike; 423-745-5800,
800-329-7466, fax 423-745-7192. BUDGET.

Gail's Country Buffet—the name says it all at this homey local   **DINING**
favorite. Look for the classic Southern dishes from fried chicken
to catfish at this bargain spot where you don't have to wait long
for your meal. Closed Sunday. ~ 2935 White Street; 423-745-
9852. BUDGET.

Legends is a small, family-run restaurant where you can be
sure the breakfast biscuits and the chili are made in the kitchen.

The menu is big on classics like burgers, grilled sandwiches and other diner fare and includes a half-dozen Mexican dishes (the salsa comes from a family recipe). Closed Saturday and Sunday. ~ 5 McMinn Avenue; 423-745-5833. BUDGET.

SHOPPING   For antiques, accessories and all manner of collectibles, check out the **Cottage Antiques & Gifts** shop. Closed Sunday. ~ 15 West Washington Avenue; 423-745-8527.

For window shopping, you can't beat the array of specialty and antique shops (and even an old drug store with a soda fountain) around the **McMinn Courthouse Square**, where carefully restored facades, wide brick sidewalks and extensive landscaping beat the mall any day. ~ Main and College streets; 423-745-0334.

▼▼▼▼▼▼▼▼▼▼▼▼▼▼
Ocoee River Area

The Ocoee River, the Hiwassee River and the Cherokee National Forest imbue this region, on the borders of both North Carolina and Georgia, with some of the most scenic vistas in all of Tennessee. Ducktown was a company town and lacks a cohesive center, but little Copperhill has a lively downtown where you can stand on a bridge with one foot in Tennessee and one foot in Georgia.

SIGHTS   Starting in the mid-19th century, the Overhill region was a major textile producer. The story of this Appalachian industry, which employed large numbers of women, is related in exhibits at the **Englewood Textile Museum**. The museum's organizers are restoring an adjoining historical building in order to expand the museum. Next door is a pocket park called Memory Gardens, which features a mural illustrating the history of Englewood. ~ 17 South Niota Street, Englewood; 423-887-5455.

Etowah, a small town on the edge of the Cherokee National Forest, celebrates its days as a boomtown with the **L&N Depot & Railroad Museum**. Built in 1906 and on the National Register of Historic Places, the 18-room building also houses the offices of the Tennessee Overhill Heritage Association, a good source of regional information. Look for the caboose outside. Closed Saturday. ~ 727 Tennessee Avenue, Etowah; 423-263-7840.

The historically stylish **Gem Theater** originally opened in 1927 to showcase movies and live vaudeville productions. The building it occupies dates from 1906, when it was the largest structure in town. Then it housed the postmaster, who established a clothing store and a millinery shop on the ground floor. When Hugh V. Manning converted the building into a theater, he named it The Gem in honor of his home town of Marietta, Georgia, also known as the "Gem City." The structure and theater changed hands as well as names until the property was acquired by the city of Etowah in 1993 and is now almost entirely restored. The Gem is home to a resident theater group, the Gem Players, who mount at least three productions every year. Located in downtown Etowah, this historic theater hosts live performances throughout the year, including concerts, plays and other events. Special tours can be arranged. ~ 700 Tennessee Avenue, Etowah; 423-263-7608.

Located about two miles from the Ocoee River, **Copperhill** is home to just over 400 souls; **Ducktown** has even fewer. These are the only real towns in these hills—the only ones with shops, restaurants and other facilities. It's the general beauty of the area that draws the crowds, with people coming mostly to use the river and to hike and bike. There's also some gold panning in the rivers and lots of camping.

Coker Creek Village is a sort of one-stop tourist attraction on the way to the Ocoee River from Athens. Among the sports offered are panning the local creek for gold. You can rent or purchase equipment at the store, and instructions are free. ~ Coker Creek Village; 423-261-2310.

Travelers intrigued by the sight of so many barren, rust-colored hillsides can find plenty of explanations at the **Ducktown Basin Museum**. The Ducktown Basin actually straddles parts of Georgia and North Carolina as well as eastern Tennessee, but copper mining left more of a legacy on the landscape here than elsewhere. The museum is located at the old Burra Burra Mine works; through a slide show and various exhibits, including a mock cutaway of a copper mine shaft, it interprets the process of mining as well as its effects on the community and the landscape. Closed Sunday. Admission. ~ 212 Burra Burra Street, Ducktown; 423-496-5778. Stop by the **Polk County-Copper Basin Chamber of Commerce** for more information on the area. ~ 134 Main Street, Ducktown; 423-496-9000; www.ocoeetn.org.

> Due to copper mining, the surrounding hills of the Ducktown Basin area glow with shades of red from pinkish to a dark copper color.

With all the attention lavished on the Great Smoky Mountains, out-of-staters might overlook the charms of the two-part national forest that brackets the country's most popular national park. The **Cherokee National Forest**, southern division, abuts the Smokies on the south, and its northern division serves as the Smokies' northern boundary. Both segments are bordered on the east by North Carolina, and the southeastern corner by the Copper Basin, including the towns of Copperhill and Ducktown.

Dense forests, rugged mountains, abundant streams and seasonal waterfalls characterize the Cherokee National Forest, along with deep river gorges and several lakes, the largest of which is Lake Ocoee in the southwestern corner of the forest. Visitors can obtain maps, campground information and wilderness permits at any of the three ranger district stations.

The **Hiwassee Ranger District** has the Gee Creek Wilderness, the John Muir State Scenic Trail and the Hiwassee State Scenic River. ~ The ranger station is in the L&N Depot, Tennessee Avenue, Etowah; 423-263-5486.

To the east, the **Tellico Ranger District** has 33 popular hiking trails (the district is second only to the Watauga, to the north, in terms of visitor traffic). Some of the best ones are easy to moderate (see "Hiking" in "Outdoor Adventures"). The ranger station is in Tellico Plains; 423-253-2520.

The **Ocoee Ranger District** offers easy access to the Ocoee River, popular with rafters, boaters and fishers. It, too, has abundant trails—22 in all. Headquarters are three miles east of Parksville on Route 64; 423-338-5201.

If you're interested in the scenery but don't want to hike, ask the Ocoee District ranger where to turn off onto **Forest Service Road 77**, a winding seven-mile paved road that leads to McKamy Lake. Here, atop Chilhowee Mountain, you'll find picnic areas and campsites and an easy, one-and-a-half-mile trail to Benton Falls, starting on the south side of the lake.

LODGING   The easiest place to find in all of Ducktown is **The Company House Bed & Breakfast Inn**, an 1850s bungalow that's been remodeled to create six rooms with private baths. The white-clapboard structure has a welcoming front porch, set with rockers. Inside, hardwood floors, bead board walls, floral wallpaper, antiques and quilts set a cozy tone. The place was never intended as lodging for the mining companies; rather it's located next to the old Company Bank. Full breakfast included in the rates. ~ 125 Main Street, Ducktown; 423-496-5634, 800-343-2909; www.companyhousebandb.com, e-mail companyhousemt@tds.net. MODERATE.

A couple of blocks up the street, **The White House Bed & Breakfast** occupies a restored home dating from around 1900. The rooms, which are none too large, have patterned wallpaper, chenille bedspreads and dark wood furnishings. Two of the three

SPLISH SPLASH

The southeastern corner of Tennessee—specifically the Ocoee River—made a big splash in the 1996 Summer Olympics. The torrent of water near the town of Copperhill is so challenging that the Olympic Committee chose it as the site of the first Olympic whitewater course ever offered on a natural river. The television coverage of the event provided most viewers with their first glimpse of the region, though it has been enjoying an influx of whitewater enthusiasts for more than a decade.

upstairs guest rooms share a bath. In general, this is not a good bet for people who require a lot of privacy and elbow room. In good weather, however, there's plenty of space on the wrap-around porch. Full breakfast. ~ 104 Main Street, Ducktown; phone/fax 423-496-4166, 800-775-4166; www.ocoee-white housebb.com, e-mail mardan@tds.net. MODERATE.

The only lodging between Ducktown and Copperhill is the **Ducktown Copper Inn,** conveniently located scant yards from the highway, with scads of free parking. Naturally, it's popular with kayakers who may have little interest in lingering over a leisurely gourmet breakfast with a chatty innkeeper. The 34 accommodations in this standard two-story motel aren't exciting, but they're clean and presentable. ~ Route 68/64, Ducktown; 423-496-5541. MODERATE.

Only in Europe would you expect to find a place like the **Lodge at Copperhill**. The innovative idea here is to charge per person, not according to the room size. They've made it easy: Room 1 has one large European full-size bed, suitable for one or two people. Room 2 has two beds; Room 3, three beds; and Room 4, four beds (and a balcony). The owners promise not to make anyone bunk with strangers. It's a great concept that should catch on in the U.S., especially in areas where sports, such as kayaking the Ocoee, are a major draw. Four bathrooms are shared, and a full breakfast is included for an unbelievably low price. One block from downtown, two blocks from the river and a world away from price-gouging B&Bs, this re-outfitted residence is clean, attractive and logically furnished for maximum comfort and convenience. This is the best deal in the state, unless you absolutely require turndown service. ~ 12 Grande Avenue, Copperhill; 423-496-9020; www.lodgeatcopperhill.com, e-mail lodge@copper hill.com. BUDGET.

◄ HIDDEN

DINING

When the urge strikes you to get hold of some barbecued pork, chicken or ribs, the place to go is **Tinsley's Restaurant and Barbecue.** Lunch only. Closed Sunday. ~ Route 411, one half mile north of Benton; 423-338-9118. BUDGET.

In Copperhill, about two feet across the Georgia state line, is something you wouldn't expect to see in these parts: a Japanese restaurant. Not only that, but **Michiko's** is housed in a white-and-red Hansel-and-Gretel cottage, complete with peaked roof and arched windows. But here it is: *yaki tori*, *gyoza*, tofu, tempura, teriyaki and some local delights. Closed Sunday. ~ Toccoa Avenue at Georgia Highway 5, Copperhill; 706-492-5093. BUDGET.

El Rio Mexican Restaurant & Cantina has come to Copperhill, bringing south of the border specialties like tacos and enchiladas. The place doesn't look very authentic, perhaps because this used to be a sort of saloon/restaurant. Still, it's friendly and attracts a crowd, and it's grits-free. ~ 23 Ocoee Street, Copperhill; 423-496-1826. BUDGET TO MODERATE.

Simple decor and plain, stained wood tables at the **Iron Horse Grill** keep things basic. The eclectic American fare includes filet mignon, balsamic chicken, fresh trout and pasta specials. Closed Monday. ~ 50 Ocoee Street, Copperhill; 423-496-9991; e-mail ironhorse@blrg.com. MODERATE.

SHOPPING   Crafts, jewelry, unique gifts, collectibles, fresh produce, baked goods and antiques can entertain shoppers all day at the **Benton Flea Market**. Closed Monday through Friday. ~ 284 Mull Road, Benton; 423-338-5933.

Coker Creek Village encompasses not only a restaurant but also the **Old Country Store**. It's big and wonderful for browsing, whether you're in the market for a quilt, locally made crafts or antiques and collectibles. ~ Coker Creek Village; 423-261-2310.

Though chiefly a furniture store, **The Copper Emporium** also stocks framed prints and houses The Doll House, featuring 15 major lines including Alexander, Heidi Ott, Gorham and others. ~ 71 Ocoee Street, Copperhill; 423-496-2965.

Another reason to visit the Englewood Textile Museum is to check out the **Company Store and Attic Treasures**, where 25 dealers of antiques and collectibles offer something for just about everyone. ~ 17 South Niota Street, Englewood; 423-887-5455.

NIGHTLIFE   Located in downtown Etowah, the **Gem Theater** hosts live performances throughout the year, including concerts, plays (including three by the Gem Players) and other events. ~ 700 Tennessee Avenue; 423-263-7608; www.gemplayers.com.

The old **Midway Drive-In Theater** is one of only 15 theaters of its type remaining in Tennessee. You can catch a double feature for $4 a head (or, on Sundays, for $6 per carload). They screen movies from dusk-til-dawn in conjunction with the July 4th and Labor Day holidays. ~ Route 30, between Athens and Etowah; 423-263-2632.

COPPERHILL CRAFTS

At their **Courtyard Studios**, Rip and Tammi Mann practice one of the rarest of traditional handcrafts, turning out hand-hewn bowls (made of cherry, black walnut, butternut and various maples) as well as stained glass, bath products, folk art, earthenware and watercolors. Tours are available by appointment. ~ 41 Ocoee Street, Copperhill; 423-496-5116.

HIWASSEE STATE SCENIC RIVER AND OCOEE RIVER 🏃 🦌

🚣🚣🚢 ⚓ The first river managed in the State Scenic River program, the Hiwassee includes 23 miles of Class III water that runs from the North Carolina state border to Route 411 north of Benton. There are many public access sites and boat-launching opportunities. The Ocoee River, the premier whitewater river in the Southeast, has Class I, II, III and IV rapids, and several access points. The only facilities here are restrooms; a restaurant is one mile down the road. The main catch here is trout. The park headquarters are located off Route 411 between Benton and Delano. Day-use fee, $3. ~ 407 Spring Creek Road, Delano; 423-263-0050.

▲ There are 45 primitive campsites; $11.25 per night.

Smallmouth bass are the catch of the day at the **Hiwassee River**, along with yellow perch and brown and rainbow trout.

Outdoor Adventures

FISHING

At **Tellico-Chilhowee Lakes**, April and May are the best time to fish for largemouth and smallmouth bass, followed by the crappie season (late April through May), trout (April through May, especially at night) and bluegill (June through September).

Fishing boats can be chartered year-round at the **Fort Loudoun Marina**, near Loudon. Depending on the season, you'll be trolling for bass or catfish. ~ 5200 City Park Drive, Lenoir City; 865-986-5536.

RIVER RUNNING

Don't even think of dipping a paddle in the Ocoee River unless you're an experienced paddler. If you just can't stand the idea of missing out on the river that hosted the Olympic whitewater events, sign up for a guided raft trip with an outfit like **Cherokee Rafting Service, Inc.** ~ Route 64, P.O. Box 111, Ocoee, TN 37361; 423-338-5124, 800-451-7238; www.cherokeerafting.com.

More than a dozen outfitters ply the waters of the Ocoee, which is a dam-controlled river with regularly scheduled water releases. USA **Raft** has a fleet of whitewater craft and includes kayaks, various-sized rafts and two types of "ducks," a cross between a kayak and a raft that is stable, sturdy and easy to maneuver. USA Raft also offers a choice of levels—Family Class, Adventure Class and World Class—as well as of types of trips—single-day or overnight. The minimum age for these trips is 12. ~ 800-872-7238; www.usaraft.com.

The **Ocoee Adventure Center** is a full-service guide shop with whitewater rafting, mountain biking, horseback riding and hiking tours as well as kayak instruction. Bike rentals and guided raft trips are available. Their website is a wealth of information and includes the calendar for rafting days on the Middle Ocoee.

~ Route 64, Copperhill; 423-406-4430, 888-723-8622; www. ocoeeadventurecenter.com.

Adventures Unlimited offers canoeing, kayaking, scenic floating and whitewater rafting, in addition to caving trips, in the Cherokee National Forest and on the Ocoee River. ~ Route 1, Ocoee; 800-662-0667; www.adventureunlimited.net.

Another well-established organization is **Southeastern Expeditions**, which can arrange trips on the Ocoee combined with other river outings, overnight excursions or simple half-day adventures. ~ Ocoee Outpost, located three miles east of Route 411 on Route 64, Ocoee; in Tennessee, 423-338-8073, 800-868-7238.

Nantahala Outdoor Center also runs these rapids, with names like Hell Hole, Broken Nose and the Doldrums, a respite before hitting Surprise Rapid. Trips run three and a half hours, with about one and a half hours on the water. ~ 13077 Route 19 West, Bryson City, NC 28713-9114; 800-232-7238.

ROCK CLIMBING

At **O.A.R.** (Outdoor Adventure Rafting), beginners are introduced to rock climbing and rappelling on a natural 45-foot-high rock bluff as well as at a manmade rock climbing wall. (Owners Rob and Susan Paden also offer water rafting.) ~ Welcome Valley Road, off Route 64 between Ducktown and Ocoee; 423-338-5746, 800-627-7636; www.raft.com.

GOLF

Golf courses are few and far between in the Overhill Region— possibly because there is no urban area from which people need to escape.

The first nine holes at the **Riverview Golf Course** are laid out along the Tennessee River; the back nine are mostly surrounded by woods on hilly turf. ~ Huff Ferry Road, Loudon; 865-986-6972.

RIDING STABLES

You can take guided rides up into the Blue Ridge Mountains with the **Eagle Ranch**. If a three-day, two-night Ranch Camp adventure sounds like a hoot, be sure to call ahead. ~ Copperhill; 800-288-3245; www.eagleadventures.com.

BIKING

The **Hiwassee Ranger District** of the Cherokee National Forest can supply maps to the park, directing bikers to more than 260 miles of paved and unpaved roads. This district is located between the Great Smoky Mountains National Park and the Ocoee. ~ Hiwassee District Ranger Station, Route 64 and Forest Service Road 77, Ocoee; 423-338-5201.

Within the **Ocoee Ranger District** of the Cherokee National Forest are more than 100 miles of unpaved roads where mountain bikers are welcome. Locals recommend the Greasy Creek Trail to Benton Falls as well as the Clear Creek Trail. ~ Ocoee District Ranger Station, Route 64, opposite Ocoee Lake; 423-338-5201.

Ducktown, Coker Creek
& Other Curious Names

When you look at a map of Tennessee, you've got to wonder: Where do names like Bell Buckle and Nutbush come from? It helps to understand a few things. First, many of the more exotic monikers are Americanizations of Cherokee and Chickasaw place-names. (Tennessee itself is derived from *Tanassi*, a leading Cherokee town that was on the Little Tennessee River.) Another thing to consider is Southerners are by nature storytellers.

Some of the most wondrous names—Heaven and Hell, Dumplin and Corn-bread, Hoodoo and Heartbreak—defy research. Places like Reliance, Difficult and Defeated may not have traceable lineage, but were likely named for the attributes of the locals or the territory. But in many cases, the legends of the names give travelers a little insight into Tennessee history and humor.

Since Ducktown is next door to Turtletown, the uninitiated might think animals inspired these names, but in fact the former got its name from a local Cherokee leader, Chief Duck.

Located on a rise north of Chattanooga, Cheap Hill got its name because of an old general store known for its cheap prices.

Naming Sunbright wasn't too tough a job. Local legend has it that a convict assigned to the construction of the railroad stood on top of one of the hills near this Cumberland Plateau town and shouted, "Sun bright!"

Sounding like a healthy place to live, Ozone actually began life named Mammy. In 1896 the name of this picturesque mountain village was changed to Ozone because of the invigorating quality of the air.

Perry County was noted for the tanneries established along the Tennessee River, particularly at a place called Rat Tail. This yard got its name because of the rats that disembarked from a St. Louis barge loaded with hides. Rat Tail and the other tanneries are no longer in business, but Mousetail Landing was named in the 19th century to distinguish it from Rat Tail.

Twenty-five years before the 1849 California gold rush, gold was discovered at a place now called Coker Creek. The story associated with this locale is that a soldier, one of the first whites to learn about the gold in them thar hills, noticed a gold nugget necklace on an Indian woman. He asked where the nugget came from and she told him, Coqua Creek. Coker Creek is a corruption of that old Indian name.

The **Tanasi Trail System** at the Ocoee Whitewater Center is considered among the premier systems in the Southeast. (It even has a top-of-the-line titanium frame mountain bike named after it.) Originating from the banks of the Olympic whitewater course at the Ocoee River, it has more than 30 miles of trails for every skill level and lots of variety, including a paved riverside trail.

The Ocoee River is called the Toccoa River once it crosses the Tennessee border into Georgia.

The most recent addition to the trail system, the 1.5-mile Thunder Rock Express, has received a lot of positive comments from bikers such as "ripping downhill rides" and "awesome jumps."

For a full description of the trails, you can contact the **Ocoee Whitewater Center** or visit their web site. A typical outing, though, is the Chestnut Mountain Loop (8.6 miles), which is suited to good or advanced riders who can ride for two hours with several moderate climbs. The majority of the trail, which is accessed from Thunder Rock Campground, follows an old logging road (double track) through a hardwood forest. ~ 4400 Route 64, Copperhill; 423-496-5197, 877-692-6050; www. southernregion.fs.fed.us/ocoee.

If you plan to rent a mountain bike in this region, it's best to contact one of these establishments in advance: **Coker Creek Village** (800-448-9580), **High Country Adventures** (800-223-8594) or **The Outdoor Store** (423-627-7636).

HIKING

All distances listed for hiking trails are one way unless otherwise noted.

Several highly recommended trails can be found in the Ocoee Ranger District of the Cherokee National Forest and hikers could easily find themselves in another state if they don't pay attention. For a difficult hike, try combining the **Wolf Ridge, Big Frog, Grassy Gap** and **Big Creek** trails (9.5 miles). The route begins at 1654 feet and rises steadily for the first four miles, eventually reaching 4000 feet. Chestnut trees, lilies, rhododendrons and other flora add interest to this strenuous hike. Before beginning, hikers should get a map, or at least directions, from the ranger station in Benton.

A more moderate trail in the same region is the **Chestnut Mountain Trail** (1.3 miles). The trailhead is at the parking area for the Cohutta Wilderness off Big Frog Road; eventually you can connect with Wolf Ridge Trail at 3100 feet. The reason the trail is so easy is that it follows an old road that the rangers closed when the wilderness was established. ~ Ocoee District Ranger Station, Route 64, opposite Ocoee Lake; 423-338-5201.

How about a hike along a cool mountain stream? The **Bald River Trail** (5.6 miles) runs beside its namesake, a wild trout stream where you can flyfish. Allow a full day for this one-way trip, starting from the parking area on Tellico River Road at Bald River Falls. A switchback climbs 200 feet to a picnic area, followed by another steep ascent to the top of the gorge, before the trail descends sharply along a cliff past waterfalls. The climax of the trip—all of it relatively easy—is a hike past wild laurel and rhododendron.

Another long trail—also rated easy—is based on the route naturalist John Muir took en route to the Gulf of Mexico. Just think: his trail was 1000 miles; yours is only 12, each way. Start near Reliance; the **John Muir Trail** (12 miles) trailhead is at Childers Creek, although you can start at several points farther along the trail. A highlight: the trail follows a riverbank and at one point runs under a swinging bridge at the Appalachia Power House. ~ Hiwassee Ranger District; 423-338-5201.

Transportation

CAR

Southern Appalachia and the flatlands to the west are wedged between the North Carolina state line and **Route 75**. To the north is Knoxville, to the south, Georgia, to the southwest, the city of Chattanooga. The main north–south route (actually, closer to northeast–southwest) is **Route 11**, which parallels the interstate only a few miles to the west. The other major road is **Route 411**. Only small state routes crisscross the area on an east–west axis. In the mountains, the major road is **Route 68**, which runs from Sweetwater to Copperhill, right on the Georgia state line.

AIR

The closest airport is the **Chattanooga Metropolitan Airport**, which is served by Delta, USAirways and the commuter lines American Eagle, ComAir, Northwest Airlink and US Airways Express. For more information, call 423-855-2200; www.chattairport.com.

BUS

Greyhound Bus Lines (800-231-2222; www.greyhound.com) provides interstate service to the Chattanooga area. ~ 2621 Decatur Pike, Athens; 423-745-8675. Aside from airplanes, bus transport is the only public transportation to this part of Tennessee; there is no longer any train service.

CAR RENTALS

The nearest car-rental agencies are located at Chattanooga Metropolitan Airport. They include **Avis Rent A Car** (800-230-4898), **Budget Rent A Car** (800-527-0700), **Hertz Rent A Car** (800-654-3131), **National Car Rental** (800-227-7368) and **Thrifty Car Rental** (800-847-3489).

SIX

Chattanooga and Environs

If Chattanooga is forever linked with its "Choo Choo," nobody seems to mind. Railroads not only made this city famous, they made a dusty riverside town into a major metropolis, the fourth largest in Tennessee. With some 155,500 city residents and double that in all of Hamilton County, Chattanooga has changed from a quiet town to a minor-league city.

It is still a small, manageable city, however, easy to live in, easy to traverse. When Chattanooga throws a party, everyone wants to come. Annual events such as the early-summer Riverbend Festival do draw out-of-towners, but it's the kind of "street party" around which some locals even plan their vacations.

The presence of the river endows Chattanooga with much of its personality and charm, as do the mountains—Lookout, Signal and Raccoon—that guard it on three sides. Its position, in the so-called Grand Canyon of the Tennessee River Valley, favored its development hundreds of years before the steam engine was invented. Relics of the days of the American Indians are few and far between in the Chattanooga today, but one remains. The name of the city is derived from a Creek word describing Lookout Mountain as a "rock coming to a point." The region was the last capital of the once-great Cherokee Nation, one of the most highly civilized in North American history. Three centuries of European and then United States aggression doomed this American Indian civilization, bringing dislocation and death in their wake.

The Cherokee survived the 1540 arrival of Hernando de Soto, the first-known white explorer to see the Tennessee Valley. His vantage point was present-day Point Park, high atop Lookout Mountain. Although de Soto is believed to have camped for a month on an island near Chattanooga, scholars do not agree on his route through the region. One thing they do agree upon, however; very few European traders followed his lead until the late 1600s.

By then, American Indians were trading actively with various Colonial outposts. The site of Chattanooga lay in the path of the Indians. Known as the Great Indian Warpath, their route was already well established—in fact, said to be three feet deep—by virtue of heavy moccasin traffic. Part of this path, on the western slopes of Lookout Mountain, has been preserved at a nature area called Reflection Riding.

In 1663 the British established the colony of Carolina, including present-day Tennessee, not that that stopped the French who laid the same claim, encroaching from the West. A century later, at the end of the French and Indian Wars, England had acquired undisputed title to the territory, at least in terms of the Europeans. It was a different story with the American Indians, a group of whom joined Chief Dragging Canoe's resistance. These Chickamauga Indians sided with the British in the Revolutionary War, but ultimately lost out to militiamen who, against official federal policy, attacked and destroyed the main Chickamauga towns in the area in the 1790s.

American Indian lands still made up about three-quarters of the Chattanooga area when Tennessee was admitted to the Union in 1796 as the 16th state. The local Cherokee, who were joined by other members of their nation who had moved out of southern Appalachia as that territory was settled, maintained active trading with the pioneers.

John and Lewis Ross, whose grandfather was the Cherokee John McDonald, established a ferry landing on the banks of the Tennessee River in 1816. This site, today commemorated with a park and plaza known as Ross Landing, was described at the time as only a "shanty for goods and a log hut for the ferryman," but the landing thrived as a hub for trade relations between the Cherokee and the settlers. The Tennessee River was so difficult to navigate, especially at Moccasin Bend, that Chattanooga would not be able to exploit its location as a port on the nation's inland waterway system until the Tennessee Valley Authority (TVA) was created in the 1930s.

Chattanooga was officially established in 1839 by an act of the Tennessee legislature. It was not until 1850, when the railroad arrived, that Chattanooga began to develop on the south bank, where sufficient bottomland allowed for future expansion. By then, the infamous Trail of Tears had already forced the migration of Cherokee toward reservations in the West, a tragic march during which thousands died, including the wife of John Ross, the principal chief of the Cherokee for 38 years.

When Tennessee seceded from the Union in 1861, it had the full blessing of Chattanooga proper, although a majority of Hamilton County favored the Union. As in other cities of the Southeast, the Civil War still enters conversation today, especially since a number of local attractions, including Lookout Mountain, still bear witness to the fighting and destruction. The most famous battle of the five that took place around Chattanooga was the so-called Battle Above the Clouds, conducted on Lookout Mountain, where dense clouds prevented Confederate gunners from protecting their comrades on the slopes below. It was another critical battle, on Missionary Ridge, that opened the way for General Sherman's devastating March to the Sea.

Scarce capital after the war delayed the rebuilding of the city until the 1890s, and many of its prominent downtown buildings date from subsequent years, including the Flat Iron Building, the Old Carnegie Library and the neoclassical Hamilton County Court House, as well as a number of mansions.

By the beginning of the 20th century, Chattanooga made history as the site of the first Coca-Cola bottling plant, and its future as a major commercial hub was set in motion. The "Chattanooga Choo Choo" building was constructed as the Southern Railway Terminal, a beaux-arts architectural wonder that served as a gateway to the South up until 1971. Most of the commercial development in the early part of the 20th century took place south of 10th Street and west of Georgia Avenue; the area north of 10th and east of Georgia was mostly residential.

At the other end of town, the city's first "bedroom suburb," the St. Elmo neighborhood, flourished with the expansion of the electric trolley line. Located at the base of Lookout Mountain, the district claims more than 600 properties on the National Historic Register, one of the largest such districts in the United States. The Convention and Visitors Bureau gives out free maps and accompanying text to several Chattanooga neighborhoods, including the Fort Wood district, where Classical Revival, Tudor, Queen Anne, Italian Villa and Victorian Romanesque houses make it one of the most attractive residential areas.

You have to spend only a little time in Chattanooga to see that it "works." To be sure, there's commute traffic and crime, but not on the scale of other cities, even in the South. Chattanooga did have a major problem with soot, as a result of its becoming an industrial center in the 1960s. But a dogged community effort cleaned up the environment in the 1970s to put Chattanooga near the top of the clean-air list for cities of its size. In the process, the city lifted itself from its economic doldrums to become a major manufacturing center for textiles, chemicals, paper products and machinery.

These buses are one reason the city is easy (and inexpensive) to explore. Added to the mix is a fairly temperate climate, with an average mean temperature of 60° and an average rainfall of 53 inches. The driest month is October; the wettest, March. It has an average of 228 frost-free days a year, and the population takes full advantage of the weather to participate in all kinds of sports, particularly canoeing and hang gliding. Chattanooga is home to the Women's U.S. Olympic Rowing Team, and Lookout, Raccoon and Signal mountains generate ideal air currents for hang gliding.

The best times to visit are late spring and early fall, when the weather is most pleasant. The nine-day Riverbend Festival takes place in late June, a citywide celebration of its musical heritage. July and August are tough if you're not used to the high humidity of a Southern river town.

Chattanooga is a fabulous place for children, with train rides, interactive museums, the world's largest freshwater aquarium, accessible historic sites and a small scale manageable for families. The town has plenty of inexpensive places to eat and a free trolley that runs up and down the main drag.

Chattanooga is a good jumping-off place for the mountains, close to the Ocoee River and only 200 miles from the Great Smoky Mountains National Park. Nearby towns include Dayton, site of the 1925 Scopes "Monkey" trial, and Monteagle, a village spread over the top of a 2000-foot mountain that has been a favorite mountain retreat for Chattanoogans (and Nashvillians) for the past century. About 30 minutes from Chattanooga, Monteagle and neighboring Sewanee, home of the University of the South, are accessible via the steepest stretch of Route 24,

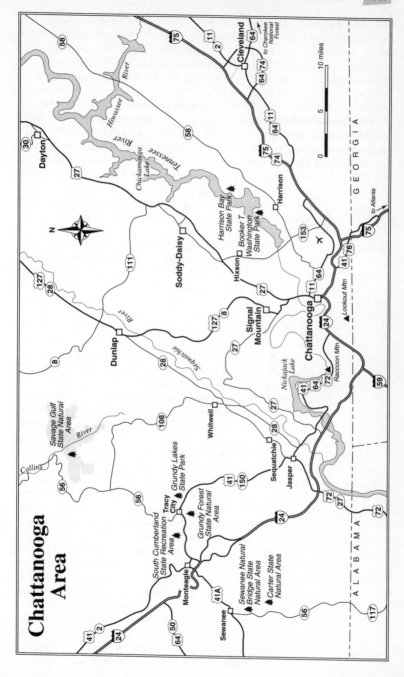

Chattanooga
Area

the main thoroughfare northwest to Nashville. Arriving by plane gives you the best overview of the region—the meandering river below, the mountains that hover near the city limits and the Appalachian range in the distance. North Georgia is also visible from the air; Chattanooga is so close to the state line that some people drive to Atlanta, roughly two hours away by car, just for lunch.

Central Chattanooga

The city of Chattanooga was founded on the banks of the Tennessee River. Long before that, it had been a hub for trade between the Cherokee and the settlers, a natural stopping place because of the treacherous curve in the river known as Moccasin Bend. Downtown Chattanooga is 665 feet above sea level. Here you will find the oldest buildings, fanning west from the river, and most of the major attractions. Since many local businesses are also located downtown, it's where you'll find the majority of fine restaurants.

SIGHTS

The majority of Chattanooga's best sights are clustered downtown and easily accessible by car. A free electric shuttle bus service loops up and down Broad Street, the main east–west artery, from morning 'til night, making a car superfluous until you want to explore farther afield. The convention & visitors bureau gives out free maps and accompanying text to several Chattanooga neighborhoods, including the Fort Wood district near the University of Tennessee campus, where Classical Revival, Tudor, Queen Anne, Italian Villa and Victorian Romanesque houses make it one of the most attractive residential areas. Restaurants in this part of town tend to be upscale, and lodging choices are either chain hotels or historic inns.

The best attraction in town is the spectacular, 130,000-square-foot **Tennessee Aquarium**, located where the city was founded on the banks of the Tennessee River. The self-guided tour (approximately two hours) begins with an elevator ride to the top, so you can walk down 12 levels via long, switchback ramps back to the entrance. But it's not an average escalator trip; video screens positioned above run footage of the interior exhibits, which are alive with fish, birds and a few mammals such as river otters. There are more than 9000 animals altogether, representing more than 575 species of fish, reptiles, birds, amphibians and mammals. The first major—and still the largest—freshwater life center in the United States, the aquarium focuses largely on the wildlife habitats of the Tennessee River. You'll see riverine habitats in seven freshwater tanks and two terrestrial environments. At the top of the aquarium is the Appalachian Cove Forest, which re-creates the mountain source of the river; walking down the ramps, you continue down to waterfalls, the Mississippi Delta and finally to an exhibit showing the wildlife and habitats of six of the world's most prominent river systems. This is the kind of place that warrants several visits over time. Allow at least an hour, if not an en-

A Family Day in Chattanooga

Chattanooga is the most family-friendly town in Tennessee. In addition to kid-specific attractions, there are places and outings that appeal to groups of all ages.

- Get an early start with a visit to the **Tennessee Aquarium** (page 148), featuring fascinating exhibits not only of fish but also of riverbank critters like otters.

- Cross the street and make a stop at the **Chattanooga Area Convention & Visitors Bureau** (page 150). They can answer any questions you have about the places you plan to visit.

- Explore **Ross Landing Park and Plaza** (page 150), one of Chattanooga's most historical spots, then stroll a couple of blocks to the **Creative Discovery Museum** (page 152) and join the kids toying with some interactive displays.

- Walk down to **Lupi's Pizza Pies** (page 158) for a lunch of pizza and a glass of iced tea before heading out to the other side of town.

- Stop for a train ride on the world-famous **Chattanooga Choo Choo** (page 154).

- Drive over to the **Lookout Mountain Incline Railway** (page 165) and take the steep ride up the mountain. Stop for ice cream when you come down.

- Take a ride out to **Reflection Riding Arboretum and Botanical Garden** (page 167), where a nature museum awaits.

- Finish the day of exploring with a visit to the **Raccoon Mountain Pumped Storage Facility** (page 167), where kids will like zooming down and up in the space-age elevator.

- Play a game of bocce ball at the courts on the bank of the Tennessee River, then order some pizza or other Italian fare at **Tony's Pasta Shop and Trattoria** (page 157), just a block from the bocce ball courts.

tire afternoon, to take it all in. An IMAX 3-D Theater seats 400 in front of a six-story screen. Admission. ~ 1 Broad Street; 423-265-0695, 800-262-0695; www.tnaqua.org.

Ross Landing Park and Plaza surround the Tennessee Aquarium, and it's worth a visit whether you go see the fish or not. Facing the river, the Tennessee Aquarium is on the left and the Chattanooga Area Convention & Visitors Bureau is on the right, but they are only part of the story. Essentially the park is an environmental piece of art, incorporating culture, history, commercialism and nature through a series of landscaped "bands" representing points in time. The closer to the river, the older the band. The entry arches are planted with ash, birch and evergreen trees characteristic of mountain forests; another band is a bridge encrusted with bottle bottoms referring to the fact that Coca-Cola's first bottling plant was established in Chattanooga; farther north are moldings of Civil War relics, stones etched with Cherokee clan names, replicas of Creek Indian neck ornaments and so forth. Look for the cornerstone at Band 131 denoting the 1815 founding of the original settlement by John and Lewis Ross at this very site. ~ 100 Broad Street.

The **Chattanooga Area Convention & Visitors Bureau,** also adjacent to Ross Landing, is excellent. You can pick up information and pick the brains of the exceptionally helpful and well-informed staff. Closed Saturday and Sunday. ~ 2 Broad Street; 423-756-8687, 800-322-3344; www.chattanoogafun.com.

After getting your bearings, you'll be eager to learn more about the city and life on the river. The beauty of the Tennessee River will compete for your attention with the running commentary on local history aboard the **Southern Belle.** The three-deck, 500-passenger riverboat has daytime sightseeing cruises as well as a smorgasbord of other options, from lunch excursions to dinner to Nashville Nite BBQ Cruise, with country music and barbecue, plus seasonal specials like Fall Color Cruises. Limited schedule January through March. Admission. ~ Chattanooga Riverboat Co., 201 Riverfront Parkway, Pier 2; 423-266-4488, 800-766-2784; www.chattanoogariverboat.com.

Occupying two floors of a 1906 schoolhouse two blocks from the Tennessee Aquarium, the **Chattanooga Regional History Museum** concerns itself largely with the history of Chattanooga from early Indian times through the 1930s. The spotty collection includes such items as a vintage jacket from the old "Chattanooga Lookouts" baseball team and exhibits on the history of television, snow and video games. More interesting is the 1930s kitchen that shows how that important room has evolved over the past century. Be sure to see *Marks on the Land,* an audio-visual show relating the history of Chattanooga from pre-Cherokee days to present.

Admission. ~ 400 Chestnut Street; 423-265-3247, fax 423-266-9280; www.chattanoogahistory.com.

Many other downtown attractions are located a few blocks away west of the river.

Sometimes you think there must be a museum devoted to every single human pursuit. Why else would there be an **International Towing and Recovery Hall of Fame and Museum**? Ernest Holmes, Sr., introduced the first wrecker right here on Market Street in 1916 and the rest, as they say, is history. And, to be truthful, it's actually interesting to see the vintage vehicles and learn the mechanics required to operate them, especially if you've never known the difference between single-boom and twin-boom wreckers. There's also a picture gallery of men and women from all over the world who have made major contributions to the towing industry. Admission. ~ 401 Broad Street: 423-267-3132; www.towing museum.com.

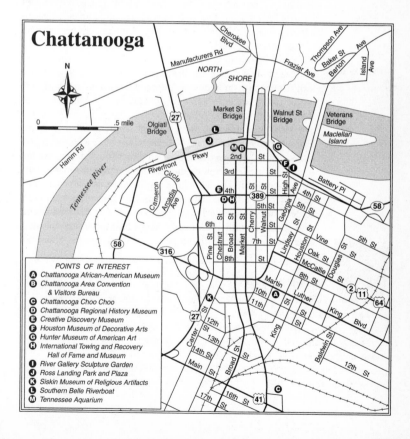

POINTS OF INTEREST
Ⓐ Chattanooga African-American Museum
Ⓑ Chattanooga Area Convention
    & Visitors Bureau
Ⓒ Chattanooga Choo Choo
Ⓓ Chattanooga Regional History Museum
Ⓔ Creative Discovery Museum
Ⓕ Houston Museum of Decorative Arts
Ⓖ Hunter Museum of American Art
Ⓗ International Towing and Recovery
    Hall of Fame and Museum
Ⓘ River Gallery Sculpture Garden
Ⓙ Ross Landing Park and Plaza
Ⓚ Siskin Museum of Religious Artifacts
Ⓛ Southern Belle Riverboat
Ⓜ Tennessee Aquarium

Around a couple of corners, a wacky turquoise tower is a clue to the delightful exhibits inside the **Creative Discovery Museum**, an interactive science museum that doubles as a godsend to the harried parent. Actually, Mom and Dad may be more entranced than the kids by hands-on exhibits such as those at the music studio, where you can pretend you're a country-and-western star. Kids can also "dig" for dinosaur bones, sculpt, paint and fiddle around in an inventor's workshop. The pint-size Little Yellow House is reserved for toddlers. Closed Wednesday in winter. Admission. ~ 321 Chestnut Street; 423-756-2738, fax 423-267-9344; www.cdmfun.org.

A few blocks to the east lies the **Walnut Street Bridge**, built in 1891. Said to be the longest pedestrian bridge in the world, it must surely be one of the most popular. In all but the worst weather, you can take the ten-minute stroll across the 2370-foot-long bridge from a dead-end street near downtown across the Tennessee River to the funky shops along Frazier Avenue in North Chattanooga. You will have plenty of company: joggers, handholding couples, moms pushing strollers and even skaters (though no skateboards allowed). ~ Walnut Street north of 2nd Street; 423-842-0177.

HIDDEN ►   East of the Walnut Street Bridge, the **Hunter Museum of American Art** contains an imposing collection housed in an equally imposing setting, an old Chattanooga mansion once home to Coca-Cola magnate and local philanthropist George Thomas Hunter. The 1500-piece collection, which includes works by Ansel Adams, Helen Frankenthaler, Louise Nevelson, Willem de Kooning, Alexander Calder, Thomas Hart Benton and Mary Cassatt, among others, is considered among the premier holdings of American art in the Southeast. The works are displayed in two strikingly different, but complementary, buildings situated on a limestone bluff some 90 feet above the Tennessee River. Even with all this room, only about one-fifth of the collection can be displayed at any given time; the displays are rotated every two to four years. The older

AUTHOR FAVORITE

sights   En route to a cappuccino, a glass of wine or dinner at a nearby restaurant, I like to meander around the **River Gallery Sculpture Garden**. This two-acre outdoor gallery on the river bluff features works by regional, national and international artists. It is accessed through a cupola upheld by columns festooned with mosaic fish and a sculptured gate representing Chattanooga's seven Tennessee River Bridges. ~ 214 Spring Street; 423-265-5033.

works (roughly from 1790 to 1950) are housed in a 1904 Classical Revival mansion; contemporary pieces can be seen in the galleries next door, in a 1975 structure built especially for the purpose. Don't see one without visiting the other. The pair of buildings works as a unit to give an impressive overview of the achievements of some of the country's most enduring artists. Closed Monday. Admission. ~ 10 Bluff View Street; 423-267-0968; www.huntermuseum.org.

Across Riverside Drive from the Hunter, the **Bluff View Art** ◀ HIDDEN
District is evolving as the most chic neighborhood in Chattanooga. It's home to historic homes, a couple of cafés, artist studios, an inn, four restaurants, a gallery and a sculpture garden. ~ 411 East 2nd Street; 423-265-5033, 800-725-8338; www.bluffviewartdistrict.com, e-mail bluff@chattanooga.net.

Anna Safely Houston opened an antique shop in 1920, just in time to fall prey to the Great Depression. But her incredible collection of 18th-, 19th- and early-20th-century glass and china was preserved in a neighbor's barn, where at one point some 15,000 glass pitchers were suspended from the ceiling. After Houston's death in 1951, a committee of interested Chattanoogans convened to preserve the collection by establishing the **Houston Museum of Decorative Arts**. Today, 10,000 pieces, including ceramics, textiles and American furniture, can be seen on periodic guided tours in the Bluff View Art District. Though the emphasis is on glassware, with fine examples of Burmese, art-nouveau and Cranberry works, there are also quilts, coverlets, toys, dolls and music boxes that still play, appropriately enough for a house dating from 1890. Closed Sunday except in summer. Admission. ~ 201 High Street; 423-267-7176; www.chattanooga.net/houston.

From the art district, take High Street south to 4th Street, turn left (4th will turn into 3rd Street) and drive about ten minutes until you see the sign for Siskin Plaza. Here, tucked away behind a rehabilitation center, the **Siskin Museum of Religious Artifacts** ◀ HIDDEN
has an extensive collection of some 450 religious objects relating to Christianity, Islam, Buddhism, Judaism, Hinduism and Confucianism, most of them dating from the 16th to the 20th centuries. Among the treasures are ceramic figures of Madonna and child in the manger, from Poland; a 19th-century Hanukkah lamp; an 18th-century five-foot-tall wooden Chinese man-god; and an ancient hand-done parchment relating the story of the Passover. Before entering, stop to look at the introductory video, which while interesting doesn't tell the whole story of how the philanthropic Siskin brothers actually went about amassing their holdings. Closed weekends. ~ 1101 Carter Street; 423-634-1700.

If you're ready for a break from driving, what about a train ride? Turn around on 3rd Street, return to Riverside Drive and follow it as it becomes the Amnicola Highway (Route 58). The divided highway runs alongside the river before intersecting with Route 153S. A couple of miles farther, you will see the turnoff to Cromwell Road; your depot is close by.

HIDDEN ▶

The **Tennessee Valley Railroad Museum** is enlightening, but not as much fun as a ride on the 1930s-era steam-powered passenger railway, the largest operating historic railroad in the South. Check out the slide show before boarding the train; it explains the founding of the museum and a bit about the dozens of vintage cars on display in the rail yard. You get an impression of how lustrous the golden age of rail travel really was in the early part of the century. Then it's all aboard for a 50-minute, six-mile round-trip journey that runs through the 986-foot-long Missionary Ridge Tunnel (built just after the Civil War) and crosses Chickamauga Creek via a modern steel bridge. Everyone disembarks at the Grand Junction Station to watch the cars spin on the turntable, then reboards for the return trip (except on summer weekends, when you can ride all the way to the Chattanooga Choo Choo). Another option is the four-hour roundtrip excursion to the Chickamauga National Park. Admission. ~ 4119 Cromwell Road; 423-894-8028, 800-397-5544.

Now it's time to explore the parts of Chattanooga south of downtown. Take Market Street from Ross Landing and turn left on Martin Luther King Boulevard.

The **Chattanooga African-American Museum/Bessie Smith Hall** comes alive with videos of blues commentators and interactive displays that allow visitors to create their own blues-band sound. Exhibits tell the story of the first lady of blues, Bessie Smith, who was born in a Chattanooga slum in 1894, began singing at the age of nine and attained fame only posthumously, following her death in a car wreck in 1937. In addition to a replica of an African hut, the museum houses a collection of historical and cultural artifacts from Gambia, Liberia and other African countries, but its scope is larger than that. Visitors can learn about the displacement of the Cherokee and its impact on slaves (even Cherokee leader John Ross kept slaves), the achievements of blacks during the Civil War and other historic episodes. A photo-mural depicts the everyday life of African Americans in Chattanooga over the past century and a half, while other displays honor their contributions in business, religion, culture and politics. Closed Sunday. Admission. ~ 200 East Martin Luther King Boulevard; 423-266-8658, fax 423-267-1076; www.caamhistory.com, e-mail museum_tours@caamhistory.com.

Back on Market Street, continue south until just before the major intersection with Main Street.

It's nigh well impossible not to start humming the tune when you visit the **Chattanooga Choo Choo**, a 30-acre complex (anchored by a Holiday Inn) in the landmark 1909 Terminal Station. A vintage trolley car rolls back and forth along a horseshoe-shaped track, the best part of which is the narration. There's a model railroad museum, where automated trains run along 100 miles of track. Unless you're a major railroad buff, this is the most overrated attraction in town. Admission. ~ 1400 Market Street; 423-266-5000, 800-872-2529; www.choo choo.com.

More than 300 kinds of trees and 900 varieties of wildflowers grow in Chattanooga, more than anywhere else with the exception of central China.

North Shore is what locals call the neighborhood north of the river; most of this area is technically still Chattanooga, even downtown Chattanooga. The main riverside drag is Frazier Avenue, which sports coffeehouses, a couple of New Age stores and even a sports store—a good place to walk and browse. It's as close to Greenwich Village as you're going to get in Tennessee!

Signal Mountain occupies the north side of the Tennessee River Gorge. The drive up to the top of Signal Mountain passes through some of the nicest residential neighborhoods in the area, including Hixson and North Chattanooga as well as Signal Mountain. To reach it, take Route 217N, turning off at Route 127; the round-trip is about 29 miles but will take more than an hour thanks to the winding gorge roads.

The **Bluff View Inn** is a complex of accommodations augmented with restaurants, all hugging a high-toned chunk of real estate above the Tennessee River. It's headquartered in a 1928 Colonial Revival mansion called the Martin House, which aims to evoke a bygone era (and a well-to-do one at that). One room belonged to the original owners, and has a balcony. Another is named for Anna S. Houston, whose glass collection is displayed in a nearby museum. The Portera/Randall Room honors the current owners, and has a view of the river. These three rooms have exquisite antiques, jacuzzis and working fireplaces. Another six rooms are located around the corner at the 1908 Victorian **T. C. Thompson House**, and are named for distinguished Chattanoogans. Four rooms are on the main level, and two suites are upstairs, both of which have gas fireplaces. A third structure, the nearby 1890s **Maclellen House**, features six rooms and one suite. All three of the the inn's buildings are in a great location if you like to walk; in fact, walking is the easiest way to get around this part of town. Still, it's the top address in Chattanooga, and since it has both a fancy and a casual restaurant, you could do worse than stay put. ~ 411 East 2nd Street; 423-265-5033, 800-725-8338, fax 423-757-0120; www.bluffviewinn.com. MODERATE TO ULTRA-DELUXE.

LODGING

The most historic hotel in town, which recently received a $10-million makeover, is the **Sheraton Read House Hotel and**

Suites, built in 1926 on the site of an 18th-century hotel that served as a Civil War hospital. The lobby, with elegant arches, walnut panels and old mailboxes once used by long-term guests, is on the National Register of Historic Places. Each of the 13 floors commemorates a different Civil War battle. The 238 rooms and suites are not luxurious, but are attractive enough, typically with dark green carpets and sophisticated floral fabrics. There are a swimming pool with waterfall, a workout room and two restaurants on site. The excellent midtown location compensates for the darkness of the decor. ~ 827 Broad Street; 423-266-4121, 800-333-3333, fax 423-267-6447; www.readhousehotel.com. ULTRA-DELUXE.

The **Mayor's Mansion Inn** is a National Register building that has been masterfully transformed into the most luxurious inn in Chattanooga. The 1889 former mayor's mansion in the historic Fort Wood neighborhood was made with 16-foot hand-coffered ceilings and floors fashioned from six types of wood. Nine rooms and suites offer dramatically distinct decor. A 16-foot domed ceiling distinguishes the Civil War Room, which has a ten-foot-tall door with silver engraved hinges. ~ 801 Vine Street; 423-265-5000, fax 423-265-5555; www.innjoy.com. ULTRA-DELUXE.

It took the owners nearly two years to get their boutique hotel, the **StoneFort Inn,** ready for occupancy. Since the building is on the National Register of Historic Places, they wanted to maintain as many of the original architectural elements as possible, including arched nooks, heart of pine stairwells, balconies and floors. They must have had fun decorating the 16 guest rooms, some of which have a fireplace, a two-person jet tub and/or a private balcony. Antique chandeliers, custom upholstery and different color schemes (a yummy one has lustrous lemon custard–colored walls) distinguish each stylish accommodation.

AUTHOR FAVORITE

Swimming in the rooftop pool at **The Chattanoogan** is an ideal way to unwind at the end of the day. The hotel is like a mini-resort, complete with exercise facilities, two restaurants and a coffee shop as well as a conference center and day spa. Most of the 202 guest rooms and suites at this five-story property, which opened in 2002, have views of the city's south side and of Lookout Mountain. The Chattanoogan is especially suited to business travelers or others who need a work space and internet access. ~ 1201 South Broad Street; 423-756-3400, 800-619-0018, fax 423-756-3404; www.chattanooganhotel.com, e-mail chattanooganinfo@benchmarkmanagement.com. DELUXE TO ULTRA-DELUXE.

The inn has high-speed Internet connections and a restaurant. ~ 120 East 10th Street; 423-267-7866, 888-945-7866, fax 423-648-7806; www.stonefortinn.com, e-mail contact@stonefortinn.com. DELUXE TO ULTRA-DELUXE.

A convenient place to stop overnight if you're coming from or going to Atlanta, Georgia, the **King's Lodge Inn** provides refrigerators, coffeemakers and cable TV in all 139 rooms, many with views of Lookout Mountain. Twenty-four suites also have microwaves. Special features include a pool and small-pets policy. ~ 2400 Westside Drive; 423-698-8944, 800-251-7702, fax 423-698-8949. BUDGET.

DINING

◄ *HIDDEN*

Unexpectedly romantic, the **Back Inn Cafe** is tucked into the rear quarters of the tony Bluff View Inn. It's especially charming when a moonglade fills the river below with a blanket of silver light. Inside, low-ceilinged, gray-walled rooms are attractive, but more fun (in good weather) are the wrought-iron tables set on three levels outside, warmed with heat lamps. Lamb chops, cioppino and New York strip with polenta and a pungent tapenade are typical entrées. You can also mix and match pizzas, pizzettas and pastas such as a roasted-duck-and-mascarpone-filled sage ravioli. Check out the excellent wine list. ~ 412 East 2nd Street; 423-757-0109, fax 423-757-0120. MODERATE TO DELUXE.

A bocce ball's throw away from the Back Inn Cafe, **Tony's Pasta Shop and Trattoria** is as casual as its neighbor is cool. Pasta, pizza and related fare are served outside on a cozy brick patio, on the covered deck or in the slightly cramped upstairs room inside. ~ 212 High Street; 423-256-5033, ext. 6. BUDGET TO MODERATE.

◄ *HIDDEN*

Virtually the only waterfront restaurant in town, the **Boat House Rotisserie and Raw Bar** specializes in Gulf Coast foods such as oysters, shrimp and po'boys, the classic Louisiana sandwich. The half-dozen entrées, all of which come with olive fries, include wood spit–roasted chicken, brisket, smoked pork and fried seafood. On nice days, there's seating on the deck. Takeout is available. ~ 1011 Riverside Drive; 423-622-0122; www.boat housechattanooga.com, e-mail boathousegrill@comcast.net. BUDGET TO MODERATE.

Sekisui, a second-floor restaurant within view of the Tennessee Aquarium, is a study in restraint, with a quiet color scheme of gray and black. The menu is the usual Japanese-American list except for some offbeat items such as lamb teriyaki. ~ 200 Market Street; 423-267-4600. MODERATE.

Thai Smile is a typically pristine Southeast Asian restaurant, a low-key option half a block from the Tennessee Aquarium. Dozens of appetizers like chicken satay and steamed vegetable rolls can be split among diners or combined for a full meal. Real entrées include ginger chicken, *pad thai* and deep-fried whole duck. Closed Sunday. ~ 219 Market Street; 423-266-2333, fax 423-266-7198. MODERATE.

Housed in a former Coca-Cola building, the **Tortilla Factory** is Tex-Mex to the core. The menu includes fajitas, quesadillas, tacos, burritos—the whole enchilada. The restaurant's claim to fame is its stock of more than 60 tequilas from all over Mexico, which can be enjoyed on the Roof Bar with views of the aquarium and the river. ~ 203 West 2nd Street; 423-756-6399. BUDGET TO MODERATE.

From tasty soups (say, a seafood bisque) to killer desserts, everything at **212 Market Restaurant** receives a knockout presentation on plates specially selected to show it off. Despite plantation shutters and a dusty pink-and-mossy-green color scheme, 212 has a vaguely Southwestern feel, but the cuisine is definitely international, with mango, anchovies, chiles, red peppers and Thai sauces showing up here and there. A regular favorite is the crisply grilled salmon with orange-dill sauce. Six tables on an overhang and another six outside augment the main dining room, where the ceiling is so high there's space for a hanging sculpture of full-sized kites. ~ 212 Market Street; 423-265-1212. DELUXE TO ULTRA-DELUXE.

The elegantly appointed, high-ceilinged room sets the stage for innovative contemporary American cuisine at **Nathan's** in the StoneFort Inn. How innovative? What about pepper-seared rare duck breast with kohlrabi, crisp pancetta and balsamic cherries. How contemporary? Try the line-caught Maine halibut with lemon-rosemary roasted potatoes and a wild mushroom vinaigrette. Other dishes reveal the influence of southern France and northern Italy as do some of the many wine selections. Closed Sunday and Monday. ~ 120 East 10th Street; 423-209-2944. DELUXE TO ULTRA-DELUXE.

The aroma of fresh-baked breads and pastries will perk up the appetites of anyone who comes close to **Panera Bread** for breakfast, lunch or dinner. Soups, sandwiches and salads are available for consumption on the cozy premises or for takeout. ~ 417 Market Street; 423-266-2253, fax 423-266-6289 (second location at 1810 Gunbarrel Road; 423-899-2253). BUDGET.

You've never seen a pizzeria like **Lupi's Pizza Pies**. Located in a former auto parts store and typical of the downtown resurgence, Lupi's has purple walls, a string of leatherette booths in different primary colors and a counter held up with posts made to look like papier-mâché trees. Refreshed by this perky decor, diners can nosh on thin-crust pizzas, calzone, bruschetta and salads that come in various guises. If you're on your own, grab a stool and sit at the counter in the middle. Closed Monday. ~ 406-A Broad Street; 423-266-5874. BUDGET.

The **Broad Street Grille**, far more upscale than its name implies, is an enormous high-ceilinged room with a wall of brick and glass on the ground floor of The Chattanoogan hotel. Try to ignore the groaning boards of a cornucopia of salad ingredients and more than a dozen housemade desserts until you've read the menu. Serious entrées run along the lines of zinfandel-braised short ribs with goat cheese grits, housemade seafood sausage, grilled quail and sautéed jumbo shrimp with a curry-buttermilk sauce. Now: Ready for the double chocolate chip cake? ~ 1201 South Broad Street; 423-424-3700. DELUXE TO ULTRA-DELUXE.

Need to refuel while shopping Warehouse Row or the antique district? Drop by **Mom's Italian** for some homemade lasagna, manicotti, pizza or ravioli, or perhaps just a bowl of minestrone. Mom may not be Italian, but her high-ceilinged, low-key restaurant is. You'll have to clean your plate if you expect to get some of her cheesecake. Oh, and don't dress up or you'll feel out of place in this old brick building with red-and-white tablecloths and slightly peeling paint. Closed Sunday. ~ 1257 Market Street; 423-266-2204. BUDGET.

St. John's Restaurant, located in a restored former hotel lobby, is one of Chattanooga's fanciest dining rooms. Not just because of the decor—lots of Tennessee marble and elaborate molding and capitals evocative of the original space built in 1915—but because of the sophisticated seasonal menu. The chef makes a concerted effort to incorporate local ingredients such as fiddlehead ferns, asparagus, cushaw squash and heirloom tomatoes to accompany foods such as bacon-wrapped monkfish, roasted Sequatchie Cove chicken with gnocchi, Kobe beef flatiron steak and, believe it or not, Broken Arrow Ranch antelope loin. ~ 1278 Market Street; 423-266-4400. DELUXE TO ULTRA-DELUXE.

AUTHOR FAVORITE

Although Chattanooga promotes itself as a family destination, it has more than its share of chic restaurants. My recommendation is the **Southside Grill**, housed in a revamped brick, early-20th-century meatpacking plant. It features service as exquisite as the cuisine. An ambitious menu stars savory dishes such as quail breasts wrapped in maple-cured bacon, grilled pork tenderloin and seasonal specialties. Twosomes may prefer seats in the more intimate side room or, in good weather, at one of the patio tables. Oenophiles should request the separate reserve wine list, one of the best in the state. Closed Sunday. ~ 1400 Cowart Street; 423-266-9211, fax 423-266-0927. DELUXE TO ULTRA-DELUXE.

Get your Memphis-style 'cue right here in Chattanooga at **Smokey's Barbecue**. You can get dry ribs (slow cooked with spices) or wet ribs (with Smokey's special sauce), but these are the most expensive items on the down-home menu. The fresh onion rings, in all sizes, are another specialty that can be devoured here or taken out. There's not much to keep you here—a gray-and-black interior, some sports memorabilia and a counter in the center with a few seats. Look for extra-cheap daily specials in addition to full dinners anchored by beef, chicken or pork shoulder. ~ 3850 Brainerd Road; 423-622-8996. BUDGET TO MODERATE.

HIDDEN ▶

Sushi Nabe of Kyoto looks like just another Denny's-type structure—except for the huge Japanese lanterns flanking the entryway. Not much enlivens the interior other than booths and mismatched Japanese lamps. However, the place offers some real deals on sushi and features other Japanese-style dishes such as tempura and chicken teriyaki, as well as combinations beginning with sashimi. ~ 6921 Lee Highway; 423-899-5049. BUDGET TO MODERATE.

NORTH SHORE DINING   On the other side of the river from the aquarium are a variety of places to eat, from barbecue joints to homey spots, accessible via either the Market Street Bridge or the pedestrian-only Walnut Street Bridge.

From fresh crab to shrimp and oysters (fried, broiled or steamed), the **Northshore Grille** covers the waterfront. More importantly for barbecue fans, they serve pulled barbecue pork and rotisserie-roasted chicken. The menu also includes fried catfish, steak and biscuits and—rare in these parts—vegetable platters. Housed in an old brick building with a tin ceiling, the restaurant bills itself as a "smokin' crab shack and canteen," but it's a lot more upscale than that, despite the bargain prices. ~ 16 Frazier Avenue; 423-757-2000, fax 423-757-0002. BUDGET TO MODERATE.

Although Coca-Cola was introduced in Atlanta, Georgia, in 1886, the first bottling plant was erected in Chattanooga in 1899.

The **Vine Street Bakery** is a popular northside stop just a couple of miles from downtown. The owners concentrate on all-day service of hearty soups, salads and sandwiches (made with house-baked breads) and, at night, gourmet-to-go. The latter include things like casseroles and vegetable lasagne. Closed Sunday. ~ 13113 Hanover Street; 423-266-8463. BUDGET TO MODERATE.

For more than 40 years, **Town & Country** has been the place to go for high-quality home-style cooking. Especially recommended are the baked squash and the corn muffins. Surprisingly for such a casual spot, they also serve cocktails. No lunch Saturday; no dinner Sunday. ~ 110 North Market Street; 423-267-8544. BUDGET.

A wall of snapshots, purportedly of satisfied customers, blocks out the parking lot glare at **Ichiban Japanese Steak House**, situated in an unprepossessing suburban strip mall. Inside, four dining areas are divided, Japanese style, with carved wood partitions. Order something "teppanyaki" and the chef will whirl and flourish his knives as he prepares your meal right before your very eyes. For more excitement, order the flaming shrimp appetizer. Or stick to tradition with beef, steak, chicken or seafood dinners, which can be prepared at an open hibachi in the center of your table. Be sure to say *"arigato"* to the nice man. ~ 5425 Route 153N; 423-875-0404. MODERATE.

Seafood is the specialty at the **Formosa Restaurant,** which clearly has a versatile chef. Cantonese cuisine is available, but the house specialty is Mandarin, Hunan, Szechuan and Shanghai cooking. This is a good place to try something you don't see every day, such as Rose Shrimp (marinated in egg white, served in a white-wine sauce), scallops in five-flavored sauce, whole steamed fish or a mixed seafood platter with lobster, shrimp, sea scallops and king crab. The decor in this three-room restaurant, once you get past the little aquarium (note: don't order puffer fish), is simple, with black-and-white bamboo paintings offsetting dark green carpeting. ~ 5425 Route 153; 423-875-6953. MODERATE.

SHOPPING

Cutting-edge work in various media fill several small rooms at the **River Gallery** in the Bluff View Art District. Sculptures, paintings, textiles and unusual framed pieces vary widely in price, but it's too late in the game for any real steals in the folk art department; most of the regional artists who dominate this gallery have already earned reputations beyond Tennessee's borders. The gallery also represents national and international artists. ~ 214 Spring Street; 423-267-7353.

Head to the south side if you're in the market for antiques. The area around Broad and 14th streets has a number of shops. Among the most elegant is **Antiques on the Southside,** which specializes in 18th- and 19th-century American, French and English furniture as well as decorative accessories, silver, linen and glassware. Closed Monday. ~ 1401-C Williams Street; 423-265-3003.

High Point Antiques is the place to check out if you need lighting fixtures to accessorize an old home, especially if you're looking for restored antique chandeliers. Closed Sunday. ~ 1704 Cummings Highway; 423-756-9566.

Fly fishermen flock to **Feather & Fly** for equipment as well as accessories such as boots and sunglasses. The shop also offers guided trips and instruction, including fly-tying classes. ~ 2401 Broad Street; 423-265-0306.

Everything for the kitchen—except the proverbial sink—is for sale at **Mia Cucina,** known for its quality cookware. ~ 307 North Market Street; 423-265-4474.

NORTH SHORE SHOPPING   You'll find interesting shops along Frazier Avenue. New Age books, music and accessories are the stock in trade at the **New Moon Gallery**. ~ 36 Frazier Avenue; 423-265-6321. If you're planning any serious outdoor activities, especially on the river, check out the outerwear at **Rock Creek Outfitters**. ~ 100 Tremont Street; 423-265-5969. The **In-Town Gallery** features original paintings, jewelry, photography, pottery, clay and metal sculptures and other craftwork. ~ 26-A Frazier Avenue; 423-267-9214.

Out toward Hixson, one complex in particular offers one-stop shopping. Ceramics, textiles, regional crafts, mugs, vases and jewelry make **The Plum Nelly** the best of the lot, especially if you are in the market for a bread-and-butter gift. The Plum Nelly tradition originated in 1947 at an outdoor art show held in a backyard on Lookout Mountain. The spirit—and the name, which comes from the phrase "plum out of Georgia and 'nelly' out of Tennessee" (we swear)—lives on in this all-American crafts store. Closed Sunday. ~ 515 Tremont Street; 423-266-0585.

SIGNAL MOUNTAIN SHOPPING   The **Flowering Pot** has four cottage-style rooms packed with pots, sculptures, fountains, birdhouses and even homes for bees, butterflies and ladybugs. ~ 1904 Taft Highway; 423-886-9246.

Collectors of ceramics should check out **Mole Hill Pottery**, which sells a variety of dishes, kitchen accessories and decorative pieces. ~ 1210 Taft Highway; 423-886-5636.

NIGHTLIFE   To find out what's going on around Chattanooga, check with the 24-hour **Arts Line** for details on performances at various venues, as well as for appearances by the Chattanooga Symphony and Opera. ~ 423-756-2787.

The Chattanooga Symphony, touring performers and local groups are presented at the fabulously restored 1920s **Tivoli Theater**, the so-called Jewel of the South, which is on the National Register of Historic Places. ~ 709 Broad Street; 423-757-5042.

AUTHOR FAVORITE

I always find incredible bargains at the **Warehouse Row Factory Shops**, one of the best—and most attractive—outlet malls in the southeastern U.S. You can find deep discounts at the likes of Ralph Lauren Polo, Tommy Hilfiger, Ellen Tracy, Kasper, Izod and Geoffrey Beene, and more than 30 other stores. The handsome interiors feature barewood floors and gleaming brass railings, housed in a complex of eight abandoned railway warehouses only a credit card's throw from the Chattanooga Choo Choo. ~ 1110 Market Street; 423-267-1111, 888-260-7620; www.primeoutlets.com.

From award-winning dramas such as *Driving Miss Daisy* to new local works to children's productions, the **Chattanooga Theatre Centre** offers a full season, capped by holiday specials at the end of the year. ~ 400 River Street; 423-267-8534; www.theatre center.com.

You've probably never seen a place like **Rhythm and Blues**, a piano bar that features regular comedy acts on the keys, including Jerry Lee Lewis–style piano rolls. On Wednesday and Thursday, other entertainment includes solo or rock performers and on Friday and Saturday, various bands play hits from the '50s to the '90s. Closed Monday and Tuesday. Cover. ~ 221 Market Street; 423-267-4644.

Head upstairs to the **Comedy Catch**, where most nights start with local comedians opening for bigger names, including folks who've cracked up crowds on HBO and the "David Letterman Show." Sunday is usually open-mic night. Arrive early (8 p.m.) and grab a little dinner at the Giggles Grill. Cover. ~ 3324 Brainerd Road; 423-622-2233.

SIGNAL MOUNTAIN NIGHTLIFE   Unless you're heading to deep Appalachia, you're unlikely to find as good a spot for bluegrass music as the **Mountain Opry**. It happens on Friday night, is good old-fashioned fun and is free (although you should follow everyone else's lead and drop a little something in the hat). ~ Walden Ridge Civic Center, 2501 Fairmount Park; 423-886-3252.

ROSS LANDING PARK AND PLAZA   Ross Landing Park and Plaza is so much part of the landscape that you almost have to be told it's there. Within it are the Tennessee Aquarium and the Chattanooga Area Convention & Visitors Bureau, but they are only part of the story. Essentially the park is an environmental piece of art, incorporating culture, history, commercialism and nature through a series of landscaped "bands" representing points in time. The closer to the river, the older the band. Look for the cornerstone at Band 131 denoting the 1815 founding of the original settlement by John and Lewis Ross at this very site. The entry arches are planted with ash, birch and evergreen trees characteristic of mountain forests; another band is a bridge encrusted with bottle bottoms referring to the fact that Coca-Cola's first bottling plant was established in Chattanooga; farther north are moldings of Civil War relics, stones etched with Cherokee clan names, replicas of Creek Indian neck ornaments and so forth. Facilities are limited to restrooms. ~ 100 Broad Street.

PARKS

TENNESSEE RIVERPARK   The Tennessee Riverpark is still under development; so far there is an eight-mile trail along the Tennessee River where you can bicycle, run or walk, or head for the picnic areas, playground and fishing piers. Along the way you'll probably see plenty of wildlife: bluebirds, butterflies, frogs, wood ducks and sometimes great blue herons, and after sunset, screech owls, raccoons and the occasional bat. Eventually the trail will extend 22 miles from the Chickamauga Dam to Moccasin Bend. ~ 4301 Amnicola Highway, Route 58; 423-493-9244, 423-842-0177.

Within Tennessee Riverpark, Coolidge Park features a fully re-stored antique Denzel carousel with 52 carved animals—leaping tigers, stylish frogs, iridescent fish, and friendly dinosaurs—arranged in three rows.

BOOKER T. WASHINGTON STATE PARK 🏃 🏊 🚤 🛥 One of two parks on the south shore of Chickamauga Lake, this 353-acre park is a little closer to downtown Chattanooga than its neighbor to the northeast, Harrison Bay State Park. Facilities include a concession building, fields for soccer and frisbee, hiking trails, a swimming pool and a volleyball court, as well as a short fishing pier. Day-use fee, $3. ~ From downtown Chattanooga, head out Route 58, which runs to the northeast toward Decatur. It's at 5801 Champion Road; 423-894-4955, 866-836-6757.

▲ There are no facilities for individuals to camp overnight, but there is a group camp lodge with a kitchen, which can accommodate up to 40 overnight guests. There is also a group camp that accommodates up to 96 people; closed November through April.

HARRISON BAY STATE PARK 🚲 🏊 🚤 🛥 When the Tennessee River flooded the old town of Harrison northeast of Chattanooga, it also covered the last Cherokee Campground, three villages once ruled by Chief Joe Vann. Today, this 1200-acre site on the south side of Chickamauga Lake is well equipped for both day use and overnight camping. You can pick up something at the snack bar, have lunch in the restaurant, turn the kids loose in the playground, buy food at the grocery store and cook it on the grill, play tennis and swim in the lake or a swimming pool. Facilities include restrooms, marina, picnic tables, picnic shelter and showers. Day-use fee, $3. ~ Located 24 miles north of Chattanooga; take Route 153 to Route 58, then go 12 miles to the lake; 423-344-6214, 866-836-6757.

▲ There are 174 campsites, some with water and electric hookup; $11 per night for tents only; $17.25 for RVs.

Lookout Mountain

Lookout Mountain, the site of one of the Civil War's most crucial battles, is also the best place in town to catch a view. You can ride the Incline Railway to the top, or drive up the hairpin-curve roads that are usually jam-packed in summer. At the base of Lookout Mountain, the St. Elmo neighborhood claims more than 600 properties on

the National Historic Register, one of the largest such districts in
the United States.

Broad Street leads south from the river to Route 41, where
you turn off for both the Battles for Chattanooga Museum and,
just down the road, the street to the Incline Railway.

Take Broad Street south of Central Chattanooga, through a section of town that includes fast-food franchises (and the occasional
barbecue joint) and auto repair shops, following the signs for Lookout Mountain. Broad Street heads south of the river to Route 41
just before it turns right at the curve in the river known as Moccasin Bend. This is where you turn off for the Battles for Chattanooga Museum and for the street that leads to the Incline Railway.

The **St. Elmo neighborhood**, located at the foot of Lookout
Mountain, flourished with the expansion of the electric trolley line.
The Chattanooga Area Convention & Visitors Bureau distributes
free St. Elmo neighborhood tour maps, which lead architectural
buffs past such attractions as the neoclassical revival **Judge Gavin
House**, circa 1912. ~ 121 Ochs Highway.

The **Mayor Seagle's House** is a multilevel Victorian home with
beveled glass at the front door and cobblestone fencing all around.
~ 4701 Tennessee Avenue.

The **Forest Hills Cemetery** is where members of some of the
city's wealthiest families have been buried over the past century,
in graves marked with a great variety of tombstone styles. ~ 4016
Tennessee Avenue.

The **Battles for Chattanooga Museum** is a Civil War buff's
idea of heaven on earth. Formerly called Confederama, this simple museum has a large-scale model of the areas where five major
battles—including the surprise assault at Brown's Ferry, the
Battle Above the Clouds and General Sherman's attack on Missionary Ridge—were fought during the War Between the States.
During a half-hour narration, different colored bulbs are lit to
indicate the points of engagement. Admission. ~ 1110 East Brow
Road, just outside of Point Park on top of Lookout Mountain;
423-821-2812; www.battlesforchattanooga.com.

A couple of blocks farther south on Ochs Highway, look for
the turnoff for the Incline Railway.

Lookout Mountain is the kind of attraction you read about
on billboards for miles around. But who needs billboards? You
can actually see the mountain from miles away. And vice-versa.
From the mountaintop on a clear day, you can see all the way to
the Great Smoky Mountains, some 200 miles away. The half-mile-
long **Lookout Mountain Incline Railway** runs two cars up the steep
side of the 2100-foot mountain at a 38° angle, except at the very
top, when the rate of incline is 72°, although you may suspect it's

even steeper than that. Two simple cable cars tote thousands of passengers (and even local commuters who live at the prestigious Lookout Mountain address) at the rate of 10 mph. A car departs about every 15 to 20 minutes, but by mid-morning the lines can be long, so get there early or you'll have to while away the wait slurping ice cream (surprisingly good ice cream, at that) from the vendor in the station. Once you arrive at the top, allow time for visiting Point Park and maybe strolling through the residential neighborhood, established almost a century ago as a summer resort getaway. Admission. ~ The termini are at 827 East Brow Road and 3917 St. Elmo Avenue, Lookout Mountain; 423-821-4224; www.lookoutmtnattractions.com.

In 1998 the **Tennessee Civil War Museum** opened across the street from the Incline Railway depot. Its mission: to honor the common soldier. Instead of focusing on officers, as many museums do, this one focuses on the enlisted man—his exploits, hardships, valor and struggle for survival. Uniformed mannequins, bayonets, batons, canteens and other artifacts convey the story of both Federal and Confederate soldiers. There are beautifully mounted exhibits on black Confederates, signal decoding and specialty troops, plus several interactive displays and an 11-minute multimedia presentation that purports to be steadfastly non-partisan. Admission. ~ 3914 St. Elmo Avenue; 423-821-4954; www.tncivil warmuseum.com.

On the far side of Lookout Mountain are two of Chattanooga's top attractions—the first one famous with tourists, the second a beloved local site. To reach them, you must return to Route 41 and follow it another mile or so beside the river until you spy the turnoff for the Scenic Highway. The only way to see **Ruby Falls Caverns** is to take the hour-long guided tour that leads some 1100 feet inside Lookout Mountain (accessible by elevator), where you are rewarded with the sight of a 145-foot-high waterfall. The falls aren't actually red; they were named for the wife of the man who discovered them. The caverns have calcite formations that will particularly fascinate school-age children who have never before been inside a deep cave. The Lookout Mountain Caverns were used as hideouts by American Indians as well as various outlaws over the centuries, and as camping grounds for both Union and Confederate troops during the Civil War. Try to arrive when the gates open at 8 a.m. in the high season, and allow time for coffee or a snack on the patio. Consider saving this excursion for hot, cold or rainy days when you don't want to be out and about too much. Admission. ~ 1720 South Scenic Highway, Lookout Mountain; 423-821-2544; www.ruby falls.com.

Half a mile farther up Ruby Falls is the turnoff to the **Cravens House**. Built in 1856 by an ironsmith, Robert Cravens, the two-story white-clapboard home commands a view of the river and surrounding countryside. It was temporary headquarters for Confederate Brigadier General Edward C. Walthall, before the Union Army drove out the rebels during the Battle Above the Clouds. Today, the home and its relics are the centerpiece of this historical site, which includes cannons and other memorials. Guided half-hour tours are available. Closed Labor Day to mid-June. Admission. ~ Off Route 148; 423-821-7786.

Return to Route 41, turn left and drive for another mile or two until you see the turnoff for Alford Hill Road, and get ready for a real treat.

Most visitors are probably perplexed when they hear locals talk about **Reflection Riding Arboretum and Botanical Garden.** ◄HIDDEN
Like a lot of great ideas, this one is beautiful in its simplicity: a 375-acre nature preserve you can tour in the comfort of your own car. Trees and wildflowers, ducks and horses, the mountainside and reflecting ponds can also be toured on foot. However, it's a treat, sort of a meditation, just to drive slowly through, spending 30 minutes or so driving three miles—during which it's just about impossible not to relax, appreciate nature and be, well, reflective. Signs along the one-lane, one-way road indicate some of the species of plant life, including more than 300 species of wildflower and 1000 species of native trees. Amid this bucolic splendor, it should be remembered that key battles have been fought in this area. Cherokee Chief Dragging Canoe lost to John Sevier's militia here following the Revolutionary War, and the Union Army scored a significant victory during the Battle of Chattanooga during the Civil War. Admission. ~ 400 Garden Road; 423-821-9582; www.reflectionriding.org.

AUTHOR FAVORITE

sights   I know it sounds weird, but a visit to the **Raccoon Mountain Pumped Storage Facility** is really worth a detour. Located about a ten-minute drive up Route 41 from Lookout Mountain, this is the best place to learn how the TVA accesses and pumps water from the river to be used when the demand for electricity peaks. Highlights include a high-speed elevator descent 1160 feet into the limestone mountain and a look at the massive hydraulic generators, all painted in bright primary colors in a setting that looks right out of a James Bond movie. Last tour begins at 3 p.m. (There are some picnic tables scattered around the reservoir, but no recreational facilities.) ~ Off Route 41 or off Route 24; 423-825-3100; www.tva.com.

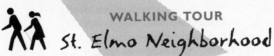

With more than 600 properties on the National Historic Register, this area at the foot of Lookout Mountain offers a pleasant look at early-20th-century architecture, with styles ranging from Spanish Revival to ornate Victorian, as well as some sites that afford a glimpse into the city's history. Zoom up the Lookout Mountain Incline for an overview of this neighborhood, then get ready to take an easy stroll through St. Elmo. For a map and more details, contact the **Chattanooga Area Convention & Visitors Bureau.** ~ 2 Broad Street; 800-322-3344.

MING TOY SHOP HOUSE   Head to your right on St. Elmo Avenue after visiting the Incline Railway and check out the Ming Toy Shop House, built in the early 1900s in Spanish Revival style. ~ 4102 St. Elmo Avenue. Also on this block between 41st and 42nd streets are private residences with Victorian and Neoclassical trim, surrounded by gardens.

ST. ELMO FIRE STATION   Continue down St. Elmo Avenue, cross 45th Street, and on your right will be the St. Elmo Fire Station, a Tudor-revival, multicolored brick structure that was built around 1934 and sports a red board-and-batten door trimmed with heavy black iron work braces. ~ 4501 St. Elmo Avenue.

ST. ELMO PUBLIC SCHOOL   Stop at the corner of 47th Street; on your right is the St. Elmo Public School. The original red brick structure cannot be seen from the front, so try to take a peek.

MAYOR SEAGLE'S HOUSE   Turn left onto 47th Street and go three blocks until this street melds with Tennessee Avenue. On your right will be a

The pint-size **Tennessee Wildlife Center at Reflection Riding** lets children get up close to raccoons, snakes and raptors on a regular basis, or sign up for canoeing, owl prowls or other special programs. Admission. ~ 400 Garden Road; 423-821-1160; www.tnwildlifecenter.org.

Raccoon Mountain lies north of the Tennessee River Gorge, accessible via Route 27 and Route 41; getting there and back takes about 30 minutes, if you don't make any stops.

Open year-round, **Raccoon Mountain Caverns** offers daily 45-minute walking tours of the Crystal Palace in June and July. Wild cave expeditions are also available, but involve quite a bit of hiking, stooping, crawling and sliding along the way. Adventurers should wear old clothes—long pants and long-sleeved shirts and sturdy shoes with tread—but can borrow helmets, lights, gloves and kneepads. Admission. ~ 319 West Hills Drive, Signal Moun-

fascinating structure, the Mayor Seagle's House, built around 1910 and featuring many levels, nooks and crannies typical of Victorian homes of the era. Note the cobblestone fencing along both streets. ~ 4701 Tennessee Avenue.

JENKINS HOUSE Continue three more blocks on Tennessee Avenue to see the Jenkins House, an asymmetrical Queen Anne with a side veranda. ~ 5201 Tennessee Avenue.

HENDERSON HOUSE Walk another block to see the late-19th-century Henderson House, one of the oldest homes in the district. Check out the ornate ironwork vents in the fountain. ~ 5310 Tennessee Avenue.

GILLESPIE HOUSE Loop back to St. Elmo Avenue by turning right at the first street after the Henderson House and crossing Georgia Avenue; turn right on St. Elmo Avenue and look to your left. Here is the Gillespie House, a prime example of Dutch Colonial style that has a second-story porch on the north side and half-moon motifs on the board-and-batten shutters. ~ 5201 St. Elmo Avenue.

FOREST HILLS CEMETERY Return to 47th Street and take a right on Alabama Avenue, where a number of notable houses are lined up on the right side of the street. Walk all the way back to 41st Street, turn right and cross Tennessee Avenue. Here you will find Forest Hills Cemetery, where members of many of Chattanooga's oldest and wealthiest families have been laid to rest to rest since the 1880s. ~ 4016 Tennessee Avenue.

tain; 423-821-9403, 800-823-2267; www.raccoonmountain.com, e-mail raccoon1@raccoonmountain.com.

LODGING

One of the few accommodations in Chattanooga featuring riverfront balconies, the ten-room **Sky Harbor Bavarian Inn** is right around the corner from Ruby Falls. Decor is pared-down Bavarian: white panel walls, hardwood floors, and clothing racks instead of closets. A special feature is the private balcony off each room and suite, furnished with rocking chairs and tables and separated from the river below only by a carved wooden balcony and a couple hundred yards of fresh air. Eight rooms and two suites are divided among three buildings. Suites come with kitchenettes. There's also a two-bedroom, two-bath condo suited for families. ~ 2159 Old Wauhatchie Pike; 423-821-8619, fax 423-825-1184. BUDGET TO DELUXE.

HIDDEN ►

On the back side of Lookout Mountain, just down the Scenic Highway from Ruby Falls, the **Alford House** is a three-story brick B&B perched on a modest point of land. The public areas—living and dining rooms—are filled with what's known as "Victorian clutter," the owner's collection of glass baskets, porcelain dolls, teddy bears and other knickknacks. The three rooms upstairs are painted in varying shades of intense pastels and decorated with antiques and lace curtains. One is a two-room honeymoon suite with a heart-shaped jacuzzi. Guests are welcome to join in a healthy light breakfast weekdays and a full breakfast weekends. ~ 5515 Alford Hill Drive; 423-821-7625; www.bedandbreadfast.com. MODERATE TO DELUXE.

In the years following the Lookout Mountain Incline Railway's inauguration in 1911, the cars were powered by steam, but now they run on a cable system.

DINING

In a neighborhood chockablock with fast food outlets, you'll find **Mount Vernon** a blast from the past, the kind of place where the Kiwanis mix with ladies-who-lunch in a series of four dining rooms, each with its distinct decor. And they've been doing it since 1954, here at the foot of Lookout Mountain. Older ladies seem to prefer the garden room, which has glass tabletops and white linens, while the working class crowds into the clubby front rooms. Fresh seafood, chicken and plenty of vegetable choices are found on this traditional Southern menu. Closed Sunday. ~ 3509 South Broad Street; 423-266-6591, fax 423-266-4216. MODERATE TO DELUXE.

PARKS

POINT PARK Just a two-plus-block walk from the top of the Lookout Mountain Incline Railway is Point Park. It's a great introduction to Tennessee's many Civil War sites. The smaller of two visitors centers for the 8000-acre Chickamauga and Chattanooga National Military Park (headquartered just over the Georgia state line), this huge, sloping park is the oldest and largest military park in the country. The battles fought here, and the soldiers who fought them, are explained in simple exhibits in the modest Ochs Museum, down a walkway and a couple of flights of stairs. There are no facilities here. Admission. ~ 1101 East Brow Road, Lookout Mountain; 423-821-7786. The park can also be reached by automobile by taking Route 148 and driving up the back side of Lookout Mountain to East Brow Road. The main entrance is down the road in Georgia at the Chickamauga Battlefield off Route 27 south of Fort Oglethorpe.

REFLECTION RIDING ARBORETUM AND BOTANICAL GARDEN
🏃 Whether visited by car or by foot, Reflection Riding is a beloved local attraction that offers 375 acres of peace and quiet, animals such as ducks and horses and over 1000 species of plant

life, which include more than 300 species of wildflower. There's also history to be savored here: after the Revolutionary War, John Sevier's militia victored over Cherokee Chief Dragging Canoe and his crew; during the Civil War, the Union army also gained a significant victory during the Battle of Chattanooga. If you're driving out from downtown Chattanooga, stop at one of the drive-through barbecue joints and get something messy to eat in the car. Slowly driving the three miles through this nature preserve is a super stress-buster, since you won't be encountering any traffic lights. Facilities are limited to restrooms. Admission. ~ 400 Garden Road; 423-821-9582; www.reflectionriding.org.

▼▼▼▼▼▼▼▼▼▼▼▼▼

Chattanooga Area

Once you're out of the Chattanooga city limits, you're in the country. Small towns like Soddy-Daisy, Dayton and Monteagle seem to exist in an earlier era. Monteagle and Sewanee are a straight shot up Route 24, unless you prefer the longer, more scenic Route 41, which goes through Tracy City. However, taking Route 24 gives you an idea of Tennessee's grandeur; there's a dramatic uphill grade just south of the exits for Monteagle. You can access Route 24 right from downtown Chattanooga; the exits are about half an hour from Lookout Mountain.

SIGHTS

Driving to **Dayton** is not going to be the highlight of your trip to Tennessee, except for the last mile of the trip, through the leafy town itself. Take Route 27 north from downtown Chattanooga (the last exit in town is just west of the Tennessee Aquarium at 3rd Street), drive for about 40 minutes (the road narrows as you approach Dayton) and take the first exit for Dayton.

The town of Dayton has an amazingly high name recognition, especially for a place with fewer than 6000 residents. That's because of the famous Scopes trial, held in the Rhea County Courthouse in the summer of 1925. The trial is re-enacted each summer during a four-day festival, the only big event in Dayton besides the annual Strawberry Festival each May, when the world's largest strawberry shortcake is produced along with fireworks and parades. For more information about the town and other Scopes trial–related sites, visit the **Rhea County Economic and Tourism Council**. ~ 107 Main Street, Dayton; 423-775-6171; www.rhea countyetc.com.

Many years after one of the most famous trials of the century, you can still sit in the very courtroom where the Scopes trial was argued. The 1891 **Rhea County Courthouse** has a museum on the lower level, but if you know anything about William Jennings Bryan, Clarence Darrow and the Monkey Trial (immortalized in the movie with Spencer Tracy, *Inherit the Wind*), just sitting in the courtroom is a moving experience. John Scopes was a high-school biology teacher who stood trial in 1925 for teaching evolution. Bryan prosecuted the case, while Darrow volunteered his services for the defense. The story of the trial, the forces at work, the guilty verdict and local history are told in the **Scopes Trial Museum** exhibits. Although Dayton may not have changed drastically since the trial, there are few other sites that recall the events that captivated the nation, drawing some 10,000 spectators to tiny Dayton (1925 population: 2000) and sensationalizing a schism still unresolved in Tennessee. Closed weekends. ~ 1475 Market Street, Dayton; 423-775-7801.

Heading northwest from Chattanooga on Route 24, you'll soon approach **Monteagle**, where the Monteagle Chatauqua Assembly has been a summer getaway favorite among Chattanoogans for most of the past century. The surrounding town (population about 1000) provides services such as grocery stores, but the focus is on families in this tree-lined enclave.

HIDDEN ▶

You don't have to own a home there to visit the **Monteagle Assembly Grounds**, though you may wish you did. For the past century, Chattanoogans have been flocking to this hilltop retreat less than an hour out of town. In summer, some just want to escape the muggy weather, but there's more to this enclave than fresh mountain air (it rests at 1238 feet). It was established as an interdenominational retreat, a center of culture, learning and, to some extent, physical well-being. Today, the ten-week summer season is open to anyone interested in various lecturers and speakers (topics are usually related to religion) or even in just using the tennis courts or the pool. Plenty of Victorian homes, lots of shade trees and slow, if any, traffic make this one of the most appealing getaways in Tennessee. It's fun simply to take a short driving tour, by asking for a map at the gate. There is also a bed-and-breakfast inn on the grounds. Admission. ~ Route 41A/74, Monteagle; 931-924-2286.

AUTHOR FAVORITE

Whether you're staying in Monteagle or passing through on Route 24, it's easy to find **Monteagle Wine Cellars** on the west side of the interstate. Vineyards were thriving in Tennessee in the late 19th century, many of them in places no one had believed arable. Prohibition put a dent in the industry and it was 1973 before the Tennessee Viticultural and Oenological Society was established. Monteagle opened 14 years later and now produces 18 varieties, some of which you can taste here. ~ Route 41/64, Monteagle; 931-924-2120, 800-556-9463.

Heading west and uphill on Route 41A, you will come to the old college town of **Sewanee** in a little under six miles. This is home to the prestigious **University of the South**, which everyone calls Sewanee (pronounced "swa-nee," not as in "way down upon the 'swa-NEE' river"). The Gothic sandstone buildings here were inspired by those in the British university towns of Oxford and Cambridge. At the stone gate, turn right onto a street that becomes University Avenue. Go one and a third miles to see the 1907-era All Saints Chapel, which has remarkable stained glass and a huge pipe organ; the 56-bell Leonidas Polk Memorial Carillion is in the chapel's Shapard Tower. This is a good place to find a parking space if you want to amble around the campus, established in 1857 on this mountaintop, a location considered safely above the the the so-called malaria line. Sewanee, founded as an Episcopal university (still owned by 28 dioceses of the church), now enrolls some 1300 liberal arts undergraduates and nearly 100 graduate students in theology. Other sights include the University View, where a large cross looks down from the Cumberland Plateau, the Green's View overlook and, for a meditative moment, the Abbott Martin Ravine Gardens, where little stone bridges cross a babbling brook, goldfish frolic in ponds, wildflowers blossom in spring and summer and benches provide a place to take it all in. Guided tours are available. ~ 735 University Avenue, Sewanee; 931-598-1286.

Encompassing a hunk of real estate between Chattanooga and Nashville, the 16,000-acre **South Cumberland State Recreation Area** sprawls northeast of Monteagle. This grand wilderness area boasts seven separate areas loaded with natural wonders. Get yourself oriented at the visitors center before heading out.

The **South Cumberland State Park Visitors Center**, headquarters for the South Cumberland State Recreation Area, offers maps and trail information. You can also check out a number of interpretive exhibits here. In all, there are eight distinct areas within the South Cumberland park region. ~ About three miles northeast of Monteagle on Route 56; 931-924-2980.

From the visitors center heading southeast along Route 41, you'll first come across the **Grundy Lakes State Park** area, the site of the Lone Rock Coke Ovens. They were constructed in 1873 and used for making coke out of locally mined coal.

Grundy Forest State Natural Area, around 212 acres, is the northern access point for the 13-mile Fiery Gizzard Trail. There are two primitive campsites along this trail.

South of Grundy Forest is **Foster Falls**, a small wild area. There are two ways to get a view of the 60-foot cascade of water. Hike in from the Grundy Forest State Natural Area, which will consume at least a day, or drive practically to the overlook. To reach

Text continued on page 176.

The Scopes "Monkey" Trial

It was a hot July day, even for the South, in 1925. The oppressive temperatures only heightened the pressures on two lawyers who helped make the trial of John Thomas Scopes a national cause célèbre. The closely watched court event achieved such notoriety that it has been known ever since as the Scopes "Monkey" trial, though it had nothing to do with monkeys, per se (although one was brought to the courthouse), and not all that much to do with Scopes himself.

Earlier in the year, the Tennessee legislature passed a law prohibiting schools and universities that received public funds from teaching theories contrary to the theory of divine creation as told in the Bible. Senator John Washington Butler, a Lafayette farmer, sponsored the bill, which its supporters claimed stemmed not from a conflict between religion and science, but from an opposition to compulsory state-sponsored public education. These kinds of issues were not new to the Deep South, nor were they resolved in the trial.

The American Civil Liberties Union (ACLU) saw things differently. It wanted to test what it perceived as an anti-evolution law and advertised for a human guinea pig. John Scopes, a coach as well as a teacher of math (and occasionally biology) at Rhea Central High School, volunteered.

Prompted by a group of leading Dayton residents, Scopes signed on to help the ACLU challenge the state law and quickly found himself charged with the teaching of evolution. Historians don't entirely agree whether Scopes ever actually taught evolution, but that issue was beside the point. Who can say whether the trial would have attained the circus-like atmosphere it did had it not been for the high profiles of the two lawyers recruited to debate the case—Clarence Darrow and William Jennings Bryan. Their celebrity attracted the attention of the major Eastern newspapers, which built the trial up as "the media event of the century." (Well, it *was* only 1925, too early to predict the O. J. Simpson trials.) Some 200 journalists from around the world jammed the second-floor courtroom at the 1891 Rhea County Courthouse to witness and report on the spectacle.

The crowds were so large—including local citizens as well as scientists and theologians—that some had to sit on the wide window ledges, deep-set into foot-thick walls. Eighteen enormous windows reach for the black, pressed-tin ceiling of the room, restored in 1979 and still in use today. The courtroom is extremely impressive, with rows of wooden chairs linked in black wrought iron, high-back leather chairs in the jury box set on its own platform and finally the judge's bench—the original—before which the merits of the case were argued.

Clarence Darrow, who volunteered his services for the defense (Scopes and the ACLU), was the most prominent defense lawyer in the country at the time. William Jennings Bryan, a silver-tongued orator who had run three times for president, been elected to Congress and served as secretary of state under Woodrow Wilson, was appointed prosecutor. The two had met before at the 1896 Democratic convention, the one that gave Bryan the first of his nominations. Darrow had been so impressed with Bryan's populism that he supported two of his later presidential bids. All affinity ended, however, when the issue on the table was religion. Darrow was an agnostic who thought religion had no place in government, while Bryan believed the law should specifically reflect Christian fundamentalism. "Government is manmade and therefore imperfect," he said, explaining away the conflict between his progressive politics and fundamentalist beliefs. "It can always be improved. But religion is not a manmade affair . . . I am satisfied with the God we have, with the Bible and with Christ."

Perhaps one reason the atmosphere surrounding the trial came to be described as "circuslike" stemmed from the presence of revival tents that were put up around the courthouse square by supporters of Bryan, the Bible and the new state law. Hot-dog stands and lemonade vendors catered to the crowds in and around the courthouse. In fact, the heat became so unbearable that the court was reconvened in a shady spot on the courthouse lawn in an attempt to stave off heat prostration.

The blistering debates, pitting the claims of the Bible against Darwinian theory, culminated in Darrow's historic cross-examination of Bryan. Testifying as an expert witness on the Bible, Bryan said under oath that he believed in the literal interpretation of the Bible, but became enraged when Darrow asked if each day of the creation lasted only 24 hours. Despite these histrionics, after eight days of trial Scopes was found guilty and fined $100. The news was immediately spread on the radio, making history as the first nationwide live trial broadcast, on July 21, 1925. Scopes, upon hearing the verdict, stood in court to declare, "I will continue to oppose this law. Any other action would be in violation of my ideal of academic freedom to teach the truth as guaranteed in our constitution."

As an anticlimax, the Tennessee Supreme Court eventually reversed the conviction on a technicality. The trial, with a few convenient instances of poetic license, was immortalized in the book *Inherit the Wind*, later made into a film starring Spencer Tracy in the Darrow role.

The Scopes Evolution Trial, as it is also known, has also been preserved in a regional festival held each summer in Dayton, where local residents perform in a two-hour play based on actual transcripts. For authenticity, the four-day "trial" is held in late July.

the parking lot, head to Tracy City from Monteagle via Route 41, turn right at the second traffic light, and continue seven and a half miles, then turn left. From the parking lot, it's about a 120-yard walk, part of which is via a footbridge that crosses the gorge, to a spot where you can view the spectacular display. For more details, contact the South Cumberland State Recreation Area in Monteagle; 931-924-2980.

Each July, students from local Bryan College re-enact portions of the Scopes Monkey trial. Admission. ~ 423-775-7206.

North of the South Cumberland State Park Visitors Center via Route 56 is the ranger station at Stone Door in the **Savage Gulf State Natural Area**. These 11,500 acres are awash with timber, waterfalls and trails. Within them are the Great Stone Door, a 150-foot-deep crevice at the crest of the Cumberland Plateau, and Laurel Falls. ~ The Savage Gulf Ranger Station is on the east side of the natural area; you can reach it by turning east off Route 56 north of Tracy onto Route 108. Turn left (north) on Route 399.

On the other side of Route 24, take Route 41 to the intersection with Route 56 at Sewanee (a little over six miles) to visit these other attractions:

Within the **Carter State Natural Area** is Lost Cove Cave, which can be reached via a two-mile hike along the Buggytop Trail.

The main attraction at the **Sewanee Natural Bridge State Natural Area** is the 27-foot-high Sewanee Natural Bridge, which overlooks the Lost Cove.

The 244-acre **Hawkins Cove Natural Area** was set aside to preserve the rare Cumberland Rosin weed. It is currently undeveloped, but future plans call for trails and a picnic area, as well as a paved parking lot.

LODGING

HIDDEN ►

The **Adams Edgeworth Inn** celebrated its centennial in 1996 and it has just about perfected the concept of relaxed privacy for its guests. It's a huge old family house, with 11 accommodations ranging from the Quilt Room, decorated with handmade family quilts from the innkeeper's grandmother and mother, to the Dutch Blue Room, which has a pencil post bed, views of the village and blue Delft tile walls, as well as an antique footed Victorian bathtub. The three suites are spacious (one has a kitchen) and all the rooms are decorated with antiques. There's also a restaurant. ~ Monteagle Assembly, Monteagle; 931-924-4000, 877-352-9466, fax 931-924-3236; www.relaxinn.com, e-mail innjoy@blomand. net. DELUXE TO ULTRA-DELUXE.

The simple but somewhat dark rooms at the two-story **Smokehouse Lodge** are a bargain. Conveniently located on the west side of Route 24, the restaurant and lodge (now part of the Best Western empire) are less than six miles from Sewanee, and only a couple of miles from Monteagle. The South Cumberland State Recreation Area is also nearby. There are 98 budget-priced accommodations in the main lodge (a restaurant is on the ground floor) and 14 one- and two-bedroom moderate-priced cabins in the rear. ~ Route 41/64 west of Exit 134 off Route 24, near Monteagle; 931-924-2091, 800-489-2091, fax 931-924-3175; www.thesmokehouse.com. MODERATE TO DELUXE.

DINING

The **Home Folks Restaurant** is the real McCoy—Southern cooking and Southern hospitality, country style. Don't expect anyone to fawn over you at this simple roadside spot. People come here for one reason and one reason only: to eat lots of good food from a buffet in the middle of a homespun room. You'll find an array of five meats, 20 vegetables and as much banana cream pudding or brownie cake as you can handle, all for peanuts. Best of all, you don't have to take off your baseball cap. No dinner on Sunday. Closed Monday. ~ 8981 Dayton Pike, Soddy-Daisy; 423-332-5724. BUDGET.

The **Dining Room** at the Adams Edgeworth Inn serves prix-fixe dinners, with a choice of five courses Wednesday through Saturday and three courses Sunday through Tuesday. Typical entrées include herbed rack of lamb, filet mignon with a portobello-bourbon sauce, grilled salmon with basil cream and macadamia nut–crusted tilapia. Guests who like wine with their meal can bring their own (no corkage fee). ~ Monteagle Assembly, Monteagle; 931-924-4000, fax 931-924-3236; www.relaxinn.com. DELUXE TO ULTRA-DELUXE.

A large room cozied up with knotty pine walls and comfy booths within sight of Route 24, the **Bluewater Lodge** makes a super pit stop for breakfast, lunch or dinner. The barbecued pork and chicken are slow-roasted over hickory and oak, the catfish is farm-raised, the meatloaf homemade, the seafood fried and the trout grilled. ~ 903 West Main Street, Monteagle; 931-924-7020. BUDGET.

The **Smokehouse Lodge Restaurant,** to the west of Route 24, is a log cabin on steroids: it just goes on forever. Keep going past the retail section and you'll find a large, dark room arranged around a hot buffet table. You can take the all-you-can-eat approach, or opt for à la carte: fried chicken, catfish, barbecue, steaks, sandwiches and the like. ~ Route 64/41, near Monteagle; 931-924-2091; www.thesmokehouse.com. BUDGET TO MODERATE.

In a structure that looks like the general store it used to be, **Shenanigan's** has a lot of built-in charm. The menu is small and focused: sandwiches (including hot ones like grilled cheese and Reubens), soup, quiche, veggie taco salad, burgers, melts, homemade desserts, plus daily specials listed on a chalkboard. Drag a chair across the wood floor and sit at a picnic table or find a spot on the small porch. Or ask for your order to go. ~ 12595 Route 64/41A, Sewanee; 931-598-5774. BUDGET.

PARKS   **SOUTH CUMBERLAND STATE RECREATION AREA** 🏃 🛶 🚣

Seven separate areas make up this 12,404-acre parcel encompassing much of Tennessee's remaining wilderness. Each has distinct features, but all offer excellent opportunities for observing wildlife, including coyotes, red and gray foxes, coyotes, white-tailed deer and, if you're lucky, wild turkeys. Check out the relief map in the visitors center to get your bearings before heading out. The challenging, 13-mile Fiery Gizzard Trail connects Grundy Forest and Foster Falls, a 60-foot fall and a popular place for rock climbing; hikers can swim in Fiery Gizzard Creek. Lost Cove is the place for exploring caves; wear your most casual clothes and take a flashlight. Sewanee Natural Bridge is a 25-foot-high sandstone arch overlooking Lost Cove. For longer hikes or backpacking, head for the trails at Savage Gulf, where you'll find sensational views and plenty of waterfalls. Here also is the Great Stone Door, a ten-foot-wide crevice at the plateau edge once used by American Indians to go in and out of the gorge. Grundy Lakes is a day-use area offering swimming, fishing, hiking and picnicking. The facilities at South Cumberland include picnic and backcountry campsites (permits required), nature trails, playgrounds, an interpretive center and canoe-access sites, as well as restrooms. ~ Forty-two miles northwest of Chattanooga in Monteagle, three miles from Exit 134 off Route 24; 931-924-2980.

▲ There are 12 primitive campsites; no fee.

▼ ▼ ▼ ▼ ▼ ▼ ▼ ▼ ▼ ▼ ▼ ▼ ▼ ▼ ▼

Outdoor Adventures

There's plenty to do right here in River City (actually, all of Tennessee's metropolitan areas could be called River City), and more farther afield. A one-plus-hour drive away is the Ocoee River, site of the whitewater-rafting portion of the 1996 Summer Olympics.

FISHING   Tennessee has the most species of freshwater fish in the country, and the region around Chattanooga has one of the country's most diverse aquatic ecosystems and fisheries. From the reservoirs around the city to the mountain streams to the east, the catch is plentiful and diverse, as are the habitats: streams cascading over stones in the highlands, rivers and their tributaries, and reservoirs and tailraces of the Tennessee River.

You'll need a fishing license from the **Tennessee Wildlife Resources Agency**. ~ 218 Genesis Road, Crossville, TN 38555; 931-484-9571.

Hamilton County's cold-water rivers and streams are stocked with rainbow trout each spring. Most of them are fished out by summertime, by which time they are warm-water rivers and streams. **Feather & Fly** arranges fly-fishing instruction and excursions. ~ 2401 Broad Street, Chattanooga; 423-265-0306.

Bass, brim and catfish are there for the catching at **Grundy Lakes** in the South Cumberland State Park area just east of Tracy City. ~ Route 41; 931-924-2980.

Fish can be taken out all year long at **Nickajack Lake**, to the north of Chattanooga. A fine largemouth bass lake, it also has stripers and white bass, which are more numerous at the upper end or beneath the Nickajack Dam than they are in the lake portion.

The **Chickamauga Lake** is a lowland reservoir with big bays and major creek tributaries at the lower end, while the upper end is more riverine. After largemouth, the best fishing is spotted bass, crappie, bluegill and shellcracker. The catfishing (flatheads, blues and channel) is terrific.

You can fish Chickamauga Lake at Booker T. Washington and Harrison Bay state parks.

> You can inline skate on most of the seven-mile Tennessee Riverpark or across the Walnut Street Bridge.

RIVER RUNNING

Beginners feel comfortable rafting on the scenic Hiwassee River. In fact, the rapids are so mild you can go down by raft or inner tube along the waterway connecting the Ocoee and the Tennessee rivers. You can rent a raft, "funyak" or tube (as well as lifejackets and paddles) from **Hiwassee Rafting Center**. These outfitters put in over at the Cherokee National Forest about an hour and a half away. ~ Reliance; 800-338-8133.

The Ocoee River is dam controlled, open for rafting only Thursday through Monday, Memorial Day through Labor Day, and on spring and fall weekends. Rapids run continuously through a beautiful gorge in the Cherokee National Forest, making the Ocoee the most popular five-mile stretch of whitewater in the entire world. Individual and group tours are offered by **Quest Expeditions**. ~ 663 Route 64, Ocoee; 423-338-2979, 800-277-4537.

North Chickamauga Creek in the Hixson area flows gently as it approaches the Tennessee River. Call **Chattanooga Out-Venture** to arrange canoe trips here. ~ 423-842-6629.

Gentle canoeing on a Class I stream is the order of the day at the Sequatchie. Scott and Ernestine Pilkington's **Canoe the Sequatchie** offers two-hour and longer outings on a river known for its spectacular scenery. Open daily from Memorial Day to Labor Day; open weekends from April through October. ~ Route 127, Dunlap; 423-949-4400; www.sequatchie.com.

CLIMBING

Anyone can climb the **Walnut Street Wall** if they're so inclined. The stone support post on the north side is fitted with anchors, holds and ropes so people can practice in a controlled environment. On Lookout Mountain, **Sunset Rock** has 250 routes to choose from and the **Tennessee Wall** has more than 200, with fabulous names like Psycho Path.

The Adventure Guild offers classes, organizes trips and certifies climbers. ~ 149 River Street, Chattanooga; 423-266-5709; www.theadventureguild.com.

GOLF

The **Bear Trace at Harrison Bay State Park** is a Jack Nicklaus–designed course where 7 of 18 holes lie along the water, with views of the Chickamauga Reservoir shoreline. The 7140-yard, links-style, bent-grass course features a couple of special holes: No. 4 is 184 yards and par 3, with a well-trapped green, and No. 8, a 434-yard, par-4 number, has a lake view. ~ 8411 Harrison Bay Road, Chattanooga; 423-344-6214, 877-611-2327; www.bear trace.com.

An 18-hole course in a residential neighborhood, **Eagle Bluff Golf Club** sits atop several bluffs overlooking Chickamauga Lake and Harrison Bay. The semiprivate course has contoured and rolling fairways and plenty of elevation changes. ~ 5808 Clubhouse Drive; 423-326-0202. The public par-72 **Moccasin Bend Golf Club** offers 18 holes, a driving range and a pro shop as well as electric carts, all close to downtown. ~ 381 Moccasin Bend Road; 423-267-3585; www.moccasinbendgolf.com. The public **Brainerd Golf Course** has 18 holes along wooded, gently rolling terrain with few water hazards. ~ 5203 Old Mission Road; 423-855-2692.

Trees line the fairways at the semiprivate, 18-hole **Windstone Golf Club**, where varied topography and water hazards provide more challenges. ~ 9230 Windstone Drive; 423-894-1231.

Long, wide fairways, gentle rolling hills and water and sand hazards characterize the **Sewanee Golf Course**, a nine-hole pub-

AUTHOR FAVORITE

Bocce ball is a popular sport in Northern California and other places with a strong Italian heritage. But it was a pleasant surprise to find the **Bocce Ball Court** on the terrace at the end of 2nd Street across from the Bluff View Inn. This court must have the best view of any in the country. You can order snacks or wine here to enjoy during your game; printed game rules are supplied and reservations required. Closed Sunday through Wednesday. ~ 423-265-5033 ext. 224.

lic course on the campus of the University of the South. ~ Route 64/41A, Sewanee; 931-598-1104.

You can find lighted courts at many places around the city, including Brainerd, 1016 Moore Road; East Chattanooga, 2409 Dodson; Lookout Valley, 350 Lookout Street; St. Elmo, 4921 St. Elmo Avenue. The 61-acre **Rivermont Park** has several tennis courts across the river from downtown. ~ 1100 Lupton City Drive in the North Shore. Call 423-697-1310 for reservations at all city courts.

Hidden away in Hixson, **Chester Frost County Park** has tennis courts on the north bank of Chickamauga Lake, where there's plenty of shade and usually a breeze blowing off the water. ~ 2318 Gold Point Circle. Tennis courts are part of the extensive offerings at **Harrison Bay State Park**, which has campsites and a marina as well. ~ 8411 Harrison Bay Road, Harrison; 423-344-6214. For more details, call the Hamilton County Parks Department at 423-842-0177.

Eventually, the **Tennessee Riverpark** will have 22 miles of trails, but for now there are just eight available for cycling, much of it right along the Tennessee River. So far, the trail is in segments of approximately one to two miles each. The Hamilton County Parks and Recreation Department has up-to-date information. ~ 4301 Amnicola Highway; 423-842-0177.

A good long ride is the **Moccasin Bend** loop. Take Manufacturers Road east to Moccasin Bend and back. Distance from downtown is about seven miles.

The **North Chickamauga Creek Greenway** is a two-mile segment north of Chickamauga Dam, adjacent to Greenway Farm. Take Lakeshore Drive from Route 153N. ~ 423-842-9480.

Take your mountain bike if you want to pedal around the **Chickamauga and Chattanooga National Military Park**, part of which is in Tennessee. For trail information, call 706-866-9241.

The **Chattanooga Bicycle Club**'s web site, www.chatbike.com, provides maps and descriptions for numerous trails in the area, including the mountain bike trails around Ocoee.

All distances listed for trails are one way unless otherwise noted.

It's more of a walk than a hike at the three completed stretches of **Tennessee Riverpark**. The two-mile upstream segment has an eight-foot-wide paved path leading from a parking area below Chickamauga Dam. You can extend the walk by looping through the parking and picnic areas. As you head downstream, the path is mostly shaded by trees that still allow views of the river. ~ Route 58 south of Chickamauga Dam. The four-mile bluff walk begins at Ross Landing at the corner of Riverfront Parkway and Chestnut Street.

From **Point Park,** you can access 25 miles of easy-to-medium hiking trails, many of which have views from the top of Lookout Mountain.

In addition to its other attractions, the **Tennessee Wildlife Center** is the setting-out point for 14 miles of trails that crisscross pine groves, oak forests and deep gorges on their way up Lookout Mountain, connecting with National Park Service Trails. You can begin either at the nature center or at Point Park, above, which covers 2000 acres. The handicapped-accessible 1200-foot wetland boardwalk also starts here at the visitors center, beginning with a wide, blacktop path and eventually leading to an elevated wooden pathway that is usually shaded and has benches for wildlife observation.

HIDDEN ►   Two waterfalls beckon at the **Laurel-Snow Pocket Wilderness,** about two and a half miles northwest of Dayton. Even though it encompasses more than 700 acres, this tucked-away park is vastly underused. You can take the **Laurel Trail** (5 miles) or the **Snow Trail** (6 miles), or both, which includes a couple of inclines of about 900 feet. ~ Walton Groves Road; 423-775-6171.

▼▼▼▼▼▼▼▼▼▼▼▼▼
Transportation

CAR

Chattanooga is a major transportation hub intersected by **Routes 75, 59** and **24.** It's within a day's drive of one-third of the U.S. population. **Route 27** runs north from Chattanooga to the city of Dayton; **Route 64** leads from Route 75 to the Cherokee National Forest and the Ocoee River.

AIR

Chattanooga Metropolitan Airport is served by US Airways jets and commuter flights via American Eagle, Delta Air Lines, Northwest Airlink and US Airways Express. For more air transportation services, call 423-855-2200; www.chattairport.com.

Another option is to take the **Express Shuttle** directly to Atlanta's Hartsfield International Airport; the one-way trip takes about two hours with frequent departures from 5 a.m. to 7:30 p.m. and costs $32. Depending on your connecting flight, it is sometimes more efficient to book a seat on one of these vans. ~ 423-954-1400, 800-896-9928; www.expressshuttle.net.

BUS

Aside from airplanes, bus transport is the only public transportation to Chattanooga; there is no longer any train service. **Greyhound Bus Lines** provides interstate service to the Chattanooga area. ~ 960 Airport Road; 423-892-1277, 800-231-2222; www.greyhound.com.

CAR RENTALS

Most of the car-rental agencies are located at Chattanooga Metropolitan Airport. They include **Avis Rent A Car** (800-230-4898), **Budget Rent A Car** (800-527-0700), **Hertz Rent A Car** (800-

654-3131), **National Rent A Car** (800-227-7368) and **Thrifty Car Rentals** (800-367-847-3489).

Chattanooga is an easy city for tourists, as long as they aren't trying to get to really remote destinations. **Chattanooga Area Regional Transit Authority** (CARTA) provides regularly scheduled transportation in the area, as well as charter service for special trips. It also operates one of the largest electric bus fleets in the United States; the free **Visitor Shuttle Service** runs every five minutes between the Tennessee Aquarium and the Chattanooga Choo Choo, essentially the length of downtown. In the summer months, service extends to Lookout Mountain. ~ 423-629-1473; www.carta-bus.org.

PUBLIC TRANSIT

Checker Cab uses regular cabs as well as vans to transport customers around town and to the airport. ~ 423-510-0586.

TAXIS

SEVEN

The Cumberland Plateau

Between the soaring Great Smoky Mountains that define Tennessee's eastern border and the mighty Mississippi on the western edge lie several interesting, occasionally even unique, geological formations. None is more dramatic than the Cumberland Plateau, a large tabletop that rises more than 1000 feet above the surrounding countryside. The plateau is roughly a parallelogram that reaches from the Kentucky border at Cumberland Gap (literally a gap) across the eastern edge of Middle Tennessee (east of Nashville) to Monteagle, at Chattanooga's backdoor. The Upper Cumberland refers to the northern section, which encompasses the area from Rugby to Red Boiling Springs and some points south. (Route 52, which links these towns as well as Celina, is one of the prettiest rural drives in this part of the state.) The Cumberland River runs through this section; on its banks such historic river towns as Celina and Carthage were established. Dams have created recreational lakes, where pleasure boats have replaced barges full of logs as the main watercraft.

Despite the flatness that characterizes much of it, the region is quite rugged. Within it is the deep Sequatchie Valley as well as other valleys such as the ones near Fall Creek Falls State Park. The challenging terrain is undoubtedly the main reason this park has remained as pristine as it has. The Cumberland, Duck and Elk rivers cut deep swaths in the plateau; as a result, portions of this area are among Tennessee's most scenic.

Moderate temperatures and plentiful rainfall have tempted humans to try to tame this terrain, to little avail until the late 19th and early 20th centuries. One geologist compared it to the Great Wall of China—only higher and wider—in that it served as a formidable barrier to westward expansion.

Understandably, then, major cities are few. Which is not to say there aren't some fascinating settlements. Red Boiling Springs was established around the hot mineral waters that bubble up on the Eastern Highland Rim. The mineral content of the waters here—enhanced by the long contact with iron sulfide—gave rise to a number of resorts at the turn of the 20th century. The water was so pure that Coca-Cola established a bottling plant in Red Boiling Springs to exploit it. In its heyday, Red Boiling Springs evolved from a bunch of rustic cabins to eight hotels and more than a dozen boarding houses that, each spring, attracted thousands of people intent on taking the waters to heal what ailed them. No one knows why the town eventually lost its cache, but advances in modern medicine—combined with the financial devastation of the Great Depression—were obviously contributing factors.

No town in the state was founded on more pure philosophical ideals, perhaps, than Rugby. Thomas Hughes, an English social reformer, politician and novelist, founded the colony in 1880, hoping to return to the values of living off the land. He had in mind as settlers England's "second sons," the disenfranchised siblings of the upper class who were denied the inheritance of their older brothers. Although the project did in fact attract a number of English colonists, the majority of settlers drawn to Hughes' utopia were actually American. Poor management and discouraging weather trends helped dash the high hopes of the settlers, but not before they had built a small town of buildings mostly inspired by English architecture. Now some of the homes are private residences and several of the original public buildings, including the stunning library—with one of the best collections of Victorian literature in the country—have been preserved and can be toured by visitors.

Perhaps because of its length and girth, the Cumberland Plateau is one of the least homogenous regions of Tennessee. But it has a multitude of quirky charms to attract both nature lovers and history buffs.

Upper Cumberland Plateau

The hamlet of Cumberland Gap, on the border of Kentucky and Virginia, grew up around the key geological pass from Tennessee and the early colonies to the western frontier. The gap had long been the natural choice of migrating buffalo, warring American Indians and eager settlers—as well as frontiersman Daniel Boone. It was also a natural choice for the establishment of a 20,271-acre national park, the Cumberland Gap National Historic Park, intended to preserve and interpret this well-known parcel of Americana. (The park entrance is located across the state line in Kentucky.)

Rugby was founded in 1880 as a class-free utopian colony dependent on agriculture, temperance and Christian principles. But bad weather and poor management doomed the venture. After the village was put on the National Register of Historic Places in 1972, tourism replaced earlier endeavors and now the town is thriving. Part of its appeal lies in its proximity to the Big South Fork country, virtually at the backdoor.

SIGHTS

The **Abraham Lincoln Museum** in Harrogate, practically next door to Cumberland Gap, is considered one of the top-five Lincoln museums in the country. There's a Lincoln death mask, the cane he carried to Ford's Theater on the night of his assassination and family memorabilia among the 25,000 artifacts, including just about every photograph ever taken of the man. You can kind of gauge the popularity of this museum when you see the bust of Abraham Lincoln, with a nose rubbed glossy by people walking by. There is also an exhibit on the contributions of African-American Union soldiers during the Civil War. Admission. ~ Lincoln Memorial University, Cumberland Gap Parkway, Harrogate; 423-869-6235.

Situated west of Harrogate and the Cumberland Gap on the southern border of the Big South Fork National River and Recreation Area, **Rugby** is one of the most intriguing towns in Tennessee. To get there from Harrogate, take Route 63 to Route 75, go north to the intersection with Route 63, and take Route 63 west to Huntsville, where you will take Route 27 south for eight miles before turning west on Route 52 for another seven miles. It would take a half-day to make this trip, as the last portion is on small roads.

Guided tours of the historic colony of Rugby begin at the **Schoolhouse Visitor Centre**, where classes were held until 1950. Everything on the tour is within a few minutes' walk. Admission. ~ Route 52, Rugby; 423-628-2441; www.historicrugby.org.

The **Christ Church Episcopal** is a lovely specimen of Carpenter Gothic architecture built—like everything else in the early days —of the Cumberland Plateau's plentiful virgin pine, walnut and poplar. ~ Across Route 52 from the Schoolhouse Visitor Centre, Rugby.

The most fabulous of the 18 original structures still standing is the **Thomas Hughes Library**, which has remained almost unaltered since the day it opened in 1882. It is the library of every English major's dreams, with scores of first editions (Dickens, among them) and ancient copies of *Punch*, the British magazine, dating from November 1869. Visitors must wear gloves and avoid touching anything. Some of the other structures are once again private residences, but picture taking is allowed. Guided tours are by appointment. ~ Across Route 52 from the Schoolhouse Visitor Centre, Rugby.

Nearby is the **Laurel Dale Cemetery**, the final resting place of many early colonists. ~ On Canyon Avenue, Rugby.

Another high point of the tour is **Kingstone Lisle**, the "English Rural Style" cottage designed by the American landscape architect Andrew Jackson Downing. Hughes lived here for a while, and the house has been repainted in its original colors—definitely a piece of arcane Americana the likes of which you won't see anywhere else. ~ Off Route 52, Rugby.

Lying northwest of Rugby is **Jamestown**, known not for its own features, but for its proximity to several attractions, particularly two major parks—Big South Fork National River and Recreation Area and Pickett State Park.

Stop by the **Jamestown/Fentresss County Chamber of Commerce** to pick up regional maps and other information. ~ 114

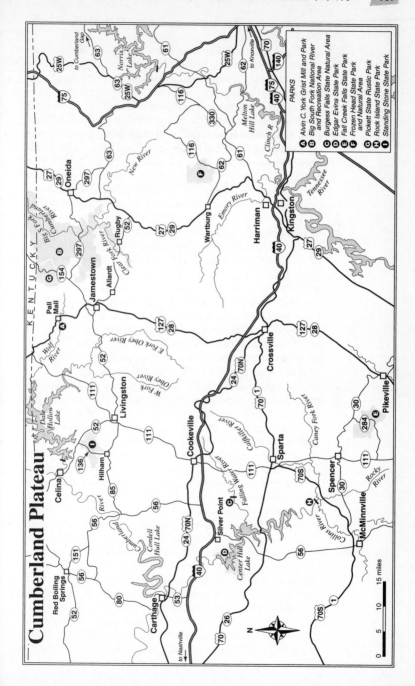

Cumberland Plateau

PARKS
- **A** Alvin C. York Grist Mill and Park
- **B** Big South Fork National River and Recreation Area
- **C** Burgess Falls State Natural Area
- **D** Edgar Evins State Park
- **E** Fall Creek Falls State Park
- **F** Frozen Head State Park and Natural Area
- **G** Pickett State Rustic Park
- **G** Rock Island State Park
- **H** Standing Stone State Park

Central Avenue West, Jamestown; 800-327-3945; www.james towntn.org.

Highland Manor Winery, housed in an English Tudor structure in southeast Jamestown, is the oldest winery in Tennessee. It offers tours of the entire winemaking process, from crushing to fermentation to bottling. Whether or not you take the tour, you can drop by the cozy tasting room to sample some of the 11 varieties made here and pick up some snacks for a picnic. There is something of a winemaking tradition in these parts; early colonists planted vineyards around Rugby in the late 1800s. ~ 2965 South York Highway (Route 127S), Jamestown; 931-879-9519, fax 931-879-2907.

The World War I hero Alvin C. York was born and raised near Jamestown, up the road in the scenic Valley of the Three Forks of the Wolf River. The area—a quilt of farms and forests in the shelter of soaring ridges—must look much as it did when the poor son of farmers joined the service for a two-year stint that led to a fateful encounter with German soldiers in France's Argonne Forest. After the war, York was rewarded with 45 Allied decorations. York's life in Fentress County and his wartime days are recounted at the **Sgt. Alvin C. York Historic Site,** located ten miles north of Jamestown. Here you can tour the home where York lived out his postwar life; the house is a shrine, with poignant reminders of his life. If this genuine hero interests you, be sure to ask questions of the ranger—none other than York's son, Andrew. ~ 2700 Route 127, Pall Mall; 931-879-3657; www.alvincyork.org.

The surrounding countryside is crisscrossed with two-lane roads that are a pleasure to drive, but there is little reason to leave your car once you are west of town.

That is, until you arrive at a most unusual spot, **Red Boiling Springs,** where only a couple of hotels remain out of more than two dozen lodgings that thrived in the early 1900s, when the little town was developed as a mineral water health resort. If you want to stroll the old-timey sidewalks and streets of this historic village, you can pick up maps of Red Boiling Springs at the **Chamber of Commerce.** Closed Saturday and Sunday. ~ 166 Dale Street, Red Boiling Springs; 615-699-2011.

LODGING   The Tudor brick **Cumberland Gap Inn** extends the English metaphor with Victorian-style furnishings in all 30 rooms plus an executive ultra-deluxe suite. Don't let the antiques fool you; each guest room has a whirlpool bath, a refrigerator, a coffeemaker and a microwave—and some have fireplaces. It's basically an upscale motel, with two floors and a residential feel to the rooms. ~ 630 Brooklyn Street, Cumberland Gap; 423-869-3996, 888-408-0127. MODERATE TO DELUXE.

Two-day Getaway

Cumberland Plateau

Day 1
- Start your drive around part of this vast portion of the state in **Cumberland Gap** (page 185). This village is right on the border with Kentucky, which you will visit if you drive through the multi-million-dollar tunnel through the mountains. Stroll around Cumberland Gap and take the half-mile hike up from the **Iron Furnace**, a path that leads virtually straight uphill.

- Enjoy lunch at **Ye Olde Tea & Coffee Shoppe Restaurant** (page 192).

- Head west on Route 63 from Cumberland Gap to the intersection with Route 75. Take Route 75 north to the exit for Route 63, then head south on Route 27. Take Route 52 west to visit **Rugby** (page 186), which was founded in the late 19th century as a utopian settlement. **Christ Church Episcopal** and the **Thomas Hughes Library** are both open on guided tours.

- Spend the night at **Grey Gables Bed 'N' Breakfast Inn** (page 190), where you will be served a full dinner that is included in the room rate. Breakfast is almost as big a meal.

Day 2
- Head west on Route 52 through the rugged countryside to Jamestown and then north to the **Sgt. Alvin C. York Historic Site** (page 188) in the village of Pall Mall, where you can learn all about the World War I hero who once lived here.

- Return to Jamestown and take Route 154 up to the **Big South Fork National River and Recreation Area** (page 194), which offers myriad opportunities for hiking and camping.

- Retrace your path to Jamestown, where you can get an inexpensive cafeteria-style meal at **Ruth's** (page 193). Head west on Route 52 after lunch. Pick up Route 85 in Livingston and continue to the intersection with Route 56. Take the scenic Route 56 south to Route 40.

- Make a detour to **Carthage** (page 197), home of former Vice President Al Gore, by taking Route 70N west from Cookeville. It's less than an hour to Carthage, where you will find a number of antique stores.

Grey Gables Bed 'N' Breakfast Inn looks as if it might have weathered Cumberland Plateau winters for decades, but in fact the attractive gray structure was built in 1990 by native Rugbyite Linda Jones and her husband, Bill. Wall-to-wall carpeting, country print and striped wallpaper in pretty pastels and ceiling fans adorn the ten guest rooms. A three- or four-course dinner is also included in the price—which is understandable, since there are precious few dining options in the Upper Cumberland—and is served in the comfortable dining room. Breakfast is an even bigger spread. After dinner, rock for a spell on the veranda; on sunny days, there are two decks for relaxing with a book. ~ Route 52, Rugby; 423-628-5252, 877-781-5252; www.rugbytn.com, e-mail greygablestn@highland.net. DELUXE.

Right in the heart of the settlement, the 1880 **Newbury House** offers cozy accommodations amid full Victorian splendor, including the original sideboard, period light fixtures, washstands and somewhat loud carpets. Like many old homes, this one's a wee bit cramped but definitely has the corner on charm. Three of the five guest rooms have private baths, and breakfast at the nearby Harrow Road Cafe is included in the rate. The inn also handles accommodations in the Pioneer Cottage, a historic structure that sleeps up to ten, and the Victorian Gothic Percy Cottage, which has a single upstairs suite. ~ 5517 Route 52, Rugby; 423-628-2441, 888-214-3400; www.historicrugby.org, e-mail rugbytn@highland. net. MODERATE.

HIDDEN ► Only one set of visitors at a time is accepted at **Delia's Guest House**, located about three miles south of downtown Jamestown. That's because the three-bedroom, two-bath house is considered one unit. The decor is country simple, with light colors and floral upholstery throughout. Guests receive a complimentary continental breakfast but have the use of a complete kitchen where they can prepare full meals. There's even parking for RVs and boats. In addition to the basic price for two, up to four additional people can stay for an extra $10 a head. ~ 1277 Bertram Road, Jamestown; 931-879-2511. MODERATE.

Charit Creek Lodge, situated within Big South Fork National River and Recreation Area, is accessible only by foot or horse. The shortest way in is via the Twin Arches Trail, which leads beneath and over a sandstone formation. This is a real getaway, with primitive accommodations and running water but no electricity. Instead, each cabin has wood-burning stoves; showers are heated by solar energy (although, depending on the season, showers may not be available). There are two cabins (with freestanding restrooms) and two sleeping rooms in the lodge, each of which sleeps 12. Both dinner and breakfast are included in the room rate. Barebones packages are also available. ~ Big South Fork National River

War Hero Alvin C. York

The most decorated hero of World War I is commemorated in an exhibit in a Fentress County park named in his honor. His heroism was such that he is also remembered in France. But first the story.

Alvin York was raised in a poor farming family in Fentress County, in the scenic Valley of the Three Forks of the Wolf River. The farmland and the forests on the outskirts of Jamestown probably look much as they did in the early part of this century. Except for the two years he spent in military service, York lived his whole life in the valley, receiving little formal education but learning valuable lessons about survival. Hunting in the backwoods of Tennessee, York developed the marksmanship skills that would one day make him one of the most admired and acclaimed men in America.

The story of Sergeant York's heroism unfolded on the morning of October 8, 1918. His platoon had set out to capture a railroad under German control, but the assault was stalled by heavy fire from the enemy's machine gunners. Sergeant York was ordered to lead a squad behind the German position and attack, but most of the squad was wounded or killed in the heavy exchange of gunfire. Armed with a rifle and a Colt .45, York returned fire. His youthful lessons in the woods served him well, as he picked off soldier after German soldier. In all, 25 enemy soldiers had fallen by the time the Germans decided to give up their weapons and surrender. Then York and seven of his men rounded up their captives, taking more prisoners, and they made their way back to the American lines. By the time they arrived, they held 132 prisoners in captivity.

More than 40 Allied decorations, including the Congressional Medal of Honor, were showered on the young soldier. He was also decorated by French Field Marshal Ferdinand Foch with the French Croix de Guerre; Foch described York's feats as "the greatest thing accomplished by any private soldier of all the armies of Europe."

True to his humble roots, York was stunned when he returned from the war in 1919 and besieged by requests for business endorsements. He returned to his native valley, but was hardly forgotten. Warner Brothers Studio convinced York that a film about his heroism would be good for patriotism. Gary Cooper, in the title role of Sergeant York, turned in an Oscar-winning performance that made the movie a classic. York married his longtime sweetheart, spent much of his life in public service to his mountain neighbors and, upon his death in 1964, was buried in the Wolf River Cemetery in the Valley of the Three Forks.

and Recreation Area, 250 Apple Valley Road, Sevierville; 865-429-5704; www.charitcreek.com, e-mail reservations@charitcreek.com. BUDGET TO MODERATE.

You have to turn off the highway and head through town to find the **Armours Hotel**, but it's worth the detour. The hotel, which has a residential feel, was built in 1924. Today it's the only one in the state with an operating mineral springs spa—albeit a down-home version. The 21 rooms (on two floors) are average in size, with turn-of-the-20th-century decor and lots of prints. It's quite a friendly place, and you don't have to be an overnight guest to book a mineral bath or a country-style dinner in the dining room. Overnight rates include breakfast and dinner. ~ 321 East Main Street, Red Boiling Springs; 615-699-2180; www.armours hotel.com. DELUXE.

The **Thomas House** is another original, looking a bit like a sanitorium on the edge of downtown. Set on ten acres, its red-brick facade, double porches, swimming pool and knoll-top location give it an air of rural grandeur. The 14 guest rooms are actually snappy, with bright colors (lavender and green, for instance) and whimsical touches. Built in 1890 as the Cloyd Hotel, it was remodeled in 1920, reopened in 1924 and has been operating on and off since then. Both breakfast and dinner are included in the rate. ~ 520 East Main Street, Red Boiling Springs; 615-699-3006; www.thomashousehotel. BUDGET TO DELUXE.

DINING

The best restaurant in Cumberland Gap is within walking distance of the Cumberland Gap Inn (as is, of course, just about everything else). **Ye Olde Tea & Coffee Shoppe Restaurant**'s three buildings, built in 1890, were originally a bank, a general store and a hardware store before an interim incarnation as a traditional

AUTHOR FAVORITE

Situated between Pickett State Park and Big South Fork, the **Wildwood Lodge** is a hybrid motel and bed and breakfast. The roadside inn looks like a two-story motel with a balcony tacked on. Inside, each of the ten accommodations is decorated a bit like a small inn, with local pressed wildflowers in frames and various crafts scattered about. In the back is a deck overlooking several acres of forests with some short hiking trails. Full breakfast is included, and guests may make reservations for dinner here Saturday through Tuesday. A cottage and four cabins are also available. ~ 3636 Pickett Park Highway (Route 154), Jamestown; 931-879-9454; www.wild woodlodge.ws, e-mail wildwoodlodge@twlakes.net. MODERATE.

English tea room, hence the name. It seats 404 diners in seven different environments, from the rather formal Victorian Bank Room to the Social Dining Club to the Casual Garden. In good weather, the best daytime choice is on the deck, the better to enjoy views of the town as well as the Cumberland Mountains beyond, capped by the Pinnacle Overlook. Closer to home, the house specialty is prime rib in various portions (up to a whopping 22 ounces). For something lighter, there are the filet medallions (sautéed in garlic and olive oil with mushrooms and scallions) as well as pork tenderloin, ribs, chicken, pasta and grilled seafood dishes. ~ 527 Colwyn Avenue, Cumberland Gap; 423-869-4844. MODERATE TO DELUXE.

The other dining option is cattycorner from the Tea Shoppe, as the locals call it. **Webb's Country Kitchen** is big on down-home cooking—fried chicken, salmon patties, meatloaf, catfish and, if you're lucky, chicken and dumplings. It's the only place in town for an early morning cup of coffee. Closed Wednesday. ~ 602 Colwyn Avenue, Cumberland Gap; 423-869-5877. BUDGET.

Sandwiched among a frenzy of fast-food franchises, **Ruth's** is a simple serve-yourself restaurant that is mighty appealing after a spell of driving around country roads. In one big room with pale pink walls and plum-colored seating, you'll find a cold bar, hot bar, salad bar and dessert bar. Meats usually include several choices such as chicken, pork chops and catfish. No dinner on Sunday. Closed Monday. Heading north on Main Street, look to your left for Ruth's about half a mile from the intersection of Routes 52 and 126, just off of Route 127. ~ 331 North Main Street, Jamestown; 931-879-8182. BUDGET.

◄ HIDDEN

You don't have to be an overnight guest to enjoy dinner at the **Armours Hotel** dining room. The country-style food isn't fancy, but it's served in a cozy Victorian setting. ~ 321 East Main Street, Red Boiling Springs; 615-688-2180. MODERATE.

Likewise, nonguests can join in at dinner at the **Thomas House**. Advance reservations are required for simple dinners featuring two meats (one is always country ham) and several vegetables. Reservations required. ~ 520 East Main Street, Red Boiling Springs; 615-699-3006. BUDGET.

All the shops in Cumberland Gap are on the same street, including the intriguing **Cumberland Gap General Store**, which isn't so much a general store as a retail discount outlet specializing in figurines, crystals and collectibles like eagles, angels and wolves. It opens at the crack of dawn, good news for those who are both early risers and compulsive shoppers. ~ 503 Colwyn Avenue, Cumberland Gap; 423-869-2282.

SHOPPING

The **Rugby Commissary** represents more than 100 regional craftspeople and also sells products from Great Britain. It's a faithful reconstruction of the original co-op that functioned as a combination hardware–dry goods store. The **Board of Aid Bookshop** can be found within the Rugby Commissary. Aside from local lore, the store sells reproductions of period wall hangings advocating good manners. ~ Route 52, Rugby; 423-628-5166.

The **Lightning Bug Gift Shoppe** can really light up your life. You'll find every conceivable shape, color and size of table lamp here, along with other crafts, collectibles and gifts. ~ 1906 Michigan Avenue, Allardt; 931-879-2273.

Just north of the Alvin C. York Grist Mill and Park and directly across the road from the grist mill, look for clothing, brooms, buckets and antiques displayed on the porch of the **Craft Shop of the Three Forks**. It's a cross between a general store and a collectibles collective, housed in a wonderful old building on the verge of dilapidation. ~ Route 27, Pall Mall.

NIGHTLIFE   Friday night often brings mountain string music, an a cappella gospel group or even a bit of hog callin' at **Webb's Country Kitchen**, where the owner has been known to regale the audience with "Will the Circle Be Unbroken." ~ 602 Colwyn Avenue, Cumberland Gap; 423-869-5877.

PARKS   **Cumberland Gap National Historical Park** is located just across the state line in Kentucky.

BIG SOUTH FORK NATIONAL RIVER AND RECREATION AREA
It would take ages to visit the far corners of this 115,200-acre area that stretches into Kentucky. The south fork of the Cumberland River and its main tributaries—Clear Fork, North White Oak and New River—drain some 1300 square miles in both Tennessee and Kentucky. Kayakers and canoers will

AUTHOR FAVORITE

In the heart of sweet little Rugby, the 80-seat **Harrow Road Café** was built in 1985 to conform to the town's historic architecture. Each wood-beamed dining room has a wood-burning fireplace for winter and plenty of working windows to let in the plateau breezes in warm weather. True to Rugby's origins, the café serves Welsh rarebit, shepherd's pie, fish and chips, and bangers and mash, as well as American-style meat loaf, grilled chicken and deep-fried catfish at lunch and dinner. Full breakfast is also available daily. No dinner January through February. ~ Route 52, Rugby; 423-628-2350. BUDGET TO MODERATE.

find more than 80 miles of navigable (Class I and Class IV) free-flowing water in this recreational wonderland. Permits are suggested but not required for backcountry camping. Hiking and backpacking trails abound—approximately 150 miles of them. ~ The park visitors center is 15 miles north of Oneida. Access from Jamestown is via Route 154; from Rugby, via Route 52; from Oneida, Route 297. 4564 Leatherwood Road, Oneida, TN 37841; 423-286-7275, fax 423-569-5505.

▲ There are 50 sites with water only, $15 per night; 100 with water and electricity, $18 per night.

FROZEN HEAD STATE PARK AND NATURAL AREA 🏃 🚴 🐎
Tennesseans outnumber out-of-state visitors nine to one at this popular park at the southernmost tip of the Cumberland Mountains. The last remaining tract unaffected by coal strip-mining in these mountains, the 11,562-acre parcel is home to thousands of old black cherry trees standing on the ridge tops. Frozen Head, named for the usually ice-capped 3324-foot mountain, also offers some of the best wildflower viewing in the state, second only to the Great Smoky Mountains National Park. It also rivals the Smokies in terms of fall color, when the oak, beech and maple leaves change in the latter part of October. In all, the park claims 14 peaks that tower above 3000 feet, making for sensational hiking and backpacking along 50 miles of trails that twist through the area. You'll also find 32 picnic sites, playgrounds, horseshoe pits, volleyball and basketball courts and plentiful trout in Flat Fork Creek, which is stocked regularly March through April. There's a playground and a picnic area. Day-use fee, $3. ~ Located six miles southeast of Wartburg off Route 62, 964 Flat Fork Road, Wartburg; 423-346-3318, fax 423-346-6629.

▲ There are 19 tent sites (some accommodate pick-ups and small trailers) and 11 backcountry campsites; $13 per night. Closed November to March 15.

PICKETT STATE RUSTIC PARK 🏃 🚴 🛶 🚤
Beautiful timberlands and abundant wildlife, natural sandstone bridges and bluffs and a 15-acre lake distinguish this 11,752-acre park, which borders Big South Fork on the west. This is one of the best places in Tennessee for hiking in the wilderness, in a parcel donated in 1933 by the Stearns Coal and Lumber Company. One of Tennessee's oldest parks, it boasts a floral diversity second only to that of the Great Smoky Mountains. It's about 12 miles northeast of Jamestown, and runs to the Kentucky state line. It also is adjacent to Big South Fork. (If you're hiking, bear in mind that the easternmost rim of the park falls into the eastern standard time zone.) ~ 4605 Pickett Park Highway, Jamestown; 931-879-5821, 877-260-0010.

▲ There are 31 sites with water and electricity (nine without hookups), and 15 family cabins; $11.25 per night for campsites, $78 to $125 per night for cabins and villas. For reservations call 877-260-0010.

ALVIN C. YORK GRIST MILL AND PARK   An old grist mill is the centerpiece of this idyllic riverside park, which consists only of sloping lawns, some picnic tables and the mill itself. It's a pleasant place to take a snooze and when the weather is good, you can take a dip in the Wolf River. ~ Route 27, Pall Mall, ten miles from Jamestown; 931-879-4026, 931-879-6456.

STANDING STONE STATE PARK 🕺 🛶 🚣 ♪   It's not easy to hide 11,000 acres, but people from out of state have a bit of trouble finding this rustic park. A curving, scenic two-lane road leads visitors past small farms and hamlets on this drive about 40 miles outside Jamestown. It's especially worth visiting in the spring, when wildflowers are abundant; ten miles of hiking trails traverse a diverse landscape. Standing Stone is ideal for sports lovers: there are volleyball and basketball courts, a croquet course, a place for horseshoes, tennis and badminton courts and fields for softball and other sports. The 69-acre lake is a joy, in part because no motorboats or other private craft are allowed; just the rowboats rented here. By the way, the park gets its name from an eight-foot-tall rock set upright on a sandstone ledge; according to legend, the ledge served as a boundary between two American Indian nations. The rock fell, and the Indians put what was left up on a makeshift monument (the stone is not here but in Monterey, Tennessee). The park is also home to the Rolley Hole National Championship, a festival of marble trading, marble making, bluegrass music, square dancing and marble-playing demonstrations, usually held in September. ~ 1674 Standing Stone Park Highway, Hilham; 931-823-6347, 800-713-5157.

Bald eagles visit Dale Hollow Lake during the winter; the south side is the best area for sighting these birds. ~ Resource Manager station, 5050 Dale Hollow Dam Road, Celina; 931-243-3136.

▲ There are 36 campsites with water and electricity; $17.25 per night. The 25 cabins are simple but attractive, set up like a little village. Each one of them is slightly different, but don't expect any memorable interior decor. You'll pay for all this splendid solitude, however; the accommodations run $49 to $104 per night. For cabin reservations: 800-713-5157.

Lower Cumberland Plateau

The Lower Cumberland region extends from the Tennessee River in the east all the way to Murfreesboro and south to the state line, just west of Chattanooga. Although Monteagle and South

Cumberland State Park are on the plateau, they are so close to Chattanooga that we have included them in Chapter Six. This chapter covers the plateau only as far south as Fall Creek Falls State Park.

Southwest of Red Boiling Springs is **Carthage**. The main square is pretty low-key, but there are some historic homes in the area. You can get a driving tour map at the Smith County Chamber of Commerce (130 3rd Avenue West; 615-735-2093; www.smith county.org), the Welcome Center on Route 40 or at the Carthage Antique Mall downtown.

SIGHTS

The red-brick **home of former Vice President Al Gore** can be found down a country road on the outskirts of Carthage. From the intersection with Route 53, head southeast on the Cookeville Highway about two and a half miles. It's on the right, and is closed to the public.

◀ HIDDEN

A small city of about 26,000 people, **Cookeville** is better suited as a headquarters for exploring than as a destination in itself. There are few lodging choices beyond the cluster of chain motels near the interstate exits.

For detailed information on the region, visit the **Cookeville Area–Putnam County Chamber of Commerce and Convention & Visitors Bureau**. ~ 1 West First Street, Cookeville; 931-526-2211; www.cookevillechamber.com.

Heading south on Route 111 from Cookeville and turning onto Route 70S, you'll run into **Rock Island State Park**. This 883-acre park offers up two pieces of history alongside its natural wonders. Built in the 1870s as the Fall City Cotton Mill by Asa Faulkner, the textile mill is on the National Historic Register; operation stopped in the late 1800s. The hydroelectric plants, one of the state's firsts, are operated by the TVA. ~ 82 Route 70S (Beach Road), Rock Island; 931-686-2471.

One of the best side trips you can take is to the **Joe L. Evins Appalachian Center for Crafts** near Crossville. Set on 600 acres above Center Hill Lake and operated by the Tennessee Technological University, the center offers formal classes and has galleries featuring glass, fiber, clay and other kinds of crafts. ~ Six miles south of Route 40 on Route 56, Smithville; 615-597-6801, 931-372-3051.

About 15 miles down Route 70S is **McMinnville**, incorporated in 1826 and boasting several historic landmarks such as the Colonial Revival Post Office and the art-deco City Electric Building. Aside from a few good antique shops, its main value to visitors today is its proximity to some outstanding state parks. One of those parks, Fall Creek, is about halfway between the cities of McMinnville and Dayton, on the eastern rim of the Cumberland Plateau.

◀ HIDDEN

Swing by the **McMinnville/Warren County Chamber of Commerce** for handy brochures. ~ 110 South Court Square, McMinnville; 931-473-6611; www.warrentn.com.

You don't have to stay at the elegant **Historic Falcon Manor** to take a peek at the rooms. Tours of this 10,000-square-foot Victorian mansion—which was built as a private residence before being transformed into a hospital from 1946 to 1968—are offered daily. Admission. ~ 2645 Faulkner Springs Road, McMinnville; 931-668-4444; www.falconmanor.com, e-mail falconmanor@fal conmanor.com.

Heading east out of town, the **waterfalls** at **Fall Creek Falls State Park** are hard to reach and famed for their scenic beauty. (Fall Creek Falls is 265 feet.) Several vantage points allow excellent views, and there are swinging bridges in two locations. See "Parks" below for directions; allow about an hour and a half to get there. The southern entrance to the park is located about 40 miles from McMinnville via Route 111. ~ Route 3, Pikeville; 423-881-5241.

Kingston, located about 40 miles west of Knoxville, is a quiet town best known for being the state capital for a single day, Sept. 21, 1807, when the Tennessee House of Representatives convened here. Nearby **Harriman** got its start in 1890 with the "Great Land Sale" on February 26, when men from 18 states came to the future town founded as a utopia for the temperance movement. Although its main appeal is for the surrounding countryside, Harriman does feature some historic homes from the late 1800s, particularly in the Cornstalk Heights Historic District.

The **Roane County Courthouse,** one of only seven remaining antebellum courthouses in Tennessee, was built by slaves using bricks that were made by hand on the site. There are some local history exhibits on the ground floor and it's worth at least a drive-

AUTHOR FAVORITE

sights The weird formations at **Cumberland Caverns** have inspired monikers like the Three Chessmen, Moby Dick, the Pipe Organ and the Twin Trolls. It's kind of like imagining galloping horses in the clouds, but it's also fun to see how people came up with these ideas. You're unlikely to find a 50-seat underground ballroom—capped with a three-quarter-ton crystal chandelier—in any other cave in Tennessee. Tours are offered daily from May through October and at other times by reservation. Admission. ~ 1437 Cumberland Caverns Road, McMinnville, seven miles southeast of town via Route 8; 931-668-4396, fax 931-668-5382; www.cumberland caverns.com, e-mail info@cumberlandcaverns.com.

by, even if you don't have time to see the lobby or the county museum inside. ~ 119 Court Street, Kingston; 865-376-9211.

Located inside the courthouse, the **Roane County Museum of History** is cramped, but it packs a lot of wallop with displays from the prehistoric, Mississippian, woodland, archaic and Paleo-Indian periods. There are also some amazing exhibits on the Civil War; you can literally see 1860s writing on the wall where the curators have left the sheetrock off the repaired structure. Closed Sunday. ~ Roane County Courthouse, 119 Court Street, Kingston; 865-376-9211.

The only fort in the state to be reconstructed on its original foundations, **Fort Southwest Point** occupies—again—a 30-acre hilltop above Watts Bar Lake. So far, there are barracks, a blockhouse and some 250 feet of palisade walls. Military activities began here in 1792 when the blockhouse was built for territorial militia troops under the command of General John Sevier. The site was chosen because present-day Kingston was near the Avery Trace, the major route between Knoxville and Nashville. As settlement increased, hostilities between the white settlers and the American Indians grew. The story of the fort's establishment and its waning importance are told in exhibits and a self-guided tour. Closed mid-December through March. ~ 1226 Route 58 (South Kentucky Street), Kingston; 865-376-3641.

LODGING

In 1896, an entrepreneur named Clay Faulkner fashioned a mansion next to his woolen mill a couple of miles from what was then a very small town. The **Historic Falcon Manor** is now a destination in itself. Since tours of the place have become so popular, rooms in the mansion itself are no longer available for guests, but there are four different places to stay on the property: the Carriage House Room, adjacent to the Victorian carriage house, has a view of the grounds and imposing antiques; the Honeymoon Suite, a 17-by-17-foot room semi-attached to the main house, boasts a king-size bed made of brass and marble, original wainscoting and a bath fashioned out of an old pantry; the General Manager's Cottage offers a choice of the three-room Jacuzzi Suite or the two-room Cottage Suite. ~ 2645 Faulkner Springs Road, McMinnville; 931-668-4444, fax 931-815-4444; www.falconmanor.com, e-mail falconmanor@falconmanor.com. DELUXE.

From McMinnville, it's about 33 hard miles to the entrance to Fall Creek Falls State Park. The roundtrip, including some time in the park, will consume most of a day.

The accommodations at **Fall Creek Falls State Park** are remote and rustic. The 20 cabins are woodsy but a little dark; each has a fireplace and polished wood floors. The 10 "villas" are rather grand, with three rooms to enjoy, right on the lower part of the lake. The nearby inn offers 145 rooms, conveniently close to the restaurant, which serves three meals a day, including a Friday-night seafood buffet. ~ Route 3, Pikeville; 423-881-5278, inn and cabin reservations 800-250-8610; www.tnstateparks.com. MODERATE TO DELUXE.

The origin of **Bushrod Hall Bed & Breakfast** may be unique in the annals of Tennessee lodging. Its construction was the upshot of a contest between Frederick Gates, one of Harriman's founders, and one S. K. Paige to see who could build the fanciest house. Gates won, but Paige may be laughing in his grave since his 1890s house still stands while Gates' is history. That rivalry seems to explain the decorative woodwork—eight types of wood were used, including red oak, burled walnut, maple and sycamore. Each of the three guest rooms is decorated with different antiques, rugs, chenille bedspreads and individual window coverings. Especially nice is an ivory-hued number with a four-poster bed. The public rooms of this knoll-top inn are done in rich colors like plum and forest green. It's named for a former owner, Bushrod W. James, and opened for business in 1997. ~ 422 Cumberland Street Northeast, Harriman; 865-882-8406, 866-500-2010; www.bushrod hall.com, e-mail info@bushrodhall.com. DELUXE TO ULTRA-DELUXE.

DINING

HIDDEN ►

You'll find a pleasantly extensive menu at **El Tepatio**, where you can order a substantial dinner for as little as $5 or as much as $17. In addition to the usual selection of tacos, burritos, enchiladas and quesadillas, the list includes fajitas, tamales, pork dishes and a special entrée with ribs, chorizo, shrimp, chicken and beef. Service is sudden and pleasant and portions are large at this roadside spot with fresh, simple decor and only a hint of Mexico—well, there is a spangly sombrero or two but that's about it. Look for the Best Western Thunderbird just off Route 40; the restaurant shares a portico. ~ 900 South Jefferson Street, Cookeville; 931-372-0246. BUDGET TO MODERATE.

HIDDEN ►

Mama Lea's Café, secreted away at the Joe L. Evins Appalachian Center for Crafts, is in a big room across from the galleries. It's the place for soups, sandwiches and excellent pastries. No dinner. Closed Saturday and Sunday. ~ 1560 Craft Center Drive, Smithville; 615-597-9812. BUDGET.

The entryway into **Fiesta Ranchera** is through a tiny door barely visible in a modest shopping center, past a couple of arcade games. Bubblegum-pink booths, a low ceiling festooned with piñatas and U.S. and Mexican flags, and a general air of festivity make this a real shot-in-the-arm for weary travelers. Locals swear by the cooking though, an assortment of fajitas, carnitas, chimichangas, enchiladas, taquitos, burritos, tacos and quesadillas as well as combinations, including a few vegetarian versions. ~ 202 McMinnville Plaza, Route 56, McMinnville; 931-506-8912. BUDGET TO MODERATE.

Homemade breads and desserts, a chicken salad like no other and daily specials draw a devoted crowd of locals to **Miss Marenda's Tea Room** on historic Liberty Square. ~ 5 East Maple Street, Sparta; 931-836-2542. BUDGET TO MODERATE.

About the only alternative to chain food in Harriman is the home cooking at **Dixie's**. "Dinner," served from lunchtime until 7 p.m. (earlier on Sunday), dishes up catfish, roast beef, ham, shrimp, hamburger steak, a ream of sandwiches and a shot at the buffet of meats and vegetables. Located across the street from the landmark Temperance Building, this diner gives new meaning to the word "plain," but Dixie and her minions warm the place up with their hospitality. No dinner on Sunday. Closed Saturday. ~ 313 North Roane Street, Harriman; 865-882-1802. BUDGET.

For a mix of classic American diner food and south-of-the-border fun, head down to **Reno's Roadhouse**. Choices include Southwestern grilled chicken, char-grilled steak, fajitas, quesadillas and Gulf shrimp. ~ 1889 South Roane Highway, Harriman; 931-590-0002. BUDGET TO MODERATE.

SHOPPING

In a souped-up cabin you'll find oodles of blown-glass ornaments as well as crafts like metal wind chimes and ceramics of all kinds at **The Silver Point Gallery**. ~ Route 56S (one-quarter mile south of Route 40, Exit 273), Silver Point; 931-858-3269.

The Vintage Rose carries furniture, jewelry, porcelain and a wide variety of other things of many vintages. ~ 1409 Interstate Drive, Cookeville; 931-520-6365.

For a wide assortment of merchandise, especially interior decorations, stop in at **Home Sweet Home Antiques & Collectibles**. ~ 535 West Main Street, Cookeville; 931-537-3884.

◄ *HIDDEN*

Near Crossville, the **Joe L. Evins Appalachian Center for Crafts** has fiber, metal, wood, glass and clay works available for sale. ~ Six miles south of Route 40 on Route 56, Smithville; 615-597-6801.

The Collection comprises several specialty shops under one roof; in addition to antiques, gifts, children's toys and furniture,

AUTHOR FAVORITE

The pink-walled **Victorian Tea Room** at Falcon Manor is open daily for formal tea, complete with scones and finger sandwiches. Reservations are advised, whether you are taking a tour of the mansion or not. Lunch is also available; the menu is limited to chicken-salad croissant or ham-and-cheese melt, with fried sweet potatoes, fruit salad, brownies and lemonade, all served in a basket at the table. ~ 2645 Faulkner Springs Road, McMinnville; 931-668-4444. BUDGET.

original art, glassware and jewelry, there's a selection of porcelain dolls. ~ 216 East Main Street, McMinnville; 931-473-1666.

The **Victorian Gift Shop at Historic Falcon Manor** is a natural, with old-fashioned toys like jacks and marbles and porcelain dolls, and period music boxes, hat racks and prints. ~ 2645 Faulkner Springs Road, McMinnville; 931-668-4444.

If you're in the market for handcrafted saddles, leather goods, battle re-enactment apparel or period clothing and supplies from the Civil War era, hie thee to **Hamilton Dry Goods**. ~ 4075 Roberts-Matthews Highway, Sparta; 931-739-6061.

NIGHTLIFE   Musicals (*State Fair*, for example), dramas and original works are presented on two stages year-round at the **Cumberland County Playhouse**, which has been one of the most popular places for family entertainment in this region since 1965. ~ 221 Tennessee Avenue, Crossville; 931-484-5000.

PARKS   **EDGAR EVINS STATE PARK** 🏃 🚤 🚢 ⚓ This 6280-acre park in the Caney Fork River Valley is a big draw for fishermen, boaters and other water sports lovers. You can rent watercraft from jet skis to houseboats to explore the clear-water coves near Smithville. Located north of Smithville and south of Route 40 on Route 96, this wheelchair-accessible park has an exceptionally scenic beauty, thanks to the forests that cling to the steep valley walls. Day-use fee, $3. ~ 1630 Edgar Evins Park, Silver Point; 931-858-2446, marina 931-858-5695.

▲ Sixty sites have water and electricity; $18 per night. There are also 34 fully equipped one-bedroom cabins; $78 per night. For cabin reservations: 800-250-8619.

BURGESS FALLS STATE NATURAL AREA 🏃 This 135-acre park looks quite modest from the parking lot, but once you turn off your motor you can hear the trickle of waterfalls. The first falls you come upon are nice enough, but less than half a mile down a forested path, you hear a real waterfall, where the river drops more than 50 feet into a bowl of limestone, flanked by hundred-foot cliffs. Impressive as this is, you're still not at Burgess Falls.

GOOD TO THE LAST DROP

South of Route 40, about a half-an-hour's drive from Cookeville, are the fantastic **waterfalls** at Burgess Falls State Natural Area. Even if you don't have the time or inclination to hike very far, you will be able to see one of the more modest falls just steps from the parking lot. See the "Parks" section above for directions.

Another quarter of a mile brings you to the bluffs above the big one, where limestone bluffs stand witness to the Falling Water River as it drops 130 feet. It is powerful, exciting and spectacular. The torrents are at their peak in the spring, which is also when the most wildflowers bloom. There is a small viewing area flanked by a banister where you will want to stand for a while before returning along the trail beside the river, or another one slightly inland. There's a picnic area back near the parking lot. Day-use fee, $3. ~ Route 6, 4000 Burgess Falls Road, Sparta; 931-432-5312.

ROCK ISLAND STATE PARK Easy to get to and easy to like, this 883-acre wooded park is at the confluence of the Collins and Caney Fork rivers. There's a natural sand beach on Center Hill Reservoir and Big Bone Cave to tour (by appointment only), as well as picnic sites, ten cabins, tennis courts and a playground. The setting is dominated by a limestone gorge with overlooks, waterfalls and deep pools for fishing and rock hopping. Also here are a 19th-century textile mill and one of the state's first hydroelectric plants. Day-use fee, $3. ~ 82 Beach Road (Route 70S); 931-686-2471.

▲ There are 60 sites with water and electricity; $16.25 per night. Cabins are $120 per night.

FALL CREEK FALLS STATE PARK This is one of Tennessee's full-service parks, and if you're planning to go see the waterfalls, plan on making a day of it. The park is a long way from anywhere, and the access roads are winding and steep. After you see the three major falls, you'll want to stay overnight, anyway. This place has most of the amenities of private resorts, plus some extras. The Nature Center has exhibits on the flora and fauna of the region; the 345-acre lake has great fishing; and the swimming pool is in a terrific setting. Accessible from two entrances, the park extends nearly 20,000 acres, so there's plenty of room to spread out. ~ Route 3, Pikeville; 423-881-3297.

▲ There are 228 sites with water and electricity; $18.50 to $20.50 per night. There are 30 cabins and villas and a 145-room inn at the park; see "Lodging" section above for more information.

Outdoor Adventures

FISHING

Several marinas are located at Dale Hollow Lake, in both Tennessee and Kentucky. The closest to Celina is the **Horse Creek Marina**, which rents boats as well as cabins. The fishing is good for catfish, bluegill, trout, muskie and largemouth, smallmouth and white bass. ~ 1150 Horse Creek Road, Celina; 931-243-2125, 800-545-2595.

The 69-acre **Standing Stone Lake** is popular year-round for catching bass and bluegill; you can even rent a boat to get out on the water, but you'll have to row: No motored craft are allowed.

~ Standing Stone State Park, 1674 Standing Stone Park Highway, Hilham; 931-823-6347, 800-713-5157.

GOLF

Some of the few courses around can be found near Cookeville. One is **Ironwood Golf Course**. ~ 3801 Ironwood Road, Cookeville; 931-528-2331. Another one is **Southern Hills Golf Course & Country Club**. ~ 4749 Ben Jared Road, Cookeville; 931-423-5149. **Fall Creek Falls State Park** has an 18-hole golf course in some of the most scenic parts of the park. ~ Route 3, Pikeville; 615-881-3297.

CANOEING

Cumberland Gap Outfitters and Dive Shop takes folks out in canoes and tubes to see wildlife and a variety of terrain. ~ 124 Brooklyn Street, Cumberland Gap; 423-869-2999, 800-401-6523.

BIKING

Mountain bikers can use the horse trails throughout the 125,000-acre Big South Fork National Recreation and River Area. There are also two designated trails, including the **Collier Ridge Loop**, an eight-mile ride suitable to all levels. The 5.3-mile **Duncan Hollow Loop** also starts at Bandy Creek. The gravel road is marked. The trail descends when you reach the power lines; all riders should be able to handle this single-track trail. The best route for views is the **White Oak Horse Trail**, which is accessed by the Collier Ridge horse trail. It is 20 miles roundtrip, longer if you visit overlooks. Another option is to follow the Gap Blevins road, heading left along a six-mile horse trail that leads to the White Oak overlook. ~ Bandy Creek Visitor Center; 931-879-3625.

HIKING

All distances for hiking trails are one way unless otherwise noted.

Some of Tennessee's best rugged hiking territory can be found at Big South Fork National River and Recreation Area. The **Twin Arches Loop Trail** (5.9 miles roundtrip) begins at a trailhead off Twin Arches Road. One of the most popular destinations in the area, the trail passes a primitive campsite at an old abandoned

AUTHOR FAVORITE

After a long drive, I was thrilled to set out on the short (1.5 miles roundtrip) hike, from the parking lot to **Burgess Falls**. Actually there are several waterfalls, culminating in the spectacular namesake torrent, but also the scenery is lovely: towering beech trees, as well as white oaks, big-leaf magnolias and statuesque hemlock trees. It's not a difficult hike, but the edge of the trail is steep and children should be kept in hand. ~ Route 6, Burgess Falls Road, Sparta; 931-432-5312.

farmstead as well as the hostel, Charit Creek Lodge. Several other historic sites and structures can be seen en route. There is a steep ascent from the lodge to the base of the arches; from there, you have a choice of paths to South Arch or North Arch. The loop is rated difficult, as is the **Honey Creek Loop Trail** (5 miles round-trip). This trail is one of the most beautiful in the park, and while it is not as spectacular as some other trails, it does feature small waterfalls, rock formations and rock houses once used as shelter for American Indians during their hunting expeditions. If you're up for a moderate-to-difficult trail of some 260 miles, check out the **Sheltowee Trace National Recreation Trail** that begins at the Hidden Passage Trailhead in Pickett State Park, runs along the John Muir Trail and leaves Big South Fork to cross the Kentucky state line. ~ 931-879-3625.

Several trails in Frozen Head State Park and Natural Area offer both challenging excursions and scenic outlooks. Physically fit visitors with a hankering for good views of the southern Cumberland Mountains opt for the **Chimney Top Trail** (6.6 miles). From the visitors center, it's steep, rugged terrain interspersed with astonishing vistas, culminating in a giant sandstone caprock. The shortest of several return routes is the **South Old Mack Trail** (2.4 miles). For wildflowers, waterfalls and an easier stroll, try **Panther Branch Trail** (2.1 miles), a loop alongside a creek that's especially nice in springtime and hooks up with South Old Mack. The trailhead is about three-fourths of a mile from the campground and can be accessed by vehicle. For a glimpse of the old black cherry trees for which this park is known, head for the **Lookout Tower Trail** (6.9 miles). It begins at the campground and climbs to the crest of Little Fork Mountain. From Mile 3 to Mile 6, in Cherry Log Gap, is the highest concentration of cherry trees. ~ Six miles southeast of Wartburg off Route 62; 423-346-3318.

Several day-use trails lead to some of the prettiest areas of Fall Creek Falls State Park. Most trailheads are near the North Entrance in the vicinity of the Nature Center adjacent to Cane Creek Falls. The trails are color coded for convenience. The shortest trail to Fall Creek Falls is the **Woodland Trail** (.8 mile), which crosses Cane Creek Cascades across the swinging bridge, then heads up to the overlooks. Along this easy path are plenty of wildflowers, particularly evident in the spring. At the top of the stairs is the **Campground Trail** (.2 mile); taking a left will lead you to the Overflow Campground. Also off Woodland is the **Gorge Overlook Trail** (1.1 miles), which leads to the right and loops around the bluff atop the huge Cane Creek Gorge. This moderate trail takes you to three overlooks, and is especially popular for birdwatchers.

Pine Falls Trail (.25 mile) is an easy hike from the parking area to the Piney Falls Overlook and across the long swinging bridge over Piney Creek. Another easy hike, though much longer, is on the **Paw Paw Trail** (4.6 miles), which begins in the Nature Center parking lot. Allow a couple of hours to cross Rockhouse Creek, mount the hill and walk near Cane Creek Falls; along the way you will be able to see Fall Creek Falls. On the Paw Paw Trail, take a left after crossing Rockhouse Creek to follow the **Cable Trail** (.25 mile), which leads down to the base of Cane Creek Falls. This hike is rugged; a cable is provided to help hikers keep their balance. Hiking-trail maps are available at the ranger station. ~ Route 3, Pikeville; 423-881-3297.

Tennis buffs will find courts at Fall Creek Falls, Rock Island and Standing Stone state parks.

Transportation

CAR

Route 40 runs east–west at about the center of the Cumberland Plateau. Aside from Cookeville, the towns in this section are located far from freeway exits. The major north–south roads are **Route 127**, which runs north from Route 40 to Jamestown; **Route 80**, which runs from Route 40 north to Red Boiling Springs; and **Route 56**, which runs south from Route 40 to McMinnville, and north from Route 40 toward both Red Boiling Springs and Dale Hollow Lake. Other intercity routes are mostly curvy two-lane roads. One of the most scenic routes is **Route 151**, which runs between Route 56 and Red Boiling Springs. Another scenic drive, Route 52 links Rugby, Jamestown and Red Boiling Springs.

AIR

There are no major airports in this region. Cumberland Gap and Rugby are best served by the **McGhee Tyson Airport** (865-970-2749), located 12 miles southwest of downtown Knoxville. Carriers include Delta, Northwest, United and US Airways. Commuter airlines servicing Knoxville are Air Tran, American Eagle and ComAir. See Chapter Three for information about flight service and car rentals.

Red Boiling Springs, Cookeville and McMinnville are within a couple of hours' driving time of the **Nashville International Airport** (www.flynashville.com). Air Canada, American and American Eagle, Continental, Delta, Frontier, Northwest, Southwest, United and US Airways all offer regularly scheduled flights. See Chapter Eight for more information about flights and car rentals.

BUS

Greyhound Bus Lines has a number of terminals serving the Cumberland region. ~ 800-231-2222; www.greyhound.com. Major stations are in Knoxville at 100 East Magnolia Avenue; and in downtown Nashville at 200 8th Avenue South. In the smaller towns, there are terminals in Cookeville at 241 Palk Way Drive; 931-526-9212; and in Crossville at 4084 Route 127N at Route 40; 931-484-5859.

EIGHT

Nashville

To paraphrase Barbara Mandrell's popular song, Nashville was country way before country was cool. There may be an ongoing dialogue, especially among musicologists and historians, about the exact origins of what we call country music, but few would argue that Nashville is now the epicenter.

It's also the capital of the state of Tennessee and its second-largest city, but sometimes those facts are dwarfed by the town's moniker, Music City. That nickname is now getting some competition from an older one, the Athens of the South. With a plethora of universities and fine public buildings, Nashville pursued its image as a Mecca for education, architecture and the fine arts, erecting a replica of the real Parthenon in 1897. Today there is a renaissance of that cultural pride, thanks to the opening of the Frist Center for the Visual Arts, funding for a new concert hall for the Nashville Symphony, a grand main library and, of course, the impressive Country Music Hall of Fame, which opened in 2001.

Like all great Tennessee cities, Nashville is a river town—in this case, the Cumberland River, which runs alongside the oldest part of town before looping north and west into a horseshoe pattern. The first-known inhabitants of the area were, in fact, the deer who frequented the nearby salt lick, followed closely by the American Indian hunters who knew it. When the French arrived and set up a trading post in the early 18th century, they dubbed the place French Lick. The French lost rights to the little fur trading center under the Treaty of Paris in 1763, around the time a French-Canadian trader named Timothy Demonbreun came on the scene. Demonbreun, who is memorialized with a major street name, is considered the first settler; he was followed by the English, led by James Robertson. The town grew from there, becoming a major shipping port servicing the farms and plantations established in surrounding counties.

Nashville's development was also prompted by its position at the northern terminus of the Natchez Trace. What had begun as a path for migrating buffalo and then for the Indians who hunted them was later established as the major overland route from the Gulf of Mexico to the interior. From Nashville, ships sailed down to the coast; the Trace was the logical return route. After steamboats came into use, the Trace was largely abandoned, though it has been recently reestablished and is paved all the way from southwest Nashville to the Mississippi state line and farther south.

James Robertson, who had led the English settlers into this part of the frontier, helped found the city in 1779. The city flourished as a cotton center and later as a railroad hub. In the mid-19th century, Nashville built turnpikes, some 410 miles of roads that linked it to outlying communities and farms. It became the state's permanent capital in 1843. Less than 20 years later, Nashville was abandoned to Union troops and became a crucial base for the rest of the Civil War.

After the war, Nashville's burgeoning prosperity was reflected in the grandeur of some of its architecture—notably the state capitol, the Gothic Revival University of Nashville and various mansions on the outskirts of the city such as Belmont and Belle Meade. Then came the era of the railroads—the Nashville and Chattanooga Railroad (1854), the Louisville and Nashville Railroad (1859) and then the Nashville and Decatur Railroad (1860), which linked the city with Memphis and the state of Alabama to the south.

Nashville also distinguished itself with the establishment of numerous universities, including Fisk, Roger Williams and Vanderbilt. Today, the city boasts 141 institutions of higher learning, 10 of which offer graduate programs.

In the early part of the century, neighborhoods began to evolve away from downtown. One of the most prominent was the Belmont–Hillsboro area, which boomed after a streetcar line linked it to the city center. Seven years later, in 1908, a streetcar line also boosted the Hillsboro–West End neighborhood, today one of the most desirable places to live in Nashville.

Between the Great Depression and the onset of World War II, Nashville saw perhaps its greatest development, including a new airport, the Percy and Edwin Warner Parks and numerous government buildings constructed around the state capitol. Where the Public Square once flourished, a new Davidson County Courthouse was built in 1937, replacing the original antebellum structure.

By this time, Nashville was setting the stage for its emergence as the premier country music town in the United States. Since 1925, radio station WSM had been presenting country music; in 1943 it began broadcasting the Grand Ole Opry from the stage of the Ryman Auditorium. No one could have predicted the widespread appeal of the music, largely because so many of its fans and practitioners were spread all over the hills, hollers and plains from one end of Tennessee to the other, and beyond. Today Nashville tops the charts in producing country music. It's also the number-two overall music recording center in the nation (Los Angeles is number one). The local entertainment industry counts on the talents of some 25,000 people. Music means a lot to Nashville's economy.

It is estimated by the Country Music Association that half of all single records produced in the United States come out of Nashville. Not only did Elvis record some 200 titles here—in RCA's historic Studio B—but the economic boom of the 1960s helped boost the local record industry. And it's never stopped growing.

Nashville is one of the South's major investment banking centers and also a force in the insurance and health care industries. Fans of the original Grand Ole

Opry may recall that, after all, the show was broadcast on WSM, the station belonging to the National Life and Accident Insurance Company (We Shield Millions).

A major factor in Nashville's robust economy is its location, within 600 miles of nearly half the U.S. population. The area has more than 100 freight terminals and 150 major freight lines, as well as a growing network of highways and interstates, such as the currently expanding southern portion of the Route 840 outer beltway.

Fabulously beautiful in the spring with dogwoods and other seasonal blossoms, Nashville, at an elevation of 550 feet, can be gray and bleak in the winter months.

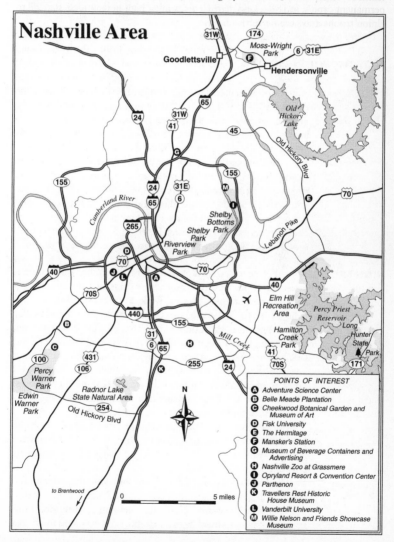

Nashville Area

POINTS OF INTEREST
A Adventure Science Center
B Belle Meade Plantation
C Cheekwood Botanical Garden and Museum of Art
D Fisk University
E The Hermitage
F Mansker's Station
G Museum of Beverage Containers and Advertising
H Nashville Zoo at Grassmere
I Opryland Resort & Convention Center
J Parthenon
K Travellers Rest Historic House Museum
L Vanderbilt University
M Willie Nelson and Friends Showcase Museum

The average low in January is about 27°; the high, a not-so-hot 46°. June days average a high of nearly 90°, with a low of just 65°. Average humidity is 58 percent; rainfall, less than 50 inches. The city limits are coterminous with the Davidson County line. More than half a million people live in the city, and another half-million are settled into surrounding communities.

More than any other city in Tennessee, Nashville is a place for blue jeans and Western shirts—at least for tourists and people in the music business. You'll want to dress up for evening performances of the ballet, symphony or orchestra, but if you plan to spend some time at the small bars and restaurants where local groups are playing, you'll look out of place in a tie, suit or high heels (unless they're attached to some mighty expensive boots).

Downtown Nashville

For much of the late 1990s, the area around 2nd Avenue North near Riverfront Park looked more like a construction zone than a cosmopolitan urban center. Two nightspots (the Wildhorse Saloon and the Hard Rock Cafe) were just getting their finishing touches, inviting yet another wave of immigrants. In the 1800s, this area bustled with the business of whiskey dealers, cotton merchants and tobacco planters. In the 1980s, the city's preservation work and foresight paid off, luring many shopkeepers back to the area. Gradually, this infusion of capital has begun to show in cleaner streets and more visitors. There are some cool clubs and one-of-a-kind music stores in the neighborhood, roughly a five-block zone. A few blocks away from the riverfront are the Convention Center and the inevitable blockbuster hotels that cater to conventioneers, and beyond that, the elegant grounds of the state capitol.

SIGHTS   A good place to start your visit to Nashville is the **visitors center**, inside the Nashville Arena and across from the Convention Center. Here you can pick up **City Walk**, a free self-guided map distributed by the Nashville Convention & Visitors Bureau. The walk begins near the Cumberland River at Fort Nashborough, runs along Church Street and along 6th Avenue and meanders over to Charlotte Avenue, passing the Ryman Auditorium and other historical buildings including the state capitol. ~ In the Gaylord Entertainment Center, 501 Broadway; 615-259-4747. Maps are also available from the **Metropolitan Historical Commission.** ~ 209 10th Avenue South, Suite 414; 615-862-7970.

The best resources for exploring the city are available at the **Nashville Convention and Visitors Bureau.** ~ 211 Commerce Street. ~ Suite 100; 615-259-4700, 800-657-6910; www.music cityusa.com.

The Country Music Hall of Fame and Museum, which relocated from Music Row to a spectacular, $37-million building in 2001, instantly became Nashville's defining institution. Constructed of native stone, it spans an entire city block on the banks of the Cumberland River within steps of the legendary Ryman Auditorium and the honky tonks along Lower Broadway. Any initial visit should begin in the Ford Theater, located off the glassed-in rotunda, which screens a film exploring and explaining the impact and variety of country music around the world. Then it's on to the marvelous exhibits, complete with videos of performers both famous and arcane as well as myriad artifacts. Industry insiders, scholars and serious fans also appreciate the extraordinary library and archive, which houses more than 200,000 recorded discs and thousands of photographs, films, videotapes, songbooks, posters, sheet music and audio tapes. An adjunct of the museum is Studio B on Music Row, "Home of 1,000 Hits," where Dolly Parton, Elvis Presley, the Everly Brothers, Roy Orbison and countless others recorded over the years. Admission. ~ 222 5th Avenue South; 615-416-2001, 800-852-6437; www.countrymusichalloffame.com.

If you have ever hummed along to a country-and-western song, you'll have to make the pilgrimage to the **Ryman Auditorium**. It's

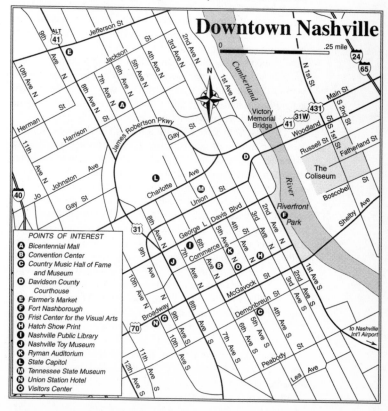

Downtown Nashville

0   .25 mile

POINTS OF INTEREST

Ⓐ Bicentennial Mall
Ⓑ Convention Center
Ⓒ Country Music Hall of Fame
   and Museum
Ⓓ Davidson County
   Courthouse
Ⓔ Farmer's Market
Ⓕ Fort Nashborough
Ⓖ Frist Center for the Visual Arts
Ⓗ Hatch Show Print
Ⓘ Nashville Public Library
Ⓙ Nashville Toy Museum
Ⓚ Ryman Auditorium
Ⓛ State Capitol
Ⓜ Tennessee State Museum
Ⓝ Union Station Hotel
Ⓞ Visitors Center

located between the major downtown hotels and the river. The Grand Ole Opry, which was presented here from 1943 to 1974, has long since relocated to Opryland, but you can almost feel the spirits of Hank Williams, Sr., and Minnie Pearl and the dozens of legends (and doubtless hundreds of lesser souls) who graced these planks. Displays encircle the auditorium room—Marty Robbins' sparkle-plenty boots and the like—but for the full experience, sit in on the talks by one of the tour guides, and be sure to take them up on the offer to set your foot on the actual stage where modern country-music broadcasting was born and nurtured. The building now accommodates country, bluegrass, inspirational and classical performances. Backstage tours offered. Admission. ~ 116 5th Avenue North; 615-254-1445 for general information, 615-889-6611 for box office; www.ryman.com.

Half a block down Broadway, you can actually buy posters and postcards at **Hatch Show Print,** the oldest-known poster print shop in the country. Elvis Presley and Bessie Smith as well as Patsy Cline and Roy Acuff had their posters done by Hatch, which has been relocated from its original site several times. Most people probably visit just to see the wonderful visuals created by a business that's been operating since 1879; many of the methods employed have been used almost since the beginning, despite developments in the industry that allow mass production. Thousands of wood and metal blocks are stored along one long brick wall in this busy shop, which now does posters for the current generation of musical legends. Closed Sunday. ~ 316 Broadway; 615-256-2805; www.halloffame.org.

The **Frist Center for the Visual Arts** is a masterpiece in itself, located in a lovingly and lavishly restored beaux arts–style post office built in the early 1930s. While it has no permanent collection of its own, the museum hosts a wide range of exhibits from such prestigious institutions as the Philadelphia Museum of Art and London's Tate Gallery. With more than 20,000 square feet of exhibit space, there's room for special galleries devoted to community arts, education and contemporary artists. The center also offers interactive opportunities, media and technology resources and a chance for visitors to create their own works. Admission. ~ 919 Broadway; 615-244-3340; www.fristcenter.org.

Now a hotel by the same name, the grand **Union Station** was built in 1900 by the Louisville and Nashville Railroad. The exterior of the massive stone building looks like you'd expect a station to look, but it's a different story on the inside. There are several restaurants and bars where you can take a break, which you'll need after taking in the elaborate stained glass and detailed woodwork—all original—that give this Richardsonian Romanesque structure a lot of its pizzazz. ~ 1001 Broadway; 615-726-1001.

A few blocks north on 8th Avenue North, the **Nashville Toy Museum** is a very personal museum, curated over a lifetime by Ted Lannon. Lannon fell in love with toys on childhood trips to the Smithsonian Institution. Wooden boats and ships, German teddy bears, model cars, all-steel fire trucks and much more fill every nook of this single-story roadside attraction. The collection includes several extremely rare boats as well as offbeat circus figurines, but most visitors will remember the trains. Models include American Flyer and Lionel trains from the 1920s and '30s, pre–World War I British trains and marvelous layouts including a wind-up version Lannon put together that uses no electricity whatsoever. Of course there's a gift shop. Who wouldn't want to exploit all that excitement? Admission. ~ 162 8th Avenue South; 615-742-5678.

The elegant main branch of the **Nashville Public Library** is actually worth a visit even if you don't plan to check out any books. The Nashville Room on the second floor is a trove of tomes on regional history and culture, such as *The Journal of Southern History*, *The Civil War Times* and the *Tennessee Historical Quarterly*. Also worth a peek is the area set aside for children, which includes pint-sized seating, computers and a theater where marionette shows are offered on a regular schedule. ~ 615 Church Street; 615-862-5800; www.librarynashville.org.

Several blocks from the Cumberland River, the **Tennessee State Museum** vies with the Ryman as the most important sight in Nashville. The carefully crafted displays document the state's history, beginning with its first residents—the mastodons. From pre-Indian communities through the Revolutionary War, settlement, displacement of the American Indians, the Civil War and into the present day, this contemporary, multilevel museum ex-

sights

AUTHOR FAVORITE

Even if you, like I, can't carry a tune in a bucket, you ought to step on the stage of the **Ryman Auditorium**. The former home of the Grand Ole Opry feels more like a church than an auditorium; the exhibits do elicit reverence. Not surprising, considering that the 1892 building was constructed as the Union Gospel Tabernacle. It was Lula C. Naff, one of the early managers of the hall, who transformed it into Nashville's cultural center, featuring a diverse array of performers from John Philips Sousa to Isadora Duncan. As Naff said, "Who wanted to hear Billy Sunday when you could go see Mary Pickford for a dime?" See page 211 for more information.

DRIVING TOUR

Nashville Country Music Tour

Nashville isn't pure country music anymore, but no city offers as much of the genre as Music City does. From morning until night, you'll find places to visit and entertainers to enjoy all over town.

MUSIC ESSENTIALS Step onto the stage following a tour of **Ryman Auditorium** (page 211), the "mother church" of country music and former home of the Grand Ole Opry. Head south on 5th Avenue one block to Broadway and duck into **Gruhn Guitars** (page 220), on the corner to your right, to see hundreds of guitars and other stringed instruments beloved by country musicians.

HONKY TONK ROW Return to Broadway and turn left, towards the river. On either side of the street are the venues that comprise Honky Tonk Row, where many clubs feature live music from morning past midnight. On your left will be **Tootsie's Orchid Lounge** (page 220), easy to find because of its lavender exterior. A couple of doors down is **Robert's Western World** (page 220), where popular acts like BR-549 and Brazilbilly have performed.

RECORDS AND PRINTS Cross the street to check out **Ernest Tubb's Record Shop** (page 220), holding strong after more than half a century. Keep walking towards the river and you'll see **Hatch Show Print** (page 212), which makes the posters that have featured Hall of Famers Hank Williams and Bill Monroe as well as contemporary musicians.

COUNTRY MUSIC HALL OF FAME Head south on 5th Avenue South to visit the Country Music Hall of Fame and Museum (page 210).

STATION INN Drive or walk back up to Broadway and then eight blocks to 12th Avenue South. Take a left and look for Station Inn (page 221), a small club boasting some of the best bluegrass in the state.

plains the who, what, when, where and why of Tennessee, with an impressive assortment of artifacts, photographs, exhibits and audio-visual aids. The only thing left unexplained is the presence of an Egyptian mummy donated by a generous citizen. Closed Monday. ~ 5th Avenue North and Deaderick Street; 615-741-2692; www.tnmuseum.org, e-mail info@tnmuseum.org.

The museum is across the street from the imposing **Tennessee State Capitol.** Even the architect, William Strickland, was so impressed that he asked to be buried here. Indeed he is, in the north-

MUSIC ROW   Take the short drive to Music Row (page 223), ground zero of Nashville's booming music industry. Head south one block on 12th Avenue South to Division Street, make a right, and, at the traffic circle, look for the 17th Avenue South turn on the right. This one-way, tree-lined street is chockablock with the offices of the industry's top record labels, publishers, promoters and performing-rights organizations.

RADIO CAFÉ   From Music Row, you have a choice of visiting clubs on opposite sides of town. To reach Radio Café (page 221), located in historic Lockland Springs just east of downtown, continue along 17th Avenue South to Wedgewood and turn left. Take the on-ramp to Route 65 North, which is about a mile away. You'll turn left after the overpass and be heading back towards downtown Nashville. Stay on Route 65 North and look for the Shelby Street exit to the right. Take Shelby Street for six blocks until you reach 10th Street and turn left, heading for the intersection with Woodland Street. Turn right onto Woodland and go four blocks to the four-way stop. Radio Café is on the far left corner. (Now that you know where it is, you can come back after dark to listen to country, blues and jazz and grab a bite to eat.)

MORE THAN FOOD   If you want to visit the **Bluebird Cafe** (page 234), you can reach it from Music Row by continuing on 17th Avenue South to Wedgewood, turning right and traveling for several blocks until turning left onto 21st Avenue South. This route will take you past the popular breakfast hangout **Pancake Pantry** (page 226) (where even the stars have to wait in line). Continue through Hillsboro Village (around here, the name changes to Hillsboro Road) and continue past Route 440 and through the shopping area known as Green Hills. Pass the Green Hills Mall on the right and the HG Hills grocery shopping complex, and then keep an eye out for the café, a nondescript storefront in the middle of a strip shopping center on the left, where you can enjoy an intimate evening of singer-songwriter entertainment.

east corner in a tomb of his own design. Also on, or in, the grounds are President James Polk and his wife. The grounds are elegant, located on a knoll clearly visible from the grand Bicentennial Mall constructed in time for the 1996 statewide celebration. The building itself, constructed between 1855 and 1859, has a large stone block basement, Ionic porticoes on each end and a cupola inspired by the Lysicrates monument in Athens—all in keeping with Nashville's claim as the "Athens of the South." Local limestone and marble from around Knoxville are incorporated in the capitol, which can be visited whenever the legislature is in session. Guided tours are offered six times daily. Self-guided tour maps are available here and at the Tennessee State Museum across the street. Wheelchair access is on Charlotte Avenue. Closed weekends. ~ Charlotte Avenue between 6th and 7th avenues; 615-741-0830.

HIDDEN ▶   The **Bicentennial Mall**, a 19-acre urban mall constructed just in time for the 1996 celebration of 200 years of Tennessee statehood, lies west of the Tennessee State Capitol. Dead-end and one-way streets can make it very hard to reach in a car; your best bet is to park near the capitol and walk from there. If it seems vaguely familiar, it's because it was patterned after the National Mall in Washington, D.C. Besides the relief map of Tennessee near the main entrance, the mall is not terribly exciting if you're not a native, to whom the Walk of the Counties—a sidewalk formed of 95 disks representing the state's counties—would mean something. ~ 598 North James Robertson Parkway, bounded by 5th and 8th avenues; 615-741-5280.

Bicentennial Mall is a pretty place to walk and, best of all, it's across the street from the **Farmer's Market**, an 11-acre smorgasbord large enough for 200 vendor stalls beneath a soaring ceiling supported by wood trusses. ~ 900 8th Avenue North; 615-880-2001.

Modern art aficionados may want to take a detour west on Jefferson Street to Fisk University. The **Carl Van Vechten Gallery** here claims the best collection of modern art in all of Tennessee. Even if you're not a student, you are welcome to tour the two-floor gallery. The permanent Stieglitz Collection includes more than 100 works by painters such as Picasso, Cézanne, Renoir, O'Keeffe and Toulouse-Lautrec, as well as African sculpture and other pieces. Closed Sunday and Monday. ~ 1000 17th Street at Jackson Street; 615-329-8543.

To resume your civic-edifice tour from the Bicentennial Mall, head southeast to the **Davidson County Courthouse**. The original antebellum structure is no more; it was destroyed in the 1930s to make way for a new building, one graced with Doric columns,

MUSIC CITY MEANDERINGS

If you'd like a bit of guidance around Nashville, contact **Historic Nashville**, which offers group walking tours by reservation. The tours begin at 9 a.m. from Fort Nashborough. Fee. ~ 615-244-7835. Another option is the **Nashville Black Heritage Tours**, which offers a look at Music City from an African-American perspective. Fee. ~ 5188 Almaville Road, Smyrna; 615-890-8173.

perhaps to help quiet vociferous opposition to the destruction of the old Greek Revival structure. The blend of art-deco elements with the classical qualifies it as "WPA" (Work Projects Administration) in style, a hybrid incorporating aspects of history with the future. The murals by Dean Cornwell fairly scream WPA with their images of industry, commerce, agriculture and statesmanship. Ask for a brochure at the lobby desk. The courthouse stands at what used to be the Public Square, the details of which are obscured by modern razing and building. ~ James Robertson Parkway, between 1st and 3rd avenues north; 615-862-5000.

Just a few blocks south of the courthouse, right on the Cumberland River, is **Fort Nashborough**. The fort is a reconstruction of Nashville's first settlement, which was established only a couple of blocks away. Smaller than the 1779 original, and with fewer cabins, the replica in what is now Riverfront Park nonetheless has stockaded walls and exhibits of pioneer implements that give visitors an idea of pioneer life, and interpreters are usually on hand to answer questions. ~ 170 1st Avenue North at Church Street; 615-862-8400.

The beaux arts–style **Hermitage Hotel**, built in 1910 as Nashville's first million-dollar hotel, has recently undergone a $15 million restoration project. The new owners reconfigured the interior spaces to create 123 rooms and suites but have left the stunning lobby intact. ~ 231 6th Avenue North; 615-244-3121, 888-888-9414; www.thehermitagehotel.com. ULTRA-DELUXE.

LODGING

The gay-friendly **Savage House Inn**, set in an 1840s Italianate townhouse on the National Register of Historic Places, offers six comfortable rooms with private or shared baths. Furnished in period style furnishings, guest rooms include TVs, microwaves, coffeemakers and mini refrigerators. Full breakfast included. Reservations recommended. ~ 165 8th Avenue North; 615-244-2229, fax 615-254-1261. MODERATE TO DELUXE.

The focus at the **Wyndham Union Station Hotel** is now strictly on inbound traffic. The best feature of this 1900 National Historic Landmark, extensively restored in 1986, is its magnificent lobby. A vaulted glass ceiling soars above a second-tier balcony, evoking images of Orient Express grandeur. All the guest rooms have cherrywood furniture, damask-covered walls and green berber carpet. The nicer rooms on the balcony level are glassed in on the lobby side (floor-to-ceiling drapes provide privacy). With 111 rooms and 13 suites carved out of the old train station (seven levels in all, some of them below the street), the hotel retains a smidgen of glory, albeit of the slightly faded variety. ~ 1001 Broadway; 615-726-1001, fax 615-248-6143. DELUXE TO ULTRA-DELUXE.

DINING

Located in the lobby of the Country Music Hall of Fame, the **SoBro Grille** offers a snazzy but limited menu to the general public during museum operating hours. Typical options range from meatloaf to pasta to vegetable plates, plus a daily assortment of homemade cakes, cookies and other sweets. No dinner. ~ 222 5th Avenue South; 625-254-9060. BUDGET.

Close to attractions like Fort Nashborough, **The Melting Pot** is a blast from the past. If you've always kind of missed the fondue restaurants so popular in the '70s, this is your place. Chicken, sirloin and even lobster get the melted cheese treatment, although many dishes also can be ordered cooked in court bouillon instead. Save room for chocolate fondue desserts. ~ 166 2nd Avenue North; 615-742-4970, fax 615-726-6328. MODERATE TO DELUXE.

Downtown workers gather even before the noon hour in the cool, dark recesses of **Market Street Brewery & Public House**. Some grab tables along the wall in the long, long bar room; others make the trek to the back room, where dark glossy woods and Victorian wallpaper evoke an upscale British pub. Diners may settle for inexpensive pub fare like "Brewtus's Caesar Salad" (with chicken), Tap Room Five-way Chili or Creole-style Backstage Red Beans and Rice with andouille sausage. The menu also lists gumbo, crawfish étouffée and steaks and chicken. ~ 134 2nd Avenue North; 615-259-9611, fax 615-242-9851. BUDGET TO MODERATE.

You don't have to be on an all-beer diet to dine at **Big River Grille & Brewing Works**, but it would be a shame to miss their special lagers, ales, stouts and pilsner. Distinguished by exposed brick walls, semi-industrial decor and a TV always tuned to sports, the grille has a seasonal menu that may highlight steak, hazelnut-crusted chicken or chicken-fried steak. ~ 111 Broadway; 615-251-4677. BUDGET TO MODERATE.

Magenta walls, hardwood floors and marble-topped bar tables constitute the decor on the ground floor at another popular

AUTHOR FAVORITE

I had to pace myself at **Monell's**, where platter after platter of food arrives in quick succession. Dishes such as cheese grits, corn casserole, fluffy biscuits, country ham, pancakes and fried chicken are all served family style. And that's just for breakfast. I even bought some housemade peach preserves to take home from this remodeled circa-1880 red-brick residence. No dinner Sunday and Monday. ~ 1235 6th Avenue; 615-248-4747 (second location at 530 Church Street; 615-248-4744). BUDGET TO MODERATE.

downtown restaurant, **The Merchants**, a former hotel now on the National Register of Historic Places. If it's nice weather or you're in a hurry, you can dine out on the patio or in the ground-floor bar-and-café. For more elegant dining, ask to be seated upstairs. The ambience is dated in a nice kind of way, but not the menu. Shrimp scampi, ahi tuna, veal rib chop, roasted pork tenderloin and other contemporary dishes attract a regular clientele. ~ 401 Broadway; 615-254-1892, fax 615-254-3012. MODERATE TO DELUXE.

For a fast, cheap but dependable lunch, drop by **Amy's**, where you can get a weekday meal of meat-and-three for less than $10. No dinner. Closed Saturday and Sunday. ~ 500 Church Street; 615-320-1740. BUDGET.

Of several inexpensive food stands at the Nashville Farmers Market, the one that doubles as **El Burrito Mexicano** and **Joe's Barbeque and Fish** offers the widest selection. The Mexican menu includes tacos, nachos, quesadillas, a couple of full platters and plenty of sides, while Joe's leans to regional fare like catfish sandwiches, hamburgers and fried okra. ~ 900 8th Avenue North; 615-255-0136. BUDGET.   ◄ HIDDEN

You may not find it on your first try, but don't give up on the **Mad Platter**. If you like Nashville and you like restored neighborhoods, you'll love this place. Housed in an old brick store on a corner near several fixed-up Victorian homes, this is at heart a neighborhood spot—but for obvious reasons, outsiders just keep on comin' in for innovative meals served in one large high-ceilinged room. The ever-changing menu marches to its own drummer, a mix of innovative interpretations of favorites like salmon portobello, crabcakes, gnocchi, pasta, salads and some heartier fare like grilled pork loin, pan-seared duck breast and veal piccata. Try to be seated near the wall of bookshelves while you wait. Lunch Monday through Friday and dinner by reservation. Closed Sunday. ~ 1239 6th Avenue North; 615-242-2563, fax 615-254-0934. DELUXE TO ULTRA-DELUXE.   ◄ HIDDEN

Closed during the $15-million renovation of the Hermitage Hotel, the lower-level **Capitol Grille** reopened in early 2003 with a menu devoted to Southern fusion cuisine. ~ 231 6th Avenue North; 615-254-6909. DELUXE TO ULTRA-DELUXE.

One of the hippest restaurants in Nashville can be found on the far side of Route 5 from downtown. On most warm nights a line forms at **Cafe One Two Three**; Nashvilleans know this wood-paneled restaurant is *the* place for a different kind of Southern cooking. Ostrich quesadilla, mushroom strudel, buffalo and homemade desserts are among the dishes offered. There are a few more prosaic items on the menu, but for adventure in dining, this is the spot. Dinner only. Closed Sunday. ~ 123 12th Avenue North; 615-255-2233, fax 615-259-2957. MODERATE TO DELUXE.

SHOPPING   If you're in the market for a guitar, you can't do much better than cruising into **Gruhn Guitars** and checking out their assortment of classic Gibson guitars. Closed Sunday. ~ 400 Broadway; 615-256-2033.

You can shop for the absolutely coolest boots at **Robert's Western World**, which showcases some of Nashville's hottest talent at night. ~ 416 Broadway; 615-244-9552.

Jam-packed with country-music audiotapes, videos, CDs, albums, sheet music, books and magazines, **Ernest Tubb's Record Shop** is an obligatory stop for lovers of the genre, if only for the vibes. If you see a title that sparks your interest, ask the clerk to play it while you peruse the stacks and make up your mind. ~ 417 Broadway; 615-255-7503.

In addition to art supplies, books, framed posters and decorative arts from around the world, the **Frist Center Shop** offers some merchandise not ordinarily associated with art galleries, including scented candles, CDs and videos. ~ 919 Broadway; 615-244-3340.

One of several shops in the 8th Avenue Antique District, **Michael Taylor and Company** offers an extensive collection of antiques, collectibles and rugs. Closed Sunday and Monday. ~ 2108 8th Avenue South; 615-292-9944.

The **Downtown Antique Mall** is a 13,000-square-foot warehouse filled with collectibles and antiques from furniture to knickknacks. ~ 612 8th Avenue South; 615-256-6616.

Even if you're not preparing meals while you're in town, do drop by the **Nashville Farmer's Market** for a peek at regional fruits, vegetables and much more. ~ 900 8th Avenue North.

NIGHTLIFE   The **Wildhorse Saloon** is a cavernous facility that opened in 1994 claiming state-of-the-art technology. Thursday through Monday there are live country-music bands; the rest of the time, the place operates as a danceclub with a variety of recorded music and videos. Nightly dance lessons offered. Cover. ~ 120 2nd Avenue North; 615-902-8200, 615-902-8218.

Tootsie's Orchid Lounge treads a fine line between museum and nightclub. Fairly rank with years of alcohol and smoke but

AUTHOR FAVORITE

Talk about boot-scootin' music. Between sets performed by the latest and hottest local bands at **Robert's Western World**, you can shop for the right boots to wear on the dancefloor. Cover. ~ 416 Broadway; 615-244-9552.

also redolent of musical memories, Tootsie's was a favorite hang-out of Patsy Cline, Willie Nelson, Kris Kristofferson, Roger Miller, Waylon Jennings and dozens of other successful performers whose photos line the walls; scenes from the movies *Coal Miner's Daughter* and *W. W. and the Dixie Dancekings* were filmed here. Tootsie Bess, by the way, bought a place, called Mom's, back in 1960 and renamed it after she came in one day to find a painter had redone her place in a bright pink orchid shade. If you can't wait 'til night-fall to hear live music, head for Tootsie's, where musicians some-times begin as early as 2 p.m. The joint stays open until 2 a.m. ~ 422 Broadway; 615-726-0463.

Aside from giant Elvis stamp paintings on the walls, there's not a lot of visual interest at **3rd and Lindsley**, but that's not what draws crowds to this long-standing favorite. It's the blues, stupid—that and a little jazz, R&B and some alternative bands. Cover. ~ 816 3rd Avenue South; 615-259-9891.

Top local bands entertain at restaurant-nightclub **12th & Porter**, on the far side of Route 65 from downtown. Cover. ~ 114 12th Avenue North; 615-254-7236.

Bluegrass is king at the **Station Inn**. Cover. ~ 401 12th Avenue South; 615-255-3307.

Nashville is the best place to see up-and-coming singers and songwriters, and a good spot for picking tomorrow's country music stars is the **Radio Café**. Closed Sunday. Cover. ~ 1313 Woodland Street; 615-262-1766.

The Coliseum, home to the NFL's Tennessee Titans, sits across the river from downtown. In the offseason, the venue hosts various events, including the CMA Music Festival, a sum-mertime country music extravaganza. ~ One Titans Way; 615-565-4200 (tickets), 615-565-4300 (office); www.www.titanson-line.com.

SYMPHONY, THEATER AND DANCE   The **Nashville Symphony Orchestra** has a year-round schedule of classical and pops concerts at the Tennessee Performing Arts Center at 505 Deaderick Street. ~ 209 10th Avenue South; 615-255-5600; www.nashvillesym phony.org.

Recognized as one of the leading regional opera companies in North America, the **Nashville Opera** presents two performances each of three different operas in October, January and May at the Tennessee Performing Arts Center at 505 Deaderick Street. ~ 1900 Belmont Boulevard, Suite 404; 615-255-2787; www.nash villeopera.com.

Nashville Children's Theatre is a nonprofit professional the-ater that presents material aimed at younger audiences. For dates, times and a list of performances, call the office. ~ 724 2nd Avenue South; 615-254-9103.

The **Nashville Ballet** season runs from October through April at the Tennessee Performing Arts Center. ~ 3630 Redmon Street; 615-297-2966; www.nashvilleballet.com.

Established in 1949, **Circle Players** is Music City's oldest community theater. Productions like *The Importance of Being Earnest* and *The Rocky Horror Picture Show* are acted by an all-volunteer cast during the September through May season at the Tennessee Performing Arts Center at 505 Deaderick Street. ~ 615-254-0113.

GAY SCENE The **Jungle** is a popular gay-and-lesbian lounge/ restaurant that sometimes offers drag shows on the weekends. ~ 306 4th Avenue South; 615-256-9411.

Tribe is a straight-friendly gay club where pop video music reverberates on the main floor, the stylish rectangular bar serves as the centerpiece, and a quieter room upstairs is filled with couches and cocktail tables suitable to mingling and conversation. Behind the little cement dancefloor is a restaurant. ~ 1517-A Church Street; 615-329-2912.

Housed in an 1840s Victorian townhouse and situated right next to the Savage House Inn, **Gas Lite Lounge** is a friendly neighborhood bar. Thursday is karaoke night. Occasional drag shows also take the stage. ~ 167½ 8th Avenue North; 615-254-1278.

Located south of downtown, the **Chute Complex** offers a choice of diversions in six themed bars. The main bar has a dancefloor to go along with the tribal/dance/rhythm-and-blues tunes; drag shows are a hit Monday, Wednesday, Friday and Saturday. In the back, you can either chill out in the patio or get up and dance at the country-and-western bar. The leather bar also has a patio, with high-energy dance music streaming through the room. The piano bar allows private time with its conversation lounge and cozy fireplace. Although the clientele is mostly gay men, women are always welcome. Cover. ~ 2535 Franklin Road; 615-297-4571.

Popular with trendy lesbians, the **Lipstick Lounge** is a rather swank jazz den where the house specialties are top-shelf martinis, elegant appetizers and dessert fare; there's an upstairs room for smoking cigars and shooting pool. ~ 1400 Woodland Street; 615-226-6343.

▼▼▼▼▼▼▼▼▼▼▼▼▼▼▼▼▼▼

Music Row to West End

Broadway and Church Street are major arteries leading west from downtown. Eventually, Broadway becomes West End Avenue, and Church forks to the south, eventually turning into Hillsboro Pike. This area lies mostly inside the Route 440 perimeter and encompasses Music Row, just off Broadway, Vanderbilt University and a neighborhood called Elliston Place.

The West End area of Nashville has a plethora of attractions, not the least of which is trendy West End Avenue itself.

Music Row is not a row at all, but a neighborhood devoted almost exclusively to the production, promotion, consumption and adulation of country music. Unlike, say, Hollywood, the industry is not run out of highrises or ritzy studios, but in bungalows that have been revamped to house businesses. If you're not in the business, you'd probably never know that these little houses aren't residences, but money-making machines. The row is roughly bounded by Demonbreun Street, Music Square West, Grand Avenue and Music Circle. The cognoscenti say that if you don't have an office in Music Row, you might as well use the pay phone at Shoney's.

Even from inside your car, you can appreciate **Musica**, a new sculpture in the middle of the Music Row roundabout. The arrangement of male and female nudes was sculpted by Alan LeQuire, whose best-known work is his re-creation of the an-

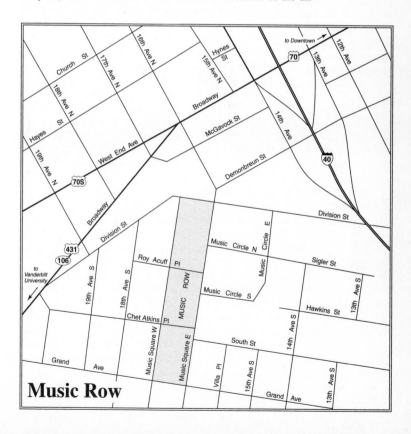

Music Row

cient Greek "Athena Parthenos," housed in the parthenon in Nashville's Centennial Park. *Musica* is believed to be the largest bronze figure group in the country. ~ 615-862-8400.

The **West End** is a lively area where families have refurbished old houses and bungalows. Some blocks are particularly nice; this neighborhood claims former governor Lamar Alexander as a resident. The neighborhood extends roughly from 19th Avenue North to Centennial Park, and about three blocks on either side of West End Avenue.

Tennessee's big cities are loaded with monuments to antiquity (think about the very name Memphis), none more impressive than Nashville's **Parthenon**. Construction of the only existing full-scale replica of the Parthenon in Athens, Greece, was undertaken by the city to house the international art exhibition of the 1897 Centennial Exposition. Typical of that era, citizens fell in love with this grand, if not grandiose, symbol of their city, the "Athens of the South." In 1921 they reconstructed the brick, wooden lathe and plaster structure with permanent materials; it was renovated again in 1987. Four galleries display changing exhibits, but the Parthenon's crowning glory, appropriately enough, is the 42-foot statue of Athena, which was created over five years by Nashville sculptor Alan LeQuire. Also, in the Neos (the larger of the Parthenon's two halls) are casts of the Elgin Marbles that the British excavated in Greece and whisked away to the British Museum in London. Closed Monday. Admission. ~ Centennial Park, 2600 West End Avenue at Elliston Street; 615-862-8431.

Tennessee's official animal, the ubiquitous raccoon, can be spotted throughout the state, but its most notable sighting is as the Tennessee Titans' feisty mascot.

Founded in 1875 and sponsored by the Methodist Church—though not as a denominational college—**Vanderbilt University** severed all its ties with the church in 1914. The school's Victorian Gothic buildings, along with its elaborate landscaping planted with hundreds of different trees and shrubs, helped boost Nashville's claim as the "Athens of the South." The campus layout today is based on the 1905 plan of George Kessler. ~ Located on West End Avenue between 21st and 23rd avenues.

A couple of buildings worth a gander include the Romanesque-influenced **Mechanical Engineering Hall** (now incorporated into the Owen Graduate School of Management Building) and the **Old Gymnasium**, designed by Peter J. Williamson and built in 1880. ~ West End Avenue and 23rd Avenue North.

Also on the campus is the **Fine Arts Gallery**, which has over 5000 works and presents five exhibitions during the year, including traveling exhibits and thematic selections of the Vanderbilt Art Collection. Closed Sunday and Monday. ~ 23rd and West End avenues; 615-322-0605.

Only those who are truly crazy about dolls should bother visiting the **Hartzler-Towner Multicultural Museum** at the Scarritt- ◄ *HIDDEN*
Bennett Center. True, there are permanent and temporary exhibits of cultural items from around the world, but they are not very well documented. However, the 700 dolls in the International Doll Room can be seen Monday through Friday (by appointment only). ~ 1104 19th Avenue South; 615-340-7481.

Hillsboro Village is a commercial hub in the Vanderbilt University neighborhood. You'll find some good restaurants favored by locals, along with shops selling art and imported items.

An 8-by-14-foot wood carving of "The Last Supper," copied from Leonardo's painting, and an 8-by-20-foot stained glass window with a Pentecost theme can be seen in **The Upper Room Chapel and Museum**. Also here are art galleries of religious subjects painted between 1300 and 1990, English porcelains, manuscripts, books and seasonal displays of nativity scenes and Ukrainian eggs. Closed Saturday and Sunday. ~ 1908 Grand Avenue; 615-340-7207.

A beautiful brick-red residence in the trendy Hillsboro-Belmont   **LODGING**
district deserves a more descriptive name than **Four Walls**, but ◄ *HIDDEN*
there you go. The woman who transformed the place has a background in design, and it shows in the understated decor. Think unfussy furniture and lots of off-white and taupe. Three upstairs rooms all have fireplaces and, to accommodate business travelers, can be set up with internet access. Guests can hang out on the wraparound porch or the rear deck with views of the Nashville skyline. ~ 1804 Blair Boulevard; 615-292-7162, fax 615-292-1538; www.fourwallsbedandbreakfast.com, e-mail mk4walls@aol.com. ULTRA-DELUXE.

The low-key sub-neighborhood of Elliston Place has a couple of   **DINING**
shops and restaurants, notably the **Elliston Place Soda Shop**. A bit of the '50s lives on here, a beloved neighborhood spot where you can get old-fashioned sodas as well as breakfast and lunch all day. There's nothing "cute" about this place; it sells no T-shirts or memorabilia. The decor is basic and authentic: simple black tiles, neon on the back wall and a counter down one side. The food fits the bill—burgers and fries and sandwiches like grilled chicken. Closed Sunday. ~ 2111 Elliston Place; 615-327-1090. BUDGET.

An atmosphere of Latin romance pervades **Valentino's Ristorante**, one of the West End's more classic eateries. Three dining areas—one at street level, one near the bar and another in the intimate cellar—have the kind of decor you definitely want to dress up for. The mostly northern Italian cuisine focuses on such items as veal marsala, pastas, seafood and a combination of chicken breast, veal and Italian sausage called a Triple Crown. Don't forget to save room for *tiramisu*. No lunch on Saturday. Closed Sunday. ~ 1907 West End Avenue; 615-327-0148, fax 615-327-9482. DELUXE TO ULTRA-DELUXE.

Locals say they knew Nashville had changed from a town to a city when they no longer recognized everyone at the **Pancake Pantry**. Understandable, since now there's always a line of waiting customers, from early-morning opening through midday. The legions come mostly for the variety of pancakes (Swiss chocolate chip, Caribbean, Georgia peach and a dozen more), but also for a long list of other breakfast dishes, including country ham, plus sandwiches, salads and steaks, available all day every day from 6 a.m. to 3 p.m. Seating is at dozens of tables in one great big room decorated with little more than ceiling fans. No dinner. ~ 1796 21st Avenue South; 615-383-9333. BUDGET.

HIDDEN ►

When you just can't face any more barbecue or meat-and-threes, head for **Sitar,** a pretty little spot off the beaten path and one of the few Indian restaurants in Nashville. Both rooms have white walls and some Indian art, keeping the focus squarely on the food. The buffet is quite a bargain at lunch—after all, many Indian dishes profit from steaming for a couple of hours—but the extensive à la carte menu may tempt you with kebabs, tandoori chicken and a variety of shrimp, lamb and chicken dishes. It's also a good choice for vegetarians, who will have their choice of eggplant, spinach, potatoes, chick peas and other classic Indian ingredients prepared in a variety of ways, including a sampler of three curries. ~ 116 21st Avenue North; 615-321-8889. BUDGET TO MODERATE.

At the **South Street Original Crab Shack and Authentic Dive Bar** almost everything comes with barbecue sauce. Exceptions include pasta, shrimp and crawfish enchiladas and Key lime pie. The lively main floor is open to the sidewalk in good weather, but

MUSIC ROW CLASSIC

Rotier's Restaurant is one of those classics beloved of locals for consistently good food in an unpretentious setting. It's somewhere between Grandma's kitchen and a chop house. You can have "meat-and-threes" (meat and three vegetables), or order steaks, chicken or other all-American choices, but why not order what's considered the best burger in Nashville? Chances are some bigwig from Music Row is sitting at the next booth, but you'd probably never know it unless a regular clued you in. Closed Sunday. ~ 2413 Elliston Place; 615-327-9892. BUDGET.

more special is the "treehouse," a crescent-shaped room with a view of Vanderbilt Plaza, Loew's Hotel and the offices of the Caterpillar company. ~ 907 20th Avenue South; 615-320-5555. BUDGET TO MODERATE.

As you might guess by the name, the **Sunset Grill** is the restaurant of choice of the relocated Los Angelenos who've infiltrated Nashville's music industry. There's generally a crowd here so unless you like to eat early or late, you should probably make reservations—be sure to ask for a seat in the garden room, where you can keep an eye on the door. After all, recording artists have to eat, too. If they come here, they'll find a very chic menu, about half of which is small dishes like calzones, quesadillas and various salads. Standout entrées include Vegetarian Voodoo Pasta (fettuccine New Orleans–style), sesame-crusted salmon, rack of veal and sushi. The Sunset Grill shows its California kinship by offering one of Nashville's best wine lists, heavy on Sonoma and Napa vintages but with strong representation from France, Chile and Australia. No lunch on weekends. ~ 2001 Belcourt Avenue; 615-386-3663, fax 615-386-0495. MODERATE TO DELUXE.

The Trace has a big, dark meet-and-greet room, with sunset views and tea lights to help you find a table. The dining areas are tucked out of sight beyond the bar. The menu aims to please everyone by offering dishes like grilled yellowfin tuna, filet mignon, chargrilled New York strip steak, shrimp gnocchi and pecan-crusted grouper. ~ 2000 Belcourt Avenue; 615-385-2200. DELUXE TO ULTRA-DELUXE.

Luxuriously upholstered banquettes, fine art and bronze statuary speak volumes at the **Wild Boar Restaurant**. From the popular lobster bisque through seasonal specials like Atlantic salmon, this is one of the city's most original (and most expensive) menus. Closed Sunday. ~ 2014 Broadway; 615-329-1313, fax 615-329-4930; www.wildboarrestaurant.com. DELUXE TO ULTRA-DELUXE.

F. Scott's takes its food extremely seriously. There's lots of it ◄ HIDDEN and it's very good, but unless you are a gourmet, the experience can be a little intense. That said, the art deco–decorated restaurant in the Green Hills neighborhood happily presents some of the city's most ambitious cooking, dishes such as braised rabbit manicotti, a cassoulet of pheasant sausage and quail, nut-brittled wahoo and seared scallops with Indian seasonings. ~ 2210 Crestmoor Road; 615-269-5861. DELUXE TO ULTRA-DELUXE.

Zola is off the street and not that impressive to look at beyond ◄ HIDDEN brick walls and a fabric-draped ceiling —that is, until you see the contemporary Mediterranean menu that changes seasonally. Seafood, paella and pasta dishes have brought Zola national recognition and regional cult status. Closed Sunday. ~ 3001 West End Avenue; 615-320-7778. MODERATE TO DELUXE.

HIDDEN ▶   **Roly Poly** wraps and rolls sandwiches incorporating meats, cheeses, vegetables and spreads in dozens of combinations, including a Thai Hot Tuna version. Closed Sunday. ~ 510 21st Avenue South; 615-255-4600. BUDGET.

Within months of opening in 2004, **Tayst** had acquired a reputation as the hottest restaurant with the most inventive American food in town. The place manages to be both hip and cozy, with a tan-and-brick-red color scheme, black-and-white photographs on the walls and low lighting. Despite being usually crowded, Tayst is a good place for intimate conversation. The menu is just this side of over-the-top, but the kitchen delivers exciting dishes such as crushed pecan–crusted ahi tuna, grilled mussels and avocado cheesecake; beef short ribs arrive with foie gras and caramelized apple slices. The adventure continues with an impressively international wine list that incorporates South Africa and Spain as well as lots of California offerings. Closed Sunday and Monday. ~ 2100 21st Avenue South; 615-383-1953. DELUXE TO ULTRA-DELUXE.

SHOPPING   **Bookman Bookwoman Used Books,** which stocks more than 150,000 books, including some 10,000 first editions, is a reader's dream, with so many aisles and categories you could completely lose track of time. ~ 1713 21st Avenue South; 615-383-6555; www.bookmanbookwoman.com.

For avant-garde fashions and accessories, check out **Posh**, one of Nashville's hottest boutiques. ~ 1809 21st Avenue South; 615-383-9840.

Jewelry, knit scarves and hats, handbags, table lamps and chopsticks are among the eclectic merchandise at **Fire Finch**. ~ 1818 21st Avenue South; 615-385-5090.

The merchandise is mostly **Made in France** at this chic shop. Stylish interior decorator pieces, antiques, lamps, pillows, candles and gifts make this one of the town's top boutiques. Closed Sunday. ~ 3001 West End Avenue; 615-329-9300.

A different kind of wild is the stock in trade at **Wild Animals**, a boutique that lives up to its name with jewelry, imported earth-friendly crafts, clothes and candles and more, all in a jungle motif. ~ 2813 West End Avenue; 615-321-0255.

Outloud! Books & Gifts carries a comprehensive collection of lesbian and gay fiction and nonfiction, as well as magazines and newspapers. Music, custom leatherwork and gift items round out the merchandise. ~ 1709 Church Street; 615-340-0034.

NIGHTLIFE   The first—and still the best-known—Nashville club to feature professional comedy on a regular basis, **Zanie's** has been cracking up crowds since 1983. You shouldn't expect to see such past headliners as Robin Williams and Jay Leno, but you might see their suc-

cessors. Dinner available. No live shows Monday or Tuesday.
Cover. ~ 2025 8th Avenue South; 615-269-0221.

Two main thoroughfares extend past Route
440. One, West End, turns into Harding Road,
which leads to the ritzy Belle Meade neighborhood. The other, Hillsboro Pike, heads almost
due south from downtown Nashville. This section fits between these
two main thoroughfares. In these environs, you find first more
shopping malls but eventually more parks and open space and,
eventually, some of the prize attractions in Nashville, particularly
a couple of old mansions now open to the public.

South and Southwest Nashville

Formerly known as the Cumberland Science Museum, the **Adventure Science Center** has more than a new name. In 2002, the center unveiled its Adventure Tower, a 75-foot-high interactive educational attraction that is part of a $2.9-million renovation plan.
Inside the tower, which is sized for kids but accessible to adults,
are more than 75 activities in six different scientific concept areas.
Hands-on exhibits demonstrate how a guitar works, how air resistance helps parachutes drop slowly, how mirrors and lenses
function, how water forms a vortex and how solar panels function. There are also many other exhibits as well as a planetarium.
Note: Try to avoid weekday mornings during the school season,
when the center is often overrun with visiting classes from nearby
elementary schools. Admission. ~ 800 Fort Negley Avenue; 615-
862-5160; www.csmisfun.com.

SIGHTS

◄ *HIDDEN*

Still in its infancy, the **Nashville Zoo at Grassmere** sits on a
200-acre parcel of what was once a much-larger working farm
some ten miles from downtown. (The original 1810 house—
older than the nearby Hermitage—may
one day be open for regular touring.) A
three-quarter-mile animal trail meanders
past immersion exhibits of zebras, tigers (including a Bengal), ostriches, otters, cougars
and cheetahs. One of the best habitats features
meerkats, the burrowing animals that look very
much like prairie dogs. Critter Encounters encourages getting up close to goats, sheep and very shy al-
pacas. The latest additions at the zoo include the
Bamboo Trail with six exhibits of animals found in bamboo
forests around the world. Clouded leopards, ring-tailed lemurs,
red pandas and the large, flightless birds of Australia and New
Guinea called cassowaries are among the new residents along the
trail, which winds through the exhibit area to a koi pond, a viewing shelter and bamboo garden with a wide variety of plant
species. Summertime visitors will also appreciate a pavilion

> Look closely at the limestone
> columns on the front porch of
> Belle Meade Plantation and you
> can still see bullet scars from
> a cavalry skirmish that took
> place on the front lawn.

equipped with misting nozzles for refreshing and a jungle terrace with a shaded picnic pavilion. Admission. ~ 3777 Nolensville Road; 615-833-1534; www.nashvillezoo.org.

The **Lane Motor Museum**'s collection of 100 cars and motorcycles does not quite run from A to Z (the E and Q are missing) but does include these makes and models: Amphicar, Berkeley, Citroën, DKW, Fiat, GasGas, Honda, IZH, Jensen, Kawasaki, Lotus, MG, NSU, OTAS, Porsche, Renault, Scootacar, Tatra, Ultra Van, Volvo, Wind Wagon, Xtreme Motor Company, Yamaha and Zündapp. Among them are micro cars, amphibious vehicles and alternative fuel automobiles that are rarely seen in the U.S. as well as cars from Asia and South America. At any given time, 90 percent of the vehicles are in working order. The museum is housed in the old Sunbeam Bread Company building. Closed Tuesday and Wednesday. Admission. ~ 702 Murfreesboro Road; 615-742-7445; www.lanemotormuseum.com.

Whether you're a musician or not, you'll gain new appreciation for fine craftsmanship at **Gibson Guitars**, where you can watch artisans fashioning fretted instruments (mandolins, banjos—mostly guitars here, though) that range in price from the hundreds to thousands of dollars. The shop also sells accessories and sheet music. ~ 433 Opry Mills Drive; 615-514-1000.

Follow West End beyond the perimeter road, Route 440, until it turns into Harding, into the posh suburb called Belle Meade. Nine buildings, built over the course of some 70 years, constitute **Belle Meade Plantation**. As soon as you see the stately columns of the imposing Greek Revival–style mansion, you feel you really ought to have arrived by horse-drawn carriage. The mansion, built in 1853 by William J. Harding, became a Confederate headquarters during the Battle of Nashville in 1864. After the war, Belle Meade established one of the country's first stables for thoroughbred horses; the house is the showpiece of what was once a 5300-acre spread. The thoroughbred stud farm and nursery no longer exist, but several outbuildings, including an 1890 carriage house and stable with antique carriages, and a 1790 log cabin (one of the oldest houses in Tennessee) are fun to tour with guides in period dress. Admission. ~ 5025 Harding Road; 615-356-0501, 800-270-3991; www.bellemeadeplantation.com.

Continue southwest on Harding Pike, keeping an eye out for signs to Edwin and Percy Warner Park. The most elegant estate in all of Nashville can be found at nearby **Cheekwood Botanical Garden and Museum of Art**. If you're in the mood to stroll, get some gardening inspiration and, while you're at it, find a different kind of inspiration in an impressive collection of fine art, set aside an afternoon to visit this 1920s mansion and the 55 acres of botanical gardens and lawns that surround it. Well-marked paths lead past clearly identified plants—be sure to pick up a map at the guard gate—and meander along as if by happenstance. In spring, the Burr Garden and the Connell Garden are the best places to tour; native plants and wildflowers can be found in the Howe Garden, and trees and annuals are all over the place. For a more intense experience, head over to the Botanic Hall, which houses major flower shows and gardening exhibitions, as well as classrooms. Up the hill is the Cheek Mansion itself, where you can see three floors of 19th- and 20th-century American art (paintings as well as porcelains), as well as the occasional traveling exhibition. Admission. ~ 1200 Forrest Park Drive; 615-354-6380; www.cheekwood.org.

To the east, not far from Route 65 and Route 31, is a more modest home. Judge John Overton built a Federal-style home in the boondocks back in 1799, just after Tennessee became a state. **Travellers Rest Historic House Museum** has now been encircled by development, but none of that is visible once you finally locate the 11-acre homestead. Touring the 13-room house (known for a large collection of made-in-Middle-Tennessee furniture) and grounds, you begin to understand what life was like on the frontier when homesteaders of means used smokehouses and weaving houses as part of everyday life. The grounds also include a prehistoric American Indian village and burial site, and Civil War headquarters. The gift shop here has an exceptionally fine collection of local history books. Admission. ~ 636 Farrell Parkway; 615-832-8197, 615-832-2962; www. travellersrestplantation.org.

◀ *HIDDEN*

> Judge John Overton was a planter/lawyer who served as Andrew Jackson's presidential campaign manager.

Bright colors, Mexican tiles and organic foods distinguish **The Cat's Pajamas**, a bed and breakfast run by Denise Jarvis and her singer/songwriter husband. They are eager to accommodate musicians and performers with flexible breakfast hours, discounts on accommodations and parking for 15-passenger vans. The three second-floor guest rooms are accessible via private entrance. ~ 818 Woodland Street; 615-650-4553; www.bbonline.com/tn/cats pajamas. MODERATE TO DELUXE.

LODGING

Top O'Woodland has a lot of charm but is not recommended for people put off by the sight of chipped paint and mismatched furnishings, however endearing. Opened in late 2002 in a large Queen Anne Victorian, this B&B has but two accommodations that share a bathroom on the ground floor. The Library has a four-poster bed and a working fireplace; the Rose Room, a queen-sized bed and a garden view. If you need more space, an adjacent cottage has beds in each room. Pets are welcome with advance notice. ~ 1603 Woodland Street; 615-228-3868, 888-228-3868; www.topofwoodland.com. DELUXE TO ULTRA-DELUXE.

◀ *HIDDEN*

Conveniently located near Vanderbilt University, the Hillsboro Shopping Center and Music Row, the **Hillsboro House** was one of Nashville's first bed and breakfasts. It's a modest-sized yellow-frame Victorian home that's been restored, with the additions of private baths for each of the three guest rooms, private phone lines, cable television and feather beds. All are furnished with antiques, though each one is a bit different. One has deep burgundy walls, for instance, and another, a floral chintz bedspread. The public rooms seem a little too lived-in, but in nice weather you can always hang out in the garden. A full breakfast is included. ~ 1933 20th Avenue South; 615-292-5501, 800-228-7851, fax 615-297-5046; www.visitnashville.net. DELUXE.

Close to the Nashville International Airport, the two-story **Econo Lodge Southeast** offers 120 standard rooms and an outdoor pool. There's cable TV and good news for travelers with small pets in tow. ~ 97 Wallace Road; phone/fax 615-833-6860, 800-553-2666. BUDGET.

HIDDEN ► Located on a pretty winding road where lots are large enough for keeping horses, the **English Manor B&B** is perched on a knoll with views from some of the upstairs accommodations. In fact, the manor does keep horses, though they are not for the guests. Seven rooms (including three suites), arranged on both floors of this Colonial home, are decorated nearly to death with pillows and floral fabrics. But it's a quiet spot and a full breakfast is included. ~ 6304 Murray Lane, Brentwood; 615-373-4627; www.english manor.com. MODERATE TO DELUXE.

HIDDEN ► The roadside **Brentwood Steeplechase Inn** comprises four two-story brick buildings. The name is a bit misleading because, while it's a godsend for stressed-out, budget-busting travelers, it is neither old nor particularly elegant, nor is there a horse in sight. It is, however, the kind of place you could be happy in for days on end, because of the convenient location on the north side of Brentwood and the well-thought-out amenities. Twenty-four of the 48 accommodations are spacious suites, which feature kitchenettes and a dining/living area. Decor is faux residential—attractive though obviously mass produced. Colors run to subdued maroons and dusty pinks, with lots of lamps and steeplechase-related prints on the walls. The proximity of Route 65 is either a convenience or an eyesore, depending on your point of view. ~ 5581 Franklin Pike Circle, Brentwood; 615-373-8585, fax 615-371-9259. BUDGET TO DELUXE.

DINING

HIDDEN ► If you know and like Vietnamese food, or at least enjoy new taste sensations, track down **Kien Giang** in the otherwise undistinguished Hillsboro Shopping Center. Dishes include spring rolls, beef, chicken, shrimp, fried squid and, amazingly, *banh mi*, which translates to po'boy sandwich (the French-bread submarine famous in the South). The Kien Giang version has various meats spiced with soy, chile sauce and coriander. Decor is virtually nonexistent, but West End residents dine here as do local Vietnamese Americans and Vietnamese immigrants probably homesick for a bowl of *pho*. Closed Monday. ~ 5825 Charlotte Pike; 615-353-1250. BUDGET TO MODERATE.

Humble though it may be, **Las Palmas** is usually packed with fans who have discovered the joys of south-of-the-border standards lovingly prepared. Portions of enchiladas, tacos and the like are large, and the staff is friendly. ~ 5511 Charlotte Pike; 615-352-0313. BUDGET TO MODERATE.   ◄ HIDDEN

Considered by many locals to offer the best Chinese food in Nashville, **Chinatown Restaurant** is also quite attractive. Brass and glass separate the booths, and indirect lighting sets a nice tone, along with handsome Oriental prints on the walls. Located in yet another small shopping center, Chinatown doesn't offer a lot of hard-to-find entrées; it's just that the food is far above average. Among the more intriguing items are Hunan scallops, fresh grouper with Hunan spicy sauce and Mongolian lamb. ~ 3900 Hillsboro Pike; 615-269-3275. BUDGET TO MODERATE.   ◄ HIDDEN

Very popular with the after-church crowd, the **Belle Meade Buffet Cafeteria** can be found, if you're patient, in a shopping center. The expansive room has white walls, gold moldings and recessed ceilings that create a refined backdrop. The food is basic Southern home cooking, but the atmosphere is pleasant and you'll get the feeling some folks come here several times a week for things like beef liver with onions, chopped sirloin, rotisserie chicken, lots of vegetables and salads, and more than a dozen desserts, including lemon ice box and pecan pies. ~ 4534 Harding Pike; 615-298-5572. BUDGET.

No trip to Nashville would be complete without a pilgrimage to **The Loveless**, a landmark for more than four decades. From   ◄ HIDDEN
country singers of all stripes to Paul McCartney, this is the place Nashvilleans bring their out-of-town visitors, be they Martha Stewart or Willard Scott. The food is good and plentiful and is, as it's always been, what the café wants to serve: meat-and-threes,

AUTHOR FAVORITE

Maybe it was because Leanne Rimes was having lunch at a nearby table, but I got the impression that the **Green Hills Grille** was one of Nashville's top places to see and be seen by insiders. Tucked behind a shopping center off busy Hillsboro Pike, the restaurant does a booming business at lunch. The large, single-story restaurant has Southwestern decor and lots of booths as well as tables. Typical entrées are chicken portobello, lemon artichoke chicken and shrimp pignola pasta. ~ 2122 Hillsboro Drive; 615-383-6444. MODERATE.

fried chicken, country ham and especially biscuits. Made from scratch, they are not as fluffy as the average biscuit, but a little crunchier, very tasty and best consumed with the homemade peach, strawberry and blackberry preserves cooked up each morning. The day begins with breakfasts, of course—waffles are a specialty— and runs through lunch. Paneled walls, red-and-white plastic tablecloths and autographed photographs provide the only real decor. ~ 8400 Route 100; 615-646-9700. BUDGET TO MODERATE.

SHOPPING   High-end specialty shops (such as The Discovery Channel Store, Crabtree and Evelyn, Williams-Sonoma and Pottery Barn) are the stock in trade at the **Mall at Green Hills**. There are also some restaurants, including Ruby Tuesday's, part of a chain of fun but not exactly high-end eateries. Despite all this, Green Hills has been named the worst shopping center in Nashville because of the difficulty of parking. ~ Hillsboro Pike and Abbott Martin Road; 615-298-5478.

A couple of antique shops out on Hillsboro Road offer distinctly different selections. At **Corzine and Company**, you can find antique silverware along with contemporary, high-end lines of china, crystal, silk, linens, barware and home accessory gifts. ~ 4003 Hillsboro Road; 615-385-0140.

The top art gallery in Nashville is the **Cumberland Gallery**, which has been specializing in contemporary American works since 1980. About half the collection in this small but prestigious space is the work of regional artists; the remainder, of national figures. Closed Sunday and Monday. ~ 4107 Hillsboro Circle; 615-297-0296.

The **Green Hills Antique Mall** spreads a wider net with an array of vintage collectibles and furniture. ~ 4108 Hillsboro Road; 615-383-9852.

Levy's was voted Best Men's Clothing Store by *Nashville Life* magazine for five years running. This Green Hills clothier is where locals shop for summer suits. Closed Sunday. ~ 3900 Hillsboro Pike; 615-383-2800.

NIGHTLIFE   **Sutler's** doesn't look like much from the outside—what nightclub does?—and the interior is no big improvement. Not that anyone minds. Blues, jazz, country, rock and folk are presented by both regional and national names every night. If you want to get a good seat, arrive early for dinner Tuesday through Saturday. Cover. ~ 2608 Franklin Road; 615-297-9195.

Talented beginning singer-songwriters flock to the **Bluebird Cafe** every Monday night, as they have since 1982. This is the place to see the big names of tomorrow. All the music is original; this is where songwriters come to be heard, not to perform covers of other people's work. Writers are frequently accompanied only by a guitar or a piano, though sometimes four or five musicians, generally friends of the songwriter, will be on stage at one time. Who cares that the cafe began as a restaurant with music as a sideline? It's now a prime venue with food as a sideline. Get here early, don't talk during the performances and be grateful that the 'bird still sings. Cover. ~ 4104 Hillsboro Pike; 615-383-1461.

If you're looking for a place to take the kids after dinner, head to **Chaffin's Barn Dinner Theatre**. Although all the shows are from Broadway, they've been screened to make sure they're PG. First, dine on a Southern-style buffet; then, try to stay awake during the performance. Closed Sunday and Monday. Cover. ~ 8204 Route 100; 615-646-9977; www.dinnertheatre.com.

RADNOR LAKE STATE NATURAL AREA 🏃 This 1000-acre park, nestled among the Overton hills, is popular among Nashvilleans when they need to get away without going far. Only six miles from downtown, the area's centerpiece is the 85-acre lake. This wildlife sanctuary offers opportunities for photographers and birdwatchers, as well as a variety of hiking trails, seven miles in all. Along the way you may well encounter beavers and rabbits, red and gray foxes, white-tailed deer and even coyotes and bobcats who thrive in the woods and meadows. Closer to the lake—or in it—look for turtles, muskrats and raccoons and, in winter, some two dozen species of migratory waterfowl. This is a vast park where you can really observe the seasonal changes; wildflowers are plentiful in spring and fall and dogwood, redbud and honeysuckle bloom from early to late spring. Middle Tennessee can be pretty bleak during the winter months, but the bare landscape will make it easier for you to spot animal tracks. Amenities include a visitors center, a nature center, walking trails and restrooms in three locations. Day-use fee, $3. ~ 1160 Otter Creek Road; 615-373-3467.

PARKS

Radnor Lake was constructed as a reservoir to service steam engines in the now-defunct railroad yards.

EDWIN AND PERCY WARNER PARKS 🏃🐎🚣 This pair of suburban parks has, when put together, nearly 3000 acres encompassing forests, fields, hills and miles of paths for hiking and horseback riding. There are two golf courses, a lake for fishing, picnic areas, playgrounds, a field for flying model airplanes and, in case you brought your mount, a polo field and a steeplechase course. It's an extremely popular park, and probably Nashville's best loved. Even if the weather isn't cooperating, it's worth darting into the nature center, which has a research library, a bird-feeding area and other neat exhibits. Programs for children ages 6 to 12 include fishing, gardening, night hikes and stargazing. ~ 7311 Route 100; 615-370-8050.

▼▼▼▼▼▼▼▼▼▼
North and East Nashville

As Nashville grows, there is less and less distinction between the city and the towns such as Goodlettsville that dot the countryside. Occupied briefly by the Shawnee in the early 17th century, the Cherokee, Creek and Chickasaw drove them out before facing an influx of European settlers. The first of those were the so-called long hunters who, attracted by the region's abundant game, went hunting for long periods of time. The biggest boost to the area's population came in 1951 when the Army Corps of Engineers built a dam on the Cumberland River to create Old Hickory Lake.

SIGHTS

Among the earliest settlers around **Goodlettsville**, a town almost due north of the capital that has nearly been swallowed up by Nashville, was Kasper Mansker, who arrived in 1772 and built a fort. When Indians burned it down, he built a second one, also long gone. Today, a historically accurate replica called **Mansker's Station** stands in Moss-Wright Park. Guides in period dress act and talk as if it were still the 1700s as they take visitors through the fort and demonstrate the old ways of cooking, washing and cleaning without benefit of electricity or indoor plumbing. Across the road, the two-story brick **Bowen-Campbell House**, the oldest home in Middle Tennessee, exemplifies the gradual civilization of the settlers from hunters to plantation managers. The rest of the furniture is considered indicative of the 1780–1850 time period. Closed Sunday and Monday. Admission. ~ Moss-Wright Park, 705 Caldwell Road, Goodlettsville; 615-859-3678.

HIDDEN ►

Who would have thought of saving every soft-drink can you ever emptied? If you had, you, too, could have opened the **Museum of Beverage Containers and Advertising**, which has now reached warehouse dimensions on a remote hillside north of Nashville, near the intersection of Route 65 and Route 31W. Library-type stacks of Coca-Cola, Pepsi, Dr Pepper, RC Cola and more obscure labels—36,000 in all—are neatly organized, along with the odd 7-Up cooler, vertical collections (continuous years of a certain beverage) and special editions, including niche categories with labels depicting women, mountains, states and animals, for example; you can also view the first soda and beer cans ever produced. There's not much in the way of descriptions, but there's a lot of nostalgia, and you're bound to pick up some arcania such as the introduction in 1807 of the first carbonated drink and the industry breakthrough of producing canned drinks (instead of bulk or bottles) in 1935. Of course there is a gift shop, where, along with thousands of signs, trays, glasses and bottle caps, items like obscure campaign matchbook advertisements sell at five for a dollar. Closed Saturday and Sunday. Admission. ~ 1055 Ridgecrest Drive, Millersville; 615-859-5236, 800-826-4929; www.nostalgiaville.com/museum.

The Hermitage, the sprawling estate of former U.S. president Andrew Jackson, can be approached from Millersville, to its north, or more likely from Nashville by taking Route 40E and then Route 45N. Even kids who whine about visiting old houses will probably remember a tour of this estate for the rest of their lives. It starts with a taped orientation before a walk to the mansion itself, built between 1819 and 1821 as a simple brick Federal-style home. Subsequent additions, renovations and repairs in the wake of an 1834 fire transformed the structure considerably. Porticos were installed in the front and rear of the original structure, which was then painted white to underscore the Greek Revival style that was en vogue at the time. History interpreters in period costume lead visitors through the many rooms that were touched up early in 1996. These efforts, along with archaeological research, are ongoing at The Hermitage. The tour includes the all-important smokehouse so vital in the days before refrigeration, several outlying log cabins, the slave quarters and the Tulip Grove Mansion, which was the home of Jackson's nephew and personal secretary. Along the way, you'll learn a lot about Jackson's illustrious political career as well as family life in the early to middle 1800s. Closed the third week in January. Admission. ~ 4580 Rachel's Lane; 615-889-2941; www.thehermitage.com, e-mail info@thehermitage.com.

Opryland itself has been torn down, but there are still things to see at the **Opryland Resort & Convention Center**. And except for a ride on a riverboat, it's all free for exploring. The **Opryland Garden Conservatory**, one of three indoor gardens at the complex, is filled with more than 10,000 tropical ornamental plants, representing more than 215 species. Crowned by a one-acre skylight, the enclosed garden is a lovely place to stroll on a hot or rainy day. Visitors can also tour the two-acre **Cascades** area via an elevated walkway that winds under palms, over waterfalls and through a 40-foot-tall mountain. Like the Conservatory, the Cascades link two six-story wings of the hotel. ~ 2800 Opryland Drive; 615-889-1000; www.gaylordhotels.com.

AUTHOR FAVORITE

Of all the fantasy "interiorscapes" at the **Opryland Resort & Convention Center**, I was most entranced by the four-and-a-half-acre Delta. Planted with magnolias and camellias beneath a 150-foot-high glass roof, the Delta has an array of shops, lounges and eateries. A river runs through it, and for a fee of $4, visitors can board a flat-boat and wander along the waterway without any effort at all. See above for more information.

Located right across the street from the Opryland Resort, the **Willie Nelson and Friends Showcase Museum** seems to cover just about every country singer who doesn't have his or her own shrine—and some, like Elvis, who do. Nelson's gold and platinum albums and guitars are the main draw here, although there are items relating to Patsy Cline and, of all people, Audie Murphy. Admission. ~ 2613-A McGavock Pike; 615-885-1515, 615-885-0733.

LODGING

The vast **Gaylord's Opryland Resort** is one of those love-it-or-hate-it propositions. It all depends on how you feel about 3000-room mega-hotels, conventioneers and a lobby large enough to give you an aerobic workout just going to breakfast. Under a glass-domed skylight the size of Kennedy Airport, the Cascades is a two-acre tropical forest with palms and waterfalls. Then there's the Conservatory, also glass-topped, part of the themed indoor environment that links two six-story wings of guest rooms with restaurants and various public areas. Thousands of tropical plants, sculptures, a 72-foot-tall fountain and an actual flowing stream complete with waterfall create an illusion that you are somewhere on Planet Earth. After all this, the attractive, contemporary rooms are kind of a letdown. In 1996, Gaylord Entertainment (which owns all of Opryland) added a third indoor natural area called the Delta. They didn't stop at foliage and water; they added an antebellum-type mansion, which fits neatly inside the four-and-a-half-acre addition. Restaurants and tippling stations like the Jack Daniel's Saloon are sprinkled throughout the property. In all, the hotel has 30 retail outlets, four full-service restaurants, a food court, five lounges, 85 meeting rooms, five ballrooms and 2883 guest rooms, including some 200 suites. ~ 2800 Opryland Drive; 615-889-1000, fax 615-871-5843; www.gaylordhotels.com. ULTRA-DELUXE.

On the air since 1925, the Grand Ole Opry is the longest-running radio show in the world.

Travelers who want to attend the Grand Ole Opry have few convenient lodging options other than the inn at Opryland. The three-story **Radisson Hotel Opryland** has all the charm of a high school gymnasium, only without the glitz. The motel-type rooms are a bit dark, though they all face onto an indoor pool area with a game arcade. A better choice is one of the two one-bedroom suites. This place is operated by the same company, Gaylord Entertainment, that runs the Opryland Resort across the busy thoroughfare. ~ 2401 Music Valley Drive; 615-889-0800, 800-333-3333, fax 615-883-1230. DELUXE.

A good economical bet if you plan to visit all the sights in this area is the 66-room **Madison Square Inn**. Standard accommodations include satellite TV. The pool is a bonus, as is its proximity to restaurants and stores. ~ 118 Emmett Avenue, Madison; 615-865-4203, 800-821-4148, fax 615-868-6767. BUDGET.

Less than a ten-minute drive from the Opryland Resort complex, **End o' the Bend** is a contemporary log cabin on the banks of the Cumberland River at the 200-mile marker. There's one bedroom, a kitchen, a screened porch, a patio and a lawn down to the river. This is a real find and offers the most privacy of any lodging in the area. ~ 2523 Miami Avenue; e-mail river200mi@ aol.com. DELUXE.

◀ *HIDDEN*

DINING

A hard-to-find marina is the last place you'd expect to encounter fabulous food, but that's the case at the **Blue Moon Waterfront Cafe**. It's on the north side of town, west of Route 24. Pan-seared trout, maple-cured salmon chop, campfire trout and Siamese catfish, not to mention a variety of other seafood dishes, come out of a tiny kitchen. In fact, meals are served in a floating dining room that was tacked onto the original building in 1996 so the original kitchen could be enlarged and the bar, expanded. This is a great spot to while away an afternoon. Closed Sunday through Tuesday. ~ 525 Basswood Avenue; 615-352-5892. MODERATE TO DELUXE.

◀ *HIDDEN*

East Nashville's undisputed hotspot is **Margot**, a cozy restaurant in the heart of the neighborhood. The ground floor is where the action is; the upstairs is where you can have a relatively quiet conversation. The daily changing menu features the likes of grilled cod on garlicky mashed potatoes, steak béarnaise, duck breast and Black Angus strip steak. The well-thought-out wine list includes moderately priced Italian and California wines. Closed Sunday and Monday ~ 1017 Woodland Street; 615-227-4668. MODERATE TO DELUXE.

Inside The Hermitage is an above-average museum restaurant, **Café Monell's**. Stop in this bright, airy setting for a Southern buffet or a light lunch featuring salads with a Southern touch. Lunch only. Closed the third week of January. ~ 4580 Rachel's Lane; 615-885-5735. BUDGET.

Ristorante Volare, a voluptuously romantic restaurant in the Conservatory Garden of the Opryland Resort, specializes in traditional Italian cuisine, with an emphasis on elaborate pastas and creative desserts. Several Italian wines are available, as are a limited number of California vintages. ~ 2800 Opryland Drive; 615-889-1000. DELUXE.

SHOPPING

Of the half-dozen or so antique shops in Goodlettsville, **Rare Bird Antique Mall** stands out for its vast and varied assortment of merchandise. Old Coca-Cola signs, kitchen utensils, ceramics, furniture and collectibles such as a vast selection of horse figurines ap-

Text continued on page 242.

The Grand Ole Opry

The roots of country music run deep in the hills, valleys and plateaus of the South, nowhere more so than in Tennessee. It's been a tradition from the early settlements up to the present day. Folks would get together, after the day's work was done, and fiddle and sing with their neighbors. Back then, there was no country-music industry, and probably nobody called it country music. It was, along with the tunes and instruments brought to America from their ancestors' original countries, all they knew.

The ballads had changed since the first "folks'" music was sung some 500 years earlier in Scotland, England and Ireland. The folks who settled in the Appalachians clung tenaciously to the old ways, cut off as they were in their mountain settlements. But the music had a life of its own, a way of absorbing the influences it encountered—Cajun, Hawaiian, Mexican and cowboy tunes, newer instruments like the zither, banjo and guitar—as it does today.

Country music made history on the night of November 28, 1925, when announcer George D. Hay introduced an 80-year-old fiddler named Uncle Jimmy Thompson on a brand-new show known as *The WSM Barn Dance*. The call letters for radio station WSM stood for the motto of the National Life and Accident Insurance Company, "We Shield Millions." In the beginning, the show was broadcast out of a studio on the fifth floor of the company's building in downtown Nashville. In the early days, of course, there were no country-music stars because there was no way to hear music beyond one's own neighborhood. To the contrary, the WSM show, which later became the Grand Ole Opry, brought fame to the people who performed, live and unrehearsed, on the program.

Thousands of Americans—in fact, people all over the globe—got their first earful of country music by listening to the Grand Ole Opry every Saturday night. Few of them probably realized how the show got its name. The show, announced by Hay, a former newspaperman, followed an NBC network program called *The Music Appreciation Hour*. One evening in 1928, Hay remarked, "For the past hour, we have been listening to music taken largely from grand opera, but now we will present 'The Grand Ole Opry.'"

Before too long, the crowds that jammed into the downtown studio forced the Opry to move to its own location, Studio C, which could accommodate 500 fans. Still, the crowds kept growing. The Opry moved to southwest Nashville, to the Hillsboro Theatre, and then to the Dixie Tabernacle in the east part of town. It seems the more people who heard country music, the more the audience swelled. By 1939 the Grand Ole Opry had made its home in the new War Memorial Auditorium downtown, where fans were charged 25 cents in hopes of dampening enthusiasm. No such luck. In 1943 the Opry found its ideal locale, the Ryman Auditorium.

Built near the Cumberland River in 1892 by a riverboat captain named Tom Ryman in honor of a preacherman whose tent revivals had turned Ryman's life around, the red-brick auditorium was originally called the Union Gospel Tabernacle. Renamed the Ryman Auditorium in 1904, the performance hall welcomed the likes of Enrico Caruso, Isadora Duncan, Charlie Chaplin and Martha Graham. The Grand Ole Opry took it over and made it the "Mother Church" of country music for some 30 years. Yet, even with 3000 seats, the auditorium couldn't contain all the people who wanted to see the Opry, so a second Saturday night show was added.

At the time, the music presented was almost entirely instrumental. But in 1938, Roy Acuff, a young man from East Tennessee, performed with his band, the Smoky Mountain Boys, such songs as "The Wabash Cannonball" and overnight, singers became as welcome as pickers. Hank Williams and Ernest Tubb were among the legends who followed in Acuff's footsteps on the planks of the Ryman. The following year, the NBC Radio Network included the Opry in its network lineup, attracting performers such as Johnny Cash, Marty Robbins and Kitty Wells throughout the 1940s and 1950s, followed by Loretta Lynn, Dottie West and their contemporaries in the 1970s. Meanwhile, the auditorium, along with much of downtown Nashville, became a bit rundown. It was time, once again, to relocate.

The Opry's last Ryman show was on a Friday night, March 15, 1974. The next evening, none other than Richard Nixon joined Roy Acuff on the stage of the Grand Ole Opry House, a 4400-seat auditorium at Opryland just up the river from downtown Nashville. The Opry took not only its memories, but also a literal reminder: an eight-foot circle of hardwood from the old Ryman, now engrained at center stage at the Opry House.

There's a happy ending to the Ryman Auditorium saga. The venerable Mother Church, long since turned into a museum, was blessed with an $8.5 million renovation and reborn in 1994 as a public performance hall for all kinds of stage entertainment, including country and rock.

Today, some 70 performers are part of the Opry family, including Garth Brooks, Patty Loveless, Dolly Parton, Vince Gill and Reba McEntire. Who would have thought anyone could build a successful show on a concept that included no rehearsals and a mere 48-hour notice on who's going to appear?

George D. Hay could have predicted it, though. "The Grand Ole Opry is as simple as sunshine. It has a universal appeal because it is built upon good will, and with folk music [it] expresses the heartbeat of a large percentage of Americans who labor for a living."

peal to someone, sometime. There are even books about how to collect and what things are worth. ~ 212 South Main Street, Goodlettsville; 615-851-2635.

Opry Mills is a sprawling indoor complex of stores, entertainment venues, restaurants and food outlets. Merchandise includes luggage, jewelry, athletic goods, apparel, electronics, specialty goods and more, including the Gibson Guitars store and outlets such as Off 5th (Saks Fifth Avenue). ~ 433 Opry Mills Drive; 615-514-1000; www.oprymills.com.

NIGHTLIFE   The **Grand Ole Opry** has been going on for more than seven decades, and although it has left the stage of the Ryman Auditorium in downtown Nashville, it carries on the tradition at Opryland Resort & Convention Center, one of the few remaining attractions in the park that was dismantled in 1998. Great stars, upcoming talent and world-famous legends tread the boards here—which include sections of plank from Ryman, the "Mother Church" of country music. Closed Sunday, Wednesday and Thursday. Admission. ~ 2804 Opryland Drive; 615-871-6510.

The **Gibson Showcase Theater** prides itself on its continuously running two-hour musical production, *A Tribute to the King*, which covers the Elvis years from 1953 to 1997. Dinner is available. ~ 433 Opry Mills Drive; 615-758-0098; www.thenashvilleking.com.

PARKS   **LONG HUNTER STATE PARK** 🏃 ⛵ ⛺ 🚣 🚤 ⛴ 🛶 A nice spot to take a picnic break on the shores of the U.S. Army Corps of Engineers' Percy Priest Reservoir, this park was named after the early explorers of the 1700s, called long hunters because of the length of time they had to be away from home in order to supply their families with food. The 2315-acre park has no individual campsites, but has places where you can backpack in to spend the night. Take a fishing rod; there is a wheelchair-accessible pier on the 110-acre lake. To learn more about the park's unique fauna and flora, including an unusual cedar glade environment that is protected within the park's boundaries, stop by the visitors center. Among the amenities are a playground, a gift shop, picnic areas, a visitors center with natural-history exhibits and some personal items belonging to former congressman Priest, and 28 miles of hiking trails, along which overnight backpacking is allowed. There's an entire area devoted to handicapped accessibility including walking trails and a children's playground. Day-use fee, $3. ~ 2910 Hobson Pike, Hermitage; 615-885-2422.

▲ Primitive camping.

Outdoor Adventures

The oldest flyfishing and light-tackle guide service in Nashville is **South Harpeth Outfitters and Flyfishing School**. Their specialty: trophy trout, smallmouth bass, landlocked striped bass and, on a private preserve, Atlantic salmon. The guides take fishermen out to several Middle Tennessee locations. ~ 615-952-4186.

FISHING

At **J. Percy Priest Reservoir** east of Nashville, popular game fish include rockfish, which are plentiful April through October along creek channels and rocky banks and drop-offs; hybrid stripe, smallmouth and largemouth bass (April through October, along rocky banks and drop-offs); crappie (early spring and fall, around sunken treetops); bluegill (May through September, around submerged bushes and bluffs); and catfish (at night, May through November, along shelving rock and mud banks). ~ 3737 Bell Road; 615-889-1975.

All kinds of watercraft, including jet skis, canoes, paddleboats, fishing boats and powerboats, can be rented from **Fun Boats** for outings on J. Percy Priest Reservoir in east Nashville. Closed mid-October to mid-April. ~ 4001 Bell Road, Hermitage; 615-399-7661.

BOATING

Wave Country is open from Memorial Day to Labor Day with a freshwater pool and waterslide complex featuring three slides, two of them corkscrew slides. Closed after Labor Day until Memorial Day weekend. Admission. ~ 2320 Two Rivers Parkway off Briley Parkway; 615-885-1052.

SWIMMING

Nashville has seven municipal golf courses, plus several private courses that allow the public to play.

GOLF

AUTHOR FAVORITE

It would take a long time to explore the entire 1000-acre watershed in southwest Nashville known as **Radnor Lake State Natural Area**. A self-guided trail extends from the west parking lot to the earthen dam at lakeside; from there, you can connect to the lake trail that runs along the shoreline toward the north. These trails are covered with wood chips; boardwalks and gravel make winter hiking less hazardous. I covered only a couple of the seven miles of hiking trails here, but found that the Ganier Ridge Loop offers the best views. Keep an eye out for plentiful wildlife, including migratory waterfowl. In the more remote sections, you may even spot a coyote or bobcat.

South of the Nashville International Airport, **Nashboro Village's** 18-hole golf course has slightly rolling terrain through heavily wooded areas along its heavily bunkered long and narrow links. Bent-grass greens, Bermuda-grass fairways and a slope rating of 129. ~ 1101 Nashboro Boulevard; 615-367-2311.

The **Percy Warner Golf Course** has nine holes in scenic Percy Warner Park out in Belle Meade. Three of them have sand traps, and there are seven par 4s and two par 3s along the short, tree-lined links. ~ Forrest Park Drive off Belle Meade Boulevard; 615-352-9958.

The **Hermitage Golf Course** in east Nashville has 18 challenging holes with Bermuda-grass fairways and bent-grass greens. Teaching pros are available for lessons. ~ 3939 Old Hickory Boulevard, Old Hickory; 615-847-4001.

If you're interested in playing at the **Legends Club,** home of the Tennessee State Open, inquire at the front desk of your hotel to see if you can obtain golf privileges. If so, you can play on two 18-hole golf courses, each created by Tom Kite and Bob Cupp. Zoysia fairways, bent-grass greens and high maintenance, plus a 20-acre practice facility, make this one of the most desirable courses around. ~ 1500 Legends Club Lane; 615-791-8100.

TENNIS

Nashville has both public and private courts, including several indoor courts for year-round play.

Tennis courts can be rented day and night at the **Thomas F. Frist Centennial Sportsplex Tennis Center,** which also offers fitness facilities, ice skating and swimming. ~ 224 25th Avenue North at Brandan Avenue; 615-862-8490.

The **Nashboro Village Athletic Club,** located south of the Nashville International Airport, has four indoor and seven outdoor (six of them are clay) courts open daily to the public. Fee. ~ 2250 Murfreesboro Pike; 615-361-3242.

All of Nashville's other public tennis courts are free. For location information, call the **Board of Parks** at 615-862-8490, or drop by a Metro Public Library Branch for a free map.

BIKING

Hamilton Creek has nearly 11 miles of trails suitable to every level of mountain biker. Beginners can start on the **East Trail,** which runs along Percy Priest Reservoir; it's a scenic, somewhat demanding three-mile loop. The **West Trail** is for the more advanced rider, with rocks, ledges, elevation changes and switchbacks on seven miles of single track. ~ The East Trail head is off Bell Road north of J. Percy Priest Reservoir; the West Trail head, off Ned Shelton Road north of Bell Road.

HIKING

All distances for hiking trails are one way unless otherwise noted.

For a restorative break in the heart of the city, take the **Scarritt-Bennett Nature Walk** around ten tree-filled acres of the campus, where 75-year-old Gothic buildings give the place the ambience of a British university setting. You can check out the demonstration organic garden and take a self-guided tour of the arboretum and learn to identify 26 species of trees. ~ 1008 19th Avenue South; 615-340-7475, 615-340-7463.

SOUTH AND SOUTHWEST NASHVILLE Percy Warner Park has two trails and its brother park, Edwin Warner, six. The trailhead for the former is in the Deep Well Picnic Area. The **Mossy Ridge Trail** (4.5 miles) crosses several springs as it leads through woods and meadows. The shorter **Warner Woods Trail** (2.5 miles round-trip) is a good choice in hot weather because it runs through deep woods. On both of these trails you should see large oaks, sugar maples, hickories and tulip poplars, and wildflowers in every season except winter. In Edwin Warner, you have a choice of several short walks (under half a mile), a moderate trail called the **Nature Loop** (.7 mile), which has a written guide describing the natural history of the area and the longer **Harpeth Woods Trail** (2.5 miles roundtrip), which passes through different types of forests—beech, oak and red cedar—and bridges a rock quarry where you can see the fossilized evidence of 400-million-year-old life forms. For a chance to see some unusual wildlife, try the **Owl Hollow Trail**, accessed by the trailhead at the Little Harpeth River. (It also connects with the above Harpeth Woods Trail as a .3-mile loop). As its name suggests, you may well see barred owls, Eastern screech owls or great horned owls, and if you've never seen an owl twist its head on its neck, you're in for a treat.

NORTH AND EAST NASHVILLE Chinquapin oaks, shagbark hickories, glade forests, wading birds and waterfowl await hikers at Long Hunter State Park's **Lake Trail** (2 miles). Eight feet wide and paved, the trail loops along the shores of Couchville Lake, crossing it on the northwest end via a 300-foot railed boardwalk.

Transportation

CAR

Nashville is at the convergence of three major interstates: **Route 40, Route 24** and **Route 65**. Route 40 intersects Nashville on an east–west axis; Route 24, roughly southeast to northwest; and Route 65, south–north. The major perimeter highway is **Route 440**. In southwest Nashville is the northern terminus of the recently completed Natchez Trace, which runs from the Mississippi state line to the Belle Meade neighborhood.

AIR

Seventeen airlines make an average of 400 daily arrivals and departures at **Nashville International Airport**, transporting not only people but products as well. Several major carriers serve Nashville, in addition to the city's own passenger airline, Nashville Air (615-742-9041). AirCanada, American and American Eagle, Continental, Delta, Northwest, Southwest, United and US Airways all offer regularly scheduled flights into and out of Nashville International Airport. ~ 615-275-1674; www.flynashville.com.

BUS

The **Greyhound Bus Lines** station is located in downtown Nashville. ~ 200 8th Avenue South; 800-231-2222; www.greyhound.com.

CAR RENTALS

Nine car-rental agencies have locations at or near the airport. They include **Alamo Rent A Car** (800-327-9633), **Avis Rent A Car** (800-230-4298), **Budget Car and Truck Rental of Nashville** (800-527-0700), **Dollar Rent A Car** (800-800-4000), **Enterprise Rent A Car** (800-325-8007), **Hertz Rent A Car** (800-654-3131), **National Car Rental** (800-227-7368), **Payless Car, Van and Truck Rental** (615-275-4280) and **Thrifty Car Rental** (800-847-3489).

PUBLIC TRANSIT

The **Metropolitan Transit Authority** requires exact change on its intercity routes ($1.10); the MTA sells a seven-day pass for $15, which allows unlimited rides on both buses and trolleys Sunday through Saturday. Buses also run to the Nashville International Airport from 8:13 a.m. to 5:33 p.m. weekdays, with limited weekend service as well. You can catch the bus at Shelter C on Deaderick Street; for specific departure times, call MTA. The trip takes about 30 minutes. ~ 615-862-5959; www.nashvillemta.org.

TAXIS

Allied Taxi runs round-the-clock service around town and to the airport; credit cards are accepted. ~ 615-244-7433, 615-833-2323. **American Taxi** also accepts credit cards. In addition to 24-hour taxi service, Music City offers guided tours. ~ 615-262-0451. **Yellow Cab Metro** also operates around the clock. ~ 615-256-0101.

There are more limos in Nashville than anywhere else in Tennessee. If you'd rather get around by limo as the music millionaires do, try **V.I.P. Limousines** (615-254-1254), **Capitol Limousines** (615-883-6777), **Country Music Limousine** (615-226-9692) or **Carey International** (615-360-8700, 800-394-7433).

NINE

Heritage Trails

South of Nashville lie some of the best roads for exploring in the state. These are not remote byways, but mostly two-lane highways through the countryside of low hills and shallow dales. Within sight are dozens of beautifully preserved antebellum homes. Some of these magnificent structures are private residences, but others welcome the public to view the interiors to get an idea of how the gentry (and their families and slaves) lived well over a century ago.

The Cumberland River crosses the top of the Central Basin in Middle Tennessee, passing by Nashville, and the Elk River flows along the southern edge. Within a triangle roughly defined by Murfreesboro, Franklin and Lynchburg are the remains not only of sprawling plantations but also of a way of life that ended with the Civil War. The fertile lands supported that lifestyle and also made the region around Wartrace and Shelbyville ideal for the development of the Tennessee Walking Horse.

Lawrenceburg and nearby Ethridge, settled by German immigrants in the last century, are now home to hundreds of Amish families who, on principles of faith, eschew modern conveniences such as the automobile. You will see them driving black horse-drawn buggies along the highways.

Many smaller roads intersect the rest of the region, which is rich in Civil War heritage.

Each of the towns and small cities in this area is distinctive, but most of them have one characteristic in common: a central courthouse square. Shelbyville is thought to have the first central courthouse square in the country, but many other communities followed its lead, establishing a courthouse on a block in the center of the square, flanked by four streets of commercial buildings, all facing inward. It was a logical pattern and an efficient one since it concentrated business, commercial and political power in one easily accessible location. As cities have grown, the square has become less and less the center of action, but as a rule of thumb, the smaller the town the more the square remains an informal meeting place and a commercial hub.

Murfreesboro was built at the exact geographic center of the state, and is, appropriately, home to Middle Tennessee State University. The Public Square in Murfreesboro was designed when the city was established in 1812. The current Rutherford County Courthouse was built in 1859, and remains a Murfreesboro landmark. Though fire has destroyed or damaged many of the surrounding 19th-century buildings, the square's original layout is intact, and the neighborhood is still a vital one. Main Street boasts a number of buildings of varying architectural style and interest, most of them private residences. The city is centered a couple of miles south of the Stones River National Battlefield, site of some of the fiercest fighting in the Civil War. Although Murfreesboro's central square still exists and its courthouse survived the war (and a 1913 tornado) intact, the square was figuratively shunted in the late 1940s when the Broad Street bypass was built. Many businesses, restaurants, gas stations and motels are located along that unprepossessing commercial strip on the west side of town.

Due south of Nashville's suburbs, the first town is Franklin, another major Civil War site. Unlike Murfreesboro, Franklin has remained small and has retained much of its charm. It is fitting that so many antiques shops on Main Street and nearby have such a hefty stock of 19th-century Americana. Local promoters have dubbed Columbia Pike (Route 31) and nearby roads the Antebellum Trail and printed a guide for visitors. The map leads to various plantations and other sights in and around Franklin and Columbia, where James K. Polk, the 11th president of the United States, grew up and began his political career.

Shelbyville, farther south, bills itself as The Walking Horse Capital of the World, but the breed—the third most popular in the country—was actually developed in nearby Wartrace. Hundreds of farms beside rolling country lanes make this one of the most enjoyable driving experiences in Tennessee. The tiny town of Bell Buckle, too, has its own claim to fame. It is home to the Webb School, alma mater of former Vice President Al Gore, ten Rhodes scholars, the governors of three states and numerous other high achievers. Once threatened with extinction, Bell Buckle has now seen a restoration of a row of early-20th-century structures on Railroad Row, which must have the highest concentration of antique shops per capita in the state.

Lynchburg has become famous, too, as home to the Jack Daniel's Distillery, makers of world-renowned sour mash whiskey. Its modest town square remains its political and commercial hub.

Easily accessible on day trips from either Nashville or Chattanooga, this part of Tennessee has many kinds of heritages to share with visitors.

▼ ▼ ▼ ▼ ▼ ▼ ▼ ▼ ▼
Murfreesboro

Murfreesboro, originally named Cannonsburgh, became the state capital in 1818, until the title was bestowed on Nashville in 1826. Occupied by both Union and Confederate forces during the Civil War, the area witnessed the bloody Battle of Stones River, now memorialized in the Stones River National Battlefield established in 1927. The Nashville and Chattanooga Railway was a critical pawn in the struggle for control of Middle Tennessee. In 1862 General William Rosecrans led his army down those tracks toward waiting Southern troops, who, under

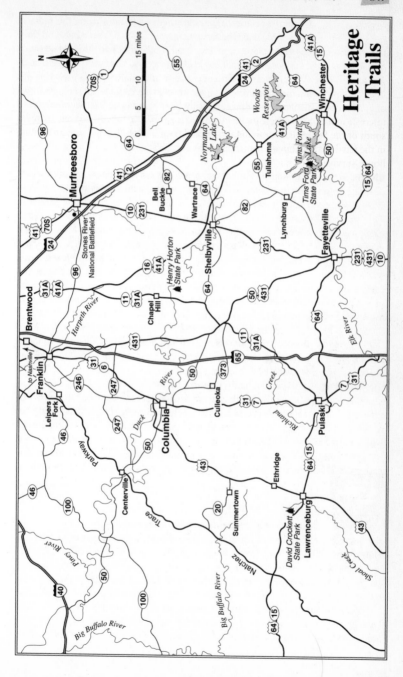

Heritage Trails

General Braxton Bragg, had themselves been using the railroad as a supply line. The fighting started on New Year's Eve, and three days and many casualties later, both sides had suffered so much damage that neither could claim victory. The battle resulted, however, in Bragg retreating south and in Rosecrans delaying his Chattanooga offensive for another six months. In the meantime, the Federal soldiers built the 200-acre Fortress Rosecrans, one of the biggest earthen-wall forts of the war; it can be seen on tours of the battlefield. Artifacts from those battles remain among Murfreesboro's top attractions.

SIGHTS   **Cannonsburgh Village** bears the original name of present-day Murfreesboro. Construction on the small village, on the banks of Lytle Creek, began in 1974 and involved relocating buildings from throughout the mid-South. The idea was to create a living-history community that blends periods from about 1800 through 1925. The small park consists of a general store, a blacksmith shop, a chapel, a schoolhouse, a doctor's office and an 1800s residence, as well as items such as a turn-of-the-20th-century fire engine and a covered wagon from the frontier days. Closed Monday and from November through April, though the grounds are open all year. ~ 312 South Front Street near Broad Street; 615-890-0355.

You can pick up literature on Cannonsburgh and other Murfreesboro attractions at the **Rutherford County Chamber of Commerce**. ~ 501 Memorial Boulevard; 615-893-6565, 800-716-7560; www.rutherfordcounty.org.

HIDDEN ►   The **Oaklands Historic House Museum** is far enough from Cannonsburgh that it's easy to believe it was once the center of a 1500-acre plantation. To get there, turn right on Broad Street, then left on Maney Avenue and continue north for a few long blocks, through two traffic lights. Originally a one-and-a-half-story home, it was built around 1815 on the property of Dr. James Maney and his wife, Sally Hardy Murfree, who inherited the property from

AUTHOR FAVORITE

sights   The museum at the **Stones River National Battlefield** is the best place to begin a tour of the largest Civil War monument in the United States. The Battle of Stones River began on New Year's Eve, 1862, and continued for more than two days, concluding with the Union forces gaining control of a key piece of Middle Tennessee. One of the country's oldest intact monuments of the war, Hazen's Brigade Monument, was put up by the survivors of the battle for Hell's Half Acre in the Round Forest, signifying a key location in the fierce fighting on this battlefield. See page 251 for more information.

her father, for whom the town was named. As their family grew, so did the house, beginning with a Federal-style addition in the early 1820s. Eventually, the Italianate facade was attached to the mansion, which wound up about five times its original size. Like many other plantation homes in the mid-19th century, Oaklands was occupied by both Union and Confederate troops. It was the site of the surrender of Murfreesboro to Nathan Bedford Forrest, who dared a dawn raid on unprepared Federal troops. After Colonel W. W. Duffield capitulated, Dr. Maney invited the warring parties to dine together in the grand banquet room, years before the war's end. Later in 1862, Confederate president Jefferson Davis stayed here while visiting the troops. Now the house is on the National Register of Historic Places and has been restored to look as it might have back then, with typical furnishings, a carpeted semicircular staircase and fleur-de-lys wallpaper popular in the period. Closed Monday. Admission. ~ 900 North Maney Avenue; 615-893-0022; www.oaklandsmuseum.org.

The largest Civil War monument in the United States is the **Stones River National Battlefield**, which is so large—584 acres, one tenth the full field of battle—you need an automobile to tour it. But that's okay; you'll need an automobile to get there, too. Leaving Oaklands, head east to Highland Avenue, turn left (north) to Clark Boulevard and go left again, then turn right onto North Maple (Route 231N), then left onto West Northfield Boulevard. Follow that around until you reach Thompson Lane, where you will see signs for the battlefield. Stop first at the museum to see the video, some Civil War memorabilia and a brochure guide or an audiotape. The national cemetery is also at the site, with 7000 graves, tablets and markers. It's open the same hours as the Battlefield. ~ 3501 Old Nashville Highway; 615-893-9501; www.nps.gov/stri.

LODGING

Several chain lodging establishments can be found along Old Fort Parkway and on Church Street.

The **Byrn-Roberts Inn** started life in 1903 as the private home of the Byrn family, including seven children. The Queen Anne–style mansion still has the same configuration, with five large guest rooms and 12-foot ceilings, along with the original fireplaces, marble lavatories and stained-oak woodwork. Unusual for such an intimate property, the inn has amenities such as private phones, dataports, televisions and VCRs in all four rooms as well as a fitness center. Full breakfast included. ~ 346 East Main Street; 615-867-0308, 888-877-4919, fax 615-867-0280; www.byrn-roberts-inn.com, e-mail byrnrobert@aol.com. DELUXE TO ULTRA-DELUXE.

DINING

The número-uno gathering spot in town is the family-owned **Demos' Steak and Spaghetti House**. In several dining areas done in dark green with old-fashioned lighting fixtures, devotees dine on spaghetti (prepared ten ways) and other pasta dishes, steaks, seafood and specialties such as pot roast, mozzarella chicken and several Mexican options. ~ 1115 Northwest Broad Street; 615-895-3701, fax 615-848-0902; www.demosrestaurants.com. BUDGET TO MODERATE.

Marina's on the Square is a haven for hand-tossed pizza lovers, but also has a full menu that includes standard pasta dishes as well as some casual Italian fare you don't see everywhere: ziti, stuffed shells, calzone and saltimbocca prepared with chicken in lieu of veal. Chicken and seafood dishes are also options at this upbeat restaurant in a restored town square building. Hanging plants add a touch of greenery. Closed Sunday and Monday. ~ 125 North Maple Street; 615-849-8885. MODERATE.

The Front Porch Café is aptly named for the portico that fronts this corner brick structure. Light luncheon fare includes burgers, various sandwiches (vegetarian, chicken, cheese and club) and a few specials such as the restaurant's "signature" meat loaf. The dining rooms are in the main-floor parlors, which are furnished with chairs and small square tables and festooned with garlands of ivy and decorated with garden-inspired murals. Closed Sunday and evenings except Friday. ~ 114 East College Street; 615-896-6771. BUDGET TO MODERATE.

The **Bunganut Pig** serves English pub fare, as well as soups and salads, at lunch and dinner. The evening menu includes heavier entrées such as pork tenderloin, filet mignon and chicken and pasta dishes. (The fanciful name comes from a British tale about piglets falling from a tree.) Closed Sunday. ~ 1602 West Northfield Boulevard; 615-893-7860. BUDGET TO MODERATE.

HIDDEN ►

For a classic Southern meal at a mom-and-pop operation, stop by the **Kleervu Lunchroom**. In what was once a country store, you can feast on hearty, home-cooked dishes served cafeteria-style. No dinner weeknights. ~ 228 South Highland Avenue; 615-896-0520. BUDGET.

The closest restaurant to Stones River National Battlefield (conveniently a stone's throw from Route 24) is **Corky's**. An outpost of the original barbecue joint in Memphis, this one is relatively fancy, a big open room with lots of windows and greenery. But it's the same great food: barbecued chicken and ribs, great slaw and unbelievably tasty fresh breads. Plus some other dishes, though only a fool would order anything but the 'cue. ~ 116 John R. Rice Boulevard; 615-890-1742, fax 615-904-2329. BUDGET TO MODERATE.

SHOPPING

Civil War buffs can have a field day at **Yesteryear,** a tiny but jam-packed shop near the Stones River National Battlefield. The collection is so interesting that a $1 admission is charged, but de-

ducted from the cost of any purchase, including some actual relics.
Closed Tuesday. ~ 3511 Old Nashville Highway; 615-893-3470.

The **Bunganut Pig Pub** features live music nightly except Sunday   **NIGHTLIFE**
and Monday, with jazz, country, classic rock or funk on various
weeknights, and R&B on the weekends. Cover on the weekend.
~ Georgetown Square, 1602 West Northfield Boulevard; 615-893-
7860; www.bunganutpig.com.

Franklin is the capital of antique shopping
in this part of the world, while Columbia   **Franklin and Columbia**
claims President Polk as its own. In addition
to the many antebellum homes open daily to the public are a handful that welcome visitors during special weekends in the spring.

Other mansions may be more grand, but there's something quite   **SIGHTS**
special about **Carnton Plantation**. Built in 1826 by Randal   ◄ **HIDDEN**
McGavock on a knoll southeast of Franklin, the late-neoclassi-
cal plantation house was a grande dame in her heyday; it played
host to an illustrious guest list that included Andrew Jackson,
James K. Polk and Sam Houston. McGavock's son and daughter-
in-law added Greek Revival elements, adding a huge two-story
veranda in the rear of the house and French wallpaper to some
of the elegant rooms. Although it is not completely restored and
refurbished, the house has a poignancy derived from its having
done duty as a field hospital during the Battle of Franklin in
1864. Hundreds of injured Confederate troops sought shelter
here; at least 150 of them died on the spot. In 1866 the McGav-
ocks set aside two acres for the reinterment of 1500 soldiers
killed in the battle, the last decisive conflict of the Civil War. The
largest privately owned Confederate cemetery in the country, it

AUTHOR FAVORITE

sights I could hardly believe I was looking at Civil War–era bullet holes
when I visited the farm office at the **Carter House**, a National Historic
Landmark. With 200 holes, it is said to be the most badly battle-scarred
building surviving the war. What had been a 288-acre cotton plantation is
now only 10 acres, much of it bearing testimony to the bloody 1864
Battle of Franklin, which incurred nearly 9000 casualties. These and
other dramatic stories are included in the exhaustive tours of the
house, the grounds and a military museum at the site. Admission. ~
1140 Columbia Avenue, Franklin; 615-791-1861, fax 615-794-1327;
www.carter-house.org.

DRIVING TOUR
Antebellum Trail

The region of Tennessee just south of Nashville is rife with Civil War sites and antebellum mansions that are easily visible from the highway. Most of the latter are
closed to the public except for special events. For a full map of the *Antebellum Trail
Guide*, or for discount trail tickets, call 800-381-1865. Note that most of the points
on the map are rarely, if ever, open to the public.

BRENTWOOD   Start your tour to pre–Civil War points of interest on
Route 31 just south of Brentwood at the **Midway Slave Cemetery**,
final resting place of many slaves who labored at the Midway Plantation.
Across the road is **Ashlawn**, an elegant 1835 Georgian home with
Greek Revival influences. Re-cross the road to see **Mountview**, one of
the last major plantation houses to be built before the war, in the classic Greek Revival style. Continue south on Route 31 until you see
Aspen Grove on the east side, an 1834 home that utilizes a number
of Greek Revival architectural elements.

FRANKLIN   Drive into Franklin to find the **Hiram Masonic Hall**, an 1823
Gothic building that was the first three-story building in the state. Continue through town; on the left you can visit the **Carter House** (page
253), which survived a pitched battle on the grounds of the farm. Across

is only a short walk from the house, and it, too, is open to the
public. Admission. ~ 1345 Carnton Lane (off Lewisburg Avenue),
Franklin; 615-794-0903; www.carnton.org, e-mail carnton@mind
spring.com.

For more information about the Franklin area, you can contact the **Williamson County Chamber of Commerce**, housed in City
Hall in the Town Square. ~ 109 2nd Avenue South, Franklin; 615-
794-1225, 800-356-3445; www.williamsoncvb.org.

Before you set off for the sights of Columbia, stop by the
Middle Tennessee Visitors Bureau. ~ 8 Public Square, Columbia;
931-381-7176; www.visitplantations.com.

Unless you count the White House, the only remaining home
of the 11th U.S. president is the **James K. Polk Ancestral Home**, a
Federal-style residence built in 1816 by James K. Polk's father.
Polk's official White House portrait and family furniture, including his wife's piano, still decorate the house, along with memorabilia from the White House and Polk's law office. Considered
elegant by standards of the period, the quarters seem somewhat

the road from the Carter House, turn east onto Cleburne Street, right on Lewisburg Avenue then right onto Carnton Lane. Here is the **Mc-Gavock Confederate Cemetery**, where 1500 bodies were buried in 1866, making it the country's largest private Confederate cemetery. Nearby is the **Carnton Plantation** (page 253), another major site open to the public. Retrace your path to Route 31 (also known as Columbia Avenue) and turn left. Just south on your right will be **Homestead Manor**, built in 1819 as an inn. Beyond it, the McKissack home was built in 1845 as the first brick house in Spring Hill. Drive on past Saturn Parkway and on your left will be **Rippavilla Plantation**, home to the Antebellum Trail; it is open daily except for Sunday mornings.

COLUMBIA   Stop in Columbia to tour two sites, **The Athenaeum Rectory** (page 255) and the **James K. Polk Ancestral Home** (page 254). Return north to the intersection of Route 50 and turn left, or west, until you arrive at the intersection with Route 243. Turn left again, or south, and in a few miles you will find the **Rattle & Snap Plantation** (page 256) on your left. This 1845 mansion is also open to the public.

BACK ON THE TRACE   You can reach your starting point by retracing your path to Route 31N, or (if you have at least half a tank of gas) you can continue your tour by returning north via the Natchez Trace. To reach it, drive south of Rattle & Snap to the intersection with Route 43 and turn right. Turn left at the intersection with Zion Road and then left again on Route 412, which leads to the Natchez Trace Parkway.

modest today, but historically it is fascinating. This registered National Historic Landmark is where Polk began the legal and political career that would lead to the state legislature, the U.S. House of Representatives and, in 1845, to the presidency. Under Polk, the United States expanded all the way to the Pacific for the first time, with 800,000 square miles added during his term. A short video at the complex, which includes the house next door and gardens, takes an informative look at Polk's political career. Admission. ~ 301 West 7th Street, Columbia; 931-388-2354; www.jameskpolk.com, e-mail jkpolk@usit.net.

Head west on West 7th Street past Walker Street, to the West 7th Street Church of Christ, then turn left and follow the markers for **The Athenaeum Rectory**, a totally revamped mansion that used to be a school. Built in 1835 for President Polk's nephew, Samuel Polk Walker, the Gothic Revival house—a refreshing change from the antebellum houses that define this region—became the home of Reverend Franklin G. Smith, who established a girls school here in 1852, using the home's ground floor as the reception room and parlors for the school, while his family lived upstairs. The school was extremely advanced for its curriculum, which ranged from natural history and chemistry to croquet and etiquette, and survived for half a century before closing down. The Athenaeum, restored and now maintained by the Association for the Preservation of Tennessee Antiquities, is open to visitors interested in a museum of late-19th-century living. Of special note are the original chandeliers in the reception room, the maple floors and the portrait of Reverend Smith over the panel. Closed Monday and from December to January. Admission. ~ 808 Athenaeum Street (off West 7th Street), Columbia; 931-381-4822; www.athenaeumrectory.com.

The **Antebellum Trail** is an automobile tour of antebellum homes around Franklin and Columbia, some of them open to the public and others completely private. One of the best homes to tour is the **Rattle & Snap Plantation**, a National Historic Landmark built in 1845 by George Washington Polk. Polk built it on land his father won from the governor of North Carolina in a game of chance called rattle-and-snap, in which dried beans were "rattled" in one's hand, then cast, like dice, with a "snap." The Greek Revival mansion is among the finest examples of its type in the country. The interior has been restored and furnished with period furnishings. Rattle & Snap is surrounded by some 1500 acres, including gardens, stables, a smokehouse, a carriage house and an icehouse, all typical of the period. Admission. ~ Route 43, six miles south of Columbia; 931-379-5861, 800-258-3875; www.rattleandsnap.com.

With its stately white columns announcing its antebellum heritage, **Rippavilla** has been restored to its original appearance and decorated with many of the family's antique furnishings. The museum room, in particular, holds a number of family heirlooms as well as some Civil War artifacts. Completed in 1855 by Nathaniel F. Cheairs as a family home, the mansion is now open for tours, as is the old mule museum. Closed Monday. Admission. ~ 5700 Main Street (Route 31), Spring Hill; 913-486-9037; www.rippavilla.org.

LODGING

HIDDEN ►

Whether or not you're traveling with a horse (or a dog, for that matter), you're welcome at **Blue Moon Farm**. And you'll have the three-room guest cottage all to yourself, as it's the only accommodation on the 15-acre farm. The unit has a kitchen and dining area as well as a sofa-bed; a porch and patio afford elbow room. A full breakfast is included and the proprietors will prepare and serve a multicourse dinner for an additional fee. ~ 4441 North Chapel Road, Franklin; 615-497-4518; www.bluemoonfarmbb.com, e-mail relax@bluemoonfarm.com. ULTRA-DELUXE.

If you ever wondered what it would be like to grow up and go to camp on a luxury scale, you'll probably love **Namaste Acres Barn Bed & Breakfast**. The Dutch Colonial–style house, sitting on 30 acres in horse country southwest of Franklin, was built in 1982, but the three suites all have a rustic ambience. On the property are a hot tub, a swimming pool and horseback and hiking trails. (The innkeepers can arrange rides.) Folks like to gather to play horseshoes, enjoy the pool or cook on the gas barbecue . . . and maybe even tell ghost stories. Full breakfast is served. ~ 5436 Leipers Creek Road, Franklin; 615-791-0333, fax 615-591-0665; www.namasteacres.com, e-mail namastebb@aol.com. DELUXE.

◄ *HIDDEN*

The accommodations at the **Henry Horton Inn** are plain and simple but well-kept. There are 65 rooms and four suites in the inn itself plus seven more-expensive cabins that sleep up to six people each. ~ Henry Horton State Park, 4358 Nashville Highway (Route 31A), Chapel Hill; 931-364-2222. MODERATE TO DELUXE.

Merridee's Bakery and Restaurant has wood-plank floors, blue-and-white tablecloths and a sprinkling of quilts (for sale). They bake their own breads, muffins and sweet treats, which you can order along with simple dishes like chicken salad and sandwiches. Closed Sunday. ~ 110 4th Avenue South, Franklin; 615-790-3755. BUDGET.

DINING

Housed in the 1899 Harrison Building and on the National Register of Historic Places, **Sandy's Downtown Grille** is a spacious affair, with high ceilings in both the bar and dining room. Main courses include grilled swordfish, pork medallions, Cajun ahi tuna and Colorado lamb. But who can resist starting off a meal with crab cakes or a smoked salmon martini? Closed Sunday. ~ 108 4th Avenue South, Franklin; 615-794-3639, fax 615-794-3842. MODERATE TO DELUXE.

You can get fish-and-chips, shepherd's pie, and other tastes of England at the **Bunganut Pig**. Also on the menu are standard sandwiches and salads, as well as a variety of steak, chicken, seafood and pasta dishes. Closed Sunday. ~ 1143 Columbia Avenue, Franklin; 615-794-4777. BUDGET TO MODERATE.

Unsuspecting pigs are painted frolicking on the side of the little pink building that houses **Nolen's BBQ**. Or you could just follow your nose until it identifies the aroma of barbecuing pork or beef. Choices are limited here—well, you do get to choose whether you want your coleslaw creamy or more vinegary—and the only seating is outdoors, overlooking the road, but the prices and taste are hard to beat. Closed Sunday. ~ 115 East James Campbell Boulevard, Columbia; 931-388-0059. BUDGET.

The **Henry Horton State Park Restaurant** decor, as unassuming as the inn's rooms, is befitting for a place devoted to straightforward Southern country food. You can pick up an inexpensive continental breakfast on weekends here; it's closed from Sunday afternoon until the Friday evening buffet. ~ 4358 Route 31A, Chapel Hill; 931-364-2222. BUDGET.

SHOPPING   Magic Memories sells estate jewelry as well as books, cards and home accessories. Closed Sunday. ~ 345 Main Street, Franklin; 615-794-2848.

The Factory is a complex of shops, restaurants and other businesses in a rehabbed 1929 factory on the National Register of Historic Places. It's home to Antiques of Franklin (615-591-4612), which specializes in antiques, rugs, collectibles and objets d'art; Times Past and Present (615-599-7020), purveyor of home accessories and folk pieces; and Treasure Trove (615-599-1022), which carries handmade glass, pottery, jewelry, wood and watercolors. ~ 230 Franklin Road, Franklin; 615-791-1777.

English, French and American furniture, Civil War artifacts, dolls and primitive pieces constitute the merchandise at Battleground Antique Mall, a big, multidealer outlet located on the east side of town. ~ 232 Franklin Road, Franklin; 615-794-9444.

The oldest antique mall in Middle Tennessee, the Franklin Antique Mall, located in the historic Ice House, may also be the largest, with 18,000 square feet and an overwhelming array of collectibles sold by more than 60 dealers. ~ 251 2nd Avenue South, Franklin; 615-790-8593.

Southern fiction, other works on local topics and children's books form the backbone of Franklin Booksellers (or perhaps we should say, the spine), but there are many more choices at this popular shop. Closed Sunday. ~ 118 4th Avenue South, Franklin; 615-790-1349.

The Garden Path stocks classic garden accessories, including furniture and fountains as well as easier-to-pack items. ~ 1178 3rd Avenue North, Franklin; 615-595-8811.

A short drive from downtown Franklin takes you to Leipers Fork—a cute village in danger of becoming terminally hip—where, at the intriguing Leipers Fork Antiques, you can find American country furniture, primitives, old-fashioned advertising signs and lots more quality merchandise. The owner, Marty Hunt, is also a fount of information about local celebrities, including the musicians who sometimes make last-minute arrangements to perform here for free. ~ 4149 Old Hillsboro Road, Leipers Fork; 615-790-9963.

NIGHTLIFE   There's live blues and Motown music most nights at the Bunganut Pig. Closed Sunday. Cover Thursday through Saturday. ~ 1143 Columbia Avenue, Franklin; 615-794-4777.

Within The Factory complex, the **Bluewind Art Bar** offers a mix of jazz, pop, swing and blues Monday through Saturday evenings. A light menu is served at antique pub tables or in the beer garden. ~ 230 Franklin Road, Franklin; 615-599-4995.

HENRY HORTON STATE PARK 🏃 ⛵ 🏕 🚤 🚣 ⛳ If you're **PARKS**
just dying to shoot trap, this is the only state park where you'll
be able to practice your skills. But the skeet and
trap range is only one of many amenities at this
1141-acre park, which was established on the old
estate of the 36th governor of Tennessee, Henry H.
Horton. Located on the Duck River, the park offers
excellent fishing. Facilities include a snack bar, a gift
shop, a restaurant, a picnic area, an 18-hole golf course,
an archery range, tennis courts, a playground and a recreation center with restrooms. ~ On Route 31A in Chapel Hill,
about midway between Columbia and Shelbyville; 931-364-2222;
www.tnstateparks.com.

> The Duck River is the longest stretch of free-flowing river left in Tennessee.

▲ There are 21 tent-only sites and 54 campsites with water and electricity; $17.25 per night.

▼▼▼▼▼▼▼▼▼▼
Lawrenceburg to Summertown

Established on the Big Buffalo River, Lawrenceburg claims David Crockett as a native son. A bronze statue of the pioneer/soldier/statesman stands in the town square, surrounded by shops, restaurants and offices. The countryside to the north is so fertile that it has attracted and maintained a sizable Amish community, as well as the best-known "hippie" communal farm in the country.

Summertown looks like it sounds—a sleepy, somewhat sprawling area with family farms and plenty of narrow winding country roads. It's a logical choice for a place like the commune. Ethridge isn't so much a town as a wide place in the road; it's notable because of the Amish population. Their black horse-drawn carriages and small plots of farmland add an intriguing element to a flat and mostly boring roadside.

Upon entering the town of Lawrenceburg, a bronze, life-size statue of David Crockett (it's the only such statue of the man in the world) greets visitors from the public square. Also here is the **Mexican War Monument**, which was raised in 1849. The monument later deterred possible burning of the Lawrenceburg County Courthouse during the Civil War. ~ Bounded by North and South Military avenues and Pulaski and Waterloo streets, Lawrenceburg.   **SIGHTS**

David Crockett Cabin and Museum is a high point of any visit to Lawrenceburg. To find it, head first to the public square, which is on Military Avenue just south of Route 64. From there, go another block and a half south to this little museum, which is housed in an unattended cabin that's free and open daily. It is a replica of his log cabin, and contains glass cases full of his writings, clothing, canteen and other memorabilia. ~ South Military Avenue, Lawrenceburg; 931-762-4231.

The **Amish community** is not a precise destination, but it's certainly an attraction. From Lawrenceburg, head up Route 43 about five miles to **Ethridge**, an extremely interesting neighborhood, though the town itself isn't very interesting. Although you'll see the telltale black horse-drawn buggies moving slowly around town, the heart of the community is a couple of miles up the road around Ethridge, where an estimated 300 to 400 Amish people live, making their living off the land. They've been here since 1944, practicing their simple way of life. Though the Amish, with their beards, wide-brimmed hats and dark dresses, are a tempting sight for photographs, most shun having their pictures taken. If you want to get up close, you can drive around and see which families are selling vegetables or candies in their front yards. A couple of stores around Ethridge sell their handmade crafts and can arrange guided tours of the community.

Granny's TV Network arranges guided trips through the Amish countryside. ~ 44 Marcella Falls Road, Ethridge; 931-829-2419.

Continuing north from Ethridge, keep a lookout for the turnoff to **Summertown**, Route 20. Follow Route 20 for about five minutes, past the fire station, looking for a green sign that says Lawrence County. You'll also see a sign for Drakes Lane. Go right, then right again at the fork, then turn right into Walker Road.

HIDDEN ► Anyone who ever identified with the hippie movement of the '60s will love a visit to **The Farm**, a commune that has been thriving for more than a quarter of a century. It's really a blast from the past. One hundred people jointly own some 1750 acres in the middle of nowhere, and a productive farm it is, too. Visitors are welcome to drive along gravelly roads past apple orchards and to stop in at the general store, a tie-died geodesic dome that sells organic juices and the like. The Farm runs a couple of private businesses, one a publishing house and the other a

AUTHOR FAVORITE
Even though there's a replica of David Crockett's log cabin in town, I prefer visiting **David Crockett State Park**, located 1.2 miles east of the town square via Route 64. Here, an interpretive center has full-scale exhibits on Crockett's life and times, and quite an education it is. (See "David Crockett, 'King of the Wild Frontier'" in Chapter Two.) ~ 1400 West Gaines Street, Lawrenceburg; 931-762-9408.

construction outfit that has built an impressive number of homes around Summertown and Columbia. Visitors are welcome, but call first. ~ 156 Drakes Lane, Summertown; 931-964-3574; www.thefarmcommunity.com.

LODGING

The **Richland Inn** is the uncontested top lodging choice in Lawrenceburg. It's one of three in southern Tennessee that cater mostly to business travelers, but it's fine for tourists as well. In an attractive two-story brick motel-like structure, 56 rooms and 4 suites are spacious and well lit, usually decorated in colors like mauve and beige. ~ 2125 North Locust Avenue (Route 43), Lawrenceburg; 931-762-0061, 800-742-4526; www.lawrence burg.com/richlandinn. BUDGET TO MODERATE.

DINING

Square Forty is an upstairs dining room housed in a falsefront brick building on the little town square. It's one huge room with polished wood floors and framed landscape prints all over the walls. Entrées at this comfy spot include seafood, chicken and pork chops; there's also a daily buffet. No dinner. ~ 40 Public Square, Lawrenceburg; 931-762-2868. BUDGET TO MODERATE.

Just off the main drag, **Rick's Barbecue** is a glorified log cabin with both a drive-through lane and a dining room of wooden booths and tables with straight-back chairs. The special barbecue sauce comes on a choice of pork, beef, chicken, ribs or "slaw dog." Closed Sunday. ~ 101 North Military Avenue, Lawrenceburg; 931-762-2030. BUDGET.

SHOPPING

The best selection of antiques in Lawrenceburg is at **Carriage House**, fronting the town square. Carriage House has delicate stuff—cut glass, pottery, jewelry and collectibles. Closed Sunday. ~ 38 Public Square, Lawrenceburg; 931-766-0428.

NIGHTLIFE

The Lawrenceburg City Administration Building is the unlikely site of the bimonthly **Tennessee Valley Jamboree**, a variety show incorporating country, bluegrass and gospel music on the second and fourth Saturday nights of each month. ~ Public Square, 1709 Deer Hollow Drive, Lawrenceburg; 931-762-6249.

Free shows are also presented on Friday nights during the summer at **David Crockett State Park**. ~ 1400 West Gaines Street, Lawrenceburg; 931-762-9408.

PARKS

DAVID CROCKETT STATE PARK Claiming 1100 acres of mostly forested high ground, this park got its name because Crockett moved his family to the head of nearby Shoal Creek in 1817. In the visitors center is a re-creation of the type of log cabin Crockett lived in, plus antique tools believed to have been his. The park is particularly popular for day use, thanks to an Olympic-size swimming pool, playgrounds, tennis courts and a restaurant. Day-use fee, $3. ~ 1400 West Gaines Street, Lawrenceburg; 931-762-9408; www.tnstateparks.com.

▲ There are 107 campsites with water and electricity; $17.25 per night.

▼▼▼▼▼▼▼▼▼▼▼▼▼
Tennessee Walking Horse Country

This region is headquarters for the Tennessee Walking Horse business, which began in Wartrace in the 1930s. As you drive around the rural roads, keep an eye out for farms where these thoroughbreds are raised. Bell Buckle and Wartrace are tiny villages where antique shops are a major tourist attraction.

Lynchburg is a small village where the biggest employer is a distillery almost as old as the town itself. Davy Crockett was an early settler here before the town was chartered in 1883. Life revolves around the Lynchburg Square, where, if you hang out long enough, you'll probably see someone whittling.

SIGHTS

You can get information about self-guided tours from the **Shelbyville Chamber of Commerce**. ~ 100 North Cannon Boulevard, Shelbyville; 931-684-3482, 888-662-2525; www.shelbyvilletn.com.

The place to see the famous Tennessee Walking Horses is at **Celebration Grounds**, a 105-acre facility (with indoor and outdoor arenas) that's the site of the world's largest Walking-Horse show, the Tennessee Walking Horse Celebration. The show began as an event attracting 8000 spectators over three nights and has grown to an 11-night event late each August that attracts about a quarter million people who come to watch 2000 horses perform. The two other annual events open to the public are the Spring Fun Show in May and the Great Celebration Mule Show in July. ~ Calhoun Street at Evans Street, Shelbyville; 931-684-5915; www.twhnc.com.

The perfect accompaniment to the Walking Horse lifestyle might just be wine. You can choose from more than a dozen dry and sweet wines at **Tri-Star Vineyards & Winery**, which makes wine from grapes as well as berries and other fruit. ~ 168 Scales Road, Shelbyville; 931-294-3062; www.tristarwinery.com.

Stop by the **Lynchburg Welcome Center** before setting your sights on Lynchburg's attractions. ~ Public Square, Lynchburg; 931-759-4111; www.lynchburgtn.com.

Most of Lynchburg's attractions are within easy walking distance of the Public Square, which is where you should park your car for a couple of hours at least.

The prisoners have long since been moved to a larger facility, but it's fun to go see the cells and to have your photo taken in front of the tiny **Old Jail Museum**, which was built even before the 1885 courthouse. ~ Public Square, Lynchburg; 931-759-4111.

Granny's TV Network

You don't have to live in the big city to have your own network channel, however humble it may be. Imagine the surprise of television audiences in Ethridge, Tennessee, to have their Nostalgia channel broadcast of a *Love Boat* rerun suddenly interrupted by footage from last summer's demolition derby. That's what happens sometimes, thanks to the amazing efforts of one Sarah Evetts.

It all started in 1982, this grandmother relates. "The community was in danger of losing its cable access channel," says Evetts. "So I contacted the FCC [Federal Communications Commission] and protested. I got a ten-watt station. It took a couple of years after that to get on the air."

Now Channel 10 is the local access channel, shared with the Nostalgia channel, which explains some of those weird segues in programming. Whether she's got airtime or not, Granny runs tape 24 hours a day, "just like the big guys," she says. Sometimes she goes downtown to City Hall to videotape the goings-on in local government, but she's no Diane Sawyer. *Your Eye on the Community* is about as serious as her programming gets.

"We tell everything that's going on in town," says Evetts. "Anyone can come and talk about what they're doing and what's going on. People send in tapes. Sometimes singers or other performers come here and talk about what they're fixin' to do. We had the costar from *Heat of the Night* in here once."

That was not Granny's only brush with fame, however. The *Late Night Show* producers got wind of her venture and called to book her. "Who?" she asked. Granny intersperses her stories with whoops and shrieks of laughter. She'd never heard of David Letterman. But she has made guest appearances with him as well as with Johnny Carson.

The wife of an automobile parts dealer and mother of seven, Granny is now in her seventies. She still has plenty of energy, which she needs to function as camera operator, technician, program director and technician. All out of the basement of her home. Between gigs, she runs a store and a tour bus business that takes visitors out among the Amish community around Ethridge.

The range of Granny's TV Network is about 20 miles, she says, but she has a core of loyal watchers who stay "glued to their TVs" for local news and weather as well as footage of birthday parties, high school football games and, yes, the demolition derby from the Lawrenceburg county fair.

The **Tennessee Walking Horse Museum** is the only one of its kind dedicated to the breed so famous for its mild temperament, stately manners and distinctive smooth gait. There are displays on the history and training techniques involved as well as interactive videotapes. Closed Sunday and Monday. ~ Public Square, Lynchburg; 913-759-5747; www.twhnc.com.

It's a bit of a hike to the distillery that made this town famous, so you should save this for last, after you've inspected the stores and restaurants around the square. Then head south on Route 55 and look to your right. Since it was founded in 1866, the **Jack Daniel's Distillery**, a short drive from the Public Square, has been synonymous with Lynchburg, a town that's not much bigger then it was 100 years ago. Jasper Newton Daniel started working in a distillery at the age of 12, bought out his partner after the Civil War and began making his own sour mash whiskey. The oldest nationally registered distillery, it has been in use longer than any other in the country. To see how the process works (the key is charcoal), take the extensive tour, which starts in the barrel house and involves a good deal of walking and climbing through various structures, ending in the stillhouse. Allow plenty of time to visit: tourists come not only from all over the U.S., but from abroad as well, to visit the Mother Church of sour mash whiskey. ~ Route 55, Lynchburg; 931-759-6180; www.jackdaniels.com.

LODGING   Within walking distance of Celebration Grounds, **Cinnamon Ridge Bed & Breakfast** is the most elegant inn in the area, where you, too, can feel like a gentleman farmer, at least for a night. This Colonial-style home has five guest rooms decorated tastefully with armoires and other antiques, some of them—such as a dresser— nearly 200 years old. This is the kind of place that has authentic Chippendales in the dining room, where guests are served a full breakfast. ~ 799 Whitthorne Street, Shelbyville; 931-685-9200, 877-685-9200. MODERATE.

sights

AUTHOR FAVORITE

Until you get up close to a Tennessee Walking Horse, you can't truly appreciate these magnificent animals. One place to get that thrill is at **Waterfall Farms**, located between Shelbyville and Wartrace on Route 64E. Trophies and ribbons are displayed in glass cases in the clublike entrance lobby. After checking them out, you'll be taken to the pristine stables where these beauties are kept and, if lucky, you'll see some of them in action in the paddock. ~ Waterfall Farms, 2395 Route 64E, Shelbyville; 931-684-7894.

The **Best Western Celebration Inn and Suites** has a lot more going for it than most motels. First, it is a short walk from Celebration Grounds. Second, it has an indoor pool and exercise room. Third, there are 12 freestanding suites to augment the 46 rooms in the main, two-story building. These are particularly nice, done in shades of blue and abutting a wooded area. ~ 724 Madison Street, Shelbyville; 931-684-2378, 800-937-8376, fax 931-685-4936. MODERATE TO DELUXE.

A couple of blocks up a gentle slope from the cluster of shops and restaurants, **The Mingle House Bed & Breakfast** is a pale yellow 1898 Victorian graced with large porches, front and back. All three rooms are furnished in antiques and have high ceilings and coal fireplaces. Full breakfast. ~ 116 Main Street, Bell Buckle; 931-389-9453. MODERATE.

It's no wonder that entertainers playing some of Nashville's bigger venues like to come down to **Goose Branch Farm** on their nights off. Goose Branch Hollow is about as far away from the bright lights as you can get. Located off a country lane off a country road, this century-old farmhouse has two suites on the second floor, each with a private entrance. The larger suite has wall-to-wall beige carpeting, blue walls and Battenberg lace at the windows. The smaller one, which is also furnished partly with antiques, has the added attraction of a desk set with a table and chairs. The suites, which can be connected upon request, have microwave ovens and refrigerators for guests who want to stock anything beyond the continental breakfast delivered in a country basket each morning. The owners raise rodeo stock cattle on their 57-acre farm, which guests are free to roam in utter privacy. ~ Goose Branch Road (Box 140, Route 3, Lynchburg, TN 37352); 931-759-5919; www.bbonline.com/gbfarmbb, e-mail gbfarmbb@aol.com. MODERATE.

◄ HIDDEN

The **Lynchburg Bed & Breakfast** is an 1877 home only two blocks from the public square and within reasonable walking distance of Jack Daniel's Distillery. It's old but a bit boring. Both rooms are decorated with antiques and have ceiling fans; there is no common room, however, other than a porch. ~ Mechanic Street, Lynchburg; 931-759-7158; www.bbonline.com/tn/lynchburg. MODERATE TO DELUXE.

Finding **Dream Fields Country Inn** is part of the fun. You follow the stenciled horse-and-buggy signs just a few short turns out of tiny Mulberry; they lead to a wonderful old farmhouse amid 260 acres. Built in 1860 (and once owned by Jack Daniel's brother Wiley), it has three rooms. The ground-floor bedroom has a high ceiling, climb-up beds, fans and assorted antiques. The upstairs ones are similar if slightly smaller. A painstaking reclamation of the house, which opened as a bed and breakfast in 1997, resulted

◄ HIDDEN

in period colors like pale moss green and understated blues. Fishing and hiking are nearby. Full breakfast. ~ 9 Back Street, Mulberry; 931-438-8875, 877-898-1998, fax 931-433-1556; www.bbonline.com/tn/dreamfields. MODERATE TO DELUXE.

The three-story **Walking Horse Hotel**, with its wonderful upstairs balconies, looks like a stage set from 1917. At least it does now. It was closed for some time and reopened in 1997. Rooms are large and quite nice, with simple color schemes and not much frou-frou; one is on the ground floor, six others are on the top floor. (All have in-room coffee makers.) One of the early owners bought and trained a horse to show in the Tennessee Walking Horse show, which was just picking up steam in 1939. That horse, Strolling Jim, won the first National Celebration. Today, the old champion is buried in the pasture out back, where visitors are welcome to pay their respects. ~ 101 Spring Street (at Route 64 and Route 269), Wartrace; 931-389-7050, fax 931-389-7030; e-mail bgj@cafes.net. MODERATE.

DINING

A tiny storefront on the town square, where the jukebox is busted and customers seat themselves, is the place for a power breakfast in Shelbyville. At **Pope's Cafe**, community notices and coat hooks line the walls on one side of a long room with a red-and-white linoleum floor. Behind a counter in the back, cooks roll out Southern-style cooking all day. Lunch and dinner choices include steak, chicken, fish, hamburger and "meat-and-threes," the standard Tennessee meal of one meat and three vegetables selected from a long list. If you like chicken livers, try the fried version here. And be sure to have pie, no matter what meal you're having. Closed Sunday. ~ 120 Eastside Square, Shelbyville; 931-684-9901. BUDGET.

In an odd little building where even the roof is off-center, you'll find the best (actually, the only) Mexican food in town. The rather subdued decor in all three dining areas at **El Mexico** is limited to two shades of pale pink, with most seating at leatherette booths. A nice feature, in addition to the usual beef burritos, chicken enchiladas and *carne asada*, is a list of vegetarian combinations, meatless *chalupas* and *tostaguac*, a flat crisp corn tortilla served with beef, beans and guacamole. ~ 713 North Main Street, Shelbyville; 931-684-0874. BUDGET.

The **Bell Buckle Cafe** is divided into large rooms (one is nonsmoking) furnished with chairs and tables with red-and-white plastic covers. Brick walls and ceiling fans, plus some old signs, add ambience. It's hard not to order homemade pie, peach cobbler or Grandma's secret-recipe oatmeal cake as a main course and just wash it down with a pitcher of fresh lemonade, but they also have lighter fare like salads, sandwiches, hamburgers, barbecue, vegetarian plates and stir-fry, as well as chicken-fried steak, rib-eye steak and a shrimp dinner. No dinner Sunday and Monday. ~ 16 Railroad Square, Bell Buckle; 931-389-9693, fax 931-389-9694; www.bellbucklecafe.com. BUDGET.

Pulled-pork barbecue is the house dish at the **Bar-B-Que Caboose Café**, but they don't mind dishing out smoked chicken, pizza and sides like Cajun red beans and rice. The 'cue is pit-smoked for 22 hours, then served with a pungent sauce on the side. How can you resist a place, however homely, whose motto is, "If you don't have fun here it's your own fault!"? Normally it's closed in the evening but on Friday nights the café stays open for dinner and music. ~ West Side Square, Lynchburg; 931-759-5180. BUDGET.

Don't miss the chance to lunch at **Miss Mary Bobo's Boarding House**. Some people make their reservations there first, and then make the rest of their travel plans. There's just one seating, at 1 p.m. (occasionally there's a seating at 11 a.m.), after which guests introduce themselves and pass the vittles, family style. There are usually at least ten dishes, like a big Sunday dinner (which is what the midday meal is called in the Old South): vegetables from the garden, biscuits or cornbread, fried chicken, ribs and homemade desserts. And endless glasses of iced tea. There are three dining rooms on the main floor of a lovely, white 1908 boarding house and two more down the steps in a brick cellar. It's an experience you won't forget. Eat up, because it's just about impossible to find an evening meal in Lynchburg. Closed Sunday. ~ Main Street, Lynchburg; 931-759-7394, fax 931-759-6334. MODERATE.

The **Iron Kettle**, on the south side of the square, is open for breakfast and lunch. You can have a full Southern breakfast or opt for something simple, like pancakes. Lunches are blue-plate specials that change from day to day in this cozy coffeehouse. Like most places around town, the Iron Kettle serves a dish—in

AUTHOR FAVORITE

The best place to eat in this region is **Emil's**, located in a century-old house. In the company of several tables of "Ladies Who Lunch," I relaxed with a generous bowl of fresh tomato soup, a filling salad topped with pecan brittle and a glass of California wine. The French-born chef/owner, Georges Martin, really knows his stuff and shows it off with elegant dinner entrées of meat, fish and poultry. No lunch on Saturday; no dinner on Wednesday. Closed Sunday and Monday. ~ 210 East Lincoln Street, Tullahoma; 931-461-7070, fax 931-461-7077. DELUXE TO ULTRA-DELUXE.

this case a hamburger—with Jack Daniel's whiskey as an ingredient. No dinner. Closed Sunday. ~ 315 Public Square, Lynchburg; 931-759-4274. BUDGET.

SHOPPING   The village of Bell Buckle is wall-to-wall shops on the main route, anchored by **Phillips' General Store**. A general store from the late 1800s until the 1940s, it still has original shelving and even a rolling ladder for retrieving hard-to-reach objects. Much of the merchandise is grouped into displays; look for old dolls, fishing tackle, architectural antiques, painted primitives and quilts. ~ 4 Railroad Square, Bell Buckle; 931-389-6547.

Bell Buckle Crafts specializes in stoneware pottery made right here and sold in this century-old bank building. Other regional handmade goods include willow furniture, folk art, clothing, quilts and more. ~ Railroad Square, Bell Buckle; 931-389-9371.

Around the corner, the **Bell Buckle Antique & Craft Mall** houses more than two dozen dealers peddling an array from crafts like rag rugs to glassware, Civil War relics, tools and books. ~ 112 Main Street, Bell Buckle; 931-389-6174.

Items for home decorating—furniture, old linens, china, silver, glassware and so forth—are the stock in trade at the **Frontstreet Showcase**. ~ Main Street, Wartrace.

Hardware items, cast-iron cookware, used whiskey barrels, local souvenirs and an entire upstairs floor filled with Jack Daniel's logo'ed merchandise (from mugs, golf shirts and caps to whiskey-infused Tipsy Cakes) makes the red-brick **Lynchburg Hardware & General Store** a fun place to browse. ~ Public Square, Lynchburg; 931-759-4200.

Lynchburg Pottery is the place to pick up local crafts (ceramic bowls, mugs, vases), as well as home and garden accessories such as birdhouses. ~ 26 Short Street, Lynchburg; 931-759-5205.

The emphasis is on the '30s, '40s and '50s at **Baker's Antiques and Collectibles**. Twenty booths are filled with a huge variety (in-

WHAT'S IN A NAME?

The folks who live in **Bell Buckle** in the heart of Tennessee Walking Horse country have a couple of explanations for their village's moniker. The favorite is that images of a bell and a buckle were found carved on a beech tree by a spring near the creek, perhaps a way of marking grazing lands. Another tale is that a large cowbell with its buckle was found by early settlers near this same location, a former American Indian camping ground. Nearby **Wartrace** was named for Wartrace Creek, reportedly because it was used by the American Indians as a route that later led all the way to Chattanooga.

cluding the inevitable Jack Daniel's memorabilia)—glassware, tools, tins, Griswold ironware and even pellet stoves. ~ Southside Public Square, Lynchburg; 931-759-4964.

NIGHTLIFE

The **Bell Buckle Cafe** hosts live country music groups Friday and Saturday nights; Sunday afternoon the café hosts a live radio broadcast. ~ Railroad Square, Bell Buckle; 931-389-9693.

Friday nights bring live music and dancing to **The Courtyard** in back of the Bar-B-Que Caboose Café (as long as the weather's warm). If you play an instrument, drop by on Saturday morning for the live radio jam session that starts around 11 a.m. ~ West Side Square, Lynchburg; 931-759-5180.

PARKS

TIMS FORD STATE PARK Fishing in Tims Ford Lake is the number one draw to this 413-acre park, especially since boats can be rented here, but its paved five-mile bike trail also beckons bikers (and you can rent bikes, too). There's also a playground, and the park is accessible to wheelchairs. Day-use fee, $3. ~ 570 Tims Ford Drive, Winchester; 931-962-1183.

▲ There are 52 campsites with water and electricity; $17.25 per night.

Outdoor Adventures

FISHING

The Duck River is popular for catfish and bass and, in warm weather, brim. If you want to try your hand, **Ted's** sells lures and gives fishing advice away for free. ~ 806 South Main Street, Columbia; 931-388-6387.

Anglers go after trout year-round in the tailwaters at the reservoir known as **Tims Ford Lake**. The lake's seasons for largemouth bass are March through June, and September through December; for smallmouth, March through April and October through November. Catfish are plentiful in April and June. ~ 570 Tim's Ford Drive, Winchester; 931-967-4457.

RIVER RUNNING

The Duck River is a Class I river that has occasional rapids. It's considered fine for beginners, yet offers enough interest for experienced canoeists. **River Rat's Canoe Rental** has equipment for canoeing the Duck River, accessible from various points near Columbia. ~ 4361 Route 431, Columbia; 931-381-2278; www.riverratcanoe.com.

GOLF

Water, water everywhere is the theme song at **Forrest Crossing Golf Club**. There is water around 16 of the 18 holes and an island green at this course, which also crosses—twice—the Harpeth River. ~ 750 Riverview Drive, Franklin; 615-794-9400.

If you're interested in playing at the **Legends Club**, home of the Tennessee State Open, inquire at the front desk of your hotel to see if golf privileges are available. If so, you can play on two 18-hole golf courses, each created by Tom Kite and Bob Cupp. Zoysia fairways, bent-grass greens and high maintenance, plus a 20-acre practice facility, make this one of the most desirable courses around. ~ 1500 Legends Club Lane, Franklin; 615-791-8100; www.legendsclub.com.

TENNIS

Six lighted courts can be reserved at **Woodland Park**. ~ 821 West 9th Street, Columbia; 931-388-8119.

BIKING

Bowie Nature Park (on some maps still marked as Fairview Nature Park), about 20 miles from Franklin, has 17 miles for mountain biking, some of which go around the six lakes within the 794-acre park. ~ Route 100, five miles south of Route 40. ~ 615-799-5544. **Tims Ford State Park** has a five-mile paved bike trail along with bike rentals. Good rides run along Route 96, which has wide shoulders, and the **Natchez Trace Parkway**, where a wide bike path extends for 400 miles between Nashville and Alabama.

HIKING

All distances listed for hiking trails are one way unless otherwise noted.

Stones River National Battleground has two miles of paved road on fairly level land within the park's boundaries. In addition, a three-mile, multi-use **Greenway** runs between the park and several trailheads in Murfreesboro, including one at Thompson Lane.

There are two miles of flat pathways for hiking within **Henry Horton State Park**.

▼▼▼▼▼▼▼▼▼▼▼
Transportation

CAR

Most of the Heritage area is within a two-hour drive of Nashville; Lynchburg is closer to Chattanooga, which is about a 90-minute drive away. Murfreesboro has two exits off **Route 24**, which runs between Nashville and Chattanooga. To the west, **Route 65** runs all the way from Kentucky to Alabama, neatly bisecting most of the Heritage area. For touring the Antebellum Trail, the best route is **Route 31**. The **Natchez Trace Parkway** defines the western boundary of this area. Most of the east–west roads and other byways are smaller state and local roads with lots of curves and plenty of pastoral scenery. The north–south route through Lawrenceburg is **Route 43**, which connects it to Ethridge and points north.

AIR

The closest airport to the Heritage Area and Lawrenceburg is the **Nashville International Airport**. Nine major carriers serve Nashville, in addition to the city's own passenger airline, Nashville Air (615-742-9041). American and American Eagle, Continental,

Delta, Northwest, Southwest, United and US Airways all offer regularly scheduled flights into and out of the Nashville International Airport. ~ www.flynashville.com.

Lynchburg is also close to Chattanooga but remember, Chattanooga is in the Eastern time zone, so allow an extra hour for the trip. **Chattanooga Metropolitan Airport** is served by US Airways jets and commuter flights via American Eagle, Atlantic Southeast, ComAir, Northwest Airlink and US Airways Express. For more air transportation services, call 423-855-2200; www.chattairport.com.

Greyhound Bus Lines provides service to several points in the Heritage area. There is a station in Murfreesboro at 2114 South Church Street; and in Columbia at 1800 Carmack Boulevard. The closest Greyhound station to Lawrenceburg is in Nashville, at 200 8th Avenue South. ~ 800-231-2222; www.greyhound.com.

BUS

Nine rental agencies are at or near the Nashville International Airport. They include **Alamo Rent A Car** (800-327-9633), **Avis Rent A Car** (800-331-1212), **Budget Car and Truck Rental of Nashville** (800-527-0700), **Dollar Rent A Car** (800-800-4000), **Enterprise Rent A Car** (800-325-8007), **Hertz Rent A Car** (800-654-3131), **National Car Rental** (800-227-7368) and **Thrifty Car Rental** (800-367-2277).

At Chattanooga Metropolitan Airport, car-rental agencies include **Avis Rent A Car** (800-230-4898), **Budget Rent A Car** (800-527-0700), **Dollar Rent A Car** (800-800-4000), **Hertz Rent A Car** (800-654-3131), **National Car Rental** (800-227-7368) and **Thrifty Car Rental** (800-847-3489).

CAR RENTALS

TEN

Northwest Tennessee and the Delta Country

Ninety miles northwest of Nashville, Clarksville is the gateway to Tennessee's recreation-oriented northwest quadrant, which includes attractions such as Land Between the Lakes and Reelfoot Lake. The Delta Country, which runs beside the Mississippi River between Kentucky and Memphis, has been agrarian since the Jackson Purchase in 1819, after which Southerners were drawn to the fertile river region to establish their own farms and plantations. Cotton, which required great expanses of land and substantial cheap labor to farm it, dictated the way of life for these people. Today, it's hard to drive more than a few miles without coming across a cotton field.

Clarksville, like neighboring Nashville, sits at 500 feet above sea level and has much the same climate, with an average high of 78° in July and 42° in January, with an average relative humidity reaching 85 percent at daybreak and lessening to 59 percent at noon. In short, summers are hot and sticky, but spring and fall are not; in fact, August and September have the least rainfall. Predictably, the weather becomes more humid closer to the Delta.

West of Clarksville, the scenery becomes dominated by lakes, both manmade (Barkley) and natural (Reelfoot). The region is extremely popular with folks who like to fish and hunt. The battlefield at Fort Donelson is one of the top Civil War sites in Tennessee, and nearby Land Between the Lakes, which extends across the state line into Kentucky, is a major recreational attraction and also home to one of the most extensive living-history programs in Tennessee.

There are no major cities between Clarksville and Tiptonville in the northwest corner near Kentucky, just small towns with names like Dover, Paris and Dresden. There is no really direct way to cross Tennessee's northwest quadrant, a result of railroading's extensive infrastructure in this part of the country. The Louisiana and Nashville Railroad ran from Henry County (west of Land Between the Lakes) southwest toward Memphis; today, the route is closely followed by Routes 70 and 79. The north–south line belonged to the Illinois Central, which ran south from Obion County (Reelfoot Lake) through Jackson. The railroads created a network of towns in what had long been a rural and thinly populated region. With no commercial or cultural hub, the main draw of northwest Tennessee is the sporting life, unless you like really small towns that seem not to have changed much in the last century except for increasing industrialization.

▼ ▼ ▼ ▼ ▼ ▼ ▼ ▼ ▼ ▼ ▼ ▼

Clarksville Area

Clarksville, situated at the confluence of the Cumberland and Red rivers, was founded in 1784–85 on several bluffs. It was named for a Revolutionary War general, George Rogers Clark, who fought with Clarksville's founder, Colonel John Montgomery. The region around the town has long been favored for a particular type of tobacco production, and in the 19th century Clarksville became a major tobacco port. The town sports a Riverwalk, allowing you to walk the length of downtown along the Cumberland.

Much of the downtown business district was devastated by fire in the 1870s, so many of the buildings that are found in the 15-acre historic district were built near the end of the 19th century. (The best collection of Victorians is in the 100 and 200 blocks of Franklin Street.) While tobacco is still important to the city's economy, so is the proximity of the Fort Campbell Military Reservation (where Colin Powell, Charles "Peanuts" Schulz and Jimi Hendrix served), which can be toured via an entrance gate across the state line in Kentucky. Clarksville, which has an estimated population of about 105,000, is home to Austin Peay State University, considered one of Tennessee's top regional universities.

SIGHTS

The **Clarksville/Montgomery County Convention and Visitors Bureau** is the place to load up on information. ~ 312 Madison Street; 800-530-2487; www.clarksville.tn.us.

At either of these centers, you can get a map for a walking tour of the **Clarksville Downtown Historic Architectural District**. The neighborhood boasts one of the state's best collections of 1870s period architecture, and a host of shops and restaurants. Also here is the **Roxy Theatre** (100 Franklin Street), which was built in 1913, burned down, was rebuilt in 1915, closed during the Depression and reopened in 1941 only to burn down again. Finally, it was constructed in 1947 and is now one of the city's favorite professional theaters.

The **Customs House** downtown has an eclectic collection to go with its eclectic architecture. Few museums in the country probably display gimmicks such as a permanent-wave machine from the 1930s, an instrument of torture in the name of vanity, or items belonging to 1920s and 1930s steamship passengers. These kinds of exhibits bring the past alive in ways that no reproduction ever could. Going further back, the museum houses a restored 1842 log home, furnished with period accessories and a miniature small-town avenue called Memory Lane where you can stroll past a firehouse, print shop and toy store. On a more modern note, there are holograms and the Explorer's Floor, where hands-on exhibits teach visitors about optical illusions, the Morse code and the creation of bubbles. The museum includes an art gallery with rotating exhibits of local and not-so-local artists. Built in 1898 as the town's post office and customs house, the building's architecture is as exotic as its contents, with Italianate ornamentation and Romanesque arches enlivened with Flemish and Gothic elements, topped with a copper turret. Closed Monday. Admission except on Sunday. ~ 200 South 2nd Street, Clarksville; 931-648-5780, fax 931-553-5179; www.customshousemuseum.org, e-mail info@customshousemuseum.org.

Follow 2nd Street north as it rounds the river bend to a quiet residential neighborhood. Drive out to Spring Street to the intersection with McClure and look up. The rich are different from you and me; they have better views. Looking positively regal atop a knoll overlooking the Cumberland River, the **Smith-Trahern Mansion** is enough to make you long for a time machine. Like other pre–Civil War homes of the era, it shows the transition between the Greek Revival and Italianate styles. Grand hallways on both floors, connected by an elegantly curved staircase, separate four large rooms on each. Looking above the Roman columns at the front of the house, you can see the widow's walk on top. Closed weekends. Admission. ~ 101 McClure Street, Clarksville; 931-648-9998.

On the same hilltop is the **Riverview Cemetery**, where pioneer leader Valentine Sevier—whose family was massacred by Indians—was buried after her death in 1800. The cemetery became public in 1805.

A life-size bronze statue of track star **Wilma Rudolph**, a Clarksville native, can be seen at the base of the Pedestrian Overpass at College Street and Riverside Drive.

HIDDEN ▶

The oldest winery in Tennessee, **Beachaven Vineyards & Winery** was established in 1986, less than ten years after the Tennessee legislature altered the laws that had shut down Tennessee grape production for decades. To reach it, cross Route 24 (at Exit 4), then take a quick right onto Alfred-Thun Road, which intersects Arcata Boulevard just before it dead-ends into Dunlop; the winery is across the road straight ahead. The family-owned business, surrounded by 16 acres of vineyards, has won dozens of awards in the intervening years, particularly for its chardonnay and merlot. If you visit in August, you can observe the harvest and all the bustle that goes into getting the grapes in the winery and pressed for fermentation. Winter is for pruning the vineyards and in spring, visitors can watch the bottling. Tours are offered daily; the tast-

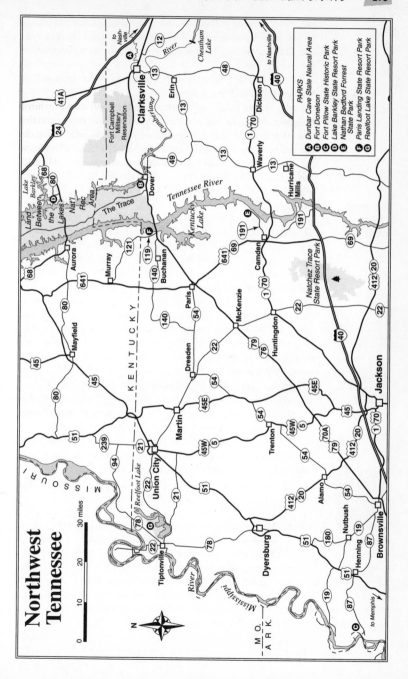

Northwest Tennessee

30 miles

PARKS
A Dunbar Cave State Natural Area
B Fort Donelson
C Fort Pillow State Historic Park
D Lake Barkley State Resort Park
E Nathan Bedford Forrest
  State Park
F Paris Landing State Resort Park
G Reelfoot Lake State Resort Park

ing room is open year-round, but champagnes are available for tasting only on weekends. ~ 1100 Dunlop Lane, Clarksville; 931-645-8867; www.beachavenwinery.com, e-mail winedude@beach avenwinery.com.

About 60 miles southwest of Clarksville is the tiny town of Hurricane Mills. It's not much, but it's kind of touching to see the mini-replica of a Coal Mine at **Loretta Lynn's Coal Miner's Daughter Museum** just outside of Waverly. The country singer known as the Coal Miner's Daughter, Lynn has collected pictures and artifacts from the Van Lear Coal Mines in Kentucky where her father once worked. These and other artifacts are on view at this 18,000-square-foot museum. Closed October through March. ~ 1877 Hurricane Mills Road, off Route 13, Hurricane Mills; 931-296-7700, fax 931-296-3378; www.lorettalynn.com.

LODGING

Clarksville has an abundance of motels and motor hotels, particularly along Holiday Road, near Exit 4 off Route 24 and near the Beachhaven Vineyards & Winery, but far from downtown.

The top spot to spend the night in Clarksville is the **Hachland Hill Inn**, where President Andrew Jackson reportedly stayed while The Hermitage was being constructed down around Nashville. Phila Hach has been operating it as an inn since 1955. Over the years, this ex-flight attendant has made herself into the Martha Stewart of north Tennessee; she writes cookbooks and is constantly producing special events for locals who want to entertain in her 300-seat grand ballroom. Sitting on a little hill not far from downtown Clarksville, the Federal-style inn has six guest rooms, decorated eclectically with many Tennessee quilts, rag rugs, knotty-pine floors and quite a few pieces of primitive antiques gathered over the decades. Also on the grounds, and available for rent, are three three-story cedar log cabins dating from the late 18th century. In addition, a fully equipped creekside cottage has five rooms and baths. The Hachland Hill Inn is not swank, but it is undeni-

AUTHOR FAVORITE

The most regal structure in Clarksville is the **Smith-Trahern Mansion.** Designed in the 1850s for wealthy tobacconist Christopher Smith, the house remained in his family until the Traherns purchased it in 1919, divided it into apartments and rented it out until 1947. Now restored by the city with new paint and wallpaper patterns typical of the mid-19th century, the house has few furnishings on the ground floor; the best restored room is the Bride's Room, which has a Victorian-era bed and armoire. See page 274 for more information.

ably not your run-of-the-mill inn. For an additional charge, Mrs. Hach will prepare three meals a day. ~ 1601 Madison Street, Clarksville; 931-647-4084, fax 931-552-3454. MODERATE.

Heading south from Clarksville on Route 13 will bring you to Hurricane Mills. Whether you want to camp out, stay in a cabin or spend the night in a motel room, or even in your own RV, **Loretta Lynn's Family Campground** has something for you. If you want upscale, though, keep driving. Accommodations are clean and simple and there's a little "downtown" to tour. Closed October through March. ~ 44 Hurricane Mills Road, off Route 13, Hurricane Mills; 931-296-7700, fax 931-296-7700; www. lorettalynn.com, e-mail campground@lorettalynn.com. BUDGET TO MODERATE.

The **Blackhorse Pub and Brewery** is a lively gathering spot that offers hearty fare and fresh brews. Appetizers are on the heavy side —think fried onion rings—but there are also substantial soups, salads and sandwiches. ~ 132 Franklin Street, Clarksville; 931-552-3726, fax 931-552-6852. BUDGET TO MODERATE.

DINING

If someone didn't tell you about **Moss's,** you'd probably never venture into this kitchen/café behind a filling station on a busy four-lane road. Well known hereabouts as the place for "meat-and-threes" (that Tennessee standby where you select one meat and three vegetables out of a long list, usually involving fried chicken, green beans, coleslaw and baked beans), and the catfish is said to be good as well. It's nothing to look at, but at least they don't charge you for the ambience. Closed Sunday. ~ 1208 College Street, Clarksville; 931-645-9415. BUDGET.

◄ HIDDEN

Arguably the most imaginative food in town is served at **Café 541.** The restaurant has been so successful it expanded from one room to three at a funky downtown corner. The eclectic menu features veal, lamb, filet mignon, shrimp and pastas, but the best bet of all is the delicious, filling crab cake salad. The place also has an extensive list of wine and beer choices, especially for these parts. ~ 541 Franklin Street, Clarksville; 931-551-9955. MODERATE TO DELUXE.

The cutest place for lunch in Dickson—or for miles around— is **Miss Mable's Tea Room.** Of course, it's hard to focus on your delectable quiche, salad or soup when you notice little teapots and other items with tiny price tags hanging off them. The food is fresh, the service is thoughtful and the surroundings a delightful break from cookie-cutter fast food and heavy-handed down-home cooking. Tea is served until 4 p.m. Closed Sunday and Monday. No dinner Monday through Thursday. ~ 301 West College Street, Dickson; 615-441-6658; www.missmable.com. BUDGET TO MODERATE.

SHOPPING   Antique stores are as plentiful as Victorians in Clarksville. A good place to explore is along Kraft Street, north of downtown. Here, **Betty's Antiques Market** specializes in old painted pieces but also has antique lamps, quilts and kitchenware. ~ 152 Kraft Street, Clarksville; 931-648-9201.

A good spot to shop for collectibles and novelties is **Traditions**. Closed Wednesday and Sunday. ~ 131 Franklin Street, Clarksville; 931-551-9800.

Off Route 179, **Grice's Antiques Mall** features 36 dealers under one roof. Closed Monday. ~ 120 West Dunbar Cave Road, Clarksville; 931-647-6682.

If you aren't looking for anything in particular but just like to browse, try **Cherry Station Antiques**, which has a wide assortment, including quilts and knickknacks. ~ 212 Warfield Boulevard, Clarksville; 931-648-4830.

More than 100 stores, including Dillard's and Old Navy, create a regional destination at **Governor's Square Mall**. ~ 2801 Wilma Rudolph Boulevard, Clarksville; 931-552-0289. Also in this general area are more than 20 strip shopping centers with smaller specialty stores.

You might say **Miss Mable's Tea Room and Gift Shops** is a restaurant or you might say it's a shop with food. Whatever, there are knickknacks downstairs and some nicer things like children's clothes and women's accessories upstairs. There's also a garden-accessories shop out back, open in summer only. Closed Sunday and Monday. ~ 301 West College Street, Dickson; 615-441-6658.

NIGHTLIFE   Stop by for a beer at the **Blackhorse Pub and Brewery**, a comfortable downtown watering hole. ~ 132 Franklin Street, Clarksville; 931-552-3726.

Austin Peay State University has an active performing arts program, ranging from the Concert Artist Series (jazz, classical and ethnic musical groups) to theatrical productions such as serious dramatic works and a revue of Broadway hits. For details, call the university. ~ Clarksville; 931-221-7011; www.apsu.edu.

The historic downtown 1947 **Roxy Theatre** presents Shakespeare, Broadway musicals and other dramatical productions year-round. ~ 100 Franklin Street, Clarksville; 931-645-7699.

PARKS   **DUNBAR CAVE STATE NATURAL AREA** 🏃 ⚓ Of several caves and sinkholes sprinkled around this 110-acre semi-urban park, Dunbar Cave is the largest. Its mouth is so big that dances and concerts were once held here, including performances of the Grand Ole Opry when Roy Acuff owned the place. Through excavations, archaeologists have determined that the cave was first occupied by humans thousands of years ago. Visitors can take guided hikes into the caves where they can appreciate the constant stream flow and natural air conditioning that first attracted their ancestors. Those who don't like enclosed spaces can fish in a small lake just outside the cave entrance. Tour schedule varies; call ahead. ~ 401 Old Dunbar Cave Road; 931-648-5526.

Land Between the Lakes Area

Land Between the Lakes (LBL) and Fort Donelson National Battlefield lie about 45 minutes west of Clarksville via Route 79. If you are staying in Clarksville, these two sites would make a good day trip. It's a bit of a stretch to try to see much of LBL if you are headquartered in Nashville, but it could be done. There are no restaurants, hotels or nightlife worth a night's stay until you get to Paris Landing State Resort Park, which is about a half-hour west of Fort Donelson along Route 79.

SIGHTS

Fort Donelson, a mile and a half east of Land Between the Lakes on Route 79, is one of the most remarkable and moving Civil War sites in Tennessee. Here, you can see the actual bunkers and easily imagine, without the aid of a Ken Burns documentary, the sound of gunfire, the falling of soldiers, the sight of blood spilled in the fight-to-the-death struggles put up by soldiers well over a century ago. Beginning in February 1862, it was the site of a pivotal battle in which Union and Confederate forces fought over the seemingly invincible Confederate-held fort for four days. The unconditional surrender on February 16 to General Ulysses S. Grant's troops marked a turning point in the Union's efforts to split the rebel forces. Along with Fort Donelson, the Confederates lost control of the Cumberland River, opening a gateway through which the Union could invade the area south of Kentucky.

AUTHOR FAVORITE

I couldn't tell the difference, but the animals at the **Buffalo Range and Trail** are technically American bison. They once ranged from Georgia to Hudson Bay, and the TVA and the LBL are attempting to establish a full-size herd here. A trail around the pasture offers the best views, except in the middle of the day, when the animals tend to congregate in the shade of trees. The herd is fed hay and protein supplements during the winter, and rotated between pastures about once a month to deter parasites. Docile by nature, the buffalo are, like all wild animals, unpredictable; do not enter through the fence for a closer encounter. ~ The Trace; 931-232-6457, fax 931-232-3032; www.lbl.org.

Even a car tour of the extremely well-kept grounds can send shivers down your spine. Before you start, stop at the **visitors center** near the entrance to see a short video and pick up a map to get the lay of the land. (You can also buy a tour tape here.) The actual fort was built between Indian Creek and Lake Barkley, a 15-acre fort constructed by soldiers and slaves over a period of seven months. But the most impressive part of the park, which is run by the National Park Service, is the River Batteries, where inexperienced Confederate gunners were defeated by Federal gunboats in fighting that was heard 35 miles away. ~ Route 79, one mile west of Dover and a mile and a half east of Land Between the Lakes; 931-232-5706, fax 931-232-4085.

Its parameters are so broad it could pass for a county, and its name so cumbersome it's often referred to as simply LBL. The **Land Between the Lakes National Recreation Area** is more than a park; it's 270 square miles of wildlands stretching from northwest Tennessee into Kentucky. A forested chunk of land situated between Kentucky Lake and Lake Barkley, it offers virtually unlimited camping and water-sports opportunities.

> The Land Between the Lakes National Recreation Area is the largest inland peninsula in the United States and the second-largest contiguous block of forested public land east of the Mississippi.

Created by President John F. Kennedy in 1963, LBL is the country's only so-called national demonstration area that blends outdoor recreation, environmental education and natural resource management—in this case, by the Tennessee Valley Authority (TVA). One of the purposes of preserving this forested peninsula was to stimulate economic growth in the region. In that, the government was successful. LBL and the lakes surrounding it are credited with creating some $400 million worth of tourism each year.

Most of LBL's acreage lies within Kentucky, but its number-one attraction, **The Homeplace-1850**, is in Tennessee. To find it, just drive north from the South Welcome Station along The Trace, the paved two-lane road that runs the length of the park. This living-history farm blends artifacts, restored structures and the traditional activities to depict typical 19th-century rural life. Around the perimeter are the special split-rail fences used in the mid-South before range laws were enacted. Built to be "horse-high, bull-strong and pig-tight," the fences served to keep wildlife out and domestic animals safe. Some 16 log structures, including two homes, a horse and ox barn and a smokehouse, are open for touring. There are also livestock representative of the period, not only pigs and cows but also rare and endangered breeds of domestic animals. You can wander about the cornfields and the gardens that have been planted with hard-to-find heirloom seeds of vegetables such as carrots, parsnips, tomatoes, squash, sweet potatoes and cabbage. In the 19th century, most food was air-dried, sun-dried, salted, pickled or preserved with sugar, while root vegetables were stored below the frost line to nourish the family during the frigid winters. Throughout, interpreters in period dress demonstrate skills like spinning, gardening, plowing and farming tobacco. The entire enterprise is the best conceivable way to learn American history. Closed December through February. Admission. ~ The Trace; 931-232-6457, fax 931-232-3032; www.lbl.org.

Who needs decor with views like these? The lakeview rooms at the gray wood-frame 130-room **Paris Landing State Resort Park Inn** are in no way luxurious, but are by far the finest accommodations for miles around. Granted, they are spare, even spartan; there's no real closet, but there's a deck with chairs, plain brown furniture, striped curtains and white walls. There are also 30 suites and 10 cabins available. ~ 400 Lodge Road, Buchanan; 731-642-4311, 800-250-8614. MODERATE TO DELUXE.

LODGING

The **Paris Landing State Resort Park Restaurant** is the only place to eat within miles. The good news is it has a sizable menu and offers the option of a bargain-priced, 44-foot-long buffet or à la carte dining. The best deal is the breakfast buffet, served up until 10:30 a.m. At night, you can choose from the buffet or order the special dinners—fried shrimp, steak, catfish, charbroiled chicken breast, chicken liver, ham and the like—which come with vegetables. Since the dining room is on the lower level, it has a close-up view of the lake. The restaurant closes for a month in winter, so call ahead. ~ 400 Lodge Road, Buchanan; 731-642-4311, 800-250-8614. BUDGET TO MODERATE.

DINING

LAND BETWEEN THE LAKES NATIONAL RECREATION AREA 🚶 🚲 🐎 🛶 🚤 This 170,000-acre wooded peninsula, which sprawls from Tennessee up into Kentucky, is especially popular with people who love to camp and fish. It also features unusual attractions such as The Homeplace-1850, a living-history museum and a buffalo range. Lake access is available at campgrounds as well as at Gatlin Point, on Lake Barkley, and Boswell Landing, on Kentucky Lake. There are primitive and family campsites as well as rustic cabins at Piney Campground. If you want to ride, you'll have to bring your own horse, but you can rent mountain bikes at Piney. There's a nature gift shop here if you want to pick up souvenirs. ~ Entrance is off Route 79, due north; 270-924-2000, 800-525-7077; www.lbl.org.

PARKS

▲ There are 378 sites, 300 with electricity, that are open from March through November, at *Piney Campground* on Kentucky Lake. The basic price is $12; for an electrical-only hookup, it's $16; add water and it's $20; with sewer it's $24. In 1996 the

TVA built some primitive cabins (read: bring your own linens); they rent for $29 a night. From Dover, drive nine and a half miles west on Route 79, then two miles north at the sign. Also at LBL are 19 primitive sites at the *Gatlin Point Campground* on Lake Barkley; $8 a night, $12 with electricity. There are chemical toilets and picnic tables available. To get there, drive three miles west from Dover on Route 79, then four miles north on The Trace, another three and a half miles northeast at the sign. For reservations at Piney Lake or Gatlin Point, contact TVA Land Between the Lakes. ~ 100 Van Morgan Drive, Golden Pond, KY 42211-9001; 270-924-2233.

PARIS LANDING STATE RESORT PARK

Perhaps the best resort park in the state, Paris Landing has a protected harbor right on Kentucky Lake, with a fishing pier, marina and free boat launch. Other facilities include a baseball diamond, basketball and tennis courts, a recreation center, a golf course, an archery range, campgrounds, picnic shelters and two swimming pools. Not to mention a lodge and a restaurant, plus facilities for washing clothes and cleaning fish, though not necessarily in that order. ~ 16055 Route 79N, Buchanan; 731-642-4311, 800-250-8614.

▲ There are 48 campsites with water and electricity; $17.25 per night. Primitive sites cost $7.

NATHAN BEDFORD FORREST STATE PARK

From 741-foot Pilot Knob, you can get a sensational view of the western valley of the Tennessee River. The spot got its name because it was used as a landmark by riverboat pilots, so it's appropriate that this 2587-acre park is also home to the Tennessee River Folklife Interpretive Center. The biggest draw here is an old work boat from the early days of musseling on the river; kids will be fascinated by "Old Betsy." Also here are unusual photographs of life in the old days, taken with a Brownie camera by one Maggie Sayre, who lived on a houseboat for more than half a century and who catalogued virtually her entire life on film. Fishing in Kentucky Lake usually turns up just about everything but trout, including bass, crappie and catfish. The park has grills, picnic sites, a playground and showers. The closest restaurants and grocery stores are about eight miles away in Camden. Day-use fee, $3. ~ North of Route 40 on Route 191 near Camden; 731-584-6356, 800-714-7305, fax 731-584-1841.

▲ There are 53 campsites, 38 with hookups; $15.25 per night with water and electricity.

▼▼▼▼▼▼▼▼▼▼▼
Tiptonville Area

A visit to Tiptonville will be dominated by the presence of Reelfoot Lake and its myriad attractions—fishing, birdwatching and nature walks. Lodging and restaurants are simple, built to service people who plan to spend most of their time outdoors.

Thousands of cypress stumps poke up from the floor of **Reelfoot Lake,** bestowing an eerie appearance on the largest natural fish hatchery in the United States. It's not off-putting to fishers, though, or the thousands of visitors who come to see the bald eagle, America's national bird, up close in a native habitat. Formed by earthquakes nearly two centuries ago, the lake may look familiar to film fans who saw the 1957 movie *Raintree County,* some of which was filmed here. ~ Route 21, Reelfoot Lake; 731-253-2007, 800-250-8617.

SIGHTS

Even if your plans do not call for an extended visit to Reelfoot Lake State Resort Park, the **State Park Visitors Center** is worth a visit. Several exhibits on the formation, natural history and diversity as well as the future of the lake are informative, especially the displays explaining how special boats called stump-jumpers had to be developed to negotiate the submerged cypress stumps that dot the lake bottom. Out back are habitats for endangered birds, usually including a couple of rescued bald eagles. ~ Route 21/22, Tiptonville; 731-253-9652, 800-250-8617.

Three-fifths of Reelfoot Lake State Resort Park is under water, encouraging the thriving population of 57 species of fish and practically every kind of shore and wading bird in existence, as well as the golden and American bald eagles.

If you're not interested in fishing Reelfoot Lake—or at least in seeing this unique setting— then Tiptonville may not hold much appeal for you. Unless, of course, you happen to be a fan of rock-and-roll. Then there could be the once-in-a-lifetime opportunity to see **Carl Perkins' boyhood home.** You can't go inside, however, though there's not a lot to see in this old wooden bungalow with its peaked roof and sturdy front porch, which is precisely the point. It's living proof that Carl ("Blue Suede Shoes") Perkins, like a lot of Tennessee's best-known recording artists, started life in a poor family and made it on his own. If the house were in its original location, it would probably tell us more about Perkins' rural roots, but rock-and-roll fans should be glad this modest home was preserved at all. It's not hard to find, but there is no address. Look for a very, very large sign with a guitar on it. It's on the right-hand side of Route 78 heading into Tiptonville, between Robertson and Church streets; the closest street address is 220. ~ Route 78, Tiptonville.

If elegant ambience is your highest priority, **Reelfoot Lake Inn** is probably not the place for you. If you're interested in fishing or bird watching, however, you're in luck. In a concrete compound resembling military barracks, you'll find 50 guest rooms (clean and comfortable albeit spartan), each with a lakeview balcony,

LODGING

and a pool enclosed with chain-link fence. Winter is prime bird-watching time here; the resort will book a tour for you, although you'll probably catch sight of the soaring birds as you sip your morning coffee in the lobby. Anglers will find an abundance of crappie, blue gill and bass. You can bring your own boat or rent one here. Continental breakfast is included. ~ Reelfoot Lake; 731-253-6845; www.reelfootlakeinn.com, e-mail keefes@reelfoot lakeinn.com. BUDGET TO MODERATE.

Sportsman's Resort is right on the shore of the lake. You have your choice of a three-bedroom duplex that sleeps up to 12 people or one of several one-bedroom cabins with air conditioning and a porch. Rooms are paneled in pine and have plaid bedspreads but are otherwise undistinguished. All accommodations have TVs and a fully equipped kitchen. There's also a campground with full RV hookup and tent campsites. This modest little resort offers fishing and lodging packages, rents boats and tackle and has a grocery store that sells bait and licenses. From March to June, only three- to seven-night packages are available; they start at $219 per person and include three days of fishing. ~ Route 1, ten miles north of Tiptonville; 731-253-6581, fax 731-253-8543; www.reelfootlake.com, e-mail sportsmansresort@reel footlake.com. MODERATE.

DINING

You'll know you're in deep country when you enter **Boyette's Dining Room**, across the street from Reelfoot Lake's visitors center. Dark paneled walls, lots of smokers, plenty of steaks, catfish, crappie and Tennessee country ham on the menu, plus an all-you-can-eat buffet provide all the evidence you need. What you might not expect on this menu are quail and frogs' legs. No wonder it's popular with the locals, who tend to congregate here with their families on Sunday afternoon. ~ Route 21, Tiptonville; 731-253-7307. BUDGET TO MODERATE.

PARKS

REELFOOT LAKE STATE RESORT PARK 🏃 ⚓ 🚣 🚤 🛥 ⚓
Reelfoot Lake was formed in the early 19th century by a series of violent earthquakes centered in New Madrid, Missouri. With 25,000 protected acres (15,000 of them are water), it is so large that it lies in two counties, Lake and Obion. The park's 280 acres are divided in ten segments along 22 miles of shoreline. Abundant plant and animal life, dominated by the cypress that hug the shoreline, make this a wonderland for nature lovers. Fishing and boating are extremely popular at the park, as are camping, picnicking and birdwatching, particularly the daily eagle tours in winter. Campsites are available on a first-come, first-served basis. Amenities include restrooms at the visitors center and snack machines. ~ Route 1, Tiptonville; 731-253-7756, 800-250-8617.

The Legend of Reelfoot Lake

Legend has it that, early in the 19th century, a mighty Indian chief ruled the rich bottomlands of northwest Tennessee. Although he was a wise and benevolent chief, his heart was heavy, for his one and only son had been born with a deformed foot that caused him to walk and run with a rolling motion. People called him Kalopin, meaning "reel foot." When his father died, Reelfoot became the chief. Unable to find a maiden to marry, he traveled south, to the land where beautiful maidens were said to dwell. There he found Laughing Eyes, the girl of his dreams, but her father, the Choctaw chief, forbid her to marry a clubfoot, chieftain or not. Reelfoot thought of abducting her, but then heard the words of the Great Spirit reminding him that no Indian may steal his wife. If Reelfoot carried out his fantasy, the Great Spirit would cause the earth to rock, and the waters to swallow up his people. But Reelfoot's passion overcame his good sense, and he stole the princess. The night he brought his bride home, his people rejoiced and celebrated, but in the midst of the festivities the earth began to pitch and roll. No one could escape. The Great Spirit stamped his foot in anger at Reelfoot's defiance, and where he stamped the earth, the mighty Mississippi formed a beautiful lake, where Reelfoot, his bride and his people lie forever in a watery grave.

That's the Indian legend. The truth is almost as weird. In the winter of 1811–12, the New Madrid (Missouri) earthquakes occurred. A series of 1874 tremors, three of which are said to be the strongest on record in the United States, were felt as far away as Boston and New Orleans. The climax, on February 7, 1812, struck the continent with such force that the Chickasaw country area in northwest Tennessee sank 20 feet, making the Mississippi River run backward long enough to create a lake over what had been cypress and cottonwood groves. Incredibly, artist/ornithologist John James Audubon was there to record the bewildering event that gave birth to Tennessee's only natural lake.

It makes sense that Audubon was in the neighborhood: more than 250 species of birds find refuge in Reelfoot Lake State Resort Park's 25,000 acres. None is more revered than the bald eagles. Whenever a cold front pushes down from the north during the winter, up to 200 eagles seek refuge at Reelfoot.

▲ There are 100 campsites, each with water and electricity; $17.25 per night. The airpark campground is open year-round; the Spillway campground is closed mid-November through March.

▼ ▼ ▼ ▼ ▼ ▼ ▼ ▼ ▼ ▼
Henning and Brownsville

One of West Tennessee's most famous natives spent his childhood in the rural region less than an hour's drive from Memphis. A small private museum honoring him makes Henning worth finding. Henning is a small town that time and the highway passed by. Alex Haley made it famous in interviews about the origins of his blockbuster book, *Roots*.

SIGHTS   In a neighborhood of similar one-story family homes, the birthplace of author Alex Haley might not stand out were it not for the commemorative plaque and gravesite on the corner of the property. It was on this porch that Haley always said *Roots* was born. It was here in his grandmother's kitchen that he would sit on the windowsill and ask endless questions about his heritage, about his third great-grandfather, Chicken George, and many of the other characters he researched back in Africa who made the book a bestseller and the miniseries one of the most popular in history. **Alex Haley Historic Site and Museum** is a gray clapboard structure with a porch swing where it's easy to imagine him spending long summer evenings with his family in the years between 1921 and 1929. This is not so much a museum as a shrine, with touching family mementos like a photograph of a six-month-old Haley, bedspreads handmade by his mother and aunt, and pictures of relatives who would never have imagined becoming household names. Tour guides are happy to lead you around. Haley, who died in 1992, would be proud. Closed Monday. Admission. ~ 200 South Church Street, Henning; 731-738-2240.

Located about 18 miles west of Henning is **Fort Pillow**, erected in 1861 by the Confederate Army. This 1650-acre state historic area serves as a wildlife observation park where you can catch sight of turkey, deer and numerous birds. (See "Parks" section below.) ~ Off Route 51 on Route 87.

Brownsville is a small, flat city best known for its proximity to Nutbush, where Tina Turner grew up. Now that she is a living legend, there will doubtless be more travelers asking how to get to her hometown just up the road.

For maps and information on local activities, drop by the **Brownsville/Haywood County Chamber of Commerce**. ~ 121 West Main Street, Brownsville; 731-772-2193; www.brownsville-haywoodtn.com.

Opened in 1999, the **West Tennessee Delta Heritage Center** celebrates the cultural and natural history of the area. Regional towns and attractions are showcased in the Tennessee Room;

area talent from Carl Perkins and Eddie Arnold to Tina Turner are highlighted in the Music Museum; the entire river watershed and ecosystem are explored in the Scenic Hatchie River Museum; and the impact of cotton on the region and its population is the focus of the Cotton Museum. Don't miss the gift shop here. Closed Monday. ~ 121 Sunny Hill Cove, Brownsville; 731-779-9000.

Blues fanatics will love the part of the West Tennessee Delta Heritage Center that includes the house where legendary guitarist Sleepy John Estes was living at the time of his death in 1977.

The story of the region's earliest inhabitants, the American Indians, provides the starting point for all the exhibits at the **Haywood County Museum**. Then it's on to the Westward expansion period and continues with today's high-tech world. In all, there are eight 25-year segments that rely on artifacts, documents, photographs and memorabilia to bring history to life. Closed Saturday and Sunday morning. ~ 127 North Grand Avenue, Brownsville; 731-772-4883.

Don't expect to find any cute or cozy B&Bs in Brownsville, but there are a couple of generic motels not far from Route 40. One of these is **Comfort Inn**, which has 52 rooms in the usual two-story configuration. You get free cable TV, movies, continental breakfast and the use of a pool, but no restaurant. ~ 2600 Anderson Avenue, Brownsville; phone/fax 731-772-4082. BUDGET TO MODERATE.

LODGING

Just down the street, **Days Inn** is a little smaller with 43 rooms. Rates include free cable TV and movies, but there is neither a pool nor a restaurant. Surprisingly, however, the inn accepts small pets in the smoking units. ~ 2530 Anderson Avenue, Brownsville; 731-772-3297, fax 731-772-2576. BUDGET TO MODERATE.

Like catfish? They fix it just about any way you want it at the **City Fish Market**. Or if you're feeling adventurous, you can try the buffalo, a seldom-seen white catfish. Bear in mind that this informal eatery located down by the railroad tracks is open only on Friday and Saturday. ~ 223 South Washington Street, Brownsville; 731-772-9952. BUDGET.

DINING

Barbecue dominates the menu at the **Backyard Bar-B-Q**, where you can also get burgers and a side of potatoes. Closed Sunday. ~ 703 East Main Street, Brownsville; 731-772-1121. BUDGET.

FORT PILLOW STATE HISTORIC PARK 🏃 🛶 🚤 🛶 This historic fort was the scene of an 1864 Civil War battle instigated by Nathan Bedford Forrest, the Confederate general who attacked and took the fort when his demands for release of prisoners were refused. Controversy still surrounds this battle, due to the high number of Union casualties and the presence of an unusual num-

PARKS

ber of African-American troops. Situated on 1650 acres atop the Chickasaw Bluffs of the Mississippi River, Fort Pillow was constructed by the Confederate Army in 1861. Remains of the earthworks have been well preserved, and now there are picnic and camping sites and a visitors center with a museum. At the north end of the park, the interpretive center exhibits various displays and offers audio-visual programs. ~ 3122 Park Road, Henning; 731-738-5581, 731-738-5731, fax 731-738-9117.

▲ There are 38 tent-only campsites; $8 per night.

Outdoor Adventures

FISHING

CLARKSVILLE Around Clarksville, everybody fishes the Cumberland and Big Red rivers. If you need a fishing pole (or plumbing, electrical, hunting or sporting goods or darn near anything else), head to **Grandpa's**. ~ 1894 Fort Campbell Boulevard; 931-647-7800

Farther afield, Kentucky Lake claims to offer the best crappie and largemouth bass fishing in the country. More than 100 species of fish lurk in secluded coves and are scattered over big stretches of fresh water. Crappie and largemouth bass fishing are excellent, but there are also five species of catfish (channels, blues and flatheads in particular), including the world-record catch for a blue catfish weighing in at 115 pounds. Crappie bite all year long, but are particularly plentiful from late March to mid-May, when the fish move into shallow water to spawn. Sauger and walleye are most often caught in December and January, while June and July produce the best catches of bluegill.

> Catches of 100 or more crappie are common during the peak season at Reelfoot Lake.

You can fish from the shoreline, or find a guide through the **Lake Barkley State Resort Park and Marina** in Cadiz, Kentucky. ~ 800-325-1708.

LAND BETWEEN THE LAKES AREA There are several lake access points in the Land Between the Lakes National Recreation Area where you can fish from shore. They include Gatlin Point (Lake Barkley) and Boswell Landing, Piney Campground and Rushing Creek Campground (Kentucky Lake).

TIPTONVILLE AREA More than 50 species of fish swim in Reelfoot Lake, and there are no limits on crappie. The other most common game fish are bream, largemouth bass and catfish. In the summer, bluegill fishing is excellent, with four- to seven-pound fish a common catch. A number of local guides can help you find what you're looking for, and navigate the special boats necessary for successful hunting. The **Sportmans Resort** (731-253-6581) near the park entrance on Route 1 has bait, tackle, boats and guides. Other options are **Bo's Landing** (731-253-7809), **Gray's Camp** (731-253-7813) and **Reelfoot Lodge** (731-253-7756).

CLARKSVILLE   Several municipal golf courses in Clarksville offer enough variety to keep visitors busy for an entire vacation. **Swan Lake Golf Course** has bent-grass greens, Bermuda fairways, a pro shop and a concession area, as well as rental carts. ~ 581 Dunbar Cave Road; 931-648-0479.

LAND BETWEEN THE LAKES AREA   The prettiest place to play golf in this neck of the woods is the **Paris Landing State Resort Park Golf Course**. The 6800-yard 18-hole championship course is carved out of some 300 acres of woods, hills and hollows alongside Kentucky Lake. Bent-grass greens and big trees make this an exceptionally popular place to play. It may be worth it for the one hole in which the golfer must drive from an elevated tee to a green far below, because the view from the tee is one of the best around. Closed two weeks during the Christmas holidays. ~ 16055 Route 79N, Buchanan; 731-641-4465, 800-250-8614. Nonmembers are welcome at the **Paris Country Club**, which has a nine-hole course four miles east of Paris. Water, bunkers, doglegs and hills help compensate for the shortness of the course. Greens and fairways are Bermuda; an automatic sprinkler system maintains the look even during the heat of summer. Closed to the public Saturday through Monday. ~ 195 Country Club Road, off Route 79; 731-642-0591.

Between municipal courts, high school courts and the courts at Austin Peay State University, Clarksville offers 40 places to play tennis but only one run by the city. The **Swan Lake Tennis Complex** courts off Saunders Road are available on a walk-in basis or by reservation. Clinics are also available through the Clarksville Park and Recreation Department. ~ 931-645-7476.

   Austin Peay State University has eight outdoor courts available for free, located between the Municipal Stadium and Dunn Center. ~ Drane Street near College Street. The APSU athletic department also oversees indoor courts. The **Governors Indoor Tennis Center** allows play on four lighted indoor courts from 9 a.m. to 9 p.m. on a walk-in basis or by reservation. Fee. ~ Sumner Street near Drane Street; 931-221-6101.

CLARKSVILLE   For fooling around on your mountain bike in Clarksville, head to **Cedar Hill Park**, just east of Route 24 on Old Hickory Boulevard. Trails are mostly single track, have steep up-and-down grades and include about three miles of twists and turns.

   Cheatham Wildlife Management Area is just down Route 12 from Clarksville (toward Ashland City), where you'll find 35,000 acres. The Brush Creek Trail is the best of several trails, some of which are rough, a few of which are gravel, and many are in real backcountry. Beware heading into the wilderness during the fall hunting season, however.

The Bicycle Center is the place to go for information—and especially detailed instructions—on bike riding in the area around Clarksville. They also offer some group rides in good weather. Closed Sunday. ~ 1450 Madison Street; 931-647-2453.

> Old logging roads and extensive backroads make Land Between the Lakes ideal for bikers of all levels.

There's a technical course in **Rotary Park**, four miles from the Bicycle Center. Take Route 41A south to the Kmart Center, turn right at the light, and the entrance is 200 yards down the road on the left. It's single track, so it's not for little kids but for the hard-core mountain biker who likes to pedal through woods and over rocks and stumps.

LAND BETWEEN THE LAKES AREA   Land Between the Lakes (LBL) offers some of the best riding in the region. One trail, the 18-mile Energy Lake Trail, is in Kentucky, but the **Jenny Ridge Trail**, in Tennessee on the Kentucky Lake side of LBL, starts at the Jenny Ridge Picnic Area and runs for 12 miles over intermediate terrain. Park at the Golden Pond Visitors Center or the Jenny Ridge Picnic Area and enter the trail at the visitors center. The 14.2-mile **Canal Loop Trail** is an easy-to-moderate combination hiking and biking trail with a 120-foot change in elevation. In addition to the new trails, look for old dirt jeep roads here, which are marked on maps available at the welcome center. ~ The Trace; 931-232-7956.

HIKING   All distances listed for hiking trails are one way unless otherwise noted.

CLARKSVILLE   Besides the walk into the cave, there are three short trails open year-round at the 110-acre Dunbar Cave State Natural Area: the **Lake Trail** (.8 mile), the **Short Loop** (1 mile) and the **Recovery Trail** (2 miles). Keep an eye out for small caves and sinkholes. ~ 401 Old Dunbar Cave Road, Clarksville; 931-648-5526.

LAND BETWEEN THE LAKES AREA   Land Between the Lakes is a hiking paradise. There is even a trail for disabled athletes called the **Pawpaw Path**, named for a group of trees at the south end of the double loop. The shorter loop is a flat asphalt trail about 200 yards long; the longer one, nearly half a mile, has a sawdust tread and gentle grades. They lie in a shallow basin dissected by a small stream that runs through open woods. Along the way, signs interpret the natural history of the area, indicating specific trees and even groundhog holes.

The **North/South Trail** (65 miles) runs the entire length of LBL. Five open-air metal shelters along the trail are available for overnight camping; they have enough room for four hikers and their equipment. On the Tennessee end, the terminus is at the South Welcome Station. The trail is rated moderate to strenuous, with 200-foot elevation changes along gravel road, logging roads and foot paths. Along the way, hikers encounter fields and forest stands in various stages of development, from mowed fields to old-growth forest.

The **Fort Henry Trail** (26 miles) is a National Recreation Trail in southwest LBL. The trail leads along gravel roads, logging roads and footpaths, but hikes can be as short as a three-mile loop. At trail sign number 10, hikers can take a one-mile link to the North/South Trail. Keep an eye out for deer and wild turkey as you pass through hardwood and pine forests. The trail is a moderate one, with a 100-foot change in elevation.

Transportation

CAR

An automobile is essential to tour northwest Tennessee. No interstates cross this portion of the state, which is bounded by **Route 24** on the east, near Clarksville, by the Mississippi River on the west, and by the Kentucky state line on the north, which extends south almost to **Route 40**, the interstate linking Nashville and Memphis. **Route 79** connects Clarksville with Land Between the Lakes and Paris Landing State Resort Park before turning to run southwest.

The region's roads are mostly state routes, almost entirely two-lane affairs, with the occasional four-lane U.S. highway such as the north–south **Route 51** in the western portion. To reach Reelfoot Lake from Paris Landing, the most direct route is to turn west on **Route 54** to Dresden, then **Route 431** to Union City, then **Route 22** to the lake and then to Tiptonville. To reach Henning from Reelfoot Lake, link up to **Route 78** heading south to the congruence with Route 51 at Dyersburg. This is a major thoroughfare that passes near Henning en route to Memphis. From Henning, the best route to Brownsville is via **Route 87**, a lightly trafficked country road. Brownsville is five miles north of Route 40, the best route into Memphis in the southwestern corner of the state.

AIR

The closest major airport to Clarksville is the **Nashville International Airport**, which is about a 90-minute drive. **Memphis International Airport**, about 110 miles south of Tiptonville, is the closest major Tennessee airport to Reelfoot Lake, Tiptonville and the rest of the Delta. See the "Transportation" sections in Chapters Eight and Eleven, respectively, for more details.

BUS

Clarksville is served by **Greyhound Bus Lines**; the station is at 11 Jefferson Street. The bus stops in Union City at 1605 West Reelfoot Avenue (Route 51) and in Brownsville at 3796 Anderson Avenue. ~ 931-647-3336, 800-231-2222; www.greyhound.com.

TRAIN   The last train to Clarksville has left the station. There is no passenger service to Clarksville or the towns along the Delta.

PUBLIC   The **Clarksville Transit System (CTS) runs daily except Sunday.
TRANSIT**   The fare is 75 cents, 35 cents for seniors over 65. ~ 931-553-
              2430; www.clarksvilletransit.org. There is no public transportation in Tiptonville.

**CAR   Several national car-rental agencies have offices in Clarksville.
RENTALS**   **Dollar Rent A Car** has one at 809 Kraft Street. ~ 931-648-8200,
              800-800-4000. **Enterprise Rent A Car** is located at 2609-E Fort
              Campbell Boulevard. ~ 800-325-8007. Several other agencies
              have outlets near Fort Campbell across the Kentucky state line.

ELEVEN

Memphis

Perched on the western border of Tennessee, Memphis is so far from Nashville that it is sometimes referred to by Middle Tennesseans as the capital of northern Mississippi. Geographically, at least, the moniker fits. In northern Mississippi, a great cliff rises some 100 feet above the Mississippi River's edge at the end of a finger of the Tippah Highlands. It was from this bluff that the Spanish explorer Hernando de Soto probably first saw the Mississippi River, in 1541. De Soto may have imagined what lay beyond the river the Chickasaw Indians called the "Father of the Waters," but he never found out. He died here and was buried in the mighty Mississippi.

But the future of western Tennessee was already destined.

These bluffs had been occupied for centuries by advanced American Indian cultures that had created great temple mound towns here and elsewhere in the South. The resurrected remains of one such place, Chucalissa Village, are open to the public in south Memphis today. The Chickasaws, who were not nomadic at all but raised corn and beans to supplement their hunting and fishing, lived in well-built homes in planned towns. Nonetheless, they were eventually driven out.

The French governor of Louisiana, Sieur de Bienville, ordered a fort built on the bluff in 1739, with the intention of ridding the region of the Anglophile Chickasaws. Too far from the original colonies to have been affected by the Revolutionary War, the bluff was also perceived as a strategic stronghold by the Spanish, who built their Fort San Fernando nearby in 1795, intending to pursue their colonial ambitions against the United States.

By 1797 the American flag was hoisted above Fort Adams on the site of the former Spanish fort, laying the groundwork for the founding of Memphis. Already the Chickasaws had signed disastrous treaty agreements with the Americans, leading to the Jackson Purchase in 1819 that ended all Chickasaw landholding in western Tennessee.

A close friend of President Andrew Jackson, Nashville judge John Overton envisioned an American settlement on the Chickasaw bluff, and the same year the purchase was signed, Memphis was established. Overton, who founded the city along with General James Winchester and Andrew Jackson, laid the town out with wide streets, public squares and a riverfront promenade. Named for the ancient Egyptian capital, the "place of good abode" had a head start. Unlike most riverfront towns, it was founded nearly 30 feet above the highest water, making flooding unlikely if not impossible.

Quickly, Memphis evolved into a rough river town popular with Indian traders and river gamblers. The Wild West image lingered until the mid-19th century, almost until the eve of the Civil War. Memphians, unlike their brothers to the east, quickly supported secession, but the town was one of the first to fall to Union troops. Spared much of the damage that cities like Atlanta suffered, Memphis actually boomed in the postwar years, particularly because of its capacity to ship cotton by both rail and steamer. By 1850 it was one of the country's busiest ports. It was in this boom period that some of the city's elaborate Victorians were built by the most successful men in business.

The yellow fever epidemics in the 1870s brought a halt to economic advances, when much of the population either succumbed to the disease or fled town to escape its ravages. A greater proportion of white citizens were affected than freed slaves, who apparently carried a natural immunity in their blood inherited from their African ancestors. The decimation of the populace along with the desertion of businessmen and officials was so crippling that the city's charter was revoked as a result, and Memphis did not become a municipality again until 1893.

By then, Memphis was becoming the most important hardwood market in the world, aided by the steamboats and loggers who fueled the boom. As the river trade escalated, many African-Americans resettled in Memphis, a large percentage of them settling in the Beale Street neighborhood that covered 15 city blocks in its heyday. By the early 1900s, blues music began to rival cotton and hardwood as the city's signature export, thanks to W. C. Handy and other musicians who evolved this all-American art form in the saloons on Beale Street. Later, Sam Phillips would create Sun Studio to record the result of blues' fusion with other mainstream American sounds, a hybrid called rock-and-roll. When Phillips recorded "Rocket 88" at Sun, it was widely received as the first rock-and-roll record. But Sun will probably always be best remembered as the label associated with Carl Perkins, Elvis Presley, Jerry Lee Lewis and Roy Orbison.

The city was brought to a virtual standstill in 1968, after Dr. Martin Luther King, Jr., was assassinated at a downtown motel. Today the Lorraine Motel is the site of the National Civil Rights Museum, which provides an overview of the long, slow struggle toward civil rights.

After the slump years of the 1970s and 1980s and urban renewal projects that threatened the very existence of Beale Street, Memphis is working to revitalize the downtown area with improved trolley service, a convention center and new hotels. South Main is already seeing signs of life, but the Pinch historic district, the northern terminus of the trolley line just beyond the Pyramid (a 32-story multipurpose arena on the bluff), has been slower to recover. Other neighborhoods, such as the midtown Cooper-Young Historic District, have come alive with restaurants, nightclubs, antique stores, coffeehouses and boutiques.

Text continued on page 298.

With a population of more than 650,000 (and more than a million in the metropolitan area), Memphis is the biggest city in Tennessee. Long established as one of the country's major distribution points, Memphis has become the world's busiest cargo airport since the success of locally founded Federal Express.

Spring and fall are the most popular times to visit Memphis, which has an average annual rainfall of 49 inches and an average temperature of 62°. Summers average 81° and winters, 41°.

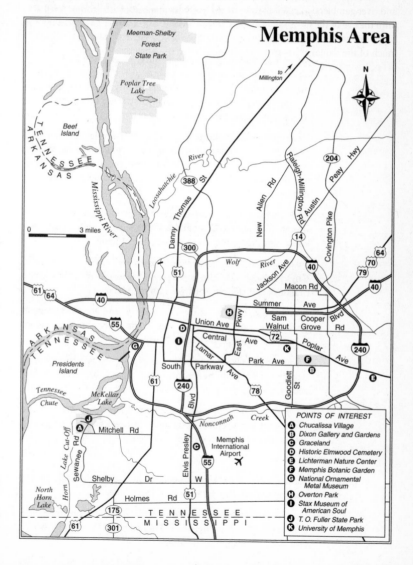

Memphis Area

POINTS OF INTEREST
- Ⓐ Chucalissa Village
- Ⓑ Dixon Gallery and Gardens
- Ⓒ Graceland
- Ⓓ Historic Elmwood Cemetery
- Ⓔ Lichterman Nature Center
- Ⓕ Memphis Botanic Garden
- Ⓖ National Ornamental Metal Museum
- Ⓗ Overton Park
- Ⓘ Stax Museum of American Soul
- Ⓙ T. O. Fuller State Park
- Ⓚ University of Memphis

Memphis

Day 1
- Check into your hotel. The best place to stay is downtown, where you'll be closest to the greatest number of attractions. You'll also be near the Main Street Trolley line and within blocks of the Mississippi River.

- Before you head out to tour, make sure you've made dinner reservations. Weekend evenings can be especially busy, even at inexpensive restaurants. The top-tier restaurants may require reservations several days in advance. If you plan to attend a show, you'll need reservations if the performer is a big name.

- Head out to **Graceland** (page 324), Elvis Presley's home, for a guided tour. The crowds don't usually get big until late morning so the earlier, the better. If you have to wait, spend your time shopping for souvenirs in the complex across the street from the mansion.

- After shuffling through the Graceland home and grounds, you can stretch your legs at **Chucalissa Village** (page 324), an archaeological site that is also on the south side of town.

- Swing around to the east side of town and follow your nose to **Corky's** (page 321), the homegrown barbecue emporium where ribs, pork and chicken are always on the menu.

- Spend the remainder of the afternoon in and around **Overton Park** (page 315). Start with a visit to the **Memphis Zoo** before touring the **Memphis Brooks Museum**.

- If you arrive back downtown before 5 p.m., you will have time to stop by the lobby of **The Peabody** hotel (page 303) to see the legendary ducks.

- For your first night in town, live it up at **Cielo** (page 311). It's one of the best and prettiest restaurants in town, and is located in a neighborhood known as Victorian Village.

Day 2
- Hop aboard the Main Street Trolley and head south to the **National Civil Rights Museum** (page 300).

- Stroll back up Main Street and stop for lunch—a hamburger or a blue plate special, perhaps—at **The Arcade** (page 307), where Elvis used to nosh.

- Saunter up and down **Beale Street**, poking into clubs and stores along the way. Tour the **Memphis Rock 'n' Soul Museum** (page 302) then head to the **Memphis Police Museum** (page 301) and the **A. Schwab** store (page 302).

- Enjoy a casual dinner at the **Blues City Café** (page 312) before crossing the street and catching a show at **B. B. King's Blues Club & Restaurant** (page 307).

Day 3
- Walk over to the Mississippi waterfront and take in the view. Head north past Adams Street and take the monorail or walkway west across the water to **Mud Island River Park and Museum** (page 298). The **Mississippi River Museum** is well worth a visit.

- Stroll a couple of blocks east to see the oldest structure in Memphis, the **Magevney House** (page 304), a white-frame home where the owner married his bride in the first Catholic wedding service conducted in the city.

- Continue farther west down Adams Avenue to **Cielo** (page 311) for a tasty and exotic meal.

- Cruise the Mississippi River aboard the **Memphis Queen** (page 298). The captain will regale you with lore about the mighty river and the people who contributed to its colorful history.

- Join the hip crowd at **Automatic Slim's Tonga Club** (page 310), where the menu ranges from Southwestern to Caribbean to New York specialties.

▼ ▼ ▼ ▼ ▼ ▼ ▼ ▼ ▼ ▼ ▼ ▼ ▼ ▼
Downtown Memphis

This is where Memphis began, on the banks of the Mississippi River. And this is where much of the town's history lies, in the cotton factors' warehouses and the saloons of Beale Street. The neighborhood extending from the river to Route 240, bounded by the North and South parkways, could use a little jazzing up, but there are plenty of bars and restaurants in the area, two excellent hotels and some of the town's best sights. Union Street is the dividing line between north and south street addresses.

SIGHTS

Beat your feet across the mighty Mississippi to **Mud Island River Park and Museum** if you want to see a spectacular flowing scale model of the entire 1000-mile Mississippi River. (You can either walk across the bridge or take the monorail.) This island (technically, a peninsula located west of downtown) was once considered such an eyesore that there was talk of demolishing it, but finally it was saved and turned into a monument to life on the river. The **River Walk**, made of concrete, slate and steel, shows every curve and twist of the river, each town, city and bridge in topographical detail. Stroll the banks and get the picture of how massive this system is—it's even acceptable for the kids to splash about in the very shallow water. The scale is 30 inches to the mile, so you can walk from Cairo, Illinois, all the way to New Orleans in a matter of minutes. The Gulf of Mexico is represented by a one-acre pool. Most of the remainder of the 52-acre island is devoted to the **Mississippi River Museum**, where 18 different galleries tell the story of the river, the boats, the people and the historic incidents that are part of its lore. The walking tour takes about an hour and includes a replica of an 1870s steamboat and the decks of a Union gunboat, all enhanced with a sound background featuring banjos and fiddles, honky-tonk piano music, blues, rock-and-roll and even the sounds of earthquakes, explosions and gunfire. Closed Monday from mid-April to late May and early September through October; closed November to mid-April. Admission. ~ 125 North Front Street; 901-576-7241, 800-507-6507; www.mudisland.com.

More relaxing is an actual river tour, via the **Memphis Queen Riverboats**, which dock a few blocks south of the bridge to Mud Island. These riverboat excursions take about 90 minutes, during which you will have to fight to stay awake to hear the captain's excellent commentary. The problem is that it's just too relaxing, especially on a sunny day when you can sip a beer or a soda on the deck and watch Old Man River rolling along. The *Memphis Queen III* offers a Friday moonlight cruise April through October. Closed December through February. ~ Foot of

Monroe Avenue; 901-527-5694, 800-221-6197; www.memphis
queen.com.

Just as Nashville built its Parthenon, Memphis has built a
Pyramid in keeping with its namesake. The 32-story triangle of
stainless steel is the site of major sports competitions plus mega-
concerts. You can stroll around yourself or take a guided tour of
the backstage area. Be sure to pick up tickets in advance; there's
only space for 22,500 people. ~ 1 Auction Avenue; 901-521-7909;
www.pyramidarena.com.

The story goes that the tunnel leading from a secret room in
the basement of the **Slave Haven Underground Railroad Museum
(Burkle Estate)** was part of the Underground Railroad before
Emancipation. It's believed that this was one of the ways slaves
escaped to freedom. While the rest of the house, built in 1849 by

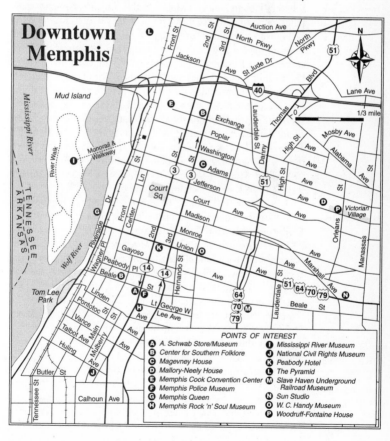

Downtown Memphis

POINTS OF INTEREST

- Ⓐ A. Schwab Store/Museum
- Ⓑ Center for Southern Folklore
- Ⓒ Magevney House
- Ⓓ Mallory-Neely House
- Ⓔ Memphis Cook Convention Center
- Ⓕ Memphis Police Museum
- Ⓖ Memphis Queen
- Ⓗ Memphis Rock 'n' Soul Museum
- Ⓘ Mississippi River Museum
- Ⓙ National Civil Rights Museum
- Ⓚ Peabody Hotel
- Ⓛ The Pyramid
- Ⓜ Slave Haven Underground Railroad Museum
- Ⓝ Sun Studio
- Ⓞ W. C. Handy Museum
- Ⓟ Woodruff-Fontaine House

German immigrant Jacob Burkle, is not particularly interesting, the artifacts (including advertisements and news of slave auctions) from the mid-19th century are startling. Tours are provided by Heritage Tours. Closed Sunday, and Monday from June through September. Admission. ~ 826 North 2nd Street; 901-527-3427, fax 901-527-8784.

HIDDEN ►

You'll need a car (or a cab) to reach the **National Ornamental Metal Museum,** accessible via the Metal Museum Drive exit of Route 55N just before it crosses the river into Arkansas. Set on a bluff overlooking the mighty Mississippi is the only museum in the United States devoted solely to fine metalwork. It's a wonderful place to see why metalworking is both an art and a craft. The National Ornamental Metal Museum is in the middle of a three-acre park and adjacent to a working metal shop, the Schering-Plough Smithy. Exhibits in this intimate, two-story museum rotate roughly every two months; they may include jewelry, hollowware, sculpture or architectural ironwork. One of the most impressive examples of the latter can be seen at the front entry gates. Designed especially for the museum by Richard Quinnell of England, they represent the work of more than 160 metalsmiths from around the world. When the pieces were done, they were assembled on site in eight days. At the next-door smithy shop, metalsmiths teach classes, do restoration work and create metalworks as varied as a weathervane for the Memphis Zoo and a silver tea service for the USS *Tennessee*. You can watch them work Saturday and Sunday. Closed Monday. Admission. ~ 374 Metal Museum Drive; 901-774-6380, 877-881-2326, fax 901-774-6382; www.metalmuseum.org.

HIDDEN ►

If you return to Route 55 heading north and exit immediately onto Crump Boulevard, you'll be getting close to the **National Civil Rights Museum.** In the two-story lobby is the provocative 14-by-21-foot bronze sculpture *Movement to Overcome.* But that's just the beginning. Extensive multimedia displays in a succession of high-ceilinged rooms tell the story of the movement and the people, including King and Rosa Parks, who led the fight for equality between the races. It is intense and informative, and the most poignant site in Memphis. Admission. ~ 450 Mulberry Street; 901-521-9699; www.civilrightsmuseum.org.

The **Peabody Place Museum** is a mind-boggling trove of rare and priceless Asian and European art and artifacts, including jade sculptures, lacquer boxes and cloisonné animals, not to mention the thrones of emperors. Founded by Jack and Marilyn Belz, the museum also includes Scandinavian art glass, Italian mosaics as well as fossils and a very extensive exhibition of scrolls, exquisite Judaic objects, paintings and bronzes. Closed Monday. Admission. ~ 119 South Main Street, Pembroke Square; 901-523-2787.

Just a few blocks west of the museum is a historic part of Beale Street. Even if you don't go inside a single door, walking around **Beale Street Historic District** is a fine way to spend an afternoon or evening. You can't help hearing blues, day and night, most of it live music, pouring out of the bars and restaurants. In the lyrics of the father of the blues, W. C. Handy, ". . . see Beale Street first." Redevelopment projects have left this four-block neighborhood of nightclubs somewhat isolated, though it is only a few blocks from the river. Think of it as Bourbon Street with soul. ~ Between Front and 3rd streets; www.bealestreet.com, e-mail info@bealestreet.com.

A modest wood-frame home with a postage stamp–size porch, the **W. C. Handy House Museum** honors the "Father of the Blues" with artifacts and memorabilia. It's not an extensive collection, but it's touching. Closed Sunday. Admission. ~ 352 Beale Street; 901-527-3427.

The Center for Southern Folklore offers walking tours of Beale Street and a great deal more. It's a combination bookstore, gift shop, café and folk art gallery, with photography and other works by Southern artists such as Hattie Childress, Bertha Bachus, James "Son" Thomas, Preacher Frank Boyle, Lamar Sorrento and Joe Light. The center also screens films about music, folk arts and regional topics. It's open late Thursday through Sunday to offer dinner and, often, music. ~ 119 South Main Street in Pembroke Square at Peabody Place; 901-525-3655; www.southern folklore.com.

In the midst of Beale Street's bars and restaurants sits the **Memphis Police Museum**, the country's only police museum housed in an operating police station. It looks like a movie set, except for the exhibits and photographs of brave officers, but it's the real McCoy. Better yet, it's the only museum you're likely to find that's

AUTHOR FAVORITE

If I had to pick one place to visit in Memphis, it would be the **National Civil Rights Museum**. On April 4, 1968—a day as memorable to many Americans as the day President Kennedy was shot—Dr. Martin Luther King, Jr., was assassinated outside room 306 in the Lorraine Motel. In 1982 the motel—which had hosted the likes of Cab Calloway, B. B. King and Nat King Cole—was saved from foreclosure for use as the first civil-rights museum in the United States. See page 300 for more information.

Victorian Village

Stunning antebellum homes can be found in this Memphis neighborhood a short drive from the downtown core. A few are open to the public.

ST. MARY'S EPISCOPAL CHURCH   Start your tour at the intersection of Poplar Avenue and Orleans Street with a visit to St. Mary's Episcopal Church, the oldest Episcopal church in the South (although the present building replaces an earlier Gothic Revival wood number erected in 1857). ~ 672-692 Poplar Avenue.

LEE HOUSE   Head down Orleans Street two blocks and turn right on Adams Street and continue to the Lee House, part of which was built in 1848. ~ 690 Adams Avenue.

MALLORY-NEELY HOUSE   Return towards Orleans Street and three other houses will also be on your left. The Mallory-Neely House (page 304) was originally built in 1855. It is open to the public. ~ 652 Adams Avenue.

CLEO BARTHOLOMEW HOUSE   Continue to the Cleo Bartholomew House, constructed by attorney Benjamin A. Massey between 1844 and 1849; Jefferson Davis dined here often with later owners. ~ 664 Adams Avenue.

open 24 hours a day. ~ 159 Beale Street; 901-579-0887, 901-525-9800.

Established in 1876, **A. Schwab** is, to some, a dry-goods store. To most, it's a veritable institution, with its banged-up floors, old-timey clothes and even voodoo paraphernalia. It's almost redundant to find an actual museum upstairs that provides a fascinating time warp of old Memphis. ~ 163 Beale Street; 901-523-9782.

True music fans can watch instruments being made at **Gibson Guitar–Memphis**, a combination factory, museum, café and gallery. ~ 145 Lt. George W. Lee Avenue; 901-578-5199, 800-444-2766.

Housed upstairs in the same building as Gibson Guitar–Memphis is the **Memphis Rock 'n' Soul Museum**, which opened its doors in 2000. Stage outfits from Jerry Lee Lewis and Elvis Presley, the handwritten original lyrics to "Heartbreak Hotel," and the podium from Dick Clark's "American Bandstand" show are among

WOODRUFF-FONTAINE HOUSE   A few steps away is the Woodruff-Fontaine House (page 305), one of the best examples of Second Empire style in the South. Built by Amos Woodruff, it was later sold to Noland Fontaine, who entertained lavishly in this house. ~ 680 Adams Avenue.

MOLLIE FONTAINE TAYLOR HOUSE   Cross the street to the Mollie Fontaine Taylor House, a Queen Anne that was built in the late 1880s as a wedding gift from Noland Fontaine to his daughter Mollie. ~ 679 Adams Avenue.

WRIGHT CARRIAGE HOUSE   Turn right onto Orleans Street and right again at the next corner, onto Jefferson Street. The Wright Carriage House belonged to the now-demolished house of Luke Edward Wright, the first U.S. ambassador to Japan and Secretary of War under Theodore Roosevelt. ~ 688 Jefferson Avenue.

ELIAS LOWENSTEIN HOUSE   Return to Orleans Street, cross it and stay on the left side of the street to see the Elias Lowenstein House, the most important Victorian Romanesque house in town and one of the finest of its style in the South. ~ 756 Jefferson Avenue.

PILLOW-MCINTYRE HOUSE   Retrace your steps to Orleans Street and turn right. Near the corner of Orleans Street is the Pillow-McIntyre House, one of the few antebellum Greek Revival houses still standing in Memphis. ~ 679 Adams Avenue.

the treasured artifacts. Six galleries detail the development of rock and soul music, from life and leisure in the rural South in the 1920s up through the Civil Rights movement of the 1960s and 1970s to present-day efforts at cultural preservation. You can also hear rare interview tapes with Memphis musicians on long-term loan from the Smithsonian's National Museum of American History. Admission. ~ 145 Lt. George W. Lee Avenue; 931-543-0800; www.memphisrocknsoul.org.

Just as Key West has its daily sunset ritual, so Memphis celebrates the nightly retreat of the **Peabody Ducks**. A quintet of cosseted quackers appears each morning at 11, departing the elevator to the strains of John Philip Sousa's "King Cotton," and spends the day splashing about in the one-piece-of-travertine-marble-carved fountain in the lobby of The Peabody hotel, a short walk north from Beale Street. Then, at 5 o'clock, after a crowd of 100 or so camera-strung tourists has assembled, the ducks are herded out of day care, down a ramp and along a red carpet to the waiting elevator, which whisks them to their penthouse roost—to the tune of "Red, White and Blue" ("Be kind to your web-footed friends. . ."). It's the best free show in town that doesn't involve blues music. ~ The Peabody, 149 Union Avenue; 901-529-4000, 800-732-2639; www.peabodymemphis.com.

Carriage Tours of Memphis runs carriage rides around the downtown area for $45 per half hour for a group of four. ~ 393 North Main Street; 901-527-7542.

From The Peabody, head north five blocks on 3rd Street to begin a tour of some of Memphis' oldest residences. Compared with the elaborate mansions gracing the Southeast (including nearby Victorian Village), the **Magevney House** looks quite modest. Nineteenth-century schoolmaster Eugene Magevney bought this little white-frame home in 1837 and married his bride in the parlor in the first Catholic wedding conducted in Memphis. Though most of the furniture is not original in this, the oldest structure in Memphis, some of the Magevney's personal possessions, including a secretary and a trunk Mrs. Magevney brought with her from Ireland, are on view. Closed Sunday and Monday, and from January through February. ~ 198 Adams Avenue; 901-526-4464; www.memphismuseums.org/magevney.htm.

Despite its evolution as a rather rough-and-ready town, Memphis became quite prosperous in the latter half of the 19th century, especially before the yellow fever epidemics. Many graceful Victorian mansions were commissioned by the town's business leaders, and the best assortment of those that survive can be found in a neighborhood north of downtown dubbed **Victorian Village**.

If you're going to tour just one old home in this neighborhood, make it the **Mallory-Neely House**, a short drive east of the Magevney House. It's one of the best-preserved Italianate Victorians in the United States. Built in the late antebellum period, the 25-room mansion was expanded by Memphis merchant James C. Neely, who installed a tower as well as stained glass, elaborate stenciling, a parquet floor and other improvements, making it one

MEMPHIS SAFARI

In addition to weekend blues excursions out of the city, Tad Pierson's **American Dream Safari** takes visitors and other music fans on highly personal, deep-background tours of Memphis itself. The drive, in a 1955 Cadillac, covers Beale Street as well as some "early Elvis" sites like the Lauderdale Courts, plus record shops, barbecue joints and, inevitably, Sun Studio. ~ 99 South 2nd Street; 901-527-8870, fax 901-527-3700; www.americandreamsafari.com, e-mail tad@americandreamsafari.com.

of the most attractive homes in the Victorian Village and in fact in the entire town. The original stenciling can still be seen on the walls and ceilings in the double parlor. Admission. ~ 652 Adams Avenue; 901-523-1484; www.memphismuseums.org/mallory.htm.

The nearby **Woodruff-Fontaine House** is one of several along what was once known as Millionaires' Row. This 1870 Second Empire mansion has more than 16 rooms, most of them filled to overflowing with period pieces collected to refurbish the house in its original style. Amos Woodruff had the house built after he moved to Memphis from New Jersey, and lived here with his wife and children from 1871 to 1874. An extremely successful and ambitious businessman, Woodruff encountered disastrous economic conditions brought on by the yellow fever epidemics of those years that decimated the city's population. He sold the home to the Fontaine family, whose successors sold it to Miss Rosa Lee, who, in turn, used the premises for an art academy. In the late 1950s, the local chapter of the Association for the Preservation of Tennessee Antiquities bought and restored the home and then opened it to the public in 1964. Closed Tuesday. Admission. ~ 680 Adams Avenue; 901-526-1469, 901-525-2695.

See the "Walking Tour" for a longer jaunt through Victorian Village.

If you have any old Sun recordings lying around the house, you probably know better than to give 'em away. **Sun Studio,** where Elvis Presley, Carl Perkins (his rendition of "Blue Suede Shoes" was the first to top the pop, country and R&B charts.) and Johnny Cash have recorded, as well as Bob Dylan and Tom Petty, still exists in downtown Memphis. The guided tour tells the story of how Elvis began his recording career, following in the footsteps of Ike Turner, B. B. King and Howlin' Wolf, all of whom cut their first sides here. It winds up in the gallery, filled with photos, instruments and other priceless memorabilia from the early days of rock-and-roll. Of course, you can buy shirts and jackets emblazoned with the Sun Studio logo. If you're lucky, somebody famous (U2 or Tom Petty?) will be recording during your visit, and you may get to listen in. For a price, you can even get recorded yourself. Admission. ~ 706 Union Avenue; 901-521-0664, 800-441-6249; www.sunstudio.com.

LODGING

The freshest, most contemporary accommodations in Memphis belong to **Talbot Heirs Guesthouse,** a revamped hostelry only a block and a half from Beale Street. There are two kinds of travelers in the world: those who would prefer the full-service Peabody across the street, and those who like to imagine they're staying at their own pied-á-terre in the heart of downtown Memphis. Bleached pine floors, residential furniture (in some rooms, it's painted white), walls painted in appetizing shades such as melon or coffee and highly individual decor provide a refreshing change from traditional hotel rooms. Each of the nine suites, all located on the second floor, is thoughtfully stocked with coffee, a coffee-maker, muffins and fruit juice. There's an efficiency kitchen, but other than takeout from nearby Automatic Slim's, you'd be hard pressed to find something to cook in downtown Memphis. ~ 99 South 2nd Street; 901-527-9772, 800-955-3956, fax 901-527-3700; www.talbothouse.com, e-mail reservations@talbothouse.com. ULTRA-DELUXE.

The Peabody needs no introduction. It's the most famous hotel in Memphis, in fact in all of Tennessee. A grand old lady on the order of New York's Plaza, San Francisco's St. Francis or other world-class hotels (before they were bought by corporate inter-ests), it is a scene of constant action. Even if you don't stay here, you must attend at least one episode of the marching ducks that entertain daily by arriving on the lobby level in the morning and departing at 5 p.m. via elevator. The 468 rooms and 16 suites are big and swank, with handsome floral upholstery and gleaming, high-quality furnishings such as armoires made from maple burl. You could spend days here without leaving the hotel, dining (four restaurants), having your hair done and shopping. If you want to hook up with friends in Memphis, ask them to meet you in the ritzy, open lobby bar, where you'll be flanked by marble columns, gilded railings on the mezzanine and polished woodwork that speak of the golden age of travel. After all, The Peabody has been an institution here for well over a century. The lower-level exercise facilities (machines, pool, sauna and whirlpool) are available for an additional charge not only to hotel guests, but to travelers staying at certain other hotels as well. ~ 149 Union Avenue; 901-529-4000, 800-732-2639; www.peabodymemphis.com. ULTRA-DELUXE.

Still can't believe Elvis Presley is dead? We can't help you there, but if you want to, you can eat fried peanut butter and banana sandwiches in the kitchen and listen to old albums in his living room. With the exception of Graceland, Elvis lived in the **Lauderdale Courts** longer than anywhere else in Memphis. The teenage home of the king was saved by fans and local preservation organizations and placed on the National Register of Historic Places. Now renamed Uptown Square, the old complex houses apartment #328, which has been restored and redecorated in 1950s style, right down to authentic period pieces and appliances including 1951 Frigidaire refrigerator, Vesta stove and free-standing sinks. The two-bedroom suite is available for overnight guests, who will probably appreciate contemporary amenities such as a microwave oven, a flat-screen television, free wireless internet ac-cess and a DVD/VHS player with a selection of Elvis movies. No

HIDDEN ▶

wheelchair access. Two-night minimum. ~ 185 Winchester Street; 901-521-8219; www.lauderdalecourts.com. ULTRA-DELUXE.

Corporate Lodging Associates offers dozens of listings in carefully selected private homes. They also arrange stays in condominiums, luxury apartments and carriage houses. Three-night minimum required. ~ P.O. Box 111141, Memphis, TN 38111-1141; 901-327-6129; fax 901-458-1003; e-mail hvdenton@aol.com. DELUXE TO ULTRA-DELUXE.

DINING

The **Arcade** is part restaurant, part folk museum. It's not the food but the ambience that's kept this place alive since 1919, making it the oldest café in town. The pale-green-and-yellow booths are pure '50s, and so is the menu. This is the kind of place for standard Southern breakfasts (fresh house-made cornbread and buttermilk biscuits) and lunch-counter lunches, strong on sandwiches, hamburgers, down-home cookin' and milkshakes. New owners took over in 1996, adding pizza (by the slice), focaccia and specialty coffee drinks to the menu—and jazz and brass-band sounds to the soundtrack, which historically has been entirely rock and soul from the heyday of the Sun Studio sound in the '50s. While you're there, ask the waiter to show you which was Elvis' favorite booth. ~ 540 South Main Street; 901-526-5757. BUDGET.

As the menu declares, **B. B. King's Blues Club & Restaurant** is a b-a-a-a-d place for a diet. Maybe if you avoid the Southern-fried chicken fingers, the sausage and cheese plate, the fried Delta catfish bites and the Lucille burger topped with bacon and cheese, you could get out for under 2000 calories. You could, after all, make a meal of grilled Cajon catfish, red beans and rice or a club salad. This lively restaurant doubles as a blues club from late afternoon into the night. ~ 143 Beale Street; 901-524-5464. MODERATE.

B. B. King arrived in Memphis at the age of 22 with $2.50 in his pocket and a guitar in his hand.

Can't face any more barbecue? Try one of the deep-fried hamburgers at **Dyers Burgers,** which originally opened in 1912 in a truck elsewhere in town. (Let's hope they've changed the grease since then.) ~ 205 Beale Street; 901-527-3937. BUDGET.

On the ground floor of one of the newer downtown buildings, **Java Blues** is a sort of super-coffee shop that serves more than hot espresso and cold fruit drinks. Aside from sweet things, the deal here is a list of sandwiches and wraps you can order with ham, turkey, chicken, pineapple or tuna, available on traditional bread or variously flavored tortilla shells. No dinner. ~ 125 South Main Street; 901-527-5282. BUDGET.

Chez Philippe, The Peabody's deluxe restaurant, offers some of the most elegant dining in Memphis. Surrounded by white pillars and wrought iron and served by formally dressed waitstaff,

Text continued on page 310.

The Early Days
of Rock-and-roll

Rock-and-roll may not have been invented in Memphis, but no other city in America had a bigger role in nurturing the genre—if not to adulthood, at least into adolescence. Just as Nashville made country music famous, and Beale Street popularized the blues, so Memphis became the epicenter for the groundbreaking fusion of blues, rhythm, country and rockabilly we now know as rock music.

Then Elvis came to town. Not that anyone took much notice—in the beginning. There was too much going on. As the largest city in the Delta region, Memphis was in a prime location, a natural crossroads with Chicago to the north and New Orleans to the south, the mountains, east, and St. Louis, west. At the beginning of the 20th century, an Alabama man named W. C. Handy had been listening to Delta-style blues in Mississippi. In 1911 he wrote "Memphis Blues," ostensibly a campaign song, which became his first big hit. Handy established a publishing company on Beale Street and began turning out hits like "Beale Street Blues" and "St. Louis Blues," which was the most-recorded song in the U.S. before the advent of rock.

The blues derived from spirituals, ballads and "field hollers," as well as percussive music, imported from Africa during the decades of the slave trade. (For an erudite explication of the history of blues music, see Robert Palmer's *Deep Blues* [Penguin Books, 1982]). Throughout the teens and '20s, blues music, with its distinctive flattened third (or blue) note, flourished in the Beale Street neighborhood, where African Americans lived largely segregated from white society. The genre took a back seat to big bands during the Depression, although it never went away. But it certainly was co-opted. The 1940s saw the ascendancy of rhythm-and-blues, incorporating amplified sound in the mix. It, too, was black music, in form and content.

Robert Gordon, who wrote *It Came from Memphis* (Faber and Faber, 1995), offers this definition of rock-and-roll: "Rock and roll was white rednecks trying to play black music. Their country music background hampered them and they couldn't do it." The closest anybody ever came (certainly before 1953) was Elvis Presley. He blended—no, embodied—a hybrid of R&B and country that came to be called rockabilly.

Memphis R&B distinguished the sound coming out of Sun Records, the legendary studio that brought Elvis to the world. Local deejay Sam Phillips opened the Memphis Recording Service in 1950, renting the studio to people such as Ike Turner and B. B. King who wanted to cut their own discs.

When Phillips amassed sufficient capital, he began organizing his own sessions, producing Jackie Brenston's "Rocket 88" in 1951. The song topped the R&B charts and was covered by Bill Haley; it's often cited as the first rock-and-roll recording. In 1952 Phillips bankrolled Sun Records and set up shop on Union Avenue.

Meanwhile, the future King had come to town in 1948 from Tupelo, Mississippi. Before he made it big and bought Graceland in 1957, he, his parents and his grandmother lived at several undistinguished addresses around town. In 1953, Elvis forked over the $4 fee to record a birthday present for his mother, accompanying himself on acoustic guitar on "My Happiness" and "That's When Your Heartaches Begin." The legend gets a little fuzzy around this point, but apparently Phillips was underwhelmed by this disk and a subsequent one.

What changed Phillips' mind about Elvis? Elvis had agreed to an audition session with guitarist Scotty Moore and bassist Bill Black, but nothing much happened until Elvis started doodling around with Arthur Crudup's "That's All Right (Mama)" and Phillips, with his talent for picking potential hits, started taping. He cut a single (with Bill Monroe's "Blue Kentucky" on the flip side) and sent it to WHBQ deejay Dewey Phillips (no relation), famous for his iconoclastic approach to broadcasting. If Phillips liked a song, he would play it time after time, whether it was country or blues or whatever; if he didn't, he wouldn't, sometimes even snatching the arm off the phonograph in mid-song, sending a screech over the air.

As soon as Dewey Phillips heard Elvis' song, he called Elvis' mother and asked her to find her son and get him to the station. Elvis, found in a movie theater, rushed over to meet Phillips and wound up with the first hit rock-and-roll record by a white artist. Those early Sun recordings by Elvis—five singles in 1954 and 1955—are pricey collectibles these days, but so are several others. Phillips built his stable of rockabillies, recording Carl Perkins ("Blue Suede Shoes"), Johnny Cash ("I Walk the Line"), Jerry Lee Lewis ("Whole Lotta Shakin' Goin' On") and Roy Orbison ("Ooby Dooby"), among others. One of the most famous impromptu recording sessions of all time—since dubbed the "Million Dollar Quartet"—included Lewis on piano, Cash, Perkins and Presley, who had dropped by one December afternoon in 1956, though he was by then signed to RCA.

Phillips closed Sun Studio and moved over to the Sam Phillips Recording Service on Madison Avenue. The original Sun Studio was not used for recording until 1987, when Gary Harding, a Memphis musician, took it over. Now restored, the place offers tours by day and is used for recording at night. At the next-door Sun Studio, visitors can chow down on soul food at the very place where Elvis signed part of his RCA contract (over a cheeseburger), back when the place was Ma Taylor's Diner.

diners may feast on innovative cuisine such as salmon with potato beignets, bouillabaisse with lobster, caramelized grouper,
roasted rack of lamb and smoked filet mignon. ~ 149 Union
Avenue; 901-529-4000. DELUXE TO ULTRA- DELUXE.

In 2002, The Peabody hotel added the **Capriccio Restaurant,
Bar and Café**, a 170-seat Italian restaurant featuring a wood-
burning oven and display kitchen. The bar, in close proximity to
the restaurant's impressive wine cellar, also serves food and provides live evening entertainment Thursday through Saturday. The
café sells deli fare and pastries. Breakfast, lunch and dinner served.
~ 149 Union Avenue; 901-529-4199. MODERATE TO DELUXE.

When you're ready to substitute blinis and borscht for barbecue sauce, think of the **Cafe Samovar**. Serious Russian cuisine,
focusing on meat dishes with the occasional salmon entrée, is the
order of the day here. Ground beef shows up in main course like
goluzi (stuffed into cabbage), but you could also opt for lighter
fare like the chicken-in-mushroom-sauce blini. This attractive
restaurant has large stylized folk murals—including one of Saint
Nicholas—that underscore the ambience of the menu. On Friday
and Saturday nights, you can start with Beluga caviar and cap
your evening watching Russian gypsies belly-dance. Closed Sunday. ~ 83 Union Avenue; 901-529-9607, fax 901-529-9638. DE-
LUXE TO ULTRA-DELUXE.

Hip when it opened in 1991 and hip it remains, **Automatic
Slim's Tonga Club** is the coolest-looking restaurant in all of
Memphis. Maybe it's the colorful modern furniture or the zebra
skins or the artful arrangement of tumbleweeds over the door,
but this high-ceilinged rendezvous spot seems to put people in a
convivial mood. The menu is a culinary melange of Southwestern
and Caribbean. Imaginative salads, fresh fish, crab and other
seafood dishes—the Caribbean voodoo stew incorporates mussels, shrimp and crab—and changing specials make Slim's the
kind of place you can enjoy time and time again. Closed Sunday.
~ 83 South 2nd Street; 901-525-7948. DELUXE TO ULTRA-DELUXE.

AUTHOR FAVORITE

Beale Street doesn't get any more authentic than at **Blues
City Café**, where chef Bonnie Mack rules the kitchen to make sure the
Gulf Coast shrimp is spicy enough, the catfish crisp enough and the barbecue ribs just right. The loud corner restaurant is as plain as a mud fence,
but the good vibes are infectious, the prices unbeatable and the menu
slightly unpredictable. ~ 138 Beale Street; 901-526-3637, fax 901-526-
6931. BUDGET TO MODERATE.

Don't order beef if you want to look local at **Rendezvous,**   ◄ *HIDDEN*
which has been a Memphis favorite since 1948. You'll want to have
the pork, and you'll want to order it "wet," meaning with lots of
sauce, instead of "dry." But what the heck: you're not local, and
the chicken and the beef are said to be just as good as the pork.
To reach this underground labyrinth, which looks like it used to
house a speakeasy, find General Washburn Alley, a tiny north–
south street across Union Street from the main entrance to The
Peabody hotel. Once you get there, do not become separated
from your party or you may never find them again amid the many
rooms laden with so many musical instruments, beer steins and
what-nots that you may think you're in a very, very interesting
museum. Closed Sunday and Monday. ~ 52 South 2nd Street;
901-523-2746. MODERATE TO DELUXE.

For a fast, filling breakfast of Southern comfort food, drop
into the ultra-casual **Memphis Grits**. Surprisingly, they do serve
beer and wine at lunch. No dinner. Closed Sunday. ~ 22 South
Main Street; 901-577-9937. BUDGET.

Located in Victorian Village, **Cielo** is a sensational addition to
the local dining scene. Brought to you by caterer/entrepreneur Karen
Carrier, who gave us Automatic Slim's, Cielo is located across the
street from the Woodruff-Fontaine House in an 1886 mansion—
built over the course of four years as a wedding gift for the daughter of Noland Fontaine—that has been wildly renovated with gauzy
curtains and fantasy furniture and decorated with handblown glass
bowls on every table. The best seats are on the ground floor; upstairs, where there is also a bar, things are a bit less cozy. Entrées
may include tuna encrusted in peppercorns, Kansas City veal
strip, Thai-spiced pork loin and sea bass filet. But first you have
to get through a mouth-watering list of appetizers that include
scallops with braised endive and pistachio-crusted calamari. Closed
Sunday and Monday. ~ 679 Adams Avenue; 901-524-1886, fax
901-526-6642. DELUXE TO ULTRA-DELUXE.

You can get take out or grab a booth or one of the few tiny outside tables at **Another Roadside Takeout**, located inside Miss Cor-   ◄ *HIDDEN*
delia's market. Lunchtime choices range from smoked chipotle
honey turkey sandwiches to roasted red pepper, eggplant and goat
cheese terrine. A larger list of take-out and delivery items (some
full-blown entrées) can be ordered in advance. ~ 737 Harbor Bend
Road; 901-578-8646, fax 901-526-4644. BUDGET TO DELUXE.

Odds are you don't need size-74 pants, size-60 dresses or 40   **SHOPPING**
types of suspenders, unless you've been putting in overtime at the
barbecue pit. But it's nice to know these items are among the
classic merchandise at **A. Schwab**, a dry-goods store that's been
doing business at the same address since 1876. ~ 163 Beale
Street; 901-523-9782.

If you like riding the trolley, you can pick up souvenirs and gifts at the **Trolley Store**. ~ 61 South Main Street; 901-274-6282.

An extensive collection of rare Chinese art, with an emphasis on the Manchu dynasty, is found at the **Peabody Place Museum & Gallery**. Stunning pieces from the last dynasty before the 1911 revolution include jade, ivory, fabrics, paintings and furnishings. ~ 119 South Main Street, Concourse Level; 901-523-2787.

The Map Room is the wild brainchild of a couple of young women who wanted to create a kind of global crossroads where people could congregate, have a cup of coffee and get a map, a travel book or an interesting conversation any time of day. ~ 2 South Main Street; 901-579-9924.

The **South Main Arts District** is a neighborhood of galleries, hip restaurants, trendy shops and open markets. On the last Friday of each month, you can take a free Art Trolley Tour from 6 to 9 p.m. ~ 901-578-7262; www.southmainmemphis.org.

One of the more distinctive sources for art along South Main is **D'Edge Art & Unique Treasures**, which has two floors of folk art, blues-related pieces and other arts and crafts. ~ 550 South Main Street; 901-521-0054.

Durden Gallery carries an affordable mix of traditional and contemporary art in a variety of media. Note that the entrance is on Huling Street. ~ 408 South Front Street, No. 11; 901-543-0340; www.durdengallery.com.

One of the region's largest contemporary art galleries, the **Jay Etkin Gallery** specializes in painting, sculpture and works on paper by local, regional and nationally recognized artists. It also has an extensive collection of Latin American and African art. Closed Sunday and Monday except by appointment. ~ 409 South Main Street; 901-543-0035; www.jayetkingallery.com.

TONIC is considered among Tennessee's most stylish boutiques, with women and men's designer apparel, custom design, vintage, home and life accessories designed by New Yorker Katrina Shelton. Closed Sunday and Monday except by appointment. ~ 431 South Main Street; 901-578-8000.

Memphis artist Arnold Thompson owns the **Universal Art Gallery**, which specializes in fine contemporary art from Memphis and abroad. ~ 111 G.E. Patterson Avenue; 901-522-9398; www.universalartgallery.net.

NIGHTLIFE   Famous names like Clarence Carter appear at the **Blues City Café**, along with a diverse roster of blues groups of all kinds. Cover. ~ 138 Beale Street; 901-526-3637.

Down and across the street, the **Rum Boogie Cafe** has live music and dancing nightly. Get there in daylight so you can see the extensive display of guitars that once belonged to some of the greats. Cover after 8:30 p.m. ~ 182 Beale Street; 901-528-0150.

Artists such as the legendary Fieldstones, Daddy Mack Blues Band, Di Anne Price, Blind Mississippi Morris, Mose Vinson and other regional artists and performers appear at the **Center for Southern Folklore** Thursday through Saturday nights. ~ 119 South Main Street in Pembroke Square at Peabody Place; 901-525-3655.

Bands that draw big crowds—and around here, it's rarely jazz or New Age—often book into the **New Daisy**, which has a capacity for crowds of up to 1000 maniacs. Closed Sunday. Cover. ~ 330 Beale Street; 901-525-8979.

During the week, **Sleep Out Louie's** is just another great bar and grill, but on Friday nights in the warm-weather months, there's a band and the party spills out into the adjacent alley. ~ 88 Union Avenue; 901-527-5337.

Locals say the best place in town for jazz is **Precious Cargo**, a gourmet coffeehouse by the bluff that also sponsors poetry readings. Occasional cover. ~ 381 North Main Street; 901-578-8446.

Major rock concerts (and sporting events such as basketball games) fit neatly into the 22,500-seat **Pyramid**. ~ 1 Auction Avenue; 901-521-7909.

THEATER, OPERA, SYMPHONY AND DANCE The 1928 **Orpheum Theatre**, originally a vaudeville palace, has been spiffed up and is once again Memphis' premier performing-arts hall. It is home to both the Memphis Concert Ballet and Opera Memphis, and is the preferred venue for touring Broadway shows. ~ 203 South Main Street; 901-525-3000; www.orpheum-memphis.com.

Ballet Memphis is a well-established company that has been presenting dance performances since 1985, including the annual production of *The Nutcracker* each holiday season in the Orpheum Theatre. Four productions are scheduled in the months of October, December, February and April. ~ 901-737-7322; www.balletmemphis.org.

Opera Memphis has been producing classical opera and Broadway musicals since 1956. The season is sporadic, but usually in-

AUTHOR FAVORITE

You can't miss **B. B. King's Blues Club & Restaurant**, in a corner location at the top of Beale Street. It's owned by the legendary guitar-playing blues man. In 1990 B. B. (short for Riley "Blues Boy" King) opened this joint and now books some of the best live blues on Beale Street. There are two levels, and you can dine on the ground level. Arrive early for a good seat. Occasional cover. ~ 143 Beale Street; 901-524-5464.

cludes four operas performed at the Orpheum Theatre, presented in October, November, January and either late February or early March. ~ 901-257-3100; www.operamemphis.org.

The **Memphis Cook Convention Center** plays host to various consumer (automobile, home) and trade shows as well as to a gigantic December consumer sale. The 2000-seat Cannon Center for the Performing Arts opened in time for the 2002 season of the Memphis Symphony Orchestra. ~ 255 North Main Street; 901-576-1200; www.memphisconvention.com.

The **Memphis Symphony Orchestra** performs a full season of classical, pops and chamber music from September until May in its permanent home in the Memphis Cook Convention Center. The 80-piece orchestra also plays a spring date at the Dixon Gallery and Gardens in midtown. ~ 255 North Main Street; 901-323-0060; www.memphissymphony.org.

PARKS

MEEMAN-SHELBY FOREST STATE PARK 🚶 🚲 🐎 🛶 ⛵ You could spend a week in this 13,500-acre park—maybe without seeing the same people twice. The western edge of the park runs along the Mississippi River for some eight miles. There is fishing—for bream, catfish and largemouth bass—in 125-acre Poplar Tree Lake. In fact, if you rent one of the six housekeeping cabins here, you can fish practically from your front door. Or you can rent little boats or fish from the bank or a fishing pier. The swimming pool is Olympic size, and there is room for volleyball, badminton and a softball field. The visitors center has maps of trails that crisscross the park, including five miles of paved biking trails. Deer, turkey, beaver and some 200 species of birds live in the park. During the summer, there are games, movies, hayrides and guided tours, plus other special events. Hot showers are available in the bathhouse. Day-use fee, $3. ~ 910 Riddick Road, 16 miles north of Memphis, Millington; 901-876-5201.

▲ There are 49 campsites with water and electricity; $16.25 per night. Six cabins (one double bed, two single beds and two rollaways, two bedrooms, kitchen, central air and heat) are $63 Sunday through Thursday, $73 Friday and Saturday.

▼▼▼▼▼▼▼▼▼▼▼▼▼
Midtown Memphis

In the area delineated by Route 240 on the east of Highland Avenue on the west are some of the most interesting neighborhoods and largest attractions in Memphis. In particular, the Cooper-Young Historic District, nearly five miles east of downtown, is the city's most diverse and lively neighborhood. It stretches from Poplar Avenue, on the south edge of Overton Park, south along McLean and Cooper streets nearly to Route 78. Plenty of shops and restaurants provide the best walking-around blocks in town.

SIGHTS

The largest park in central Memphis, **Overton Park** is Tennessee's answer to Central Park. Wide boulevards lead to the Memphis Brooks Museum of Art and the Memphis Zoo, both within the boundaries, which are Poplar Avenue, North and South parkways and McLean Boulevard. Overton Park also has a bandshell near the Memphis Brooks Museum of Art that was built during the Depression by the Work Projects Administration (WPA). It's used for outdoor summer concerts; famous performers in the past have included Janis Joplin and Elvis Presley, who made one of his earliest public appearances here. Some concerts are presented free of charge; others charge admission. ~ 1928 Poplar Avenue; 901-274-6046; www.overtonparkshell.org.

The **Memphis Brooks Museum of Art** is the crowning jewel of the 342-acre Overton Park, which is also home to the Memphis Zoo. Funded by a bequest from Mrs. Samuel H. Brooks, it opened in 1916 with just two paintings. Over the years it has acquired more than 7000 pieces of art that span nearly 20 cen-

turies, beginning in A.D. 50. Galleries are designed and painted to enhance their individual holdings. They are arranged in a complex of buildings, notably the original grand marble structure now on the National Register of Historic Places. For instance, Italian baroque art is housed in a cream-and-red-brick gallery; the Northern Renaissance collection is displayed on walls painted yellow and then rag-washed to appear marbleized; the American Gallery could have been lifted straight from a historic home in Williamsburg. The focus is always on the art. Be sure to allow time to hang, as it were, with the impressionists in the French Gallery; few collections rival it. Closed Monday. Admission (except on the first Wednesday of the month). ~ 1934 Poplar Avenue; 901-544-6200, tours 901-544-6215; www.brooksmuseum. org, e-mail brooks@brooksmuseum.org.

If the kids have behaved at the museum, reward them with a trip to the nearby zoo. A top exhibit at the 700-acre **Memphis Zoo** is Cat Country, a four-acre natural habitat shared by lions, tigers, cheetahs and other endangered predators. Rocky outcroppings, grassy savannas, waterfalls and rock caves make a giant playpen for these big cats from Asia, Africa and South America. Instead of being caged, they can be seen climbing up and down trees, even hunting for fish along a riverbank, giving visitors at least some idea of how they behave in the wild. In addition, there's also Primate Canyon and a habitat for nocturnal animals. Among the newer exhibits are a butterfly habitat and a collection of komodo dragons from Indonesia. You'll find the usual fish, reptiles, elephants, hippos and bears, too, nearly 3000 animals within the 70-acre zoo. Some, like Sumatran tigers, brown kiwi and Russian cobras are rarely seen in captivity. The zoo has a three-acre panda exhibit enhanced with Chinese gardens with a traditional Chinese teahouse, 50-foot pagoda and a carved, hand-painted 25-animal carousel. Ya Ya and Le Le will have new neighbors in 2006 when the Northwest Passage exhibits opens to house polar bears, seals and sea lions. In a nice switch from the can-you-top-this approach of some zoos, this one also has an exhibit focusing on domesticated animals like horses, sheep, pigs, cattle and chickens, at Once Upon a Farm. The zoo has a train ($1) as well as rental wheelchairs. Admission. ~ 2000 Prentiss Place; 901-276-9453, fax 901-725-9305; www.memphiszoo.org.

Several blocks down Parkway and several more east on Central, you'll find one of the grandest homes in Memphis—one that was never lived in. Perhaps you've never wondered: Who invented the self-service supermarket? If you have, you probably already know it was Clarence Saunders, who in 1916 began the well-known Southern chain of grocery stores called Piggly Wiggly. The **Memphis Pink Palace and Museum** is the house that Piggly Wiggly built. Saunders built his mansion with Georgia pink marble, but was forced into bankruptcy before he even finished designing the interior. He never spent a single night in the palatial house, which Memphians had already dubbed the "pink palace." Empty from 1976 to 1996, it has been reopened by the city and houses an eclectic collection. Top on the list is an exhibit on 19th-century Memphis "From the Boss to the King" (meaning "Boss" Crump and Elvis Presley). Permanent exhibits cover topics as varied as the Civil War, medical history and dinosaur fossils. There is also a planetarium with scheduled laser light concerts and other shows. Admission. ~ 3050 Central Avenue; 901-320-6320; www.memphismuseums.org/museum.htm.

Memphis' official city flower is actually a shrub: the crepe myrtle. Summer is the best season to enjoy its showy blossoms of pink, fuschia, lavender and white.

Just up the street there's another treat in store for the pre-adult set. **The Children's Museum** more or less doubles as a child-care facility for parents who've run out of ideas. Like many other similar "discovery" museums, this warehouse-size one encourages learning through play. Kids can try shopping for their own groceries, driving their own "car," climbing on a fire engine, wandering about in a three-dimensional maze, even cashing a check at the bank in a pint-size metropolis. In addition to regular interactive exhibits, the museum hosts special programs throughout the year. Closed Monday. Admission. ~ 2525 Central Avenue; 901-458-2678, information line 901-320-3170; www.cmom.com.

The **New Overton Square**, at the corner of Madison Avenue at Cooper Street, is an informal complex of shops and restaurants. Usually a lively place with plenty of foot traffic and fun places to browse, it more or less anchors the northern edge of the Cooper-Young Historic District. ~ 901-278-0014.

If you are around on a sunny day, head for the back deck at the **Bayou Bar & Grill** in Overton Square. Cajun food tastes good in warm weather—and on the other hand, it warms your cockles when it's cold. Cajun popcorn (shrimp or crawfish), jambalaya, shrimp Creole, blackened catfish and blackened tenderloin are some of the more appealing items on a lively bar menu. The Budweiser umbrellas go up on the deck in nice weather, sheltering a fairly young clientele; or you can dine inside, seated on red chairs at square white marble tables. ~ 2100 Overton Square Lane; 901-278-8626; www.bayoubarandgrill.com. MODERATE.

DINING

Paulette's seems worlds away from laidback cafés. This sedate restaurant is popular with Ladies Who Lunch and couples who enjoy dining out together as well as businesspeople during the week. A rather Parisian decor features dark wood ceilings, white walls and south-of-France prints; an enclosed brick courtyard outback is reserved for mild days. This is the place for upscale fish dishes like grilled salmon, rainbow trout and Louisiana crab cakes, as well as specialties such as crêpes à la Bretonne, filled with scallops and shrimp in a Mornay sauce. Chocolate-banana-almond crêpe are among the many desserts at Paulette's, along with crème brûlée and elegant pies. ~ 2110 Madison Avenue; 901-726-5128, fax 901-726-5670. DELUXE.

Cafe Society is another magnet for Francophiles. More casual than Paulette's, it also has a soupçon more chic. Popular entrées include pan-seared duck breast, chicken roulade and shrimp Diane, as well as steaks. You can be seated in the all-mauve-and-wood dining room, or outside at one of four little tables set on an awning-shaded patio right on the street. No lunch Saturday and Sunday. ~ 212 North Evergreen Street; 901-722-2177, fax 901-722-2186. DELUXE TO ULTRA-DELUXE.

HIDDEN ►

If you start having sushi withdrawal while you're in Memphis, hang on 'til you get to **Sekisui Midtown**. It's on a side street off a side street, but worth the trek for fresh *maki* sushi, sashimi and other raw fish. Lots of lacquer and flowers adorn the main room behind the sushi bar. Daily specials such as skewered beef dishes augment the standing menu, which is strong on tempura and teriyaki, available à la carte or as part of a full meal. ~ 25 South Belvedere Boulevard; 901-725-0005, fax 901-725-0006. MODERATE TO DELUXE.

To look at the converted bungalow, you'd never guess it's the home of pan-Asian cuisine. **Lilly's dimsum thensome** offers a range of options, from low-priced dim sum (small Chinese savories like pork-stuffed dumplings) to full entrées. The dinner menu covers Japan, Korea, China and Thailand with Hong Kong chicken (peanuts and coconut milk), *pad thai*, wild rice–noodle dishes and both Panang and Thai curries. Lots of the offerings are vegetarian at this funky hangout popular with the neighborhood's gays and lesbians. ~ 903 South Cooper Street; 901-276-9300. BUDGET TO MODERATE.

The snazzy brick-and-neon façade at **Melange** is a good advertisement for the chic menu at this Midtown hot spot. Entrées run to filet of escolar and grilled beef medallions with bleu cheese potato gratin; imaginative second courses may include roasted shellfish bisque. Inexpensive tapas put bar food to shame and are offered in the M-bar early and late. There's also café seating in good weather. No lunch Sunday through Tuesday. ~ 948 South Cooper Street; 901-276-0002. ULTRA-DELUXE.

SHOPPING   A women's clothing shop with a wonderful selection of hats and lingerie, **Tut-Uncommon Antiques** has an astonishing selection of estate jewelry, sterling pieces and costume jewelry, particularly in the art-deco style. ~ 1920 Madison Avenue; 901-278-8965.

Just a block off Madison, you enter **Maggie's Pharm** by a residential stairway to the second floor. The first room is devoted mostly to candles and soaps, but the farther inside you venture, the more herbs, spices and New Age potions you'll find. ~ 13 North Florence Street; 901-722-8898, 800-536-8898.   ◄ *HIDDEN*

The area around Central and Cooper is great for antique browsing. **Market Central**'s antique and decorator showrooms are filled with armoires, trunks, benches, light fixtures, decorative iron and garden fountains, as well as light treasures such as porcelain. ~ 2215 Central Avenue; 901-278-0888.

The coolest place to shop for vintage furnishings, clothing and collectibles is **Flashback, Inc.**, a veritable department store known for art-deco and '50s furnishings and an awesome collection of armoires. ~ 2304 Central Avenue; 901-272-2304.

Gifts, antiques and decorative items for the home and garden plus some small pieces like lamps and tables comprise the elegant merchandise at **Chapman & Company**. Closed Sunday. ~ 612 South Cooper Street; 901-274-4438.

For a pick-me-up while you shop, cruise into the **Otherlands Exotic Gift and Coffee Bar**, which specializes in international imports plus crafts by local artisans. Full coffee bar with espresso drinks and light snacks. ~ 641 South Cooper Street; 901-278-4994.

If you have a cat, or like someone who does, pad on over to the **House of Mews**, just across the street. It's the cat's pajamas . . . and mug, and toy and everything feline you can imagine. Closed in the morning and Monday and Tuesday. ~ 944 South Cooper Street; 901-272-3777; www.houseofmews.com.

Huey's Restaurant has been in the forefront of the blues scene for the last 15 years. Its ace-in-the-hole is the willingness of professional traveling blues bands to play here for free on Sunday night. You can also get a great burger or shoot some pool at this corner hangout. ~ 1927 Madison Avenue; 901-726-4372, fax 901-278-9073.   **NIGHTLIFE**

BUYING THE BLUES

Shangri-La Records, located in a modest bungalow, is the place to look for that hard-to-find blues album or CD you've been hoping to find, whether it's vintage Jerry Lee Lewis or the latest by Memphix. Also the place for picking up information, even printed brochures, on what's happenin' in town. ~ 1916 Madison Avenue; 901-274-1916; www.shangri.com.

PARKS **OVERTON PARK** 🚶 🚲 The oldest and largest park in Memphis is home to the Memphis Zoo and a number of other attractions. It's very popular for tennis, biking and hiking, for golfing at a municipal course or for hanging out on balmy summer afternoons on shade-sheltered benches. This is also a good place for picnics. It has a golf course, sports fields, gymnastic equipment and a children's play area. ~ 1928 Poplar Avenue, off the intersection of Poplar Avenue and Parkway. Call the Memphis Park Commission for more information at 901-325-5759.

▼▼▼▼▼▼▼▼▼▼
East Memphis

As Memphians moved out of downtown in the 1970s, many of them headed east. This part of town has some fine residential neighborhoods as well as parks and the campuses of University of Memphis. Streets here tend to be wider than usual and lined with trees that provide welcome spring and summer shade.

SIGHTS Central Avenue, which intersects the University of Memphis (formerly Memphis State University), is just such a street. The **Art Museum at the University of Memphis** houses a permanent collection

HIDDEN ► of Egyptian art and artifacts, but you'll have to search for it. (Park at the visitors center on Central Avenue, walk five buildings east, go behind the theater and look for the four-story brick building on the right.) Among the holdings are a statuette of Nedjemu, who probably lived more than 3000 years ago, wearing a wraparound kilt; a painted and gilded mummy with significant evidence of the elaborate Egyptian funerary rituals of 2000 years ago; and a model granary, a typical enterprise in ancient Egypt showing men performing various functions necessary in the creation of flour. Closed Sunday. ~ Communications and Fine Arts Building No. 142, 3750 Norriswood Avenue, off Central Avenue, University of Memphis campus, 901-678-2224, 800-669-2678; e-mail artmuseum@memphis.edu.

Though at its most glorious in springtime (think: 1500 rosebushes), the Memphis Botanic Garden has been designed for year-round enjoyment; something is almost always in bloom.

On a nearby street that runs parallel to Central are two other outstanding attractions. Memphis has been blessed with philanthropists with an appreciation for fine art. Margaret Oates Dixon and Hugo Norton Dixon were two community leaders who bequeathed their home, their gardens and their French impressionist collection for the public to enjoy. In addition to priceless works by the most famous painters of their time—Degas, Renoir, Gauguin, Cassatt, Turner and Constable—the **Dixon Gallery and Gardens** houses 56 works by Jean-Louis Forain and a stellar assortment of nearly 600 pieces of 18th-century German porcelain. The Dixon home is still mostly furnished, so it's easy to imagine how it might have been to live among these and other treasures, such as the 18th- and 19th-century British portraits and landscapes collected by Hugo Dixon, who was of English heritage. Seventeen acres of Tennessee woodlands have been transformed into an English-style park, complete with greenhouses and sculpture. Gallery is closed on Monday. Admission. ~ 4339 Park Avenue; 901-761-2409; www.dixon.org.

When things get too hectic, take time out and head for the Garden of Tranquility in the **Memphis Botanic Garden**. The spacing of carefully selected plants and stones, the bridge that zigs and zags (to confuse the demons) here will chill your jets. Or perhaps the Sensory Garden would do the trick. Accessible to wheelchairs, it is filled with roses, herbs and other aromatic plants to get you in touch with your senses—especially the olfactory one. These are just a couple of the 20 different gardens planted in the 96-acre park. Admission (except Tuesday). ~ 750 Cherry Road; 901-685-1566; www.memphisbotanicgarden.com.

The **Lichterman Nature Center** brings Mother Nature to the heart of the city, with a number of interconnected, self-guided walking trails that wind through these 65 acres. Small fry will also like the butterfly garden next to the greenhouse. Admission. ~ 5992 Quince Road; 901-767-7322; www.memphismuseums. org/nature.htm.

LODGING

It's not so much the rooms that distinguish the **Adam's Mark Hotel** as it is the setting. Virtually surrounded by a manmade body of water—complete with its own ducks, though not trained in The Peabody tradition—the reflecting cylindrical structure houses 408 rooms on 27 floors, all with views of *some*thing. They are very well designed, comfortable and handsome in a CEO kind of way. The hotel caters to business travelers with a fitness room, an outdoor pool and a restaurant where the waitstaff perform Broadway classics while serving your dinner. ~ 939 Ridge Lake Boulevard; 901-684-6664, 800-444-2326, fax 901-762-7411; www.adamsmark.com. DELUXE TO ULTRA-DELUXE.

DINING

The neon pig sporting the chef's hat on his head keeps smiling no matter how long the lines are at **Corky's**. In fact, maybe those long lines are the very reason he's grinning from ear to ear. Smoke from the grill curls out over the parking lot at this popular Poplar corridor 'cue spot. Cult followers chow down on ribs (wet or dry), barbecued chicken, shrimp plates and other highly flavored fare. In a region where barbecue sauce is the stuff of dreams, Corky's is distinct and delicious. Framed fan mail decorates the busy waiting room where people sit calmly, knowing they will be seated strictly on a first-come, first-served basis. Part of the appeal is the '50s/Southern ambience, complete with cool car posters on wood-plank walls and period music, as it were, like the Everly Brothers, the Shirelles and Neil Sedaka, helping with your digestion. Everyone eats at plain tables or booths in two large rooms. ~ 5259 Poplar Avenue; 901-685-9744, 800-926-7597, fax 901-685-1102. BUDGET TO MODERATE.

> If barbecue is your poison, Memphis—the self-proclaimed Pork Barbecue Capital of the World— is the place to be.

Piñatas and neon signs brighten the interior of El Chico, which looks like a regular American Mexican restaurant in a shopping-center location. But this place offers many menu items not normally seen around Memphis, including veggie fajitas, chicken Monterey, flautas, *chalupa* salad, enchilada pie and a dynamite tortilla soup (not to mention Mexican apple pie). Service is prompt, friendly and knowledgeable in this large, upbeat restaurant. ~ 3491 Poplar Avenue; 901-323-9609, fax 901-323-5261. BUDGET TO MODERATE.

NIGHTLIFE Thursday through Saturday, local groups play a variety of jazz, blues and rock at **Satchmo's** in the Adam's Mark Hotel. ~ 939 Ridge Lake Boulevard; 901-684-6664.

PARKS **LICHTERMAN NATURE CENTER** 🏃 This 65-acre wildlife sanctuary is crisscrossed with self-guided trails; most loops take less than an hour to walk. You'll be wandering amid Southern hardwood forests, marshes, lakes and fields, containing, in all, some 350 varieties of plants, 45 types of reptiles and amphibians, 35 species of small mammals and 200 kinds of birds, including mallards and kingfishers. Also on the premises is a butterfly garden next to the greenhouse. Admission. ~ 5992 Quince Road; 901-767-7322.

Memphis Gay Scene

There's no single gay neighborhood in Memphis, but there are several restaurants and clubs that cater to a mostly gay clientele, especially in the Cooper-Young Historic District. The best source for more information is the **Memphis Gay & Lesbian Community Center**, which has recorded information and staff to answer questions each night between 7:30 and 11 p.m. ~ 901-278-4297.

DINING The Memphis Gay & Lesbian Community Center hotline recommends a few restaurants popular with gays and lesbians, including the following.

The **P&H Cafe** (for "poor and hungry") has a limited menu —burgers, melts, tamales and the occasional salmon patty (sometimes more on weekends)—but welcomes an after-theater crowd. Closed Sunday. ~ 1532 Madison Avenue; 901-726-0906. BUDGET.

SHOPPING **Bookstar** is not so much a gay bookshop as a store that welcomes everyone. A section of books is devoted to gay and lesbian issues;

a gay and lesbian book club meets here once a month in what used to be a movie theater. ~ 3402 Poplar Avenue; 901-323-9332.

The nightlife scene is a bit mercurial, but there's a trend toward fewer gay clubs offering drag shows and more gay and lesbian bars offering a chance to mingle and maybe join in some karaoke fun. Most gay bars and clubs serve beer only and are open until 3 a.m. You may usually bring your own bottle for mixed drinks. **NIGHTLIFE**

Metro Memphis features a drag show on Thursdays, when there's a cover charge (which includes a beer bust). ~ 1349 Autumn Avenue; 901-274-8010.

J-Wags is open 24/7, convenient for travelers suffering from jet lag. Tuesday is karaoke night and Friday and Saturday usually offer drag shows. The rest of the time deejays spin dance music starting at 3 a.m. It's strictly B.Y.O.B. Cover on Friday and Saturday. ~ 1268 Madison Avenue; 901-725-1909.

One of the most popular lesbian bars in town, **One More** has karaoke on Friday. ~ 217 Peabody Place; 901-278-6673.

The **Pumping Station**, a gay bar formerly called The Pipeline, is casual but discourages drag attire. Like most other gay bars, it gets rolling after 10 p.m. and is B.Y.O.B. ~ 1382 Poplar Avenue; 901-272-7600.

Retro has a full bar, a nightly happy hour and the occasional cabaret show. ~ 1394 Autumn Street; 901-274-8010.

Near Overton Square, **Back Street** attracts a mostly gay male crowd for shows and dancing. B.Y.O.B. Cover on Friday and Saturday nights. ~ 2018 Court Avenue; 901-276-5522. ◀ *HIDDEN*

The area south of South Parkway can't really be called a neighborhood. It's home to strip malls, light industry, motels and fast food outlets. There is not much to love about it, except that it's the locus of two top attractions, an ancient American Indian village and the last, great home of Elvis Presley. ▼▼▼▼▼▼▼▼▼▼▼ **South Memphis**

You don't have to be acquainted with any of the residents to visit the **Historic Elmwood Cemetery**, whose name was drawn out of a hat by its founders. Hundreds of trees shade the grounds where 70,000 people have been buried since 1852. Many of them perished in the yellow fever epidemics but you'll also come across the gravestones of two governors, three U.S. senators, 22 mayors, soldiers from all wars (including 19 Confederate generals), jazz singers, madams, suffragettes and other characters. The grounds are especially pretty in spring, when wildflowers bloom amid 80 acres studded with statuary, making it a lovely site for a picnic or a walk. Check out the 1866 Carpenter Gothic cottage topped by **SIGHTS**

◀ *HIDDEN*

a bell that tolls for each service—as it has done since 1870. ~ 824 South Dudley Street; 901-774-3212; www.elmwoodcemetery.org.

Isaac Hayes' 1972 "Superfly" Cadillac, Albert King's famous purple "Flying V" guitar and, believe it or not, a century-old church transported from the Delta are some of the 2000 exhibits at the **Stax Museum of American Soul**. Back in the 1970s, Stax Records was surrounded by so much talent it was dubbed "Souls-ville, U.S.A." And today you can tour the restored Studio A, where the legendary Stax sound was born, and listen to the gritty, raw, stripped-down music that launched America's hippest black entertainers of the era. Admission. ~ 926 East McLemore Avenue; 901-942-7685; www.soulsvilleusa.com.

HIDDEN ►

You've got to go out of your way to see the archaeological park known as **Chucalissa Village**. Drive south on Route 61, then west on Mitchell Road for four and a half miles to reach this unusual site. The Mississippian Indians who inhabited this region from around A.D. 1000 to 1500 are remembered here with a museum of prehistoric tools, weapons and pottery. The four-acre park sits atop the original site and offers a partially reconstructed village to tour. The museum is linked to the village grounds by a trench that was one of the first excavations. Along this walk through history, visitors can see a layer-by-layer view of the ancient occupation, beginning in prehistoric times. Several reconstructed huts surround the open plaza, and an audio-visual show tells the story of Chucalissa in detail. Closed Monday. Admission. ~ 1987 Indian Village Drive; 901-785-3160; www.people.memphis.edu/~chucalissa.

Flash forward to modern times by returning to Route 55, heading east and then exiting south on Route 5 (a.k.a. Elvis Presley Boulevard). The first, foremost and still the favorite tourist attraction in Memphis—or maybe all of Tennessee if you include foreign visitors—is **Graceland**. Elvis' family moved six times before he bought a bungalow on Audubon Drive in 1956 for $40,000 cash. His mom was still hanging out the wash to dry when Elvis finally figured Graceland was better suited to the superstar status he had achieved by '57. The 14-acre estate, his longtime home, is an absolute must-see for any American who's ever loved rock-and-roll, if not sequined white jumpsuits. Tupelo-born but Memphis-made, Elvis died here in 1977. He must be spinning in his grave (*located here, folks, on your right—Elvis' actual burial plot*) at the thought of millions of strangers trampling through his once-hallowed retreat. While he's at it, he might cringe: who among us would want our 1970s decorating scheme to be seen a quarter of a century later? It's all here . . . the lime green shag carpeting with matching ceiling, the mirrored hallways, the all-white living room, the 14 TV sets, the

In a career that spanned three decades, Elvis Presley performed at the Grand Ole Opry only once.

atrocious furniture in the "jungle room." Even so, it's pretty wonderful to be in the presence, more or less, of The King. Especially impressive is the Trophy Building, which houses the huge collection of gold records and awards. His recordings have sold a billion copies, a world record; if they were laid end to end, the taped commentary tells us, they'd wrap around the equator. Twice. After leaving the mansion itself, visitors return via shuttle bus to the money-making machine that is Graceland Plaza, replete with gift shops proffering everything Elvis from music boxes to coffee mugs. Separate tours, available as part of a package, include the airplanes and the automobiles. There are three restaurants on site, should you swoon. Closed Tuesday from November through February. Admission. ~ 3734 Elvis Presley Boulevard; 901-332-3322, 800-238-2000; www.elvis.com/graceland.

The one-story, 108-room **Memphis Inn** is the sole nonchain motel in the general neighborhood of the airport. There's not much to distinguish it from the outside—or the inside, for that matter—but the rooms are neat and tidy. ~ 4879 American Way; 901-794-8300, fax 901-362-5208. BUDGET.

LODGING

If The King ever does show up again, you might keep an eye out for him at **Elvis Presley's Heartbreak Hotel**. Check into the red-hot Burning Love Suite—one of the four super-pricey themed suites here—and look around in all the bedrooms and baths and even in the kitchen or dining room. Five smaller suites and a host of standard rooms are also available at this 128-room boutique hotel across the street from Graceland. The usual color scheme prevails: creamy walls, blond furnishings and framed, black-and-white Elvis photos. Amenities include continuous Elvis videos and free airport shuttle and continental breakfast. ~ 3677 Elvis Presley Boulevard; 901-332-1000, 877-777-0606, fax 901-332-2107; www.elvis.com/epheartbreakhotel. DELUXE TO ULTRA-DELUXE.

T. O. FULLER STATE PARK ⤛ Named for Dr. Thomas Oscar Fuller, a leading clergyman and educator, this 384-acre park is not one of Tennessee's fanciest. It's pleasant, with paved roads and plenty of shade trees, but its main draw is its proximity to Chucalissa Indian Village, the archaeological site administered by the University of Memphis. Trailers, motor homes and recreational vehicles are welcome to park overnight, making it a convenient location if you're planning to spend much time at either Chucalissa or Graceland, only a few miles to the east. Facilities include a swimming pool, tennis courts, picnic tables and a visitors center with a modest exhibit on major Memphis attractions, plus an 18-hole golf course laid out on the shores of McKellar Lake, a sort of inlet between the Harbor Channel and the Mississippi River. Day-use

PARKS

fee, $3. ~ 1500 Mitchell Road West, 11 miles southwest of downtown Memphis via Route 55 and Route 61S; 901-543-7581.

▲ There are 45 campsites with electricity and water; $16.25 per night.

Outdoor Adventures

GOLF

All courses rent carts unless otherwise noted. On the east side of town, the semiprivate, 18-hole **Big Creek Golf Club** has a 7000-yard championship course with bent-grass greens and Bermuda fairways. ~ 6195 Woodstock/Cuba Road, five miles south of Millington off Route 51; 901-358-0020.

Built in the early 1970s but open to the public only since 1988, the 18-hole **Stonebridge Golf Course** is one of the most challenging in Memphis. It was designed by George Cobb, who is responsible for the so-called Amen Corner at the Augusta National Golf Club. The layout is fairly long, with lots of woods and narrow tees to challenge all levels of golfers. ~ 3049 Davies Plantation Road South; 901-382-1886.

Both 9- and 18-hole municipal golf courses are managed by the Memphis Park Commission. A favorite is **Overton Park**, designed in 1906. ~ Poplar Avenue and East Parkway; 901-454-5200. **Riverside** is another popular course. ~ 465 South Parkway West; 901-774-4340. Or try the 18 holes at **Audubon Park**. ~ 4160 Park Avenue; 901-683-6941.

An 18-hole public course is south Memphis' T. O. **Fuller State Park**. ~ 1500 Mitchell Road, Memphis; 901-543-7771.

TENNIS

No matter how hot or cold it is outside, the four indoor courts at the **Leftwich Tennis Center** are dry and warm. All these, as well as some of the ten outdoor courts, are lit for night play. Reservations, in 90-minute increments, are always a good idea at this center in the neighborhood of Goodlett Street and Highland Avenue. ~ 4145 Southern Avenue; 901-685-7907.

Most municipal courts are open to the public for a fee. Among the more centrally located are those at the **Wolbrecht Tennis Center** near Park Avenue, which has six outdoor courts and two indoor, all of them lit for night play. ~ 1645 Ridgeway Road; 901-767-2889.

RIDING STABLES

Shelby Farms Stables, located near Cordova, has nearly 400 acres on which to take guided rides through pastures and woods where wildlife can be seen. To get around the place takes about an hour. ~ 7171 Mullins Station Road; 901-382-4250, 901-382-2249.

BIKING

Meeman-Shelby Forest State Park has a smooth and easily accessible four-mile paved loop that starts from the parking lot (at picnic shelter 2) and runs through a mature hardwood forest atop

a ridge, ending on the Chickasaw Bluffs. Along the way are picnic tables in grassy clearings. The trailhead is west of the park
entrance, one mile past the visitors center.

In 1996, the 177-mile Tennessee segment of the **Mississippi
River Trail** was launched. Depending on where you ride, you
may find yourself along winding forested
roads, alongside fields and river bluff or a
combination thereof. In Memphis, the trailhead begins near the Visitors Welcome Center
on Jefferson Street, where you can pick up a
map. Various excursions can be taken all the
way to Reelfoot Lake. A 30-mile roundtrip to
Meeman-Shelby Forest State Park is a good way to
start your exploration. There are six two-bedroom
cabins at the park on the shore of Poplar Tree Lake.
To make reservations, contact the visitors center there at
901-876-5215. ~ Lower Mississippi Delta Development Center,
777 Walnut Grove Road; 901-753-1400; www.bicyclemrt.org.
Bike Repairs Bikes Plus has a full-service shop and a mobile repair unit for service on the route north of Memphis. ~ 7970 Gia-
cosa Place #101; 901-385-8788.

A year-round ice-skating rink
draws the public to the Ice
Chalet, even when it's not swel-
tering outside. Skate rentals
and instruction are available.
Admission. ~ Mall of
Memphis; 901-362-8877.

All distances for hiking trails are one way unless otherwise noted.

Nearly three miles of self-guided trail loops have been created
within the 65 acres of forest, marsh, lake and field in the **Lichterman Nature Center** in east Memphis.

Thirteen miles north of Memphis, the Meeman-Shelby Forest
State Park has a number of hiking trails, including two difficult
routes. The **Chickasaw Bluffs Trail** (8 miles), at the north end of
the park just east of the Mississippi River Group Camp, begins
at the top of a ridge, then descends and follows a stream that it
crosses several times. (The trail is blazed in white.) It crosses an
old road bridge, then rises and reenters the forest to meet the Woodland Trail Juncture, which is blazed in red. It then rises steeply to
the Woodland Trail Shelter. The trail continues across a paved
road, converges with the Pioneer Springs Trail (blue), then goes
up and down a ridge, paralleling the bike trail to the left. It passes
through a horsetail thicket, then rises above a cypress-stumped
bottomland on the right. (Because this is swampy, be sure to wear
insect repellent.) Eventually the trail crosses Pioneer Springs, then
continues to Poplar Tree Lake before going up a steep hill to the
trail end at the lake parking lot.

The easy **Woodland Trail** (3 miles roundtrip) has a beginning
and an ending at the park's nature museum. After beginning as a
straight ridge-top path, it descends on a tree-root "staircase" to
a fork. To the right is a one-mile loop that is mostly level. It leads
through bamboo and hooks up with a .8-mile spur to the Dogwood

HIKING

Ridge campground. To the left of the original fork, a longer loop passes a bluff, leads through forests (with springtime wildflowers), crosses a stream and then goes up and down several times.

Transportation

CAR

Route 40 is the main east–west route connecting Memphis with Nashville to the east and St. Louis to the west. To reach downtown from the east, follow Route 40 as it loops around the northern rim of the city before crossing the Mississippi River. Then exit at Danny Thomas Boulevard and turn right toward the river on one of the westbound one-way streets. **Route 240** splits from Route 40 on the east side of Memphis, and makes the southern loop until it intersects with Route 55. **Route 55**, accessible in the southwest part of the city, runs north and south. When driving around Memphis, remember it's legal to turn right at a red light, as long as you come to a full and safe stop first.

AIR

Memphis International Airport is located off Route 240 about 11 miles south of downtown. It is served by seven major carriers, including American, Continental Express, Delta, KLM, Northwest, United and US Airways. ~ 901-922-8000; www.mscaa.com.

TRAIN

Amtrak has a station in Memphis. ~ 545 South Main Street, near Calhoun Street; 901-526-0052, 800-872-7245; www.amtrak.com.

BUS

Greyhound Bus Lines has a location downtown, near some of the larger hotels. ~ 203 Union Avenue; 901-523-1184, 800-231-2222; www.greyhound.com.

BOAT

The **Delta Queen** makes a stop at Memphis on its way up and down the Mississippi River and other waterways. New Orleans, St. Louis, Tulsa and Little Rock are among the ports. The ship docks at the foot of Beale Street. For schedule details, call American Classic Voyages. ~ 504-586-0631, 800-543-7637; www.delta queen.com.

CAR RENTALS

Several automobile rental agencies are located within a shuttle-bus drive of the Memphis International Airport, on either Rental Road or Airways Boulevard. They include **Alamo Rent A Car** (800-327-9633), **Avis Rent A Car** (800-230-4898), **Budget Rent A Car** (800-879-1227), **Dollar Rent A Car** (800-800-4000), **Enterprise Rent A Car** (800-325-8007), **Hertz Rent A Car** (800-654-3131) and **Thrifty Car Rental** (800-847-3489).

PUBLIC TRANSIT

You can ride the pretty green **Main Street Trolley** all the way from Butler Avenue (south of Beale Street) to Overton Avenue (near the Pyramid) for 50 cents each way (25 cents for seniors and persons with disabilities; free for children ages four and under). Weekdays from 11 a.m. to 1:30 p.m., there's a lunchtime fare of 25 cents. There are 11 on-and-off points along the two-and-a-half-mile route, which operates from 6 a.m. to 12 midnight Monday through Thursday and until 1 a.m. on Friday; from 9:30 a.m. to 1 a.m. on Saturday and from 10 a.m. to 6 p.m. on Sunday, plus extended hours during special events. The trolleys, which run the same route as their mule-drawn predecessors, were built between 1912 and 1940 and have been restored with brass seat and window accents and antique light fixtures. There is also a Riverfront Loop, where authentic vintage trolleys run—southbound only—along the scenic Riverside Drive parallel to the Main Street Route. To return north via trolley, passengers take the Main Street Trolley from the Butler Avenue station. ~ 901-274-6282.

For getting around the rest of Memphis, the **Memphis Area Transit Authority** (MATA) runs buses all over town. ~ 901-274-6282; www.matatransit.com.

Yellow Cab (901-577-7777) and **City Wide Cab Company** (901-324-4202) are the biggest taxi companies serving all of Memphis. The trip from Memphis International Airport into downtown Memphis takes about 20 minutes and costs around $21.

TAXIS

TWELVE

Southwest Tennessee

The southernmost stretch of Tennessee's Western Plains is home to a motley mix of towns. Tiny LaGrange was once expected to become a big city. Jackson is a big city, but seems like a town. Shiloh is not really a town, but a village, famous as the site of an exceptionally bloody Civil War battle.

Although Memphis has had nowhere to expand but eastward, it's surprising how quickly all traces of urban life fade away as you head east from the mighty Mississippi River. Most of the land is flat along the border with the state of Mississippi. Closer to Jackson, two state parks, Natchez Trace and Chickasaw, claim some of the hilliest terrain in this part of the state.

Jackson, with nearly 60,000 residents, is the second-biggest city in southwest Tennessee after Memphis. It is accessible via Route 40, about 85 miles northeast of Memphis and 125 miles southwest of Nashville. The name seemed appropriate when the place was settled early in the 18th century, since many residents were either related to General Andrew Jackson or had fought with him. The founding fathers must have envisioned a grand future for Jackson; they arranged broad boulevards all around the town's center. In 1822, when lots were auctioned off, the proceeds were considerably enlivened by a civic allocation of $20 worth of whiskey.

Occupied by both Union and Confederate forces during the Civil War, Jackson fell to Union general John P. Hatch in July 1863, not long after Memphis surrendered. Today Jackson is more linked with the name of Casey Jones than with that of its namesake. John Luther Jones was a hometown boy who became a railroad engineer with the Illinois Central line. His colleagues nicknamed him Casey because he had spent much of his childhood in the Kentucky town of Cayce, and Casey was easier to spell. Long before his date with history, Casey was known for his trademark whippoorwill train whistle. If you've heard the song "The Ballad of Casey Jones"—which Carl Sandburg heralded as the greatest ballad ever written—you know what happened on the night of April 30, 1900. Jones, 36, didn't usually engineer the fast train on the 188-mile run between Memphis and Canton,

330

Mississippi, but that night he substituted for an ill coworker. As Jones' train rounded a curve near Vaughan, Mississippi, at a 75-mile-per-hour clip, Jones saw the caboose of another southbound train right in front of him. Slamming on the brakes, Jones called for the fireman to jump. Jones stayed the course, and even though he got his train to slow down to 35, it crashed into the caboose, killing him instantly. He was the only casualty. The ballad written by Jones' friend Wallace Saunders became famous, inspiring an entire genre of railroad songs.

After Jones' widow died, their home in downtown Jackson was turned into a museum. It was then moved in 1980 to an exit off Route 40 as part of the Casey Jones Home and Railroad Museum Village.

The prettiest town in these parts is LaGrange, an outpost of antebellum architecture 50 miles east of Memphis on Route 57. LaGrange was an Indian trading post called Cluster of Pines in the early 19th century, and had become a thriving settlement by 1824, when Fayette County was formed. Situated on a 300-foot bluff above the Wolf River, it quickly became the wealthiest and most advanced Tennessee settlement west of Nashville, certainly more sophisticated than the rowdy river town of Memphis. Then it fell victim to overzealous expansionists. Like many of its neighbors, LaGrange was gripped with railroad-building fever. A group of local businessmen formed their own railway line in 1835, but the financial crash of 1837 delivered the fatal blow to the town's future as Memphis' better. Still, the town trucked along, building churches and colleges and supporting a newspaper, foundry, livery stables, jewelry and dry-goods stores and many small businesses. Unfortunately, the town occupied a perfect situation for a military outpost—the views from LaGrange extend for 25 miles—and Federal troops occupied it from 1862 until the end of the war. Perhaps because Union soldiers were living in some of the gracious antebellum homes, little structural damage was done to LaGrange—other than the burning of wooden sidewalks and fences for firewood. Touring these residential streets is now a popular tourist pastime.

Grand Junction and its centerpiece, the Ames Plantation, are in the heart of bird-hunting country. The level landscape and plentiful habitat makes this one of the state's most popular destinations for the sport, and people take it seriously in these parts. If you aren't into hunting, or at least into bird dogs, you may want to keep driving, because there's not a great deal more to see around here, and no recommended dining or nightlife.

Heading east, the next city is Savannah, but south and west of it are the major attractions along this stretch of the Tennessee River, Shiloh National Military Park and the Pickwick Dam. Allow a couple of hours for touring the legendary Civil War battlefield, and keep an eye on the gas gauge because about the only place to fill up in this neighborhood is around the intersection of Route 142 and Route 57 in Counce. Savannah is on the far side of the river, which was founded in the 1820s and survived occupation by Federal generals Grant and Sherman. Some of the very residences where the officers were headquartered can be seen today, and one is open to the public as an inn. In the 1990s, Savannah gained a modicum of fame with the television miniseries *Queen*, a story inspired by Alex (*Roots*) Haley's paternal grandmother, longtime local resident Queen Haley, who is buried in the Savannah cemetery.

Forty-five miles east of Savannah, Route 64 leads to the Natchez Trace Parkway, now a paved, two-lane highway that follows the path of the original trace from Natchez, Mississippi, to the southeast outskirts of Nashville.

▼▼▼▼▼▼▼▼▼▼▼▼▼▼▼▼

Memphis to Chickasaw State Rustic Park

LaGrange is a tiny town that packs a lot of charm and history into a few square blocks. Grand Junction and Bolivar are larger, but Bolivar is the only thing even approaching a city. Bolivar has a historic district you can tour in a car.

SIGHTS

Heading east from Memphis on Route 57, you probably won't want to stop until you arrive in **LaGrange**. Then you'll want to get out and poke around.

From time to time, tours are offered of some of the pretty old structures in LaGrange. All the homes are private residences, but visitors are welcome to drive or walk by. **Tiara**, built in 1845, got its name from a cupola that was once blown off during a tornado, carried clear to Hickory Valley ten miles away and reattached. ~ On 4th Street one block north of Route 57, LaGrange.

Two blocks east, on Commerce Street, you can enter the **Immanuel Episcopal Church**, built in 1842 in what is called the English country style. It was used as a hospital and barracks during the Civil War, when its pews were removed and fashioned into coffins for the Union casualties. ~ Commerce Street, LaGrange.

The most famous house locally, though, is **Woodlawn**, located a mile east of downtown on Route 57. A white two-story Colonial, the 1828 home was commandeered during the war as headquarters for General William T. Sherman. ~ Route 57, LaGrange.

Each October, several residential streets here are featured on an Architectural Treasures of Fayette County Home Tour. For information, contact the **Fayette County Chamber of Commerce**. ~ P.O. Box 411, Somerville, TN 38068; 901-465-8690.

Situated on some of the highest terrain in west Tennessee about 18 miles south of Jackson, **Chickasaw State Rustic Park** boasts 14,384 acres of timberland, 1280 acres of which are used for recreation. The park has 50 miles of roads and trails open for horseback riding in the summer. In warm weather, a park recreation director conducts group games, arts and crafts, evening movies, campfire programs and hayrides. ~ 20 Cabin Lane, Henderson; 731-989-5141; www.tnstateparks.com.

The **Ames Plantation** is the site of the National Field Trial Championship for bird dogs held each February. But the turn-of-the-20th-century plantation also has standing attractions, including the Ames Manor House and stables, a 19th-century farmstead (complete with smokehouse and other outbuildings) and an early-19th-century log cabin relocated here and refurbished in period pieces. Tours are available on the fourth

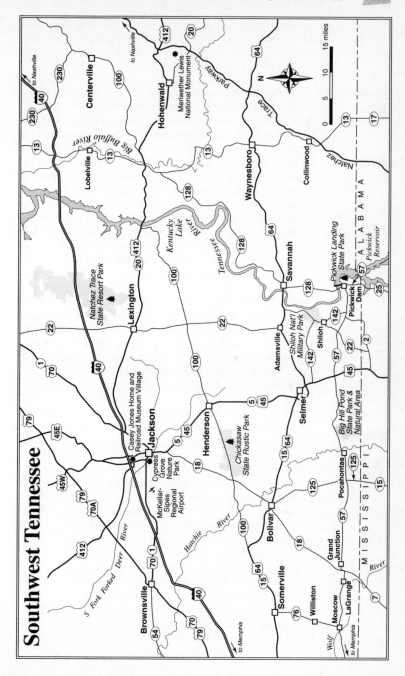

Southwest Tennessee

Tuesday afternoon of each month from March through October. Admission. ~ 4275 Buford Ellington Road, Grand Junction; 901-878-1067, fax 901-878-1068; www.amesplantation.org, e-mail info@amesplantation.org.

LODGING   Looking as out-of-place among more modern buildings as a hoop skirt at a high-school prom, **Magnolia Manor** is the belle of Bolivar. Built in 1849 for a local judge, the white-columned Georgian-style home is rectangular, with halls on both floors running the depth of the house. It's hard to prove, but lore has it that a mark on the walnut staircase was put there during the war by an enraged General Sherman; Civil War records indicate that General Grant's troops were stationed near Magnolia Manor, and that the general set up headquarters in the mansion. The manor has been restored, with period color schemes and appropriate furnishings, including chandeliers and elaborate bedsteads in four guest rooms. Since opening the inn, the owners have restored an 1849 cottage that has a bedroom, a living room with fireplace and a kitchen. Full breakfast is included. ~ 418 North Main Street, Bolivar; phone/fax 731-658-6700. MODERATE TO DELUXE.

The 13 vacation cottages at **Chickasaw State Rustic Park** are nestled among tall pines and located within easy access of Lake Placid. Some of them accommodate up to six people. All are equipped for housekeeping and have fireplaces and televisions. From June through August, they can be rented by the week. ~ 20 Cabin Lane, Henderson; 800-458-1752; www.tnstateparks.com. MODERATE.

DINING   If you want to eat around Somerville, you'll want to go to **Hut the Restaurant**. Everybody else does. The menu at this country-

AUTHOR FAVORITE

sights   As a dog person, I found the **National Bird Dog Museum** endearing. Here in prime birdhunting country, the museum has a special section devoted to the Field Trial Hall of Fame for pointing dogs. Paintings, photographs and even sculptures of virtually every type of hunting dog known to humankind fill the warehouse space at this museum, dedicated to the teamwork between human and dog that has been part of the American landscape for more than two centuries. The serious scholar, or major fan, can explore video films and a library where each breed can be studied at length. Even if you don't hunt, you may well find the portraits of setters, spaniels, retrievers and lesser-known breeds informative and rather touching. Closed Monday. ~ 505 West Route 57, Grand Junction; 731-764-2058, fax 731-764-3004; www.fielddog.com.

style place is mostly barbecue but also includes pork chops, chicken pot pies, grilled chicken salads and sandwiches, burgers and, by far the most expensive item at $10.25, a rib-eye platter. The Hut is easy to find; it's right across the street from the jail. ~ 16920 Route 64, Somerville; 901-465-3458. BUDGET.

The **Chickasaw State Rustic Park Restaurant** is open for breakfast, lunch and dinner Thursday through Sunday. Like most park eateries, it sticks to regional fare, home-style country cooking and full buffets. Closed Monday through Wednesday. ~ 20 Cabin Lane, Henderson; 731-989-7558. BUDGET TO MODERATE.

The most unusual store in southwest Tennessee is **Cogbill's General Store & Museum**, where everything old is new again. Founded nearly a century ago as a dry-goods store and co-owned by Mr. Cogbill's granddaughter, the store still sells sarsaparilla, hoop cheese and Mennonite breads and cakes, but more to the point it carries the crafts of more than 100 artisans. Birdhouses and feeders, books, Victorian prints, linens, glassware and other handmade items make browsing simply irresistible. Closed Monday through Wednesday. ~ 14840 LaGrange Road, LaGrange; 731-878-1235.

SHOPPING

You'll find a cache of English and American antiques at **Wren's Nest Antiques**, along with prints, china, lamps and one-of-a-kind gift items. Closed Saturday through Monday. ~ 308 Bills Street, Bolivar; 731-658-3235.

Small antiques and collectibles, from tea cups to handkerchiefs, tempt shoppers and diners both at **Me and My Tea Room**. Closed Monday and occasional Saturdays. ~ 111 West Court Square, Somerville; 901-465-0077.

CHICKASAW STATE RUSTIC PARK 🕴🏇⛵🚣 This 14,384-acre park is among the few in Tennessee where visitors can rent horses for riding along 50 miles of roads and trails. Named for the American Indians who lived here prior to the Jackson Purchase of 1819, the park is full of timberlands, crisscrossed with fire trails and crowned with Lake Placid. Chickasaw has 13 cabins, tennis courts, a golf course, basketball courts, playgrounds, a volleyball court, a lighted ball field and an archery court. Other amenities include a restaurant (open for dinner only on weekdays and three meals on weekends; closed Monday through Wednesday) and a lake with part of the shoreline roped off for swimming. Limited activities are allowed Labor Day through Memorial Day. ~ 20 Cabin Lane, Henderson; 901-989-5141, 800-458-1752.

PARKS

▲ There are 29 tent-only sites, $11 per night; 183 sites with hookups, $17 per night; 13 cabins, $78 per night (for more information on the cabins, see "Lodging" above).

Jackson Area

From Grand Junction, you can head north through Bolivar to Chickasaw State Park and then to Jackson, which straddles Route 40, or continue touring the region close to the Mississippi state line. If you do go to Jackson, you'll find the major attraction in this not-very-pretty industrial city to be a real piece of American history.

SIGHTS

Jackson isn't a big tourist town. Although it grew rapidly as a railroad center in the mid-19th century, it has never become really urban, but seems more like one sprawling small town. You don't have to be an aficionado of railroad lore to appreciate the **Casey Jones Home and Railroad Museum Village**—but it helps if you at least care about Americana. The museum houses a lot of memorabilia related not only to the brave John Luther Jones, who died trying to prevent the biggest wreck in Mississippi history, but also to the lore of the rails themselves. A short, well-done video also tells the story of "The Ballad of Casey Jones," which, one learns, was written by a now-obscure wiper engineer named Wallace Saunders who sold the song for a bottle of whiskey. Admission. ~ Casey Jones Village, at Route 45 Bypass at Exit 80A off Route 40, Jackson; 731-668-1222, fax 731-664-7782; www.caseyjones.com.

Now that rockabilly has regained some respect, it's not so funny that there is an **International Rockabilly Hall of Fame & Museum**, appropriately located about halfway between Nashville (home of country music and birthplace of hillbilly music) and Memphis (hotbed for early rock and roll, R&B and blues). Some folks in fact just say that Jackson is "between Graceland and the Grand Ole Opry." Both fans and those who've never much cottoned to this genre can listen to tapes and watch films narrated by stars the museum has honored, notably Carl Perkins and Roy Orbison. The museum also houses memorabilia and serves as a resource center. Tours are given from 10 a.m. to 4 p.m. Monday through Friday and at 6 p.m. Monday and 6:30 p.m. Friday. Admission. ~ 105 North Church Street, Jackson; 731-423-5440; www.rockabillyhall.org.

LODGING

Within the major roadside attraction that is Casey Jones Village is a basic motel. **Casey Jones Station Inn** has two floors and 51 rooms that are rather spacious for the price, with wooden bedsteads, paisley bedspreads and well-designed bath and dressing areas. Not much in the way of ambience, but a good landing spot, especially for railroad fans and families with kids to be entertained. There are also much smaller accommodations in an old caboose and an 1890s railcar. Buffet breakfast is included. ~ At 1943 Route 45 Bypass at Exit 80A off Route 40, Jackson; 731-668-3636, 800-628-2812; www.caseyjonesvillage.com. BUDGET TO MODERATE.

The Trail of Tears

The Cherokee, the largest single American Indian group in the southeastern United States, had developed an advanced agricultural society long before the Spanish explorer Hernando de Soto met them in 1540. Had they known what meeting white men would spell for their future, that introduction would have given them fair warning.

In 1820 the Cherokee Nation had established a republican form of government with a constitution calling for a principal chief, a senate and a house of representatives—all elective positions. The Nation created a judiciary and a legal system with powers to levy taxes, license white traders and perform other functions. Much of the credit for the Cherokees' sophisticated society is laid at the feet of Sequoyah. Half-Cherokee and half-white, Sequoyah created a syllabic alphabet of the Cherokee language and presented it to tribal leaders in 1821. Literacy led to the keeping of tribal records and, ultimately to the publication of newspapers.

By 1827 the Cherokee had relocated their capital to New Etowah, in north Georgia. The next year, gold was discovered in nearby Dahlonega, an event that inspired the Georgia legislature to enact laws stripping the tribal members of their right to own property, to sue white men or even to assemble. The Indians re-established their capital in Tennessee, where they sought redress in federal court while white men seized their former homes and property in Georgia.

Their chances were doomed, however. In 1829, the new U.S. president, Andrew Jackson, made clear his intention to force American Indians to move west of the Mississippi River, championing the Indian Removal Act as his weapon of choice. For several years, the Cherokee tried to negotiate favorable financial terms for what seemed an inevitable future. In 1835 Cherokee fate was sealed when a treaty was signed—by only a tiny fraction of tribal members—allowing all their tribal land east of the Mississippi to be ceded to the United States. Although some Cherokee had moved earlier, the majority resisted migration until the summer of 1838.

That year, soldiers approached each house and surrounded it while residents were rounded up and led out. By June the long march along the Trail of Tears had begun. The first of 13 detachments (some 13,000 Cherokee in all) encountered horrific heat; the groups that left in the fall encountered an early winter. The contractors the Cherokee had put in charge failed to carry sufficient food; malnutrition led to cholera and smallpox, which felled between 10 and 25 percent of the tribe during the six months it took to travel the 1200-mile distance to Oklahoma.

DINING   Maybe it was because he grew up a poor sharecropper's son in
Lake County, but Perkins will never be hungry again. Nor will
you, given the portions at **Suede's**. It helps to know that the joint
is named for the song Perkins wrote and recorded in 1956, a little ditty called "Blue Suede Shoes." Indeed, a pair of 'em twirls
above the restaurant, which otherwise looks like something you
might find on or near the coast of New England. Lots of steaks
anchor the dinner menu, along with fried shrimp and catfish, Cajun chicken and a whole mess o' barbecue items. Rock-and-roll
memorabilia of Perkins, Elvis Presley and Johnny Cash cover most
of the walls in the perky blue, pink and white interior. Closed
Monday. ~ 2263 North Highland Avenue, Jackson; 731-664-
1956, fax 731-664-0919. BUDGET TO MODERATE.

This part of Tennessee is especially known as the Catfish Capital, where the fish of choice is delicious fried and accompanied
HIDDEN ▶   by tartar sauce. **Barnhill's Buffet** serves this delicacy as well as
fried chicken, grilled and carved meats, fresh salads, vegetables
and breads and homemade dessert at their all-you-can-eat buffets. Friday is seafood night. This is a good place to remember if
you're hungry in the middle of the afternoon, since it's open daily
from late morning until 8 p.m. ~ 660 Carriage House Drive,
Jackson; 713-664-5163. BUDGET TO MODERATE.

SHOPPING   There's a lot of junk at **Brooks Shaw & Son's Old Country Store**,
but also some finds among the antiques and souvenirs. It's a good
place to browse before or after a meal in the restaurant under the
same roof. ~ 56 Casey Jones Lane, Jackson; 731-668-1223.

The **Carriage House Antique Market** could better be described as a 15,000-square-foot mall filled with an assortment of
antiques, art, books, children's clothing, collectibles and items
for the home. ~ 195 Carriage House Drive, off Route 40 at Exit
80 or Exit 82, Jackson; 731-664-6678.

NIGHTLIFE   The **International Rockabilly Hall of Fame & Museum** pulses
with live music—you know what kind—on Friday night, pre-
ceded by tours of the facility. They also offer dance lessons on
Monday evening. Cover. ~ 105 North Church Street, Jackson;
731-423-5440.

PARKS   **CYPRESS GROVE NATURE PARK** 🏃 A 4800-foot elevated
wooden boardwalk twists and turns through this 165-acre cypress
HIDDEN ▶   park, tucked away near a major thoroughfare. It's one of the most
peaceful parks in southwest Tennessee. For better views, the park
has an observation tower from which visitors can watch the many
birds that thrive in the preserve. Keep an eye out for red-tailed
hawks, wood ducks, green herons, owls, eagles and vultures, as

well as for muskrats, cottonmouth snakes, white-tailed deer, bull-frogs and other denizens of the forest. There is also a raptor center that houses birds of prey in an educational center. Facilities are limited to restrooms. ~ Off Route 70W, one and a quarter miles west of the intersection of Route 45 Bypass and Route 70, Jackson; 731-425-8364, 731-425-8316.

NATCHEZ TRACE STATE RESORT PARK

⬦ This park encompasses more than 14,000 acres within the 48,000-acre Natchez Trace State Forest, the largest in the state. Because of the high volume of people (and the highway robbers who preyed on travelers) moving along the original Natchez Trace (now formally known as the Natchez Trace Parkway), a western spur was developed as an alternate route in the 18th and 19th centuries. In 1814, Andrew Jackson traveled down the western route after the Battle of 1812. Within the vast, scenic park are four lakes; Pin Oak and Cub Creek are the best-developed areas. Picnic facilities, a camp store and service station, an archery range, tennis courts, an equestrian center, cabins, a 47-room inn and a restaurant are among the numerous amenities. ~ Located off Route 40, 40 miles northeast of Jackson; 731-968-3742, 800-250-8616.

▲ There are 144 campsites with water and electricity; $17 to $19 per night. Reservations: 731-968-8176, 800-421-6683.

BIG HILL POND STATE PARK AND NATURAL AREA

⬦ If you drove about 45 miles south of Jackson via Route 45 (or 75 miles east from Memphis on Route 57), you'd come across a park beloved for its varied landscape, nearly 5000 acres encompassing rivers and floodplains, swamps and lakes, meadows and hills. It's not hard to imagine why Chicksaw Indians chose to live here. Bald cypress, sweet gum, weeping willow and tupelo grow in the wetlands, while the valleys are lush with second-growth oaks, black gum, willow elm, tulip poplar, cedar, pine and birch. Naturally, it's popular with hikers, who have a choice of 20 miles of marked loop and interconnecting trails; you can hike as little as half a mile or as much as five and a half miles on a single trail. For a fabulous view of the surroundings, take the Boardwalk, Tennessee's longest wooden walkway, through Dismal Swamp and climb the 73-foot Tuscumbia Trail tower. Keep an eye out for Civil War–era earthworks (designed to fit a man or a cannon) used to protect the Memphis-Charleston railroad that runs through this area. A dam created the 165-acre Travis McNatt Lake, popular for catfish, bass and bream fishing (the bass limit is

> The passion flower, Tennessee's state wildflower, has no aphrodisiacal qualities; its name derives from early missionaries who perceived symbols of the crucifixion of Jesus Christ in the flower's stamens.

20 per person, and the fish must be at least 12 inches). Amenities are extensive for a "rustic" park and include a basketball court, a playground complete with a jungle gym, an archery range, picnic grounds and restrooms and showers near the campsites. Day-use fee, $3. ~ 984 John Howell Road, Pocahontas; 731-645-7967.

▲ There are 30 campsites, no hookups; $13 per night.

▼▼▼▼▼▼▼▼▼▼▼▼▼

Shiloh to Savannah

The presence of the Pickwick Dam dominates this wedge of southwest Tennessee, where fishing and recreation are enhanced by the reservoir. Nearby Shiloh, on the banks of the Tennessee River, was the scene of one of the bloodiest battles in the entire Civil War. Savannah, with a population of 7000, is what passes for a big city in southwest Tennessee. Except for Bolivar, few other towns are large enough to have recognizable cross streets.

SIGHTS

Heading south out of Jackson along Route 45, then east along Route 64, you'll come to the town of **Adamsville**, due north of Shiloh National Military Park. Remember the *Walking Tall* movies? There really was a Buford Pusser, and today you can tour the **Buford Pusser Home & Museum**, the residence of this latter-day Davy Crockett–Elliot Ness character. A one-time professional wrestler and chief of police, Pusser became at the age of 26 the youngest sheriff (of McNairy County) in Tennessee. In the late 1960s, he shut down 87 stills, ran gambling and prostitution rings out of town and killed two people in self-defense. He survived an assassination attempt only to perish, in 1974, in a fiery car crash—allegedly an accident. The one-story brick family home is still filled with the furniture and memorabilia; nearby is the cemetery where Pusser and his wife are buried. Admission. ~ 342 Pusser Street, Adamsville, at Routes 2 and 117; 731-632-4080.

Five miles west of Adamsville on Route 64 is a roadside plaque that commemorates the site of Buford Pusser's fatal crash.

Almost due south of Natchez Trace State Park, via Route 22, is one of the most extensive parks devoted to the War Between the States. The largest battle of the 1862 Civil War campaign for control of the railroads and the lower Mississippi River Valley was fought in a place whose name reverberates with historical meaning.

Shiloh National Military Park was established in 1894 to preserve that ground; it was consolidated into the National Park System in 1933. More than 3000 Union soldiers are buried in Shiloh National Cemetery, in both marked and unmarked graves. The Confederate dead were buried in trenches located throughout the battlefield, five of which are marked. They were buried in haste, due to health concerns of the victorious Union troops, who camped on the field of battle for weeks afterward.

These are only some of the moving sights in what is really a beautiful natural setting, nearly 4000 acres in all. The visitors center dispenses maps, including a nine-and-a-half-mile auto tour route, but visitors can walk to many of the points of interest throughout the forests and fields, which include 200 Civil War cannons, 151 monuments and some 600 troop position markers that help tell the story of General Ulysses S. Grant's victory over General Pierre G. T. Beauregard. In all, nearly 24,000 men were killed, wounded or declared missing in action. Also found in the park are prehistoric Indian mounds and a village site registered as a National Historic Landmark. Admission. ~ 1055 Pittsburgh Landing Road, Shiloh; 731-689-5275, fax 731-689-5054; www. nps.gov/shilo.

From the park, continue south on Route 22 to the intersection with Route 57, and continue east until you reach the Tennessee River. Construction on the 113-foot-high **Pickwick Landing Dam** was begun in 1934, not long after the Tennessee Valley Authority was established, and the 53-mile-long lake began to fill four years later. It was built both for flood control and to generate hydroelectric power. A series of locks allows towboats and barges to travel up and down the Tennessee River. Visitors can watch all this and also take a self-guided tour of the **Tennessee River Waterways Museum.** ~ Route 128, Pickwick Dam; 731-925-4346, 800-552-3866, fax 731-925-1640.

Up the Tennessee River about a half-hour's drive from the Pickwick Landing Dam is **Savannah,** a pretty old town with a nifty little museum. The **Tennessee River Museum,** housed on one floor of the red-brick chamber of commerce building in the heart of town, is a work in progress. Already ensconced, though, is the Riverboat Room, which tells the story of steamboats on the river through pictures and prints (and a recovered brass railing), as well

◆◆◆◆ ◆◆◆

sights

AUTHOR FAVORITE

I grew up in a Georgia city called Savannah so I was partial to the lovely old homes in Savannah's **Historic District,** a residential area off Main Street that includes several private homes dating from the late 19th century, meanders about two miles along College, Williams, Guinn, DeFord and Church streets. You'll see gems such as the 1889 Queen Anne Williams-Ledbetter House, with its ornate porch and eave trim. White Pillars, also known as the Williams House, was built in 1910 and remodeled in 1974; it's graced with Palladian windows and wraparound porches. See "Walking Tour" for more details.

WALKING TOUR
Historic Homes of Savannah

A leisurely pace suits the architecture in this historic district, where the oldest house dates to 1830 but the majority of the homes were built in the late 1800s and early 1900s.

MAIN STREET   Begin a stroll around this historic district at the oldest building in Savannah, found on Main Street down from Williams Street. The **Cherry Mansion** was built by a prominent businessman around 1830 and served as headquarters for Major-General U.S. Grant in the spring of 1862, until an outbreak in fighting at the Battle of Shiloh prompted him to depart abruptly by steamer for Pittsburg Landing. ~ 101 Main Street. At the corner of Main and Williams streets, the **Ross House** is a 1909 Colonial Revival brick home featuring an Ionic two-story portico, the first and best example of this architectural style in Savannah. ~ 524 Main Street.

WILLIAMS STREET   Head up Williams Street past DeFord Street and on your left will be the 1899 **Walker-McGinley House**, a two-story Queen Anne Victorian with a widow's walk and wraparound porches. ~ 311 Williams Street. A bit farther is the **Williams-Ledbetter House**. ~ 391 Williams Street.

as exhibits on archaeology, paleontology and the Civil War. The Trail of Tears Walking Trail begins here. Admission. ~ 507 Main Street, Savannah; 731-925-2364, 800-552-3866, fax 731-925-6987; www.tourhardincnty.org.

Ask for a map at the **Hardin County Convention and Visitors Bureau** before checking out the rest of the town. ~ 507 Main Street, Savannah; 731-925-2364, 800-552-3866, fax 731-925-6987; www.tourhardincnty.org.

LODGING   The **Inn and Conference Center at Pickwick Landing State Park** opened for business in 2001. In addition to the ultra-deluxe one- and two-bedroom suites, there are 119 rooms with picturesque views of Pickwick Lake. The inn also has a gift shop, exercise room with Nautilus equipment, an indoor/outdoor pool, laundry facilities and a day-use area with tennis courts. ~ Park Road, Pickwick Dam; 731-689-3135, 800-250-8615. MODERATE.

It's not much more than a place to lay your head, but the **Savannah Motel** is located right downtown. The one-story lodg-

COLLEGE STREET   Continue to College Street and turn left. The first house on your right will be the **Williams-Churchwell House**, a two-story Greek Revival home built in 1869 to replace an antebellum home that was destroyed during the Civil War. ~ 520 College Street. On the same side of the street, the 1920s-era **Abrams House** is an unusual one-and-a-half story structure. ~ 514 College Street. Past Williams Street on your left is the **Colonial-Revival Williams House**, built in 1874 and remodeled around 1910. ~ 606 College Street. Continue on College Street to the corner of Church Street. On your left will be the **Churchwell-McGinley House**, a two-story frame home built around 1876 but altered in the 20th century by the addition of columned porches. ~ 810 College Street. College Street jogs right on the other side of Church Street. Near the corner is the **Williams-Norton House**, a two-story Queen Anne Victorian constructed in 1901 for banker A. J. Williams. ~ 900 College Street.

CHURCH STREET   Return to Church Street and turn left. On the right will be the **Welch-Ralston House**, a Queen Anne built around 1901 featuring a tower with a conical roof and a curved porch, Palladian attic windows in gables and curved bay windows. ~ 304 North Church Street. Steps away is the 1898 **Sevier House**, with Queen Anne touches such as ornate porch trim and Palladian attic windows in the gables. One of the best examples of the style in the state, it once served as a boarding house. ~ 315 Church Street.

ing has twenty rooms, eight of them non-smoking. ~ 40 Adams Street (Route 64), Savannah; 731-925-3392. BUDGET.

The restaurant at **Pickwick Landing State Park** is huge, big enough to seat more than 180 people. The look is very modern, high ceilinged with light bare-wood walls and steel support beams, all lit with contemporary light fixtures. Southern-style cooking is the order of the day, either à la carte or via the buffet line. Catfish, shrimp, country ham, rib-eye steak and delicacies like fried chicken livers are standard offerings. There's also a Friday-night seafood buffet. ~ Route 57 at Pickwick Dam; 731-689-3135. MODERATE.

DINING

The decor is pretty much limited to historic photos of Savannah and its citizens, but that's not the reason for visiting **Woody's**. Located downtown near the courthouse, this place draws a big lunch crowd for grilled or fried shrimp, chicken dishes and side orders like house-made hushpuppies. ~ 705 Main Street, Savannah; 731-925-0104. BUDGET TO MODERATE.

SHOPPING If visiting the Shiloh National Military Park puts you in a commemorative mood, swing by **Shiloh's Civil War Relics**. Their collection of authentic muskets, bullets, cannons and uniforms might just as well belong in a museum. Closed Tuesday. ~ 4730 Route 22, just north of the park entrance, Shiloh; 731-689-4114.

Ed Shaw's Gift Shop carries Shiloh- and Tennessee-related souvenirs, as well as some original Civil War items. Closed Monday through Friday. ~ At the intersection of Routes 22 and 142, Shiloh; 731-689-5080.

Just off Main Street, you'll find an assortment of locally made crafts—from handpainted cards to knitted dishcloths—at the **Savannah Art Gallery**. Closed Wednesday and weekends. ~ 112 Williams Street, Savannah; 731-925-7529.

For antiques, furniture, vases, records, toys and old photographs, **Shaw's Antiques** is the place to go. Call ahead before setting out. ~ 2308 Wayne Road, Savannah; 731-925-7147.

PARKS **PICKWICK LANDING STATE PARK** 🚶 🛥 ⚓ 🏊 🚤 ⛳ A 24-hour marina caters to the needs of water sportspeople at this 1400-acre park on the shores of Pickwick Reservoir. From here, boaters can lock through the dam for a scenic cruise down the Tennessee River. There are tennis courts, an 18-hole golf course, rental boats, indoor and outdoor pools, an exercise room and an inn with a full-service restaurant. ~ Route 57 at Pickwick Dam; 731-689-3135. 800-250-8615; www.tnstateparks.com.

▲ There are 48 sites with water and electricity, $17.25 per night; and 100 tent-only sites, $7 to $13 per night. There are also ten cabins available; $100 to $115 per night.

▼▼▼▼▼▼▼▼▼▼▼▼▼
The Natchez Trace The buffalo that once roamed this part of Tennessee were the first travelers to form a recognizable trail from around Natchez, Mississippi, to the Cumberland River. The American Indians followed the path for years, before pioneers brought their wagons along the trail, rutting the road with their wheels. The traffic was so constant that robbers began frequenting the so-called Natchez Trace, causing many travelers to seek alternate routes farther west.

In 1800 the federal government designated it as an official mail route. Federal troops arrived to clear obstructions and construct bridges, but by 1815 travel began to decline, though records show it was in use during the Civil War.

In the 1930s, the National Park Service started construction of a parkway that follows, as much as possible, the original Trace. Today, the entire 450-mile stretch has been paved, including some 200 miles within Tennessee, and is open to both bicyclists and automobiles. The final Tennessee segment was completed only in the spring of 1996. There are dozens of access points all along the route. It is a pastoral route, with nary a billboard or fast-food joint anywhere. The speed limit, usually 50 mph, is strictly enforced, but it is such a beautiful drive that few people should be tempted to exceed the limit. The Natchez Trace Parkway now terminates near Belle Meade Plantation in southwest Nashville.

There are several access points on the Natchez Trace. From Savannah, drive east on Route 203, a two-lane road that lopes along, past farmsteads and not much else—but it's all very pleasant driving and is lightly traveled. The highway runs right into the Natchez Trace just a few miles north from where it enters Tennessee from Alabama.

SIGHTS

Don't expect to see a lot of buildings, much less a restaurant, on the Trace. Historical sites are marked with small signs, and it's easy to get off the parkway to explore side roads and nearby towns. (The larger towns, such as Columbia and Franklin, are closer to Nashville and covered in Chapter Nine.) Most notable is the **Meriwether Lewis National Monument**, at Milepost 385.9, marking the grave of the explorer. The **Meriwether Lewis Campground** here has 32 campsites, a water and comfort station, and is free. ~ 931-796-2675.

Among the famous feet that have trod the Natchez Trace are those of Andrew Jackson and the explorer Meriwether Lewis, who died in southern Tennessee under mysterious circumstances in 1809, an apparent suicide later thought to be murder.

For more information on the Natchez Trace Parkway, you can call the **Visitor's Bureau**. ~ 800-305-7417.

Close by is the town of **Hohenwald**, seven miles west of Milepost 385.9 on Route 20. Settled by Swiss and German immigrants in the late 19th century, the town still has an alpine ambience. The name is German for "tall forest," and many homes have the painted window boxes and elaborate roof moldings common in Tyrolean villages.

LODGING

If you're looking for a unique stay in the southwest area, **Natchez Trace B&B Reservation Service** can help. It specializes in bed and breakfasts located near the Natchez Trace Parkway. ~ P.O. Box 193, Hampshire, TN 38461; 931-285-2777, 800-377-2770; www.bbonline.com/natcheztrace, e-mail natcheztrace@bellsouth. net. MODERATE TO ULTRA-DELUXE.

DINING

While there are no commercial outlets on the parkway itself, plenty of dining options can be found in the towns and cities as close as 15 miles, and if you're looking for fast food, you can often find it even closer than that. Franklin (See Chapter Nine) is your best bet.

▼ ▼ ▼ ▼ ▼ ▼ ▼ ▼ ▼ ▼ ▼ ▼ ▼ ▼

Outdoor Adventures

FISHING

Bluegill, bass, crappie, chain pickerel and sauger swim the Wolf River. It's known for a good supply of yellow catfish (up to 60 pounds) said to taste as good as those from the Tennessee River. Locals recommend fishing upriver from Bateman Bridge near Moscow for bass; about a mile upstream, the river spreads into a large lake. Another option is Herb Parsons Lake, a 177-acre state lake in southwest Fayette County.

Fishing is popular on all the lakes in Natchez Trace State Resort Park. Maple Creek and Brown's Creek are managed by the Tennessee Wildlife Resources Agency. The 58-acre Cub Lake has rowboat and pedal-boat rentals; the others, including Pin Oak, have launching ramps for privately owned boats. All the lakes have bluegill, crappie, catfish and rock, hybrid and large-mouth bass.

The fishing is good year-round, except for some rainy periods in the spring, at the **Pickwick Tailwaters** below Pickwick Dam, so it's one of the most popular angling spots in the state. Still, quickly changing water levels caused by hydroelectric power mean anglers must exercise caution; life vests are required on the water. In these waters you can find crappie, sauger, catfish, bluegill and several types of bass, including yellow, striped, white, largemouth and smallmouth. ~ Located 13 miles south of Savannah on Route 57 at Route 128.

Fishing for smallmouth bass is recommended from June through September at nighttime, and at any time the rest of the year along the bluffs and the old river channel. The peak for largemouth and spotted bass is in the off seasons, March through April and October through November. Bluegill and catfish are also found in the reservoir. You can rent fishing boats at **Pickwick Boat Rentals**, at the Pickwick Landing State Park. ~ 7380 Route 57, Pickwick Dam; 731-689-5359.

You can fish for largemouth bass, blue gill, crappie, and blue and channel catfish at 550-acre **Lake Graham**, about six miles east of downtown Jackson. Bait, tackle, boat rentals, a fishing pier, ramps, a picnic area and restrooms make this a comfortable spot for a few hours of angling. ~ 300 Hurts Chapel Road, Jackson; 731-422-4171.

GOLF

If you've only got time for nine holes, your best bet is the **Hardeman County Golf & Country Club**, a well-kept course with a single pond. If you get through in a hurry, you can always go around again at this par-37 course. ~ 215 Golf Club Lane, Bolivar; 731-658-9245.

Wooded fairways, several ponds and lots of contour characterize the private **Hidden Valley Golf & Athletic Club**. Beware

No. 18, where the green is guarded by a sizable body of water. ~ 307 Henderson Road, Jackson; 731-424-3146.

Pickwick Landing State Park has a championship 18-hole course, plus a pro shop with rental clubs and pull carts. There's also a pro on duty at this tree-lined course near Pickwick Reservoir. ~ Route 57 at Pickwick Dam; 731-689-3149.

The **Shiloh Falls Golf Club,** which plays host to more than 150 tournaments every year, has 18 holes, including the signature hole, No. 15, which has an 88-foot elevation change from tee to green. ~ 220 Clubhouse Lane, Counce; 731-689-5050.

RIDING STABLES

Chickasaw State Park has a stable where visitors can rent mounts for trail rides through the rolling countryside of this 1400-acre park. ~ 20 Cabin Lane, Henderson; 901-989-5141.

BIKING

West Tennessee is mostly flat, but not at **Chickasaw State Park,** where a network of over 50 miles of backcountry roads and horse trails add up to almost endless rides. The park rangers want bikers to stay off the hiking trails, but otherwise they are welcome to wander this 14,384-acre park at their discretion.

All levels of mountain bikers should find some terrain to their liking at **Natchez Trace State Resort Park.** Constantly rolling hills, with elevation changes up to 200 feet, and spectacular scenery await riders on these well-marked trails, including horse trails, access roads and both dirt and gravel fire roads. Caution is advised during hunting season, but otherwise bikers are likely to see turkey, deer, fox and coyote as well as other wildlife.

HIKING

All distances listed for hiking trails are one way unless otherwise noted.

On the southwest side of Jackson, **Cypress Grove Nature Park** has a one-mile elevated trail that is wheelchair accessible. The

CANOEING

The Wolf River flows north from Mississippi near LaGrange all the way to its destiny with the Mississippi River at Memphis. There are no rapids, just an unspoiled environment where canoeists are likely to see cypress and gum trees, swamp roses, water lilies and wetland meadows. Recently a 12-mile stretch between LaGrange and the Bateman Bridge near Moscow has been opened up, though it's recommended only for seasoned canoeists. **Wolf River Canoe Trips** rents canoes for excursions on the Ghost River and Moscow sections of the Wolf River. Closed Saturday. ~ 1600 Old State Line, Moscow; 731-877-3958.

boardwalk is six feet wide and railed and inclines are few and mild. Throughout the 165-acre forest are not only bald cypress and water tupelo but also white ash, red maple and sweet gum trees. Royal fern and sensitive fern can be seen along the **Jewelweed Trail**, and at Killdeer Pond you can see plants that thrive in the swamp such as cattails, bulrushes and black willows; other flowers bloom in the late summer. The observation tower on Wood Duck Lake is a good stop to do some birdwatching, since owls, raptors, songbirds and waterfowl all make the park their home at one time or another.

Big Hill Pond State Park and Natural Area offers almost 20 miles of marked loop and interconnecting trails. Ranging from a half mile to over 5.5 miles in length, they run along ridges and through valleys. There are several observation points from hilltops and rocky overhangs, plus a 73-foot tower on **Tuscumbia Trail** that has views of the river bottoms to the south. The wetlands portion of this 5000-acre park has cottonwood, alders, sweet gum, bitternut, weeping willow, tupelo and several kinds of oak trees, while higher up are chestnut oak and blackjack oak. The valleys are full of second-growth tulip poplar, cedar, birch and pine. Deer are abundant, but you may also see quail, squirrels, wild turkeys, raccoons and the occasional mink or coyote. Below the dam at Travis McNatt Lake is a boardwalk (.8 mile) that allows closer views of the wetlands and waterfowl that congregate there. In spring, wild azaleas and the rare dwarf iris bloom here.

You can not only drive the Natchez Trace these days, you can hike along several portions of it. The Tennessee portion follows some of the hillier parts of the old route. The habitat varies with the terrain, as do the animals hikers can see along the way. White-tailed deer, wild turkey, red-tailed hawks and barred owls are the most common, but there are another 50 species of birds in the area. The moderate **Natchez Trace National Scenic Trail** (24.5 miles) has access points at the following parkway mileposts, listed with the appropriate parking areas: 427.6 (Garrison Creek Parking Area); 426.2 (Old Trace); 425.2 (Burns Branch); 423.88 (Tennessee Valley Divide); 422.9 (Carter Road); 415.6 (Route 7); 408 (Route 50, access along highway and Totty Lane west of Parkway).

Shiloh National Military Park offers a number of trails, most of which are easy hikes between 10 and 20 miles long. Younger hikers will probably enjoy the **Shiloh Battlefield Trail** (2 miles) and the **Shiloh Indian Mound Trail** (3 miles).

▼▼▼▼▼▼▼▼▼▼▼▼

Transportation

CAR

Jackson is located on **Route 40**, 85 miles northeast of Memphis. The major north–south artery through the city is **Route 45**. On the southern edge of the state, **Route 57** runs from Memphis through LaGrange, Grand Junction and Pickwick Dam. Savannah is linked to the Natchez Trace Parkway by **Route 64**.

Jackson is served by the **McKellar-Sipes Regional Airport**. The **AIR**
only regularly scheduled commercial service is provided by Northwest Airlink. ~ 308 Grady Montgomery Drive, Jackson; 731-
423-0995; www.mklairport.tn.org.

The closest major airport to Jackson, LaGrange, Grand Junction and Savannah is in Memphis, some 85 miles away. The
Memphis International Airport is located off Route 240 about
11 miles south of downtown. It is served by seven major carriers,
including American, Continental Express, Delta, KLM, Northwest, United and US Airways. ~ 901-922-8000; www.mcaa.com.

Greyhound Bus Lines offers bus service to Jackson. ~ 407 East **BUS**
Main Street; 731-427-1573, 800-231-2222; www.greyhound.com.

The nearest train station to Jackson and other southwestern Ten- **TRAIN**
nessee towns and cities is the Memphis **Amtrak**. ~ 545 South Main
Street, Memphis; 800-872-7245; www.amtrak.com.

Index

Lodging Index

Dining Index

HIDDEN GUIDES

Adventure travel or a relaxing vacation?—"Hidden" guidebooks are the only travel books in the business to provide detailed information on both. Aimed at environmentally aware travelers, our motto is "Where Vacations Meet Adventures." These books combine details on unique hotels, restaurants and sightseeing with information on camping, sports and hiking for the outdoor enthusiast.

PARADISE FAMILY GUIDES

Ideal for families traveling with kids of any age—toddlers to teenagers—Paradise Family Guides offer a blend of travel information unlike any other guides to the Hawaiian islands. With vacation ideas and tropical adventures that are sure to satisfy both action-hungry youngsters and re-laxation-seeking parents, these guides meet the specific needs of each and every family member.

HIDDEN GUIDEBOOKS

____ Hidden Arizona, $16.95
____ Hidden Bahamas, $14.95
____ Hidden Baja, $14.95
____ Hidden Belize, $15.95
____ Hidden Big Island of Hawaii, $13.95
____ Hidden Boston & Cape Cod, $14.95
____ Hidden British Columbia, $18.95
____ Hidden Cancún & the Yucatán, $16.95
____ Hidden Carolinas, $17.95
____ Hidden Coast of California, $18.95
____ Hidden Colorado, $15.95
____ Hidden Disneyland, $13.95
____ Hidden Florida, $18.95
____ Hidden Florida Keys & Everglades, $13.95
____ Hidden Georgia, $16.95
____ Hidden Guatemala, $16.95
____ Hidden Hawaii, $18.95
____ Hidden Idaho, $14.95
____ Hidden Kauai, $13.95
____ Hidden Los Angeles, $14.95
____ Hidden Maui, $13.95

____ Hidden Miami, $14.95
____ Hidden Montana, $15.95
____ Hidden New England, $18.95
____ Hidden New Mexico, $15.95
____ Hidden New Orleans, $14.95
____ Hidden Oahu, $13.95
____ Hidden Oregon, $15.95
____ Hidden Pacific Northwest, $18.95
____ Hidden San Diego, $14.95
____ Hidden Salt Lake City, $14.95
____ Hidden San Francisco & Northern California, $18.95
____ Hidden Seattle, $13.95
____ Hidden Southern California, $18.95
____ Hidden Southwest, $19.95
____ Hidden Tahiti, $17.95
____ Hidden Tennessee, $16.95
____ Hidden Utah, $16.95
____ Hidden Walt Disney World, $13.95
____ Hidden Washington, $15.95
____ Hidden Wine Country, $13.95
____ Hidden Wyoming, $15.95

PARADISE FAMILY GUIDES

____ Paradise Family Guides: Kaua'i, $16.95
____ Paradise Family Guides: Maui, $16.95
____ Paradise Family Guides: Big Island of Hawai'i, $16.95

Mark the book(s) you're ordering and enter the total cost here ➾ [   ]

California residents add 8.25% sales tax here ➾ [   ]

Shipping, check box for your preferred method and enter cost here ➾ [   ]

❏ BOOK RATE   FREE! FREE! FREE!

❏ PRIORITY MAIL/UPS GROUND   cost of postage

❏ UPS OVERNIGHT OR 2-DAY AIR   cost of postage   [   ]

Billing, enter total amount due here and check method of payment ➾ [   ]

❏ CHECK   ❏ MONEY ORDER
❏ VISA/MASTERCARD _____EXP. DATE_____

NAME _____PHONE_____
ADDRESS _____
CITY_____ STATE _____ ZIP_____

MONEY-BACK GUARANTEE ON DIRECT ORDERS PLACED THROUGH ULYSSES PRESS.

ABOUT THE AUTHOR

MARTY OLMSTEAD is a freelance writer based in Sonoma, California. She is the author of Ulysses Press' *Hidden Georgia* and co-author of *Hidden Florida* and *Hidden Wine Country*, as well as *San Francisco & the Bay Area* (Windsor Publications, Inc.). Her articles have appeared in numerous national and regional publications, including *Travel & Leisure*, *Appellation*, *Odyssey*, the *Los Angeles Times* and the *San Francisco Chronicle*.

ABOUT THE ILLUSTRATOR

DOUG McCARTHY, a native New Yorker, lives in the San Francisco Bay area with his family. His illustrations appear in a number of Ulysses Press guides, including *Hidden Wyoming*, *Hidden British Columbia*, *Hidden Bahamas* and *The New Key to Ecuador and the Galápagos*.